D1050338

SUMMER OF SHADOWS

SUMMER
OF
SHADOWS

A MURDER,
A PENNANT RACE,
AND
THE TWILIGHT
OF THE
BEST LOCATION IN THE NATION

Jonathan Knight

CLERISY PRESS

Summer of Shadows: A Murder, A Pennant Race and The Twilight of the Best Location in the Nation

Copyright © 2011 by Jonathan Knight
All rights reserved. No portion of this book may be reproduced in any fashion, print, facsimile, or electronic, or by any method yet to be developed, without express permission of the copyright holder.

Published by Clerisy Press
Printed in the United States of America
Distributed by Publishers Group West
First edition, first printing

For further information, contact the publisher at:
Clerisy Press
PO Box 8874
Cincinnati, OH 45208-08074
www.clerisypress.com

Library of Congress Cataloging-in-Publication Data
    Knight, Jonathan, 1976–
        Summer of shadows : a murder, a pennant race, and the twilight of the best
        location in the nation / by Jonathan Knight.
            p. cm.
        ISBN-13: 978-1-57860-467-8
        ISBN-10: 1-57860-467-2
            1. Cleveland (Ohio)—History—20th century. 2. Cleveland (Ohio)—
        Economic conditions—20th century. 3. Cleveland (Ohio)—Social conditions
        —20th century. 4. Press and politics—Ohio—Cleveland—History—20th cen-
        tury. 5. Sheppard, Sam—Trials, litigation, etc. 6. Cleveland Indians (Baseball
        team)—History—20th century. 7. Rock music—Ohio—Cleveland—History
        and criticism. I. Title.
        F499.C657K65 2010
        977.1'32--dc22
                                    2010038349

Edited by Jack Heffron
Cover designed by Stephen Sullivan
Text designed by Annie Long
The photos on pages 55, 167, 200, 215, 229, 306, and 440 appear courtesy of the
    Cleveland Public Library Photograph Collection. All others appear courtesy of the
    Cleveland Press Collection, Cleveland State University Library.

DEDICATION

For Jeannine, Mike, and Carter . . .
and whoever comes next

CONTENTS

Coming events cast their shadows before.

—Thomas Campbell,
"Lochiel's Warning"

PRELUDE: SUMMER 1969

The image of Cleveland, Ohio, as a great American city—one once known as "The Best Location in the Nation"—died at four minutes before noon on a cool, overcast Sunday morning in June.

There had been no catastrophic natural disaster, no legal declaration. The city would continue to appear on maps, and its citizens carried on with their lives. But the shining image of Cleveland as a full-color postcard of a grand dominion on the waterfront—which had gradually been curling at the edges and deteriorating for a decade and a half—literally went up in flames on June 22, 1969. In that moment, the Best Location in the Nation was blasted to smithereens and blown away in the winds whipping off Lake Erie. Cleveland became just another American city limping through a tumultuous decade.

It had been a quiet morning, the dew from the crisp summer night not yet fully evaporated by the warmth of the day. The fiery days of the season were still weeks away, and June remained, as it usually did, Cleveland's finest month of the year.

Outside the city, the day would prove historic for other reasons. Judy Garland would die that Sunday. After sixteen historic years on the bench, Earl Warren would spend his final day as Chief Justice of the U.S. Supreme Court before officially stepping down the following morning. The nation would cautiously maneuver through another day of conflict and turmoil. Having endured the stunning assassinations of three iconic political leaders in the past six years, the United States was

1

being torn apart from the inside out, its ideals clashing in a cultural civil war. Major cities had become battlegrounds for race riots. Dinner tables were divided in the debate over whether or not the United States should remain embroiled in the Vietnam War. In less than two weeks, San Francisco would be introduced to the Zodiac killer, who would terrify northern California for the next decade with random murders and taunting letters to the police. The most infamous episode of the era's madness would soon hit frighteningly close to Cleveland, at Kent State University, less than forty miles away, where four students would be shot and killed by members of the Ohio National Guard during a weekend of anti-war protests the following spring.

But on this Sunday morning in June, Cleveland was quiet, the wailing of its own racial confrontations now nothing more than chilling echoes. Yet the peaceful mood of the morning vanished when the seemingly impossible occurred. To anyone standing alongside the Cuyahoga River at the foot of Campbell Road Hill just outside of downtown, the vision appeared almost biblical—a snapshot from the Book of Revelations.

The river was on fire.

Technically, what was burning was a large slick of oil waste floating along the Cuyahoga. In the aftermath, no one could determine what caused the fire. Likely there'd been some sort of spark or fallen shrapnel from any of the waterfront industries that had created the slick in the first place by dumping their chemical extract into the river. Perhaps it was nothing more than a smoldering cigarette butt flicked away by someone who had no idea of the magnitude the action would carry.

Reaching as high as five stories, the flames floated along with the sludgy current of the river. As the slick slid beneath a pair of railroad trestles, the flames licked the weathered wood above and ignited it. The intense heat began to cook and warp the rails. Joining the sour smell of burning chemicals, great black plumes of smoke whispered through downtown Cleveland.

The response was fast and efficient. Sirens wailed throughout downtown. In less than twenty-five minutes, the fire was out. A fireboat that performed daily patrols on the river looking for just such types of oil slicks was joined by three fire battalions, and the flames were extinguished. The fire caused roughly $50,000 in damage—nothing really, compared to several of the other times the river had caught on fire in years past. The worst was in 1953, when a similar outbreak caused nearly a million dollars of damage.

But this time the damage wouldn't be solely monetary.

The fire, at first, drew little attention. The *Plain Dealer* ran a photograph of the flames on the front page of Monday's edition, but the corresponding story—just a few paragraphs long—was buried deep within the paper. The *Cleveland Press*, more attuned to what its subscribers wanted to read than what they should, also ran a front-page photo on Monday afternoon, but no story. An afterthought *Press* editorial on Tuesday sighed with fatigue and made a case that the city's industries should be encouraged to stop dumping wastes into the river.

It should have ended there. By the summer of 1969, fifteen years after its apex, Cleveland's reputation as a noble lakeside metropolis was terminal, and its death was inevitable—not unlike those of a handful of other blue-collar industrial burgs in the Midwest. But that Cleveland's came in such a publicized fashion was nothing more than a stroke of incredibly bad timing. If only man hadn't walked on the moon, Cleveland may have been spared decades of agony.

Exactly four weeks after the improbable occurred along the Cuyahoga River, America witnessed the impossible. With the landing of Apollo 11 on the moon and Neil Armstrong's first steps on that alien surface, one of the most significant moments in the history of the world played out before a live audience watching on television sets glimmering blue in the darkness of a July night. In the days and weeks that followed, news coverage of the moon landing was immeasurable as the American public fed its hunger for more information about this achievement.

Serving as the unofficial national recorder for this event was *Time* magazine, which sold millions of additional copies of its subsequent issues examining the Apollo 11 mission. And in the middle of one of those issues was an unremarkable environmental article on the Cuyahoga River fire. But because that issue of *Time* was examined by millions more readers than a typical one, the Cuyahoga River fire became a national story. Or rather, a national punch line.

"Some river!" *Time* guffawed. "Chocolate-brown, oily, bubbling with sub-surface gases, it oozes rather than flows." It even cited a joke passed among Clevelanders about the state of the river: "Anyone who falls into the Cuyahoga does not drown. He decays." It went on to outline the horrifying condition of Lake Erie, clogged with wastes from Detroit's automobile empire, Toledo's steel mills, and the paper plants of Erie, Pennsylvania.

The article went on to describe the efforts Cleveland had made in the subsequent weeks to clean the river and ensure that its industries shaped up. In the months to come, *Time* would describe the conception of the Clean Water Act, set in motion by the Cuyahoga River fire, which eventually led to the creation of the Environmental Protection Agency and a new commitment to purified air and water.

"The accomplishment, huge as it is, only fixes the price of optimism," *Time* explained. "Unfortunately, water pollution knows no political boundaries. The Cuyahoga can be cleaned up in Cleveland, but as long as other cities keep dumping wastes upriver, it will remain exactly what it is today—an open sewer filling Lake Erie with scummy wavelets, sullen reminders that even a great lake can die."

From there, the Cuyahoga River fire took on a life of its own. Johnny Carson made it—and Cleveland—a recurring joke in his *Tonight Show* monologues. Randy Newman would set the fire to music in his 1972 satirical tune "Burn On." And from coast to coast, Cleveland's nickname had been changed. Known as the Best Location in the Nation little more than a decade before, it now became the "Mistake by the Lake."

That afternoon, with the burned railroad trestles still smoldering, the last-place Cleveland Indians committed five errors in a miserable 6–0 loss to the Baltimore Orioles. Like their hometown, the Indians of 1969 were a shadow of what they once had been.

And 120 miles to the south, one of Cleveland's most infamous former citizens was busy preparing for a defining moment in his life. Once one of the most promising young doctors in Cleveland, handsome and athletic with a beautiful wife and vibrant son, Sam Sheppard had captured headlines throughout the country fifteen years earlier in a murder case that, even now, sparked debate. Now he was just over a month away from making his professional wrestling debut.

His wrestling career would begin on a steamy Saturday night in August in the cracker-box gymnasium at tiny Waverly High School just south of Chillicothe, where Sheppard defeated Wild Bill Scholl, a lolling walrus of a man, before a modest crowd of 1,500. When Sheppard entered the gym wearing a red-hooded sweatshirt and black tights, a cascade of boos flooded from the fans, who had paid two dollars for entry, with the proceeds benefiting cancer research. The loudest came from the women in attendance. They knew exactly who he was and, fifteen years ago, what he had done.

Though utterly inexperienced and outweighed by nearly a hundred pounds, Sam Sheppard won the scheduled twenty-minute match in a mere seven minutes, unveiling a move he'd invented himself. Drawing upon his medical training, when the opportunity arose, he stuck three fingers into Scholl's mouth and pressed on the mandibular nerve at the base of the tongue. The pain was excruciating. Scholl immediately screamed "Quit!" and would later challenge Sam to a fight in the locker room, calling it a dirty move. Sam claimed not only was it clean, but it was reflective of the intellect he brought to the match. "As a doctor, I had an advantage over Scholl," he said, "and the hold was not illegal." Several of the nation's top wrestling promoters were impressed. They'd come to the backwaters of Ohio to give Sam Sheppard a once-over on this summer night, and Sam had known it. In the early moments of the match, he tangled Scholl in a head-lock and held firm the pose, smiling at flashing cameras ringside.

Afterward, reporters gathered around Sam in the locker room to ask about the match, but even more about how this career shift fit into the bizarre landscape his life had become over the past fifteen years. He was asked about his new medical practice—operated out of a narrow bunker of an office in Gahanna, just outside of Columbus. Most of his patients were Medicare cases or referrals from county welfare programs. "I'm doing a lot and not getting much for it," Sam said with a chuckle.

Before the serious questioning could begin, a roar echoed from the gym, and Sam rushed back out. His trainer and partner, George

Strickland, who was wrestling in the second match of the evening, a tag-team event against a group called the Iron Russians, was in trouble. Ignoring the rules of the match, the Iron Russians were sending both wrestlers into the ring at once to fight Strickland. Sam charged into the ring to aid his friend, pulling one of the opponents out of the ring and throwing him to the floor, then kicking him. The doctor then chased him around the ring as the fans cheered hysterically.

Like the city he'd once lived in and the baseball team he'd once loved, Sam Sheppard was a different entity in 1969 than when his name was in the national spotlight in 1954. And eight months later, his death was as little a surprise as that of Cleveland's prominence itself. What made it notable was the old debates it stirred back to life—ones involving the murder of his wife and whether or not he'd done it. "He was a very tragic figure," his second wife said the day he died. "He was a victim of everything that has happened to him for the past sixteen years. He just wasn't strong enough to face up to what had happened to him." She sighed and added, "His turmoil and misery had finally ended."

"The friends of Sam Sheppard's youth and the members of his family will continue to reflect on what might have been," the *Cleveland Press* predicted, "and to wonder why such a promising life turned, instead, into a classic American tragedy."

This is the story of three American tragedies that intersected over the course of one golden, yet haunted summer. This tale recalls the triumphant hour of an empire just before its fall, the dominance and grace of a star-crossed group of warriors, and the result when the mesmerizing allure of mystery is combined with the terrifying power of fear.

This is Cleveland, 1954.

The Best Location in the Nation.

Interlude

Game 1

THE BLACK LOCOMOTIVE SLOWLY CURLED into Grand Central Station like a snake returning to its nest. It left the dawn outside and was absorbed by the smoky darkness of the tunnels running beneath New York City. Still, the coolness of the fall morning sifted through the walls, and as the passengers stepped off the train, the atmosphere of autumn in the city gently kneaded its way through their senses.

It was, for these men de-boarding the special eight-car overnight train that had scurried through the dark Pennsylvania farmland and then the growing burgs on the outskirts of New York, a World Series atmosphere—fitting, given that they soon would play the first game of baseball's Fall Classic. The mood on the ride was much different from the other trips this group had made over the course of the past six months of 1954. With many of the passengers accompanied by their wives—a special privilege awarded for this trip—much of the usual chicanery of card games and off-color jokes was suspended. Similarly, beer and cocktails were replaced by the warm aroma of coffee and cake, partially because of the presence of the women, but also

8

Drenched in the autumn sun during batting practice the day before the 1954 World Series began, the quirky dimensions of the Polo Grounds would play a pivotal role in Game One the following afternoon.

because of the magnitude of this trip.

Such a flavor in the air was nothing new for the capital of baseball. At least one New York team had played in the Fall Classic each of the previous five seasons and in six of the last seven. The streak would continue, albeit in a surprising fashion. It would be the Giants who would carry Gotham's torch into the World Series, not the mighty Yankees. For the first time in six years, the baseball gods in pinstripes would not participate in the sport's showcase—because of the men confidently marching through Grand Central Station on this Tuesday morning.

As they stepped onto the platform beside track twenty-six,

spotlights burst on, and bulky television cameras whirred to life to record the arrival of these conquering titans. A cadre of New York's finest carved an aisle through the mass of equipment and bystanders for the visitors to pass through. Photographers from New York newspapers began barking orders, telling the players how they should pose for the pictures. The players ignored them. This team had already conquered this city, and these battle-tested players weren't naïve enough to believe they owed the desperate photographers any favors. If anything, the camera hounds should be bowing and scraping, just as they did when they visited the clubhouse at Yankee Stadium, which would sit silent this week. It was this group of ballplayers, not Casey Stengel's celebrated Yankees, who had been Ed Sullivan's guests on *Toast of the Town* two nights before via a camera linkup in Cleveland.

It would be a busy day for the Cleveland Indians. After they settled in at the Hotel Biltmore and their wives headed out for a much-anticipated shopping trip, they would take batting practice at the Polo Grounds—a place of legend for most of these players, not unlike Camelot or Sherwood Forest. Then that evening, many of the players and coaches were invited to the Biltmore's grand ballroom to participate in a pre-Series radio program broadcast nationally to more than eight hundred stations on the Mutual Network, including a hundred from fourteen Latin American countries, where more than casual interest in the Series had been generated for the first time. "This autumn baseball show no longer is local," baseball commissioner Ford Frick stated, "but interest in it is felt all over the world."

Donning the new uniforms that had been tailored for them to wear in the World Series, they took batting practice at the Polo Grounds on a perfect afternoon for late September on the East Coast. Burning as brightly as it had in July, the sun boiled the city, raising the temperature into the low eighties as the Indians attempted to comprehend the nooks and crannies of the peculiar ballpark. They now realized the jokes they'd made in their final workout back in Cleveland were not, in reality, jokes. Somebody would pop a shallow fly to right and watch it be caught just a few yards behind first base. "Home run in the Polo Grounds," the batter would offer with a smile, drawing laughter from his teammates. But now they saw that the dimensions of this strange ballpark located a stone's throw from the Harlem River were no laughing matter. A routine fly ball to right field in Cleveland, one caught seventy-five feet in front of the fence, could indeed be a home run here. And conversely, a ball hit to center field would need to travel nearly twice as far—almost five hundred feet – to leave the park as one hit to right.

Yet as the Indians warmed up and took swings in the batting cage, and the outfielders started to study the tendencies of baseballs hit off the ancient outfield walls, they were not at all concerned with minor details like the dimensions of the field they were playing on. They'd won more games than any other American League team in history—more games than any major-league team had won in a half-century. They'd won in every park they'd played in, beaten every team that had dared to stand in their way in every imaginable fashion. Over the course of the summer, they'd taken the Yankees to the mat six times on their own diamond. The Polo Grounds may have been shaped like a bathtub, but after exorcising the demons of Yankee Stadium it didn't frighten the 1954 Cleveland Indians. Nothing did.

They were heavy favorites to defeat the Giants in the World Series—possibly in as few as five games, saving themselves the hassle of a return trip to New York the following week. In combined polls of 208 baseball writers conducted by the Associated Press and United Press International, 147—more than 70 percent—picked the Indians to win. They'd won fourteen more games than the Giants, but more importantly, in a tight pennant race, had stared down the Yankees, who'd won the last five World Series, including a triumph over the Giants three years earlier. Even Cleveland third base coach Tony Cuccinello, who'd spent the last two weeks scouting the Giants, couldn't see how that team could possibly beat the Indians more than twice—really, he couldn't imagine losing more than one time. And he wasn't alone.

"We don't know how many games will be required to put our lads on top," a *Plain Dealer* editorial admitted. "We happen to hold a couple of tickets for game No. 5—but if they can do it in four, we'll not complain." Thus, back in Cleveland, the latest item for conjecture during coffee breaks and lunch hours centered on how many games

it would take the Indians to put the Giants away. It was the latest item for conjecture in what had become a summer of questions: *Are we really prepared for an atomic attack? Is Cleveland about to become one of the most important trade centers in the world? Is television just a fad? Are this year's Indians the best team ever to play the game?* And, of course, there were the most asked questions of all: *What happened to Dr. Sam's t-shirt on the night of the murder? Why didn't their dog, Kokie, bark?* And the final, breathless question: *Such a nice, good-looking young doctor with a pretty wife—why in heavens did he do it?*

Everyone admitted the Giants were tough, particularly their young center fielder who'd just reached superstar status with a dynamite season after missing all of the 1953 campaign while serving in the Army. Twenty-three-year-old Willie Mays could certainly hurt them, but Cuccinello and the majority of reporters knew the Indians were too good to lose to a team with one slugger and a bunch of role players.

The Indians had a center fielder comparable to Mays both in the field and at the plate, in addition to a heavy-hitting third baseman who'd already made more impact than the heralded Mickey Mantle had made with the Yankees. They had the league's batting champion at second base, the franchise's first Latino star, who'd been contacted the previous week by the president of his home country of Mexico seeking Series tickets for himself and several members of his cabinet. A sudden celebrity, the previously unknown Bobby Avila had also been named honorary mayor of a tiny California town that bore his last name. But the hamlet's three hundred citizens were distracted from following their figurehead in the World Series when on the day before the Series began, a commercial fishing boat exploded on its docks. Seven people—the equivalent of 2 percent of the town's population—were missing and presumed dead. Some may have considered this a bad omen. But bad luck alone wouldn't be enough to vanquish the Indians.

Even if you considered the teams equal offensively, the Giants themselves had to admit that their pitching staff was nowhere near comparable with Cleveland's. The Indians brought four pitchers into the Series who would eventually be inducted into the baseball Hall of Fame. Their front-line starting rotation— better known throughout baseball as the "Big Three"—had combined to win sixty-five games during the season. On the rare occasion when one of them couldn't finish what he started, the Indians had two young aces to call on in relief—a right-hander and a left-hander, forming the franchise's first true bullpen.

Following the afternoon workout and a harried dinner back at the hotel, several of the Indians headed to the Biltmore ballroom for the 8:30 Mutual broadcast. Try as they might to remain humble, their confidence couldn't help but spill out on the air. "This is my sixth Series as a player or official," Cleveland general manager Hank Greenberg said, "and is giving me my biggest thrill because I grew up in New York, and the Giants were my first baseball love. It is a thrill playing the Giants, and it will be a still greater thrill beating them." Following that sentiment, American League president Will Harridge good-naturedly informed the radio audience that the Indians were about to bring home the junior circuit's eighth straight world championship. Fans across the nation flipped off their radios at the conclusion of the show wondering if the Giants would even be able to make things interesting over the next seven days.

The players were then free to take in the Big Apple, whose gates opened to a landscape of entertainment, from nightclubs to Broadway shows. Those seeking a more low-key evening could take in any number of movies that weren't showing back in Cleveland. One in particular that had received much attention since its New York premiere eight weeks earlier was *Rear Window*, the latest thriller from director Alfred Hitchcock, his second release of the summer. This one, like the first, centered on the nefarious plot of a husband attempting to kill his wife. Considering these visitors from Cleveland had just left a city submerged in the Sheppard case—a very similar, real-life tale—it's doubtful Hitchcock's latest spellbinder had much appeal.

Wednesday morning dawned cloudy and overcast in New York, but by noon, the sun burned off the haze and the afternoon promised to be as sparkling and bright as the day before. Appropriately, New York was experiencing an Indian summer—just as Cleveland had for the past five months. Temperatures would soar into the eighties as the day took on a flavor of June rather than one on the brink of October. Better than fifty thousand fans poured into the Polo Grounds to witness the first game, the largest crowd ever to attend a contest involving a National League ballclub. Scalpers made a mint on the streets around the Polo Grounds, taking in as much as fifteen dollars for reserved seats and an outrageous twenty-five dollars for box seats.

The game also drew a cavalcade of celebrities: Spencer Tracy, J. Edgar Hoover, Don Ameche, Lou Costello (and, of course, Bud Abbott, who together had followed the Indians for years), Sammy Davis, Jr., and Roy Rogers. Perry Como would sing the national anthem, and leading the Indians cheering section would be comedian Bob Hope, who also was a part-owner of the franchise. He said he'd been hit up for tickets by just about every star in Hollywood, and he had guaranteed he'd wrap production on his latest film, *The Seven Little Foys*, in time to attend the Series. If they hadn't, Hope explained, "we'll wind it up behind the left-field foul line at Cleveland Municipal Stadium."

Back in Cleveland, fans who'd climbed on the ever-growing bandwagon of technology and purchased a television could catch the first two games on two of Cleveland's three stations—one with local broadcasters and the other, WNBK, carrying NBC's national broadcast. WNBK even installed a television in the window of its headquarters in downtown Cleveland at East Ninth Street and Superior Avenue, and throughout the afternoon, a large crowd circled the window to follow the action. Similarly, televisions had been installed in banks and department stores—including a colossal twenty-one-inch model on the second floor of Lane Bryant—so that shoppers could follow the game action. Workmen busy six feet beneath Superior Avenue listened to the game on a small radio sending the play-by-play through an open manhole cover. Hotels hosted grand "watch parties" sponsored by local businesses, which wined and dined clients over expensive food and drink as the game played out in crisp, if colorless, images on the screens before them. With an influx of out-of-town baseball fans flooding the city, many of these same hotels also rocketed their room rates to three times the usual cost. Restaurants, also overwhelmed with new clientele, politely informed diners to request no substitutions during the World Series.

In Denver, Colorado, vacationing President Dwight Eisenhower settled in at his "summer White House" at Lowry Air Force Base to watch the first few innings on television before heading out for a round of golf. He would bring with him a portable radio to listen to the remainder of the game as he played.

At one o'clock that afternoon, Eastern Standard Time, the day's business ground to a halt. Schoolchildren with understanding teachers in both

New York and Cleveland were permitted to listen to the game on the radio, where Cleveland's own Jimmy Dudley would team up with Al Helper to describe the play-by-play action to a national audience.

In Cleveland's office buildings, elevator operators announced the score to new groups of passengers as they stepped on board. Outside, drivers of cars without radios hollered out windows at stoplights and intersections to bystanders, inquiring the score and situation. Even those without access to a radio or television wouldn't be left in the dark. By calling Greenwich 1-1212, the standard phone number to receive an automated message reading the time, Ohio Bell operators would also announce the score of the game. And right away, there was good news to report.

On the fourth pitch of the game, New York pitcher Sal Maglie—nicknamed "The Barber" because of his tendency to pitch high and tight—trimmed a little too close, hitting Cleveland leadoff hitter Al Smith squarely in the back. Bobby Avila, the league's batting champion and national hero of Mexico, then laced a single to left center, and Smith's speedy legs carried him to third. Maglie settled to retire the two most dangerous—and most historically significant—hitters in the lineup: Larry Doby, the league's first black star, and Al Rosen, the first Jewish player to earn MVP honors since his general manager, Hank Greenberg, a decade earlier. With two down and Doby and Rosen safely put away, Maglie appeared in the clear. All that stood between him and the Giants dugout was Cleveland's first baseman—a short, prematurely bald young man who looked more like an insurance salesman than a ballplayer. Few, if any, of the Giant fans in the Polo Grounds that day had heard of Vic Wertz. By the end of the afternoon, however, he would be the talk of the Big Apple.

Wertz was unusually nervous as he stepped into the batter's box. Part of the reason was that this would be his first World Series at-bat. But he was more concerned with his left index finger. He'd jammed it taking a few extra swings after the previous day's batting practice, and in the moments afterward he could tell that it would affect his grip on the bat. He decided not to tell anyone about it for fear that he would wind up on the bench for the game. Instead, that night he bought a sponge and snipped off a small piece that he would hold in his left hand between his finger and the bat to provide some relief and allow him to maintain his natural grip and swing. The night before, it seemed silly, but as he dug into the thick dirt, Vic Wertz knew his fortunes in the Series would rest on the success of a small piece of sponge.

Wertz crushed Maglie's second pitch into deep left center, where it caromed off the wall near the Giant bullpen, stationed along the warning track. Smith scored easily, and

Avila scampered around the bases with the second run as Wertz motored into third with a triple. Maglie retired the next batter to end the inning, but the damage was done. Back in Cleveland, fans cheered on every street corner. As expected, the Indians would have no trouble with these Giants. If New York's pitching couldn't contain the Cleveland bats, the Giants were in deep trouble indeed. With Bob Lemon, the kingpin of the Big Three, on the mound, Wertz's two runs might be enough to carry the day.

Lemon was wobbly through the first two innings but managed to keep the Giants off the board, while Maglie settled to keep the Indians at bay over the next two frames. In the third, three singles and a walk enabled New York to knot the contest at two. Lemon persevered, then rallied after giving up two more hits in the fourth to keep the score tied, though things could have been much worse. The Giants had stranded seven runners in the first four innings and were

a base hit from blowing the game open on three separate occasions. They'd let Lemon up off the mat and were about to pay the price. Cleveland's ace retired the next eight New York hitters and cruised into the eighth. And in the top half of the inning, the path to his third career World Series victory began to materialize.

Maglie was running on fumes. He walked Doby to start the inning, and then Al Rosen slapped a hard grounder deep in the hole at shortstop and the throw to second wasn't in time to catch Doby. Giants manager Leo Durocher, realizing the critical moment the game had reached, quickly pulled Maglie and called on part-time starter Don Liddle to put out the fire. He'd face fellow lefty Vic Wertz, who'd added a pair of singles to his first-inning three-bagger and was enjoying one of the finest days in his career, which four months before had appeared to be limping to a disappointing conclusion. Working quickly, Liddle got ahead of Wertz one-

The Indians watch in amazement as their luck
sours in the opening game of the World Series.

and-two. His fourth pitch, a
fastball, rocketed through the
shadow cast by the grandstand
that now stretched halfway across
the infield, but Wertz read it
perfectly. His hands tightened on
the handle of the bat, flattening
the tiny bit of sponge in his left
hand. He was so locked in on the
trajectory of the ball, he wasn't
even sure what kind of pitch it
was, simply that he was about to
clobber it. And he did.

"When I smacked the ball,"
Wertz would say later, "it felt so
good, and I was so sure of how

hard I tagged it that all the details were erased from my mind." It was, he added, the hardest he'd ever hit a ball in his life.

The crack of the bat echoed through the Polo Grounds like a rifle shot, and even those leaning against the rafters of the ballpark could tell that Wertz had gotten all of the pitch. The ball soared into the outfield as if fired from a rocket. The players inside the Cleveland dugout rose to their feet and watched the white fleck zoom across the blue sky. They knew Wertz had hit a game-winning, three-run home run. Such dramatics were nothing new to them. Unheralded players had risen to the occasion throughout the long, sweltering summer, winning and saving games from the clutches of defeat. This time it would be Vic Wertz's turn. A promise he'd made to Lemon on their previous trip to New York had just been delivered.

So enraptured with the path of the baseball, nobody, at first, noticed Willie Mays. Rosen, his

right leg heavily taped to comfort a nagging charley horse suffered three weeks earlier—the latest in a line of injuries that plagued him in 1954—immediately sprinted toward second, knowing that in case the ball somehow hit the wall and ricocheted back into play, he'd need every second to make it around the bases on his bum leg. Doby, as Cleveland's center fielder, was more familiar with the area the ball was carrying toward and was more cautious. He skipped halfway between second and third and paused. Not only did he know better than his teammates just how far it was to the center-field wall in this bastardized ballpark, but he also knew that the Giants' young center fielder was one of the rare ballplayers who was just as good as everyone said he was.

In that first second after Wertz's shot cleared the infield and began its course toward history, Willie Mays's actions were almost laughable. He turned with his back completely facing the plate and began running "like a scared deer," *Sporting News* would describe, toward the dark canyon just to the left of straightaway center field. Of the better than 53,000 people in the park that day, none thought Willie Mays had a chance of catching up with the ball. None, that is, but Mays himself. As the ball cruised out of the shadow of the grandstand and was illuminated by the bright autumn sun, Mays craned his head slightly over his right shoulder to follow its path. The ball began its descent right about where it would have cleared the fence in any of the other fifteen stadiums in Major League Baseball. But with the Polo Grounds fence still another forty feet in front of him, Mays now knew he had it. He had enough time, in fact, to begin his habit of slapping his glove with his throwing hand the way he did before every routine catch.

Finally, in a drawn-out moment that seemed to last much longer that it actually could have,

Mays—the "24" on the back of his jersey still squared toward the infield—held out his left hand and watched Vic Wertz's dream settle into it. Mays's cap spiraled off his head and floated into the grass behind him

In the years to come, the catch would be described as the greatest in the history of the game, one that only Mays could have made. Naturally, Cleveland fans, while impressed by the snag, scoffed at the notion. Partially it was sour grapes. But more than that, they'd seen Larry Doby make comparable catches for years, many of which he'd had to contend with outfield fences to achieve. For instance, Mays's catch paled next to that truly incredible one Doby had made in Cleveland back in July—on the night the detectives finally got Dr. Sam.

For a moment, there was no sound at all. It was as if the air had been taken out of the Polo Grounds and for one perfect instant, fifty thousand people were unable to react. But then, as the magnitude of what they'd just witnessed settled in, they did. The crowd exploded into applause as Mays skidded to a stop a few feet in front of the center field wall, turned and fired the ball back toward the infield before falling to his knees. It would have been possible for a runner with Doby's speed to tag up from second base and come around to score in the time it would take the ball to be shipped back to the infield, essentially a New York City cab ride from home plate. But Mays's throw, while harried, was on target. Doby had been able to scamper back to second, tag up, and motor to third. Rosen, pulling into second as Mays caught up with the ball, had no choice but to turn and hobble back to first without even entertaining the option of tagging up. Wertz returned to the dugout, stunned. The greatest hit of his life had turned into nothing more than what was known in the game as a "loud out."

This wasn't supposed to happen.

The thought ran through the minds of fans back in Cleveland as they watched, listened to, or heard about the miraculous catch. It had been a summer of promising omens and portents—all of them signaling that 1954 belonged to the Cleveland Indians. Every break had gone their way. Each time a key player was injured, and they'd suffered more than their share, a reserve would step up and deliver. Adversity was nothing new to the Indians, but Mays's catch marked the first time all season that fate betrayed them.

The rest of the inning is lost to history, drowned out in the thunderclap of the catch. Pinch-hitter Dale Mitchell walked to load the bases with one out, and the Indians were still in prime position to take command of the game. Had they done so, Willie Mays and the most celebrated catch in World Series history would have become minor footnotes to Cleveland's 112th victory of a blessed season. Dave Pope, a valuable pinch-hitter all season, struck out looking on a one-and-two pitch, leaving it up to eleven-year-veteran catcher Jim Hegan, who had a knack of coming through in the clutch. He also fell behind one-and-two, but then blasted the next pitch toward left. Hegan knew he'd gotten all of the pitch and watched it soar toward the upper deck, following the same path as Bobby Thomson's "shot heard round the world" homer that won the pennant here three years before. Hegan knew he'd belted a grand slam that would prove once again that these Indians were a team of destiny—that no matter what misfortune came their way, they would respond and overcome.

But as he neared first, his gaze still on the ball, he couldn't believe his eyes. From the Cleveland bullpen in right center, Hal Newhouser saw it, too. It was as if an invisible hand was pushing the ball down. Hegan saw New York's left fielder, Monte Irvin, slowing down at the base of the wall, but not in the slumped-shouldered manner of an outfielder knowing he didn't have a chance. Irvin's posture was straight as an arrow, and he was raising his left arm. Hegan realized Irvin thought he had a play.

And with another look up to the ball, Hegan saw that Irvin did. The steady wind blowing in from left field all afternoon had caught Hegan's grand slam in its stream. Instead of becoming a souvenir, the ball plopped into the glove of Monte Irvin, who had pressed his spine against the wall like a child being measured on his birthday. Irvin later said the ball missed hitting the light overhang of the scoreboard by less than six inches.

Two walks, one hit, one incredible catch, and one wind-induced fly ball. No runs. Both the land and the air had turned against the team of destiny.

Lemon was unfazed by fate's double-whammy. He glided through the eighth and ninth, and after Al Rosen was unable to bring a runner home from second with two out in the top of the ninth, the game toiled into extra innings.

With the grandstand shadow now casting darkness over the entire infield, Vic Wertz led off the tenth with a double to the gap in left center that even Willie Mays couldn't get to. It was his fourth hit of the game, and as he was lifted for a pinch-runner, the partisan Polo Grounds fans rose to their feet to offer this unlikely hero a standing ovation. A sacrifice bunt and an intentional walk put runners on the corners with one down, but once again the Indians' usually heady bench failed them when pinch-hitter Bill Glynn struck out swinging. Bob Lemon was due up next, and manager Al Lopez, already having used five players off the bench and knowing Lemon still had gas in the tank, decided to allow his pitcher to bat. Lemon, a better career hitter than most of the league's pinch-hitters anyway, lined a pitch toward right field. With a runner on first, Lemon's liner was placed perfectly to zoom past the first baseman, who should

have been at the bag holding the runner. But New York manager Leo Durocher, playing a hunch as he often did, instructed his first baseman to ignore the runner and play in his normal spot. As a result, he was standing right in the path of Lemon's line drive. He snared it, and the inning was over. Like St. Peter on the morning of the crucifixion, luck had now denied the Indians three times.

Lopez's decision to stick with Lemon still appeared solid when Lemon fanned Don Mueller to start the bottom of the tenth. But then he walked Willie Mays on five pitches, setting the climax to this operatic struggle into motion. Knowing reliable Jim Hegan was no longer behind the plate, lifted for a pinch-hitter in the top of the frame, Mays took off for second on Lemon's next pitch and made it easily. With the winning run now in scoring position, Lopez changed tacks. He had Lemon intentionally walk left-handed Hank Thompson so he would match up better with the right-handed Monte Irvin.

But Durocher countered, pulling back Irvin for substitute batter extraordinaire Jim Rhodes—better known as "Dusty"—who'd carved a niche for himself in his three-year career as a pinch-hitter, hitting .341 off the bench in 1954. Still, it was a gamble. The one time Rhodes had faced Lemon in a spring training game, he struck out on three pitches. Rhodes stepped into the batter's box at 4:12 p.m., exactly ninety minutes before the sun would settle into the New York horizon.

Lemon's first pitch, his 142nd of the day, was a sinking curve, and a good one, arriving over the plate just below Rhodes's belt. Rhodes, who intended to take the first pitch to allow himself to settle in, couldn't resist. He swung and made contact, glancing it off the top of the bat. As he completed his motion and saw the ball float awkwardly into the air, Lemon knew he'd just gotten the second out and mentally turned to how he would pitch to Davey Williams, the next batter. In the broadcast booth, announcer Al Helper's voice remained in its neutral cadence as he described the path of the baseball, certainly not slipping into the rising crescendo foreshadowing a big play. Bobby Avila saw the ball spiral off Rhodes's bat and started running to his left from his stance near second base. He figured he'd be able to get to it before right fielder Dave Pope could reach it. In another second, he changed his mind. It was carrying enough, he saw, that Pope would have the easier play. Avila slowed to a stop and watched Pope jog to his right, clearly with a bead on the ball.

But Avila noticed that Pope was also moving backward. That damned ball was carrying farther than he thought it would. He glanced back to Mays, who, dancing off second, might have a chance to tag up and advance to third.

Pope shifted again, this time shuffling to his left to follow the path of the ball. Avila's eyes widened. Pope was on the warning track and still trying to back up. *This isn't happening*, Avila thought. *This can't be happening.* The same wind that had slapped down Hegan's potential grand slam two innings before had picked up Rhodes's lazy fly ball and was carrying it toward the obscenely short porch in right field. "It was nothing," Pope would say later. "A can of corn . . . a little can of corn."

With his back pressed against the wall, just as Irvin had done to catch Hegan's drive in the eighth, Pope leaped up into the sea of hands poised two feet above his head. Though not actively reaching for the ball, the Giants rooters in the first row still leaned forward in natural anticipation as the ball neared them. It glanced off the torso of a fan, just above the tip of Pope's glove, and pinballed back onto the field. It was a home run—the cheapest in the history of the World Series.

It had traveled just 258 feet—fifty-seven feet shorter than Hegan's out in the eighth and roughly two hundred feet shorter than Wertz's. The preposterous nature of Rhodes's homer further underlined the injustice of Wertz's robbery. "Wertz hits the ball as far as anybody ever will," Lopez sighed later, "and it's just an out." Indeed, just as Wertz's blast would have been a home run in any ballpark but one, Rhodes's game-winning home run would have been a routine fly ball in any baseball park in America. Except one.

Five days earlier, *Cleveland Press* sports editor Franklin Lewis had made a prediction that turned out to be eerily accurate. "Fluke hits, such as pop fly home runs, are much more likely to be stroked in the Polo Grounds than in Cleveland," he wrote. "A 200-foot home run can turn the trend of a contest there. An outfielder's catch of a 450-foot fly ball can attain an equal effect, positive or negative, according to your rooting interest." As it happened, the rooting interest of Cleveland had been decimated by both occurrences in the space of thirty minutes.

Plain Dealer sports editor Gordon Cobbledick called it a "little-boy" homer. Most other reporters dusted off an old baseball term coined by a crusty New York writer who had disliked legendary Giants manager John McGraw and would often highlight flaws in Giant victories. The reporter, who hailed from San Francisco, an area that at the time held a dim view of those of Asian descent, would label lucky round-trippers such as the one Rhodes hit as "Chinese home runs." Naturally, Leo Durocher would defend it. "It was a home run," he announced, "nothing more and nothing less." His conviction was almost believable.

Bob Lemon lifted his glove off his left hand and fired it into the air toward the backstop with frightening force—a strikingly unusual display of anger both for the pitcher and the era. Willie Mays leaped into the air at second base, flinging his arms in circles, landed, then leaped again with the joy of a young boy on Christmas morning. In his celebration, Thompson came up right behind him at second, and Mays finally began to prance toward third at a slow pace. By the time they'd reached third, Rhodes had caught up with both, and the trio rounded the bag and jogged toward home as if part of a conga line. It was the fitting start for a night of revelry and celebration in New York City. "*A storybook finish for the New York Giants in the first game of the 1954 World Series . . .*" Al Helper told his radio audience.

Back in Cleveland, there would be no celebrating; nor would there be panic. The Giants had stolen one, fair and square. It simply underlined what strokes of luck were required to beat the greatest team in recent memory. The Indians had stranded thirteen men on base and were an incredible one-for-sixteen at the plate with runners in scoring position. Vic Wertz had delivered both runs and half of Cleveland's hits, but the rest of the lineup and each pinch-hitter had either struggled or been outright robbed. Through it all, Bob Lemon had been his usual dominant self, allowing only two hits after the fifth inning—only one if you didn't count Rhodes's lucky shot. It was just a bad day for the Cleveland hitters and a tough break for Lemon. It proved that the Giants would need divine intervention to top any of the Big Three and that all the Indians needed was a little bit of offense for everything to turn out the way it was supposed to.

"So we lost in the tenth inning, after an afternoon of blood-chilling thrills," a *Plain Dealer* editorial comforted the following morning. "But are we downhearted? Not on your life. It's only the first one, and there are plenty more to come.

"There's no reason for civic gloom. Tomorrow's another day!"

Indeed, it had been a summer of bright tomorrows in the Best Location in the Nation, days and nights filled with good news and shining optimism.

But this time, setting a heart-wrenching tone for the remainder of the century and beyond, tomorrow would never come.

PART ONE

BEFORE THE SHADOWS

FINAL 1953 AMERICAN LEAGUE STANDINGS

	W	L	PCT	GB
NEW YORK	99	52	.656	—
CLEVELAND	92	62	.597	$8\frac{1}{2}$
CHICAGO	89	65	.578	$11\frac{1}{2}$
BOSTON	84	69	.549	16
WASHINGTON	76	76	.500	$23\frac{1}{2}$
DETROIT	60	94	.390	$40\frac{1}{2}$
PHILADELPHIA	59	95	.383	$41\frac{1}{2}$
ST. LOUIS	54	100	.351	$46\frac{1}{2}$

1 - NOW OR NEVER

I t was only the first week of April, but the Cleveland Indians were already sick of the New York Giants.

In addition to the anxiety and impatience all baseball players feel as spring training grinds to its welcome conclusion, a big reason the Tribe looked forward to breaking camp and starting the regular season was that it could bid farewell to the Giants for good in 1954. As April dawned, and the Indians and Giants began their winding road home from their training camps in Arizona, they stopped in cities throughout the west and played exhibition games to generally small and disinterested crowds. On April 1, their trains pulled into Houston, where the Giants once again topped the Indians, marking New York's ninth victory in twelve games against Cleveland that spring. It was the midpoint of a slate of twenty-four preseason contests the teams would play, continuing a tradition begun in 1934. Over that twenty-year period, the teams had played more than 250 exhibition games. Needless to say, by 1954, they knew one another well.

Even without the string of losses to the Giants, it had not been a prosperous camp. The Cleveland offense, not the strength of the team to begin with, was virtually non-existent, while the pitching, the aspect on which the fortunes of the team would sink or swim in 1954, had been inconsistent. The team arrived in Tucson the last week of February filled with expectations. General manager Hank Greenberg, under fire in recent years, brashly predicted the Indians would reach the World Series. "I honestly feel you have the tools to win the pennant," he would say at a Cleveland Advertising Club luncheon before the season opener. "All you have to do is use them. If you stick together through the long, hard season ahead, I see no reason at all why we can't have a World's Series here in October." To some, Greenberg's confidence appeared desperate—a smokescreen created by a man who needed a handful of controversial decisions to bear fruit to save his job.

Long before Greenberg became the team's GM after Bill Veeck sold it in 1949, he was well known to Cleveland fans, primarily as a nemesis. For twelve years, Greenberg had riddled Indians pitching as well as that of every other team in the American League during a Hall of Fame career with the Detroit Tigers. A four-time All-Star and twice named MVP, Greenberg left a legacy as one of the greatest hitters ever to play the game. Yet his real legacy was less about his accomplishments on the baseball field than about his religious affiliation.

Greenberg, born to Russian immigrants, became baseball's first Jewish star. In an era of world history defined by the Holocaust and Adolf Hitler, the tall, lumbering Greenberg became almost a folk hero to American Jews, representing their own hopes and dreams of what could be accomplished once they overcame the hurdle of anti-Semitism. But with his playing career winding down after the war, Greenberg wasn't ready to leave baseball. Outspoken and intelligent, Greenberg was full of new ideas and wanted to showcase them as a general manager. He'd considered moving from the diamond to the front office in Detroit but was unceremoniously sold, after a contract dispute. After one final year on the field in Pittsburgh in 1947, Greenberg retired, not knowing what would come next.

A chance encounter at the World Series that October would set the course of the rest of his career. Sitting in the box seats on the first-base line at Yankee Stadium along with many other members of baseball's royalty, Greenberg happened to be placed beside Bill Veeck, the charismatic showman who had purchased the Indians the year before. As the game ended and the spectators from that section exited by crossing the field to a gate in right field, Greenberg and Veeck, hobbling along on his trademark cane to aid his amputated leg, struck up a conversation. Veeck asked if Greenberg was having dinner at Toots Shor's, the well-known restaurant on Fifty-First Street that hosted many New York celebrities and athletes. Greenberg said he was, and Veeck invited him to join him there. They met at 7:30 and stayed until the restaurant closed at 4 a.m., talking and debating baseball. Both men could see that they were of the same mind about the game, and after a few more get-togethers during the Series, Veeck invited Greenberg to join the Indians. Greenberg told Veeck he was no longer going to play, but that wasn't what Cleveland's owner had in mind. He advised Greenberg that one of the team's minority owners would soon be looking to sell his share of the team, and with a little maneuvering, Greenberg could wind up with 10 percent of the club. In the meantime, Veeck offered to hire Greenberg as his assistant so he could learn the ropes of the front office. Though at $15,000 a year he would only earn a quarter of what he was paid in his final season as a player, Greenberg saw the opportunity and agreed.

He mostly stood by as a spectator during the Indians' greatest season in franchise history, as they triumphed in an incredible four-team

In 1949, the torch of leadership in the Indians
front office passed from showman Bill Veeck (left)
to former slugger Hank Greenberg.

pennant race and captured their first World Series title in nearly three
decades. Along the way, Veeck took Greenberg under his wing and
introduced him to baseball's executive solar system. He also trusted
his new assistant as a confidant, often second-guessing Tribe player/
manager Lou Boudreau and asking Greenberg if he'd ever consider
taking over as manager. Greenberg shrugged off the idea. The following
season, Veeck put Greenberg in charge of Cleveland's vast farm system,
a colossal responsibility that Greenberg embraced, quietly laying the
parent club's foundation for the next decade.

Championing the innovative idea of creating a centralized farm system that marched in step with the parent club rather than keeping track of multiple minor-league teams with separate agendas, Greenberg rented an abandoned air base in Marianna, Florida, and built four baseball diamonds with a central platform in the center. Scouts and managers would combine efforts to create not one minor-league team, but an entire farm system. The camp soon moved to a larger complex at Daytona Beach and the program expanded. By the mid-1950s, the Indians oversaw the most fertile farm system in baseball.

After Veeck sold the team in 1949, the new owners appointed Greenberg general manager. Yet even in this new role as one of the most powerful men in the game, Greenberg still encountered some of the anti-Semitism that had haunted him in his playing career. When he attended the winter owners meetings in Phoenix, he was not permitted to stay in the same hotel as the rest of the guests because he was Jewish.

By the end of his first season as GM, two things were clear: first, Hank Greenberg was not Bill Veeck. And second, he wasn't going to try to be. Whereas Veeck was personable and charming with Cleveland reporters, Greenberg was aloof, feeling he knew more about baseball than any members of the media. During long games on hot summer afternoons at Municipal Stadium, reporters would snicker at the confident Greenberg, who would sit in his reserved box with his shirt off, soaking in the sunlight as if he were nothing more than a fan—not that any ordinary fan would be so crass as to take off his shirt in public.

It didn't take long for animosity to settle in, as reporters who'd grown accustomed to Bill Veeck quickly turned on Greenberg. Meanwhile, Greenberg began the controversial process of restructuring a good—but not great—team. Despite a strong third-place finish in 1949 and a ninety-two-win campaign in 1950, the Indians, thought Greenberg, needed to be rebuilt. He released longtime fan favorite and seven-time All-Star Ken Keltner as well as pitcher Gene Bearden, who'd won twenty games during the magical 1948 season. First baseman Mickey Vernon, shrewdly acquired by Veeck in one of his final transactions with Cleveland, was traded away after only one year, costing the Indians four of his All-Star seasons. Most notably, after the 1950 season in which many thought the Indians had choked down the stretch, Greenberg decided to pull a trigger that Veeck never could. When Boudreau announced his intention to retire as a player after 1950 and just be the manager, Greenberg felt his value to the Indians plummeted. He released Boudreau and brought in minor-league manager Al Lopez, introducing him at a press conference and shocking area reporters after flying Lopez into Cleveland under an assumed name and putting him up at his own house in Shaker Heights. While many reporters knew Lopez and thought it was a good move, Greenberg's subterfuge fueled his adversarial relationship with the press.

Without question, for better or worse, by 1951, this was Hank Greenberg's team. Yet little changed in the standings. The Indians continued to contend through much of the summer, only to finish second to the mighty Yankees three consecutive years. A fourth straight failure in 1954 would be a rebuke to Greenberg, who had yet to match Veeck's accomplishments. For all his intelligence and articulate descriptions of his plans to the press, Greenberg's tenure in Cleveland had been rocky.

"If you judge a front-office executive on his accomplishments in . . . player-juggling and talent-handling, Greenberg is a failure,"

Franklin Lewis wrote in the *Cleveland Press*. "If you add the delicate field of public relations, both with the press and the fandom, Greenberg is a flop." He did have some support among the fan base, including the proprietors of a laundry that distributed buttons to its clients that read "We're Witcha Hank!" No matter how many shirts around town displayed this message, Greenberg knew his fate would be decided on the field. Another failure in 1954—even a narrow one—would likely signal the conclusion of his duties with the Indians.

There was, however, reason for optimism. Al Lopez called the '54 Tribe the strongest team he'd had in his four years at the helm. Yet in the same breath, he revealed that only four starting positions were set. Four others would be determined in spring training, hardly the recipe for success in a league dominated by perhaps the finest team in baseball history.

To be sure, there was little about the Indians that gave the New York Yankees pause as they reported to camp. Not only had the Yankees captured five consecutive American League pennants (followed by a quintet of World Series triumphs), but in each of the past three seasons New York had been challenged by the Indians in September, only to sprint past them with the finish line in sight. In 1951, the Indians dropped ten games back by Memorial Day, then mounted a furious August comeback, winning thirteen straight and taking a three-game lead. With two weeks to go, the Tribe held a one-game advantage on New York, then went on to lose eight of the last eleven to finish five back. A year later, the Indians ripped off seven straight wins to start the season and controlled first place in mid-June before a string of nine losses in twelve games dropped them into fourth. Cleveland rallied from seven and a half back in late July to claw within a half-game of first with a dozen to play. They went on to win nine of their last ten, but the Yankees won thirteen of their last fifteen to take the pennant by a mere two games. Even the 1953 race, which New York won by a comfortable eight and a half games, was a painful experience for the Indians, who had won a remarkable twenty of twenty-three games down the stretch—yet in the process only gained six games on the Yankees.

As the Indians tried desperately to shed their reputation as choke-ups, their fans tried to get to the bottom of their September swoons. "I believe that in Cleveland, players are affected greatly by civic pressure," Harry Jones wrote in the *Plain Dealer*. "This is not true in New York. There is constant civic demand on Cleveland players, whereas the Yankees are swallowed up by the multitudes in New York once they leave the ballpark."

Ever since the Indians had triumphed over the Yankees and Boston Red Sox in their legendary pennant race in 1948, no matter what they did or how much they improved, New York was always better. Granted, the Yankees were better than everyone, but the contrast came into stark relief with Cleveland since the Indians were the only American League team capable of competing with them. In fact, since 1950, the Indians had won more games than any other team in the American League. Any other team besides New York, of course. The Indians had been good, even great, at times. But not good enough. "Ever since they won the world championship in 1948 it has been one thing or another with the Indians," *Sporting News* declared. "One year they had superlative defense but not enough hitting. The next year they battered down the fences but their infield fell apart." Reflecting this trend, as the Indians' offense exploded for sixty-five runs in their first four exhibition games of 1954, a fan hollered from the grandstand, "Save some of those runs for the Yankees!" Exhibition game or not, everyone knew the Indians needed all the help they could get.

Pushing the buttons on New York's well-oiled (and financed) machine was the oracle of baseball himself, Casey Stengel, who in his twenty years as a manager had forgotten more about baseball than most managers would ever know. After the Yankees won their fifth straight World Series the previous fall, Stengel admitted he didn't know why the string couldn't reach six or seven. Before spring training, he noted that the club was stronger than at any time since he'd been manager. Then, as if thumbing his nose at the rest of the league, he added, "The other clubs are sore and desperate. The 'Hate the Yankees' campaign will be picked up with more venom."

In a preseason poll of 197 baseball writers, 119 picked the Yankees to return to the World Series for a sixth straight season. "The Yankees will win the pennant," Stengel boldly proclaimed as the team headed home from spring training, "because there isn't a club in the American League capable of beating them." It was a direct shot at the Indians, the only team within arm's length of New York in recent years. Stengel's sentiment was reflected in the writers' poll. Of the seventy-eight dissenters, only twenty-four picked Cleveland to topple the dynasty. On the off chance the Yankees would fall, the experts said, it would not be the Indians who tripped them. And their sickly 13–16 spring record did little to change minds.

It appeared the window of opportunity to dethrone the mighty Yankees had passed. "You could pick the Indians to win the American League pennant this season and get away with it, I suppose," Harry Jones wrote in the *Plain Dealer*. "But frankly, I can't." The paper's sports editor, Gordon Cobbledick, agreed, noting that the team would have to prove it was capable of winning the big game. "They've been a long time earning a reputation as a team that looks like a champion until the chips are down," he wrote. "They have to show me that they think like champions." And they had to do it quickly, Cobbledick added, because time—defined in sports as the median age and condition of a team's key players—was running out. "The Indians as they are now constituted can't last much longer," he said. "It's now or never."

As the team began its journey across the continent back to Cleveland, so too did a young couple on their way home after an extended vacation in California. The husband, a thirty-year-old doctor named Sam Sheppard, had traveled out west to attend a medical conference and had brought his wife, Marilyn, with him. As they headed home from what would be the last trip they would ever take together, each carried a secret from the other. During part of the trip, when the young doctor had stayed at a friend's house away from his wife, he had reconnected with an old flame—a pretty medical technician who used to work with him in Cleveland—and the two had resumed their sexual relationship.

And his wife, not knowing this, also did not yet realize that her life had changed in another way. During the trip, she had become pregnant with their second child.

There was also a third secret, unbeknownst to either of them. In three months, Marilyn Sheppard and the burgeoning life within her would be murdered.

2 - EMPIRE OF FREEDOM

T he Best Location in the Nation.

It was a term that not only rolled off the tongue with a confident cadence, but also fit the city it described like a smooth leather glove.

The bold, iconic aspect of the phrase originated by accident. In 1944, the Cleveland Electric Illuminating Company launched a marketing campaign to attract new businesses to the area. Its slogan, cooked up by executive Frank Ryan for full-page ads in national publications, proclaimed Cleveland and northeast Ohio to be "the best location in the nation for many industries," with the subhead, "No other area in the U.S. offers this unique combination of advantages." The *New York Times* originally refused to publish the ad on the grounds that no area could support such a claim. The Illuminating Company provided the *Times* with its research and invited the paper to further investigate the statement. The *Times* did, and then published the ad.

Ironically, the campaign gained more attention in Cleveland than in the targeted cities. Editors at the Cleveland papers quickly adapted and modified the slogan in their copy. The final portion of the phrase was neatly omitted, leaving just "the best location in the nation." The words made Cleveland feel proud of itself, providing a verbal emblem for what its citizens already believed.

The initial purpose of the campaign was to mirror the city's dramatic population growth. In the last half of the nineteenth century, Cleveland had grown from a Midwestern wagon stop to one of the largest cities in the country. Then, as immigrants flooded across the ocean at the dawn of the new century, Cleveland's population again quadrupled, launching it from the nation's tenth-largest city to the fifth. Though the social and economic scars left by the Great Depression were still evident, as what would soon be remembered as the golden decade of the 1950s reached its midpoint, Cleveland, now the seventh-largest city in America, could lay claim to such a term and defend its position. The post-war economic boom of the late 1940s had helped Cleveland rebound, and a flurry of civic projects led by Mayor Thomas Burke had resulted in the construction of a new lakefront airport and an efficient rapid transit system. It seemed also symbolic that Cleveland earned notoriety as the best-lighted metropolitan area in the world in the mid-fifties, with more than a thousand miles of well-lighted streets and highways. After all, it was in Cleveland in 1879 that the first public electric street lighting was activated. As the *Saturday Evening Post* declared, Cleveland was "the city that forecasts the future," further exemplified that summer when it became one of the first cities in America to see its postmen use automobiles to deliver the mail.

For all its innovation, however, Cleveland still mirrored the past.

By the 1950s, Cleveland remained one of the most culturally segregated cities in America. From the outside, it gave Cleveland a European, cosmopolitan flavor. Its neighborhoods were still lit up by religious parades and social events, and the spires of countless churches and synagogues were sprinkled along the Cuyahoga Valley. Yet unlike the melting-pot neighborhoods created out of necessity in New York, Cleveland was splintered into very clear communities: Jewish or Catholic on religious grounds, or Italian, Czech, Polish, Hungarian, or Irish on ethnic ones. Early in an initial conversation with a new acquaintance, the natural question would inevitably come up: "What are you?" These communities often co-existed side-by-side—Germans flocked to Lakewood and Rocky River, Poles to Garfield Heights and Parma, Jews to Shaker Heights and Cleveland Heights, Czechs to Brecksville and Seven Hills, and so on. But rarely would they cross their invisible boundaries. A Polish girl bringing home an Italian boy, for example, would create a family scandal that would be whispered about for decades.

The suburbs were generally more mixed, but remained just as steadfast as the neighborhoods in the city in their intolerance for allowing blacks, who were essentially quarantined in a tremendous cluster of poverty on Cleveland's East Side. If word trickled into a suburban neighborhood that a black family was considering buying a home, many white families pulled up their stakes and moved elsewhere. Property values would instantly drop, leading to the unspoken agreement for anyone selling his house to not post a "for sale" sign in the yard. Realtors would spread the word and market the homes to the "right kind of people," and the entire neighborhood could rest easy.

It was one of the industrial capitals of the world, supplying steel, textiles, and other fossil fuels of manufacturing. More than 750 Cleveland companies were engaged in foreign trade, and exporting brought in more than $500 million to the city annually. And Cleveland's strength was in tune with the robust economy around the United States. In January, U.S. Steel reported its most profitable year since before World War I. General

Motors announced a $1 billion expansion program—a total more than the entire net worth of the city of Cleveland. That spring, the stock market hit peaks not seen in nearly a quarter-century, a drive spearheaded by the success of railroad companies, and would remain lofty throughout the summer. The nation's jobless rate was at a record low and the American dream was never more vivid. There were plenty of good jobs in industry and sales for men, who went off to work knowing that their wives would handle everything on the homefront. One of the few domestic debates that surfaced was reflected by an article in the *Plain Dealer*'s Sunday magazine that spring: "Should Wives Cook Breakfast?" followed by another a few weeks later: "Should Women Let Their Brains Show?"

Overseas, the conflict between North and South Korea had finally come to a close after American intervention. Still, the threat of communist domination hung over the globe like a shadow. Americans opened their newspapers in April to the first photographs of the test detonation of a hydrogen bomb over the Pacific Ocean. Official government films of the test were broadcast on television—the latest breakthrough in domestic technology. The images sent a shudder down the spine of America, particularly when the magnitude of the weapon was put into context. If a hydrogen bomb were dropped above the Terminal Tower downtown, the *Cleveland Press* helpfully speculated, the total destruction would cover a diameter of eight miles. The *Press* included a map of Greater Cleveland to outline the precise parameters of doomsday: eastbound to East Boulevard, westward to West 117th Street, and as far south as Cuyahoga Heights.

It was this kind of crackerjack reporting that had made the *Press* the greatest newspaper not only in Cleveland, but the entire state— evidenced by its catchphrase printed below the banner of each issue:

"The Newspaper That Serves Its Readers." In 1954, its readers numbered better than 311,000, giving it the largest circulation in Ohio and among the top fifteen in the United States. Every weekday, seven out of ten families in Cuyahoga County bought a copy of the *Press*. And the prince of the paper was its longtime editor, Louis Seltzer, a strong-willed, self-made pillar of the community who channeled so much power among the city's movers and shakers that he'd earned the nickname "Mr. Cleveland."

It had been a remarkable journey for Seltzer. Born in 1897 in a three-room house behind a fire station on the western bank of the Cuyahoga River, he once described himself as "a bald-pated, dried-up little dude at whom nobody might be apt to look a second time." Short and slender, his outward appearance may have been ordinary, but inside he was as unique an individual as Cleveland had ever seen.

Enigmatic Cleveland Press editor Louis Seltzer, better known as "Mr. Cleveland," remains one of the most fascinating—and polarizing—figures in American journalism.

High-strung and constantly energetic, he would vacuum his entire house late at night in an attempt to tire himself out to the point that he could sleep. He spent little time behind his desk, often hovering through the newsroom like a vulture, reading stories over his reporters' shoulders as they typed them while nibbling on candy and jelly beans they'd leave out for him.

Seltzer dropped out of school at the age of twelve to take a job as a copy boy at the *Cleveland Leader*, in time writing his own column under the byline "Louie the Office Boy." By this time, Seltzer was in love with the profession and had no desire to go back to school. At seventeen, he got a job as a reporter for the *Cleveland News*. By nineteen, he was heading the city desk at the *Press*, where he'd begun as a police reporter, but only held the city editor job for six months because he wanted to get more experience as a reporter. He was named editor of the entire paper at thirty-one. "Like Alice in Wonderland," Seltzer said, "I felt I had to run my best to stay in one place and twice as fast if I wanted to move ahead."

While the *Press* was already successful, Seltzer guided it in a new direction, namely, making it the voice of the city he loved and perhaps knew better than anyone. "My idea," he told the *Saturday Evening Post*, "has been to get back to the way of the old country editor who spent most of his time learning about his hometown. If you don't get the flavor of the town into your paper, you've missed the boat." A newspaper had "to beat every day with the hearts of our readers," and if it didn't, he wanted to know why. A reader who decided to cancel his *Press* subscription would often receive a call from Seltzer himself. The editor wasn't trying to change his mind, just to find out where his paper had failed him.

And Seltzer appealed to one of the underlying flavors of the city by nurturing a reputation for fighting corruption and standing up for the underdog. Known as the self-appointed conscience of the city, Seltzer, who didn't drink or smoke (which was highly unusual for the time), saw himself and his reporters as public watchdogs and the *Press*'s rickety old office building at East Ninth Street and Rockwell Avenue as Cleveland's citadel of truth. Seltzer wasn't afraid to criticize the police or judges or politicians when he felt they were trying to pull a fast one on John Q. Public. In theory, it sounded honorable, and Seltzer and the *Press* did much good. When a local four-year-old boy was assaulted and left for dead, Seltzer and the *Press* offered a $1,000 reward for the arrest and conviction of the perpetrator. A tip to police led to an arrest and a confession two days later, and Seltzer presented the tipster with a check—in a ceremonial photograph that, naturally, was splashed across the front page of the *Press*.

But Seltzer also was known to get carried away, seizing on the mere appearance of corruption or misconduct and clinging to it tenaciously. In 1953, he attacked one of the most honorable judges in Cleveland for conducting shady financial affairs. The eventual firestorm of attention resulted in the judge's resignation from the Bar Association, though he was acquitted of embezzlement charges. Many involved in the case were either outraged at Seltzer or simply rolled their eyes, commenting, "Louie is just trying to sell papers."

He was involved in seemingly every decision the newspaper made, and his fingerprints could be found on every article the *Press* published. Clevelanders would use Seltzer's name and "the *Press*" interchangeably, and by the 1950s, he had become known as both a "kingmaker" and a "boss-buster." With one editorial, he could shatter a political campaign or anoint a new legacy. He paved the way for Ohio Governor Frank Lausche (who in 1954 appeared to be an appealing

Democratic candidate for the presidential campaign of 1956, particularly if President Eisenhower decided not to run for re-election), Senator Thomas Burke (a former mayor of Cleveland), and most recently, new Cleveland Mayor Anthony Celebrezze, who had risen out of obscurity to defeat better-known opponents in both parties in 1953. Seltzer himself had reportedly turned down an offer to run for the Senate, in addition to plush jobs at bigger papers in bigger cities, because he refused to leave the city he loved. Needless to say, politicians and power brokers often fell over one another courting Seltzer's support.

Seltzer's passion for his hometown was reflected in a column he wrote about an ordinary return flight from a long trip. "You breathe that sense of comfort that can come from only one thing in the world—the unequaled sense of coming home," he wrote. "Of being among people, in surroundings and mixed into the traditions and life of the city you love—of that place upon Earth most important of all: Cleveland, Ohio, USA."

Along the way, he'd become a beacon of professionalism, giving countless speeches on the importance of his trade. With the nation still buzzing about the hydrogen bomb, Seltzer was the feature attraction at the University of Missouri, one of the nation's leading journalism schools, during National Journalism Week. In Cleveland and beyond, Seltzer was seen as both a role model and a dynamic showman, capable of holding people's attention for as long as he wanted it. For example, taking a distant and routine weapons test and molding the story to provide a local angle: how a nuclear holocaust would affect your neighborhood. This was a brand of reporting other newspapers couldn't offer, and while those competitors may have snickered at Seltzer's tactics, he consistently proved he was better—maybe not at effectively relaying the pertinent facts surrounding a story but certainly by selling more newspapers.

But even the *Press*'s shrill proclamations surrounding the H-bomb were soon drowned out. President Eisenhower went on television later that week and allayed the nation's worries. Clevelanders were further comforted three weeks later with the announcement that their city had been selected as one of the first in the nation to host a NIKE missile— the Army's electronic rocket response to an atomic air raid. Within days, the specter of nuclear holocaust faded into the background, as did, to some extent, the threat of a Soviet ambush fanned by the accusations of flamboyant Wisconsin senator Joseph McCarthy. With the passing of a pair of geopolitical storms that spring, Americans eased back into everyday life. The Soviet threat didn't appear quite so immediate after all.

Thus, when word trickled out of Southeast Asia that a French fort in Dien Bien Phu was under assault by communist insurgents, few gave it much notice. As the story dragged along through the spring, U.S. Secretary of State John Foster Dulles warned that the situation "may involve serious commitments to us all." In a speech to the Cleveland Engineering Society that April, the president of one of the nation's largest manufacturers of aircraft defense equipment stated that the U.S. was already committed to the conflict and would eventually "inherit" the situation. Yet the headline "Indo Crisis Could Pull U.S. In" in the *Plain Dealer* seemed melodramatic. Few readers had heard of this little country, so it was difficult to imagine the United States becoming involved. Newspapers couldn't even settle on whether "Viet-Nam" was one word or two.

But such details didn't matter. America was the world's shining empire of freedom, winning two wars in the span of a decade, and was now basking in the glow of peace and prosperity.

3 - A SATURDAY NIGHT TOWN

As it often does in northeast Ohio, April dawned cold and overcast. After on-and-off snow flurries throughout the first of the month, the temperature remained in the forties for much of the first few days of what is considered to be the calendar's official proclamation of spring.

In spite of the frosty conditions, Clevelanders were busy preparing for Easter, now just over two weeks away. Department stores such as Halle's and May Co. unveiled new fashions in bonnets and dresses, along with sales for children's formalwear. Hough Bakeries was inundated with orders for lamb-shaped Easter cakes, with jelly beans for eyes and the wool made of coconut shavings atop the white frosting. Fathers bought corsages for their wives and daughters to wear to church on Easter Sunday.

Holy Week also would mark the beginning of the baseball season, as the Indians would play their first game on Tuesday, the thirteenth of April. Of course, there would be the usual excitement in each of the thirteen cities that owned a major league team. With none south of Washington, D.C., and none west of St. Louis, the citizens of these areas saw the beginning of baseball season as more than just the start of a new sporting campaign. It was a reward for surviving a cruel winter and a harbinger of the summer days and nights to come.

While three straight close-but-no-cigar finishes may have taken some of the verve out of many Cleveland fans as they looked forward to the 1954 campaign, there were still plenty of reasons for them to take notice of the new season. For the second straight year, the home schedule would include thirty night games—including an unprecedented three on Saturday nights. This was a trend many in baseball felt was counterproductive. "Baseball under the lights has made a big difference in living conditions," Bob Feller would say that summer. "It's harder to keep the proper physical edge because no definite pattern for sleeping and eating habits can be established." Cubs owner Philip Wrigley went so far as to say that attendance would be much higher overall if there was no night baseball. More games during the day was the only way to ensure future prosperity, he claimed, because with the introduction of television into the American family room, there were too many evening entertainment choices against which baseball had to compete.

Wrigley wasn't alone. The major league 1954 schedule showed that the expansion of night baseball had ceased, making the Indians' night schedule—particularly the trio of Saturday-night games—a bold decision. But Cleveland was no ordinary baseball town. There was plenty to draw people downtown any night of the week, especially on the weekends. "Cleveland," Hal Lebovitz wrote in the *Plain Dealer*, "has become a Saturday-night town."

Night games were still relatively rare, but the thought of playing games after dark on the weekends seemed particularly risky for the Indians. Roughly half of the Tribe's weekend home crowds consisted of fans from outside of Cleveland. The team's Ohio-wide appeal led to the brilliant marketing idea of a traveling box office: a brightly decorated station wagon would cruise from town to town around the Buckeye State selling tickets. Also appealing to out-of-towners were the nine doubleheaders the Tribe was scheduled to play. Originally eight were slated, but when the team refused to play a scheduled game with Detroit on Good Friday, to respect the reverence many of its fans invested in the day, the game was switched to a Wednesday in August, setting up a rare weekday afternoon doubleheader.

The Indians, like all teams, were constantly seeking ways to lure more fans to the ballpark. One method was through a speakers bureau set up to arrange engagements for players. Yet many fans were upset to discover that players were often paid for such appearances. Star players like Yogi Berra even went so far as to employ an "agent" to organize and schedule appearances and endorsements, but Nate Wallack, head of the press office, proudly announced that, going into 1954, "None of our fellows has an agent." He further attempted to allay these concerns about players being paid for their appearances, explaining that if organizations weren't required to offer some sort of compensation, players would be inundated with requests. There actually was a precedent for such thinking, since players were paid for appearances on a pregame dugout interview television program. But these honorariums were donated by the players to a clubhouse kitty used to purchase flowers and gifts on behalf of the team.

Another controversial idea to generate interest was proposed by Hank Greenberg prior to the season. He suggested introducing "interleague play" for 1955, in which each American League team would play two home games and two away games against a chosen National League team. It was met with vociferous opposition. "You might have a couple of good hits with three teams," White Sox general manager Frank Lane commented, "but you would die with the rest. It would also harm the World Series and All-Star Game." Opponents of the plan were also concerned that such a tradition-shattering concept could open the door to even more wild ideas. What would be next, they wondered. A playoff system?

Another change, albeit not a particularly welcome one, was the Indians' decision not to televise any home games. Each road game would be televised locally on WXEL Channel 8, and all games would be broadcast on the radio on WERE-AM 1300, but in following with the general thinking of organized baseball, the only way to keep attendance from plummeting was to not give fans the option of watching games at home instead of at the stadium.

Major League Baseball struggled with the question: to televise or not to televise. The benefits were obvious. In 1953, only four of the sixteen teams finished in the black—the Yankees, Indians, White Sox, and Milwaukee Braves. And of that quartet, only the Braves, playing in brand-new County Stadium, were financially sustainable based solely on attendance. The other three finished in the clear because of their profitable agreements with local radio and TV stations to broadcast games. The Indians, for example, drew more than a million fans to home games in '53, but this was far less important to the bottom line than the $350,000 the franchise collected from broadcasting rights. Yet there was a risk to accepting such bargains. Baseball commissioner Ford Frick proclaimed his opinion that putting baseball on television was "killing the goose that laid the golden egg."

While television may have been the wave of the future, radio was still the centerpiece of home entertainment. The daily radio-programming grid that appeared in Cleveland's newspapers was still larger and more prominently displayed than the television grid. The broadcast booth was another site of change for Tribe fans in 1954. After serving twenty-one years behind the microphone as the first radio voice of the team, the legendary Jack Graney had retired, leaving play-by-play duties to his partner, Jimmy Dudley.

Two additions to the rulebook also piqued the interest of longtime fans. The first, league-wide, was initially resisted by the players. It required players in the field to bring their gloves with them to the dugout at the completion of an inning and not simply leave them in the outfield grass—a practice that had been in place since the game began. The second required all Indians players to wear plastic batting helmets over their caps when at the plate. And for the first time in two decades the Cleveland caps themselves would be noticeably different. While the red wishbone "C" logo in place since the thirties remained, placed in the middle was the small Chief Wahoo logo that had been created in 1951 and added to the sleeves of the jerseys.

As the team wrapped up spring training and headed back east, the grounds crew put the finishing touches on a new infield at Municipal Stadium. With snow still piled up around the dugouts, workers tilled the old surface, added new dirt, and smoothed it out, a process exercised every five or six years. The Indians, however, wouldn't get much use of the new diamond at first. Twenty of their first twenty-four games would be played away from home—more than a quarter of the road schedule, which would begin in Chicago.

Even though the event would take place in Chicago, 350 miles away, Tuesday was a day of celebration back in Cleveland. Festivities began at 9:15 that morning at a barbershop in the Hotel Statler with a tradition first established more than two decades before. On opening day 1932, WGAR's station manager came into the shop for a haircut and bet barber Al Klein fifteen minutes of air time that the Indians wouldn't defeat the Detroit Tigers that day. Cleveland won, and ever since, Klein had been collecting with a fifteen-minute broadcast live from his barbershop on opening day.

The biggest opening day crowd in the history of Comiskey Park filed through the turnstiles on a surprisingly beautiful afternoon. Though frigid temperatures and howling winds plagued many openers in Chicago, this one was a welcome exception: the April sun shone brightly, and the temperature climbed into the seventies. Many fans removed their coats and jackets and basked in the springtime sun in their shirtsleeves.

Al Lopez (far left) watches as the Indians storm out of the dugout to take the field at Comiskey Park in Chicago on opening day, 1954.

Cleveland's Early Wynn faced White Sox ace Billy Pierce, and for three innings they engaged in the kind of pitchers' duel expected from a pair of contending teams—and the kind of performance Indians fans had become familiar with over the past five seasons. Unlike most ballclubs, which boasted one true pitching ace on whom the team could always depend for a solid performance, the Indians had three: Bob Lemon, Early Wynn, and Mike Garcia.

By the time their careers were over, this trio would combine to win more than 600 major-league games, and both Wynn and Lemon would be inducted into the Hall of Fame. Lemon had been with the team the longest—despite being perhaps the unlikeliest player in Cleveland history to become a star on the pitcher's mound.

At the tail end of the 1942 season, reporter Ed McAuley of the *Cleveland News* sat down to interview a pair of minor-league call-ups, both twenty-one-year-old infielders. Most of McAuley's attention was spent on first baseman Eddie Robinson, whom the Indians had purchased prior to the season. But toward the end of the session, McAuley tossed a question to the quiet young man sitting beside him, a third baseman who had hit twenty-one home runs in the minors that summer. "Don't bother with me," Bob Lemon replied. "I'm in the Navy."

The Indians hadn't bothered much with Lemon in the five seasons since they'd signed him at the age of seventeen, despite an almost ethereal connection between the young ballplayer and his new team. Lemon had been born in San Bernadino, California, in September of 1920, while the Indians were in a heated pennant race that would result in their first world title. Lemon's father, a semipro ballplayer at the time, was enthralled with the Indians, particularly the way they persevered after their star shortstop Ray Chapman had been killed when hit in the head by a pitch a month before. With his wife and three-week-old Bob in tow in a small basket, Earl parked himself outside the local newspaper office for a week that October to "watch" the World Series through a play-by-play billboard posted on the front of the building. When the Indians dispatched the Brooklyn Dodgers, Earl Lemon was so moved he decided that his young son would not only one day play professional baseball, but that he would sign with no other team but Cleveland.

Yet once the Indians had him, they didn't know quite what to do with him. He'd made nine late-season plate appearances in 1941 and 1942, collecting just one hit, and was on his way into the service. When he returned for the 1946 season at twenty-five, it appeared his window of opportunity for becoming a big leaguer had passed. Veteran third baseman Ken Keltner held out during spring training, and Lemon was given a golden opportunity to win the starting position. He blew it, Keltner returned, and Lemon was shuffled to the outfield in the hopes of finding a niche. He started in center field on opening day and made a dazzling catch to save a 1–0 victory for Bob Feller, but he struggled at the plate, unable to raise his batting average above .200. He rode the bench and could hear the clock ticking down on a once-promising baseball career.

Killing time, Lemon began throwing batting practice, and his natural delivery drew attention from the coaching staff. He'd originally been signed by the Indians as a pitcher, after he'd led his high school team to a state title, but at his first stop, in Oswego, he saw a roster loaded with pitchers. Eager to play anywhere he could, he turned himself into a solid infielder. He hit well, batting .309 in New Orleans in 1939, then .301 at Wilkes-Barre in 1941. He switched back to pitcher for some intramural games in the Navy but returned to the Indians determined to find a spot in the everyday lineup. With the '46 Indians wallowing in sixth place in late June and in desperate need of reliable pitching whenever Feller wasn't on the mound, manager Lou Boudreau came up with a crazy idea. When the Yankees came to town, Boudreau asked catcher Bill Dickey what he thought about turning Lemon into a pitcher. Dickey, who'd played with Lemon in the Navy, thought it was a great idea. Meanwhile, Indians owner Bill Veeck had other plans. He had agreed to sell Lemon to Washington just before Boudreau made the switch. But when Senators owner Clark Griffith prematurely announced the deal, Veeck called it off and kept Lemon. It turned out to be perhaps the smartest thing Veeck did in his colorful stint in Cleveland.

Lemon wasn't crazy about switching to pitcher, but over the remainder of the season he appeared in thirty-two games, primarily in relief. Though his 4–5 record was not remarkable, his 2.49 ERA showed promise. Working with pitching coach Mel Harder, Lemon evolved. His stubby fingers gave him one of the most devastating sinkers in baseball, and he developed a fastball and a sharp curve to go along with a natural slider, a pitch he didn't even know he was throwing until someone pointed it out to him. He became a regular starter midway through the 1947 season and wound up winning eleven games. And in 1948, he found his stride, winning twenty with a 2.82 ERA, and helped the Indians capture the pennant. Along the way, he pitched a no-hitter against the Tigers, and then went on to win two games in the World Series against the Boston Braves. It was the beginning of a period of pitching dominance matched only by Bob Feller in the annals of Cleveland history.

Over the next seven years, no pitcher in baseball had a better record than Lemon. His 1948 campaign was the first of three consecutive twenty-win seasons, followed by two more in 1952 and 1953. On a long plane ride during this period, Cleveland coach Herold Ruel, sitting next to McAuley (who eight years earlier had all but ignored Lemon in their first interview), motioned to Lemon sleeping behind them and said, "If he isn't the best pitcher in the business, I'd like to know who is."

Ironically, the man sitting beside Lemon in that interview with Ed McAuley in 1942 wound up helping the Indians acquire the second member of the Big Three. Eddie Robinson became Cleveland's starting first baseman and helped the Indians win the 1948 pennant, but two months later he was traded to Washington along with two other players for Senators' All-Star first baseman Mickey Vernon and a mediocre pitcher with the unusual name of Early Wynn.

Wynn had been a workhorse over ten seasons with the Senators, pitching more than 1,200 innings. On the mound, he was nothing but business, working quickly, often taking less than ten seconds between pitches. But with a career record of 72–87 and an ERA near 4.00, the twenty-eight-year-old Wynn certainly was expendable. He boasted one of the most impressive fastballs in the game but had no other pitches to complement it. As he'd done with Lemon two years before, Mel Harder transformed Wynn from a thrower to a pitcher. He helped him develop a curve, a slider, a changeup, and even introduced him to the knuckleball, which would become a valuable weapon over what would become a very long career. With an arsenal of pitches surrounding it, Wynn's fastball became legendary, and he became one of the most feared pitchers in the game.

Wynn won eleven games for the Indians in 1949, but his career took a dramatic turn in 1950, as he went 18–8 with a league-best 3.20 ERA. He only got better over the next two years, going 23–12 in 1952 with a 2.90 ERA while becoming a bona fide candidate for league MVP. Pitching with constant pain in his shoulder in 1953, Wynn saw his ERA balloon a full point, but he still managed to collect seventeen wins. In the offseason, doctors recommended he lower his intake of protein and a meatless diet was prescribed. Gradually, his arm got better, and after a sterling spring, Wynn would be the Tribe's opening-day starter, looking to rebound from what he felt was a sub-par season.

The final member of the Tribe's triumphant trio rose to prominence almost in perfect harmony with Wynn. Edward Miguel Garcia, better known as Mike, had never aspired to be a baseball player growing up on a ranch in the San Joaqin Valley. Hard as this was to believe later, Garcia was a bit of a runt as a teenager, and he dreamed of becoming a jockey and riding horses to fame. As he developed physically, so, too, did his baseball skills. Originally signed by Cleveland in 1942, Garcia made his major-league debut in garbage time during the final game of the 1948 regular season as the Indians were getting pounded by Detroit, blowing the Tribe's chance to clinch the pennant that day and forcing a one-game playoff in Boston. In adverse conditions, Garcia pitched two shutout innings and set the tone for a breakout year in 1949. Like Lemon and Wynn, Garcia had been molded into an effective pitcher by Mel Harder, who taught him a nifty curve to complement his slider and power fastball. He made his first big-league start in May. He was bombed, and then sent back to the bullpen. Three weeks later Early Wynn developed hives just prior to a doubleheader against the visiting Yankees, and Lou Boudreau thrust Garcia into an emergency start.

Before 77,000 fans at Municipal Stadium, Garcia held the Yankees to one run and once again earned a spot in the starting rotation. This time, he kept it. Posting a 2.36 ERA—best in baseball—Garcia went 14–5. After a slight backslide the following year, he rebounded with back-to-back twenty-win seasons, including six shutouts in 1952. Another great year followed in 1953, along with his second All-Star selection.

Things continued to look good for the man teammates called "The Bear," so named both because of his thick black hair and because of his portly resemblance to a grizzly—he generally weighed more than 220 pounds despite standing just over six feet tall. Embracing the nickname, Garcia bought a dry-cleaning shop in Parma and renamed it "Big Bear Cleaners."

Yet 1954 got off to a sour start for The Bear. He gave up ten runs in two innings in his first appearance in spring training, and for the rest of March, he was rocked around the Cactus League, allowing forty-one hits and twenty-nine runs in his first eighteen innings. Though he claimed his fastball had returned just as camp broke, Garcia's disastrous spring and 11.35 ERA led many to wonder if he had passed his prime—and for that matter, if the Indians could still rely on the Big Three, all of whom were now in their thirties. It appeared as though Cleveland's remarkable good fortune when it came to pitching, which dated back two decades to the arrival of Bob Feller, may finally be waning. As Feller's career began to wind down after his final twenty-win season in 1951, the rise of Wynn and Garcia, along with Lemon's continued run of excellence, kept the Indians in contention. In 1952 and 1953, the Big Three had combined for 123 victories, and the law of averages, combined with the knowing voice of baseball common sense, suggested that the Big Three had just about fished their lake dry.

By 1954, the Big Four—(clockwise from bottom)
Bob Lemon, Mike Garcia, Early Wynn, and Bob Feller—
had become known as the Big Three, though Feller put
together one final magnificent season.

As Cleveland's 1954 opener reached the middle innings, Wynn
got the support he needed. The Indians shattered the scoreless game
in the fourth when Wally Westlake and George Strickland, neither a
proven power hitter, blasted back-to-back home runs that each traveled
more than 400 feet. Chicago tied it at two in the fifth, but the Indians
exploded for six runs in the next four innings to notch an 8–2 victory.
For the day, Cleveland rapped out fifteen hits. If this opening-day
onslaught was indicative of what the Indian offense would provide
its Big Three, the season might prove to be a memorable one after all.

Lopez was so impressed he labeled these Indians the best team he'd ever managed.

"Presumably they'll lose a few before the course is run," Gordon Cobbledick wrote, "but on the evidence presented today they'll also win one or two." Things looked even rosier the following afternoon when the Tribe collected fourteen hits and scored four early runs to take control of the game, then turned a key double play to snuff out a Chicago rally in the eighth to secure a 5–3 triumph for Bob Lemon.

There may have been 152 games yet to play, but the Indians would return home all alone in first place—exactly where a team from Cleveland should reside.

4 - STORM CLOUDS

I n many ways, Dr. Sam Sheppard was the embodiment of the American dream.

Baby-faced and handsome, Sam had been a popular student at Cleveland Heights High School, an excellent athlete and voted president of essentially every club he joined. In his senior year he was selected the "Most Likely to Succeed" in his class. Though a year and a half older, Marilyn Reese was drawn to Sam's charms just like many other girls in high school. Though she went off to Skidmore College while he was still in high school, their relationship continued to blossom. But after he departed for California for medical school—the Los Angeles Osteopathic School of Physicians and Surgeons—he realized he couldn't live without her. She joined him there, and they were married in February 1945.

He graduated later that year, but they stayed in California, renting an apartment, enjoying the ocean and weather and the free and open lifestyle of the West Coast, which fit their active and social natures. They returned to Cleveland seven years later, in 1952, when Sam became part of the family legacy, joining his two older brothers, Richard and Steve, and his father, Richard Sr., staffing Bay View Hospital, a Georgian-style mansion that had been purchased by Sam's father and converted into a hospital in 1948, the same year Sam's beloved Indians captured their

Newlyweds Marilyn and Sam Sheppard.

first world title in twenty-eight years. In the six years that followed, as the Indians regularly fell just short, Sam Sheppard continually came up aces. His career blossomed at Bay View as the new hospital—and its reputation—grew. Well-liked by his patients, he was referred to informally as "Dr. Sam," in part to distinguish him from his brothers and father.

Sam and Marilyn were the portrait of success. Their son, Samuel Reese (whom they called "Chip"), enjoyed a childhood in a relatively small but charming home overlooking Lake Erie in affluent Bay Village. With Sam's increasing success, he was able to pay off the mortgage in two years.

In 1954, Dr. Sam Sheppard was an Adonis in a city of champions—one which that spring had received yet another crown.

The night before the Indians' home opener on April 15, the Cleveland Barons defeated the Hershey Bears at musty Cleveland Arena to conclude the American Hockey League championship series in six games and capture the Barons' second straight Calder Cup and seventh in fourteen years. Part of the original group of teams that had founded the AHL in 1936, the Barons had quickly built a dynasty that turned Cleveland into one of the best hockey towns in the country. Another pair of Calder Cups would follow in the next decade, and the nine championships would remain an AHL record until Hershey matched it fifty years later. Of course, Hershey had played in the league for sixty-six seasons at that point, while the Barons' complete AHL history consisted of just thirty-six—meaning that they won a title, on average, once every four seasons. It was a rarity at any level of professional sport. But in the Cleveland of 1954, it was business as usual.

Still glowing from the latest crown placed atop their heads, Clevelanders treated the coronation of their triumphant Barons and the return of the Indians as a civic holiday, symbolized by the fanfare surrounding the Tribe's home opener. The *Plain Dealer* conjectured that there would be many "grandmother's funerals" that afternoon as the wheels of the workday came to a screeching halt. Fine spring weather added to the atmosphere. As fans streamed into Municipal Stadium, the sky was bright and clear, the memories of a harsh winter long forgotten.

The cost of entry was reasonable, though still considered somewhat pricey by many. A general admission ticket cost $1.25, a spot in the bleachers went for sixty cents. You could splurge for a boxed seat for $2.25. Of course, there were other, less traditional methods of acquiring tickets. With the purchase of a pair of shoes at Garfinkel's, you'd get a reserved seat ticket for the home opener. And if you were willing to spend $1,727 for a new Chevrolet sedan, you'd receive a ticket to every Indians home night game.

The home ballpark itself was enticing, as Municipal Stadium was widely considered one of the finest places to watch a game. Decades away from its reputation of being a sewage-smelling rathole that attracted swarms of prehistoric insects off the lake, the stadium in 1954 was a baseball palace, the largest in the nation. During the '54 team's first workout at the stadium, rookie Rudy Regalado hopped up the dugout steps, arched his head around the bowl of the park, and whistled. "Holy cow!" he cried with Jimmy Olsen-like enthusiasm. "This *is* a big place!"

The 40,000-plus that marched into the ballpark on the lake were treated not just to a gorgeous spring afternoon, but a myriad of improvements to the ballpark. Near Gate A, a new concession area had been constructed that resembled a cafeteria more than a lunch stand. Patrons could walk inside and purchase never-before-available offerings such as hamburgers and fish sandwiches for thirty-five cents apiece. Of course, the stand also offered the usual wares at the usual fares: beer for thirty-five cents, hot dogs for twenty, peanuts for fifteen, and coffee for ten. The staff selling beverages to fans in their seats also enjoyed a technological breakthrough. Instead of carrying a bulky carton full of bottles, Coca-Cola was placed in portable thermos jugs that were carried via backpack and poured into cups through a spigot, reducing the number of trips for supplies. On the field, a shiny red Ford convertible transported pitchers from the bullpen to the pitcher's mound—quite an upgrade over the Nash Rambler used in previous years.

By the time Ohio Governor Frank Lausche tossed the ceremonial first pitch to Mayor Anthony Celebrezze, the morning chill had burned off and the day had become a portrait of all that an April afternoon in Cleveland could be, a day in which all of the senses were pleasantly teased and tousled. The sky was bright and cloudless, a robin's eggshell covering all of northeast Ohio. The breeze off the lake still carried some of the sting of winter, but it felt fresh and clean against the skin, while the sunshine gradually warmed everything it touched. Wafting through the stadium was the scent that defined baseball: crushed peanut shells, spilled beer drying on concrete, and everywhere, the pleasant, subtle tang of burning cigarettes. The ears received the shouts of concessioners and the noodling of the ballpark organ, the only auditory elements that stood out over the low murmur of the excited crowd. In the sunlight, the Indians' uniforms looked so vibrantly white they almost hurt the eyes. Set against the emerald of the newly grown outfield grass, it was as if color had reappeared after four months of gray skies over an ashen landscape. That afternoon, life returned to Cleveland.

And like the balmy April morning, the Indians began their home opener unusually warm. After Mike Garcia enticed a double play to thwart a Tiger scoring threat in the first, the home team got going when its first two batters walked and advanced on a sacrifice bunt. As Cleveland's cleanup hitter stepped to the plate, the crowd offered an ovation. With his cropped blonde hair peeking from beneath his batting helmet and his ice-blue eyes leveling on the pitcher, he gripped the bat and flexed his tremendous forearms, which bulged from his sleeves and somehow made his uniform look smaller than those of his teammates. He was the reigning king of baseball at the peak of his career.

Al Rosen: the All-American athlete
in the All-American city.

In this moment, he was better than Yogi Berra or Mickey Mantle
or Ted Williams. He was what every kid playing in the sandlots of
Cleveland aspired to be and who every player clinging to the last thread
of his career in the minor leagues looked to for a glimmer of hope. He
was Albert Leonard Rosen, who the previous year became the first man

to ever receive the Most Valuable Player award by a unanimous vote. In the process, he'd become Cleveland's first Jewish star athlete.

It hadn't always been this way for the handsome thirty-year-old slugger. Many of the fans who now showered him with praise had taunted him in years past—never because of lack of productivity, simply because of his religious affiliation. Even opponents would ridicule Rosen early in his career. Pitchers would fire fastballs at his ribs, and when they connected, Rosen refused to rub away the pain or even wince, for fear it would only encourage them. In fact, he took the beanings as a compliment—they meant he was becoming a threat at the plate.

Born in Spartanburg, South Carolina, Rosen had endured a troubled childhood. He was plagued by bouts of asthma as an infant, and his family subsequently moved to a neighborhood outside of Miami, where they were the only Jewish family in the area. Shortly after, his father abandoned the family, and young Al quickly learned to take care of himself. He was provoked into countless fights as a youngster because of his religion, but he never shied away from his heritage. He idolized the only Jewish athlete he knew, Tigers star Hank Greenberg, and would later tell people he wished his last name was "more Jewish" so people wouldn't confuse his religious affiliation.

As his asthma slowly faded away, Rosen developed into a strapping athlete. His childhood street-fighting skills made him a good boxer, but he gained more notoriety as a baseball player. Sandwiching baseball between part-time jobs, he played American Legion ball at the age of eleven and was in a semi-pro league at fourteen. After toiling at menial jobs like a slat-painter in a venetian blind factory, Rosen was signed by the Red Sox and shipped to a farm team in Virginia. Soon after, he was released. Desperate to continue a career that seemed to have ended before it began, Rosen signed a $90-per-month contract with a Class D team in North Carolina. Eventually, the Indians took a flyer and signed him to a minor-league contract. But Rosen's long journey to the majors was only beginning.

His powerful hitting kept him in the game, but his defense was atrocious. Managers winced whenever the ball was hit to him. Even after he made the modest jump to Class C ball, his manager pulled him aside one day and said, "Listen, kid, you'd better go home and get yourself a lunch pail. Forget about baseball. You either have it or you don't. You don't." By all rights, Rosen should have quit long before. But he didn't. He kept at it, slowly trudging up the minor-league ranks. Things started to come together in 1947 when he hit .349 at Oklahoma City, earning Texas League MVP honors and his first big-league call-up for a seven-game stint in September. In Kansas City a year later, Rosen ripped twenty-five home runs while batting .327, earning the nickname of "Hebrew Hammer." His offensive prowess earned him a spot on the Indians' roster for the '48 World Series, and he pinch-hit for Satchel Paige in Game Five and, facing Warren Spahn, popped out to second.

Going into 1949, Rosen felt he had earned a spot on the roster and was stunned when he was shipped back to the minors as Cleveland stuck with aging Ken Keltner at third base. Though Keltner, then thirty-two, was coming off his finest season, his numbers dropped dramatically in 1949, and Rosen later admitted he felt that decision cost the Indians a chance to win a second straight pennant. In one of his first moves as Cleveland general manager, Hank Greenberg released Keltner on the day of the 1950 season opener. As Rosen's name echoed over the Municipal Stadium loudspeakers when he was introduced as the starting third baseman, the gigantic crowd booed. Not only had Keltner been their guy for more than a decade, now their Jewish GM had just kicked him out the door to replace him with some other Jew they'd never heard of. It stirred the darker side of Cleveland's unspoken ethnic territorialism. And when Rosen came to bat representing the tying run with the Tribe down two to the Tigers in the eighth inning, the booing began again. It amplified dramatically when Rosen quickly fell behind in the count, and a chant of "We Want Keltner" began to filter through the park. But Rosen clobbered the next pitch over the left-field wall to tie the game—the first home run of his major-league career. The boos instantly turned to cheers for the suddenly heroic rookie. Indians fans never again longed for Ken Keltner. Rosen led the American League with thirty-seven home runs and 116 RBI that year as Cleveland nearly stole the pennant from the Yankees.

Rosen would hit a total of fifty-two home runs over the next two seasons and became an All-Star. Despite his success, he maintained his yeoman work ethic and dedication. Even when he was hitting well, he would generally take early batting practice more than five hours before the start of a game. Though he collected more than twenty home runs and 100 RBI in 1951, he was bothered that these numbers and his batting average had dropped in his second full season. That winter he took a long, soul-searching vacation to South America to clear his head and try to refocus—this after a season that would have satisfied most young hitters.

After he was hit in the face by a line drive during a game in 1951, both eyes swelled shut, and he was taken to the hospital. Though doctors recommended he rest for a few days, Rosen insisted on rejoining the team, which had left for Philadelphia. After icing his puffed face all night, he was able to open his eyes the following day and, against the advice of the team doctor, he played. Another time, he confronted a teammate who complained his leg muscles were too tight for him to play in a crucial game against the Yankees. Suiting up with a broken nose himself, one of eleven in his career, Rosen was very persuasive, and the teammate played.

His commitment to the game also spilled into his personal life. After he'd broken into the big leagues, he informed his longtime fiancé, Terry Blumberg, that they couldn't get married until he hit .300. She didn't take him seriously at first but soon discovered he wasn't kidding. Leading the league in home runs as a rookie wasn't enough (he hit .287), nor was a second straight season of 100-plus RBI (he hit .265). Fed up, she called it off. Now stunned at the mistake he'd made, Rosen turned his laser-like focus on getting Terry back. As the 1952 season unfolded, he called her from every city and would ask her to marry him. And every time, she said no. Despondent, he finally stopped asking.

One night in St. Louis, Rosen's roommate, Ray Boone, got tired of watching Rosen mope around and convinced him to call Terry one more time. Rosen did, and they chatted awkwardly for a few minutes. Finally, Terry asked, "Aren't you going to ask me?"

Rosen's face crinkled. "Ask you what?"

"What you always ask me," she replied.

He sighed and once again asked the question. This time, Terry said yes. And Rosen finished the season with a .302 average.

Then came 1953.

Though he could have simply accepted his reputation as an all-hit, no-field player and reveled in his offensive success, Rosen was determined to become a better all-around player. "I've got to work and keep thinking," he once said. "When I don't, I'm bush league, or worse." Rosen arrived at spring training earlier than usual in 1953 to improve his fielding, which was still a liability. Gradually, over the course of the spring, he improved, as Cleveland coach Tony Cuccinello hit him grounder after grounder. Comfortable off the field and on it, Rosen embarked on one of the finest individual seasons in Indians history. He not only raised his fielding statistics across the board, but he upped his batting average more than thirty points to .336. But where

Al Rosen—the first player to win the American League Most Valuable Player by unanimous vote— is presented with the award.

he garnered the most attention was in his power swing. He blasted a league-best forty-three home runs and drove in 145 RBI with a robust slugging percentage of .613. Not only was he the consensus MVP of the American League, he finished one thousandth of a point away from winning the triple crown. In fact, had he been called safe on a close play at first in his final at-bat of the season, he would have taken the title. But the umpire ruled Rosen missed the bag as he ran by while trying to beat out a slow grounder to third. Though Rosen could have created a controversy and perhaps etched his name in history as a star hitter wronged (particularly in an era before instant replay and constant television highlights of every game), he publicly agreed with the call, admitting he'd missed the bag.

After being told to quit the game while in the minor leagues, Al Rosen would make $40,000 with the Indians in 1954. In the off-season, he had a plush job as an investment broker and hosted a Cleveland television show. No longer was he harassed or targeted by opposing pitchers, and he'd found a fiercely loyal following among Cleveland's large Jewish population. He'd earned the respect of players and managers alike. Prior to a game at Municipal Stadium, Casey Stengel raised a crooked finger and pointed out to Rosen taking infield practice. "That young feller," Stengel began in his usual rambling tone, "that feller's a ball player. He'll give you the works every time. Gets all the hits, gives you the hard tag in the field. That feller's a real competitor, you bet your sweet curse life."

Now, in his first at-bat in Cleveland in 1954, Rosen pounded a long fly ball to left that brought the runner home from third to give the Indians a 1–0 lead—and, due to an adjustment to the rule book for 1954, he was charged with a sacrifice fly rather than with an at-bat. Then in the sixth, after Detroit tied the contest, Rosen crushed his first home run of the season to put Cleveland ahead again. The crowd once more showered him with cheers. In the All-American town, he was the All-American baseball hero—young, strapping, blond-haired, blue-eyed, and movie-star handsome. And, as it happened, Jewish.

Garcia cruised through the top of the seventh and got the first two Tiger batters in the eighth, and the Indians were four outs away from their third straight victory to start the season. But as the Indians came to bat following the stretch, the bright promise of the day began to fade. Storm clouds slid eastward, and the sky over downtown Cleveland gradually transformed from aqua to gunmetal. The sun disappeared, the temperature dropped, and the wind picked up, a steady spring breeze turning into a chilled, blustery nuisance, swirling wrappers and abandoned scorecards around the ballpark.

As the storm moved closer, the Indians' lead became more precarious. One out away from the ninth, Garcia allowed a single, a stolen base, and another base hit as Detroit tied the contest again. He got out of the inning with no further damage, but the lead was lost in the gathering darkness. At 4:35, the stadium's lights were turned on, marking the first time they'd ever been used in a home opener. Twenty minutes later, the rain began to fall. It poured down in sheets, drenching the new infield. More symbolically, the rain seemed to rinse away the earlier excitement like a chalk drawing on a sidewalk. The soothing magic of baseball on opening day vanished as play was halted for ninety minutes while the squall trudged along the Lake Erie coastline.

It was nearly 6:30 when the rain passed and the teams returned to the field, the bright blue afternoon sky having transformed to a dark marble of gray and purple. The crowd had dwindled to a fraction of its original size, and the festive mood had been carried off with the storm. Not surprisingly, Garcia was rusty as the ninth began, walking the first two batters as the Tigers loaded the bases with one out. The winning run came home on a ground out moments later as Detroit managed to take the lead without knocking the ball out of the infield. The Indians went quietly in the ninth and nearly four hours after it began, Cleveland's 1954 home opener was history.

Over the course of the remaining seventy-six games played on that diamond over the next five months, they would lose only seventeen more times.

5 - THE CHASM OF RIDICULOUSNESS

O f all the problems facing the youth of America in 1954, none was more dangerous than the colorfully illustrated booklets found at any newsstand or drugstore.

Comic books were warping young minds, psychiatrist Dr. Frederic Wertham was convinced, and that April he testified as such to a Senate subcommittee on juvenile delinquency led by Estes Kefauver. The underlying messages and visual elements had the potential to turn ordinary kids from respectable homes into violence-prone doppelgangers of their former selves. Wertham's book, *Seduction of the Innocent*, outlined his argument in detail and became a bestseller. More importantly, it put parents on high alert. Wertham's primary targets were the gangster and horror titles that, even by the standards of future generations, were rather violent and filled with sexual innuendo.

Never one to turn down an opportunity to spread fresh paranoia to the masses, Louis Seltzer hitched the *Cleveland Press* to Wertham's bandwagon. Coinciding with Wertham's congressional testimony, the *Press* reported that Cleveland youngsters could choose from 107 horror and crime comics (though "comics" was coyly framed in quotation marks), seventy-seven of which contained themes of sex and violence. And, the *Press* pointed out, most of these titles were on sale within immediate proximity to schoolyards. In June, Cleveland police would seize thousands of comics that were for sale second-hand and turned them over to the county prosecutor, then would be ordered to arrest merchants who persisted in selling "pornographic" or suggestive comics. While some sellers agreed that many comics should be removed, others resisted, seeing the meddling do-gooders as "nothing but church people." In retrospect, the *Press* was merely clearing its throat for the hyperbole it would launch later that summer against Dr. Sam Sheppard, sparking an even more frenzied hysteria among its readers.

Though Kefauver's committee concluded that comic books were not directly related to crime, it suggested that some of the elements be toned down. Thus, publishers formed the Comics Code Authority to regulate the content of comic books and keep the lucrative industry from imploding before their eyes. The code guaranteed, among other things, that criminals would not be construed as glamorous or sympathetic, no comic book could be published that included the presence of a vampire, werewolf, or zombie, and that females would be drawn realistically, without exaggeration of physical qualities.

But Wertham also warned of the subtle dangers of superheroes, another cash crop of the comics industry. Batman and Robin were almost certainly homosexual partners (and the Boy Wonder a minor, to boot). Born in a culture not accustomed to seeing strong, independent females, Wertham also concluded that Wonder Woman was a lesbian.

Even the centerpiece of the industry wasn't exempt. Wertham labeled Superman as a fascist, teaching children that the only solution to their problems is through physical force. (The irony of this conclusion is that when Nazi propaganda minister Joseph Goebbels was introduced to Superman during World War II, he screamed, "Superman is Jewish!")

"If I were asked to express in a single sentence what has happened mentally to many American children," Wertham stated, "I would say that they were conquered by Superman." Now sixteen years old, Superman had evolved from a guest character in a fledging title to his own publication while starring in a daily radio show. And with the dawn of television, the Man of Steel anchored the first national television sensation for young viewers as millions of boys (and girls) would cease all activity and race indoors for another episode of *The Adventures of Superman*, which premiered in the fall of 1952. Though Superman was part of American culture, it would not have surprised most of his Cleveland fans that he was actually one of their own. Superman was created by two Jewish teenagers—Jerry Siegel and Joe Shuster—who'd attended Glenville High School, located on Cleveland's east side. They spent six years seeking a publisher before National Allied Publications launched both their impenetrable new hero and a new series called *Action Comics* in the summer of 1938. And though "Metropolis" would eventually become the home of Clark Kent, Lois Lane, and company, in an early issue, one panel depicted Clark Kent telegraphing a story back to his newspaper—the fictional *Evening News*—in Cleveland, Ohio.

With the second season of *The Adventures of Superman* completed in March, and the third season more than a year away, Cleveland's youngsters turned their attentions to other pastimes. One of those was following another set of heroes dressed in red and blue: the Indians. But, like Superman trapped in a room filled with Kryptonite, the Indians continued to appear weak and listless as the first month of the season progressed.

The storm clouds that had derailed the home opener remained through the weekend as the Indians dropped a pair of lopsided decisions to the White Sox. An Easter Sunday doubleheader was pre-empted by rain after the first game was called after six innings with Chicago winning 6–2. Losers of three straight, the Indians would try to turn things around in a city they'd never played in before.

Baltimore, now home to the transplanted St. Louis Browns, was ablaze with enthusiasm for their new Orioles and better than 43,000 fans watched with delight as twenty-four-year-old pitcher Bob Turley put on a show against the Indians on a chilly Wednesday night, collecting strikeouts like a toddler picking dandelions. After Turley retired the side in the eighth, he received a standing ovation and tipped his hat to the crowd, which realized its young hero was now just three outs away from the first no-hitter in the week-old history of the Baltimore Orioles.

Clinging to a 1–0 lead, Turley started the ninth with a three-pitch strikeout, his fourteenth of the night. It brought up Al Rosen, and Turley quickly collected two strikes against the Cleveland slugger. Then, with the count even at two, Rosen laced a hard single to left, spoiling the no-hitter, and, as Franklin Lewis wrote in the *Press*, leaving a "block-wide crack in the heart of young Turley." Rosen was booed magnificently—a treatment he was used to—as Larry Doby stepped into the batter's box. Historical infamy may have been avoided, but the prospect of a fourth straight defeat loomed before the Indians. Doby, who had already struck out twice, was committed to not fall victim again. Accordingly, two pitches later, on the same kind of pitch he whiffed on in the seventh, Doby crushed the baseball deep into the cold April evening, and it landed three rows into the bleachers. Turley, who moments before was destined for history, kicked the dirt on the mound in frustration. He'd gone from a man on the brink of a no-hitter to, after Bob Lemon closed out the Orioles in the bottom of the inning, a losing pitcher.

While Rosen would get the credit for interrupting Turley's date with destiny, Doby was the game's hero. It seemed only fitting that the center fielder would halt the team's first skid of the season, since the Indians' fortunes seemed to follow Doby's ebbs and flows. And over his seven years in Cleveland, there had been many.

When Bill Veeck acquired the Indians in 1946, he correctly deduced which way the cultural wind was blowing and sent scouts to scour the Negro Leagues. He instructed them to look for not necessarily the best player, but the one with the most long-term potential. And while open-minded, he only wanted one black player at first. If the experiment failed, it needed to be brought to an end quickly and simply.

The one name that kept coming up was Larry Doby, second baseman for the Newark Eagles. Though he fit the basic mold Branch Rickey had sought when he found Jackie Robinson—free of vices, educated, and articulate—Larry Doby was not Jackie Robinson. Unlike Robinson, Doby didn't have the background of a born pioneer, nor did prejudice fuel a white-hot flame within him. A descendent of West African slaves captured and brought to South Carolina in the eighteenth century, Doby grew up in Paterson, New Jersey, far from the plantations of the South. In high school in the early 1940s, his skin color was a rarity but not necessarily unique. Doby was one of roughly twenty-five blacks in a student body of 1,200, and through athletics he made many white friends. Yet even these relationships were shadowed by the cultural climate. When Doby would hit a home run or score a touchdown, his teammates would celebrate, but were careful not to pat him on the back or show any other visible signs of appreciation for fear of how it would look to the bystanders. Not surprisingly, the sensitive, introspective Doby accepted the tone of his surroundings and went along quietly. He made few close friends, and while some considered him a loner, he saw himself as independent. When he'd fail on the field, he'd retreat within himself, further fueling his reputation as moody and distant. Considering the only alternative was to release his feelings and carry the label of emotional and uppity, traits that likely would have ended his athletic career, Doby's inner struggle was his only option.

Through it all, he excelled in every sport he played, earning eleven varsity letters in football, baseball, basketball, and track. His true strength was on the diamond, and shortly after graduation, he was offered $300 to play for the Newark Eagles of the Negro National League for the remainder of the summer until he left to attend Long Island University in the fall. Thus, Larry Doby played his first professional game at Yankee Stadium against the New York Cubans on May 31, 1942, under the name of "Larry Walker" to maintain his amateur status.

The following year, with World War II raging, Doby was drafted into the Army. While playing in pickup and intramural games over the next three years, he impressed many of his comrades—one of whom was Mickey Vernon, another young athlete who'd just begun to make an impression with the Washington Senators when the war intervened. Vernon was impressed with Doby's baseball skills, even mentioning him in letters to Senators owner Clark Griffith.

In January 1946, with the war over and Doby stationed at a small island in the Pacific, a startling development from the States crackled over the Armed Forces Network. The Brooklyn Dodgers had signed Jackie Robinson to a minor-league contract, and he would play the following season for the Dodgers' top farm team in Montreal. If Robinson was going to play for a major-league team—and there was little doubt this would eventually happen—then there was no reason

Doby couldn't do the same. His success in the Negro National League, combined with praise from astute judges like Mickey Vernon, proved to him he had the necessary skills. The only thing that would have prevented him from playing Major League Baseball was the invisible color line around each team's clubhouse. But now, with the Dodgers on the brink of opening the door, Doby saw his life taking a new course. Prior to hearing this story on the radio, he had planned to finish college and become a teacher and a coach. Now he concentrated on baseball and waited for his chance.

He returned home in time to play for the Newark Eagles in '46, helping guide them to a seven-game victory over the Kansas City Monarchs in the Negro World Series. The Cleveland scout sent by Bill Veeck was impressed with Doby's talents—and with his reputation for clean living. He recommended to Veeck that Doby was his man. In 1947, the Indians offered Newark $10,000 for Doby, plus another $5,000 if he stuck with the team. Hoping Cleveland would want to tap further into what it now saw as a nearly bottomless resource, Newark's owner also offered the team's starting shortstop for the bargain basement price of $1,000. But keeping in mind Veeck's original intent, and fearing the twenty-eight-year-old shortstop was too old, the Indians passed. Thus, Monte Irvin, after switching to the outfield, would go on to enjoy an eight-year, Hall of Fame career with the New York Giants rather than the Indians.

Three months after Jackie Robinson debuted with the Brooklyn Dodgers, the Indians officially acquired Doby. Two days later, he joined the Indians in Chicago. "If Doby is a good player," Branch Rickey commented, "and I understand that he is, then the Cleveland club is showing signs that it wants to win."

Not everyone in the organization, however, shared Veeck's progressive view. Most notably, a handful of players made known their opposition to Doby joining the team, threatening to quit rather than play with a black man. Veeck caught wind of the potential mutiny and called a meeting in the clubhouse. "I understand that some of you players said that 'if a nigger joins the club,' you're leaving," he said. "Well, you can leave right now because this guy is going to be a bigger star than any guy in this room." Manager Lou Boudreau followed suit, telling his players that they "should be honored by having the first black ballplayer joining us." The flames of revolution may have been extinguished, but the embers of racism still smoldered.

Though his integration process came after Robinson's, Doby actually was far less prepared for the hatred and bigotry he would encounter. Branch Rickey had brought Robinson along slowly, allowing him to spend a year playing among only white players in the minors, and then carefully guiding him through a spring training filled with potential land mines. Doby simply appeared in the Cleveland locker room. As Boudreau walked him around the clubhouse introducing him to his new teammates, each player shook Doby's hand. Not all looked up as he did so.

The inevitable historical moment came on July 5 at Comiskey Park. With the Indians trailing in the seventh, Boudreau called back pitcher Bryan Stephens and sent Doby in as a pinch-hitter. As he strode back to the dugout, bat in hand, Stephens personified the nightmare of his teammates. Seeing the look on Stephens's face and realizing the magnitude of what had just occurred, Tribe catcher Al Lopez—who in three years would replace Boudreau as Doby's manager—shook his head and muttered, "I'm glad that he didn't hit for me." It was the beginning of a complicated, often troubled relationship between the two men. Doby struck out in that first at-bat, beginning a miserable transition to the big leagues. After the game, he was separated from his teammates and taken to a black hotel on the south side of Chicago.

While Robinson lit the National League ablaze in 1947 with his energetic style of play, Doby made little impact that first summer. He played in only twenty-nine games, mostly as a pinch-hitter, and collected only five hits. It did little to quell the opinion of bigots who felt baseball was a white man's game despite Robinson being named Rookie of the Year. But over the course of the off-season, Doby was switched to center field. And in 1948, he proved his worth, hitting .301 (including a .396 clip over Cleveland's critical final twenty games) with fourteen home runs and helping drive the Indians to the World Series. Doby's success paved the way for the Indians' signing of two more Negro League stars in a four-day period in July of 1948: the much-celebrated and ageless pitcher Satchel Paige, who added both experience and flavor to the Tribe's pennant run, and a twenty-year-old outfielder named Al Smith, who would maneuver through Cleveland's farm system over the next five seasons before bursting into the starting lineup in 1954.

Though he was the first black player in the American League, Doby was little more than a footnote to history. And though Robinson had played barely seventy games at the time of Doby's debut, Doby would forever be remembered (or not, as it were) as the one who came after. He suffered through many of the same racial attacks as Robinson, encountered the same bigotry and ignorance, and was forced to endure the suffering by turning the other cheek. But unlike Robinson, he'd never faced widespread prejudice before. The slurs, the cheap shots, the high-and-tight pitches were all new to him. When an umpire would make an obviously bad call when Doby was at the plate, he'd step out of the batter's box and casually point to the skin on the back of his hand. When the Indians and Giants made their spring-training barnstorming trip through the South, Doby was forced to stay in different hotels or even at the homes of black residents. The experience pulverized him, so much so that one year, when camp broke and the teams began their road trip, Doby asked if he could simply go back to Cleveland and wait for the team. He wasn't embraced by a forward-thinking city and its media. No books were written, no movies made telling the heroic story of his journey to stardom.

Even after his dazzling 1948 performance that helped deliver a world championship, Doby was still nothing more than a second-class citizen when the team reported to spring training the following year. When he stepped into a cab with fellow youngster Al Rosen that spring, the driver informed Doby he'd have to get out and take another cab. Before Doby could respond, Rosen, no stranger to prejudice himself, burst out of the cab, yelling at the driver and threatening to kick his teeth in. While Rosen's stance was welcome, it was rare. Few teammates stood up for Doby when bigotry arose.

Doby was even better in 1949, earning the first of seven straight All-Star selections. He led the league in home runs in 1952 and knocked in more than 100 RBI three times in four seasons going into 1954. But along the way, as he rose to stardom, he also acquired a reputation as a moody, unfriendly player. Reporters went from calling him a loner to labeling him friendless to eventually sticking him with the most unwelcome baseball label of all: head case. When he was benched twice by Lopez during the 1952 season, reporters were quick to explain it as Doby's melancholy and surliness rising to the surface. Yet when a white player slumped, his mental state was rarely questioned. Bystanders only saw what was on the surface: Doby keeping to himself, not playing cards or drinking with his teammates, spending his free time with his wife or friends outside of baseball. He was often the subject of trade rumors, with the Cleveland front office subtly suggesting they'd be willing to sacrifice Doby's wonderful statistics for a more likable player. While Jackie Robinson vocally fought the system and tried to change baseball—and the country along with it—Doby chose to fight his personal war quietly, with as much dignity as he could muster. Slowly, he began to earn the respect he deserved, becoming the highest-paid non-pitcher on the team.

Larry Doby scored 94 runs in 1954
and led the Indians in home runs and RBI.

A *Sporting News* poll of baseball writers after the '53 season labeled Doby as the "Most Nervous on the Field," "Most Temperamental," and "Unhappiest" player, along with the unenvied title of "Least Friendly to Fans." He did little to curb this impression by holding out prior to 1953, waiting for a better offer as his teammates reported to spring training. Following the season, Art Ehlers, GM of the St. Louis Browns (on their way to Baltimore to become the Orioles) made a trade proposal for Doby, offering modest outfielder Vic Wertz. Hank Greenberg wisely turned him down, not knowing a year later Wertz would become the greatest acquisition of his career.

As the 1954 season dawned, teammates and reporters noticed a change in Doby, though he would later say he felt no different that year than in any other. For starters, when Greenberg traveled to Cuba with a 1954 contract for Doby, who was playing winter ball, he signed without argument. Then Doby traveled to Hot Springs for special conditioning with Dodgers' catcher Roy Campanella a month before spring training. And once the Indians assembled in Tucson, they quickly realized this was not the same "moping" Larry Doby. Part of the reason may have been the symbolic gesture offered by the Santa Rita Hotel, the Indians' spring training headquarters, which for the first time allowed the black players to stay there—as long as they didn't use the elevator or sit in the lobby. Even the swing through the South didn't get him down. Smiling and relaxed, Doby appeared eager for 1954.

"If I had him on the Yankees," Casey Stengel would say that summer, "our sixth pennant would be a cinch." It was a bold comment, not only considering the amount of talent Stengel already had, but also that the Yankee roster was made up entirely of white players. Al Lopez countered much of the mainstream baseball media by saying he preferred Doby to Willie Mays. "For my money," Lopez said, "there isn't a ball that Mays can catch that Larry can't." And now that Doby had apparently turned a new leaf, perhaps it would help the Indians turn a corner as well.

However, though his heroics saved the Tribe from defeat in its Baltimore debut, the Orioles triumphed the next night as Mike Garcia was "H-bombed off the mound" as the *Press* put it, allowing three runs without recording an out. And things only got worse over the weekend in Detroit. For starters, the Indians' equipment trunks were inadvertently dropped off in Pittsburgh on the train journey from Baltimore, delaying the start of Friday afternoon's game an hour as the trunks were whisked to Detroit by cargo plane. As it turned out, the Indians didn't need the contents of the trunks, as they were thumped by the Tigers on Friday and Saturday. With Detroit eyeing a sweep to strengthen its hold on first place, the Indians found themselves in the American League cellar, holding the worst record in baseball. "Victims of another case of assault and battery, the Indians' clinical report today is this," Harry Jones wrote in the *Plain Dealer*, "condition critical, sinking rapidly."

Soundly beaten in six of their last seven games, the Indians resorted to desperate measures—what the Cleveland writers would call "The Big Switch." To ignite the slumping offense and, as Franklin Lewis put it, "rescue the Indians from the chasm of ridiculousness," Lopez shifted Rosen from third to first base and inserted spring training superstar Rudy Regalado into the lineup at third for his first major-league start. Rosen, who had never played first before, borrowed a glove from Detroit's Walt Dropo for Sunday's game. The Big Switch paid off as Regalado reached base four times, scoring three runs, including the go-ahead run on a tenth-inning homer by previously slumping Dave

Philley. Cleveland won the nearly four-hour marathon, 10–9, to avoid the sweep and stop the bleeding for at least a day. Yet the victory had taken a dramatic lineup shift and the use of all three members of the starting pitching trio. Though no longer in last place, the Indians looked like anything but contenders. Especially to Casey Stengel.

The Indians then traveled to Boston and sat around for two days as a hard rain pounded New England. Killing time in the lobby of the Hotel Kenmore, Lopez contemplated the Tribe's immediate future. If they ever got out of Boston, their next stop was New York for their first encounter with the Yankees. The good news was that the rain allowed Lopez to reshuffle his pitching rotation to ensure that Bob Lemon and Early Wynn would start the two games at Yankee Stadium.

Lopez's thoughts were interrupted when he was paged for a telephone call—long distance from New York.

"Hello, Al," said the friendly voice on the other end. "This is Red Patterson."

Lopez smiled. He'd known Patterson, the Yankees' often-swarmed press agent, for years.

"Hi, Red. What's up?"

"Casey wants to know who you're pitching in New York Friday and Saturday," Patterson said.

Lopez's smile curled further in amusement as he thought of his crafty old friend. What the hell was Casey up to?

"Oh, he does, does he?" he asked with a chuckle. "You tell Stengel to go jump in the lake. If he tells me who he's pitching, I'll tell him who I'm pitching."

Despite his joking, Lopez was thinking there was something strange about the call. It was one thing for a manager to try to figure out who his opponent is going to pitch, but it's another to make a straightforward phone call and ask your primary rival for privileged information.

But Patterson's reply was both dry and quick, as if the request were not unusual at all.

"Casey's going to pitch Morgan and Miller," he said. "At least that's what he said yesterday."

Lopez almost dropped the phone. All background noise in the bustling hotel lobby faded away, leaving just the sound of the rain pounding on the sidewalks and streets outside and the buzzing in Lopez's ears. *Morgan and Miller?* That's who Stengel was going to pitch against the team that was his main adversary for the pennant? April or not, both managers knew that every game against a fellow pennant contender was crucial and, as Lopez had done, they try to maneuver their rotations so that their best pitchers start as many of these key encounters as possible.

Going into the season, unproven Tom Morgan and Bill Miller had twenty career wins between them—compared with Wynn's and Lemon's combined 301. Why in the world wouldn't Stengel pitch at least one of his two aces against his primary contender?

Then the dime dropped for Lopez. That's exactly what Stengel had done. Whitey Ford and Ed Lopat were going to pitch against Chicago that week. He had indeed used his two aces against the team he saw as his primary contender. After the Indians' poor start, and perhaps their three straight September swoons, Stengel was announcing loud and clear that he no longer saw Cleveland as a team the Yankees needed to worry about.

"Well," a flustered Lopez barked into the phone, "you tell Casey I'm going to pitch a couple of young fellas against his club, too. Lemon and Wynn." He slammed down the phone and stormed back to the lobby, stewing and steaming over the slight his club had just received.

One thing was for sure—the Indians would go to Gotham that weekend with something to prove. Nobody from Cleveland would tolerate that kind of insult.

6 - A TRIPLE INTO THE GRAVESTONES

J ust across the Hudson River from where the Indians would battle the Yankees that weekend, another Cleveland icon would also be taking his show on the road. Alan Freed, WJW disc jockey (a new term in itself), would host the Eastern Moondog Coronation Ball in Newark, New Jersey, on the first Saturday night of May. Still glowing from the praise of *Billboard* magazine, which had just named him the best DJ in the country, Freed would show East Coast teens what made him—and the music he played—so special. But joining these new fans would be many of his Cleveland fans. Special trains from Cleveland to Newark were scheduled that Saturday to transport any fans wishing to see their beloved Freed light up Jersey.

After making a name for himself in Akron in the late 1940s hosting a revolutionary "call-in" radio show featuring jazz and popular music, Freed arrived in Cleveland in 1951. At first, nobody knew quite what to make of him. He was one of the first white disc jockeys to play rhythm-and-blues music—still often called "race records"—and exploded onto the airwaves with relentless energy and personality, creating his own sound effects and talking in different voices on the air. He called himself "Moondog."

His confidence stemmed from a realization pointed out by a friend who owned a record store in a black area of Cleveland. Freed saw that white teenagers were buying what was considered to be "black" music. He began receiving phone requests from white listeners in affluent areas like Shaker Heights and Lakeside. Knowing that Cleveland was already an ideal test market for new trends in music, Freed saw the future and was about to cash in.

In March of 1952, Freed organized the first "Moondog Ball" at Cleveland Arena. Before the show even began, the arena filled past capacity and police couldn't control the masses of young people outside demanding to get in. Thousands more crashed the gates, and the ball was called off before it really got started. The event may have been a disaster, but Freed's career had just taken flight. WJW quickly became Cleveland's most popular radio station, and Freed's program became the nation's top R&B show. By the end of 1953, recordings of Freed's show were rebroadcast in the New York listening area, and a new term Freed would later claim to have coined was being used to describe the type of music he played: "rock and roll."

While bobbysoxers bopped to Freed's tunes in Newark, back in Cleveland, May debuted with dramatically fluctuating weather patterns—which wasn't at all unusual. Thermometers soared into the eighties on May 1 and flowers blossomed. Four days later, they plummeted into the twenties amidst an overnight frost that withered many of those flowers. The month began with eleven consecutive days of rain, and as voters headed to the polls for the May 4 primaries leading to November's midterm elections, snow flurries floated through the air. Most races unfolded exactly as predicted, including victories for the two front-runners in the governor's race: incumbent Democrat Frank Lausche and his Republican challenger, James Rhodes. Among the bland tallies was a pair of unremarkable primary victories in races for separate seats as a judge of the court of common pleas for Cuyahoga County. Few, even those who voted for him, knew the name of the lone Republican contestant, but by the time his name appeared on the ballot again in November, Edward Blythin would be familiar across the country. Likewise, John Mahon was a virtual unknown, even after winning the Democratic primary, but by the fall, he would become another central character in one of the city's most magnetic mysteries, involving "Dr. Sam" Sheppard and his murdered wife.

When the rain finally stopped in Boston, the "Big Switch" worked once again. The Indians plated five runs in the first two innings at damp, chilly Fenway Park and cruised to a win over the Red Sox that pulled them within a game of .500. But the price was costly. Running out a bunt, Regalado strained muscles in his thigh and would be shelved for two weeks. Rather than un-switching and sending Rosen back to third, Lopez slid young outfielder Al Smith to the hot corner, though he'd only played third base twice in his brief major league career.

And for the second time in three days, a Lopez experiment paid off. In New York, before a modest crowd of just over 9,000, Cleveland jumped to a 4–0 lead in the third inning and delivered a symbolic blow. After a Larry Doby homer put the Indians on the board, Dave Philley rifled a line drive that landed in deep center field and pinballed among the monuments honoring Babe Ruth, Lou Gehrig, and Miller Huggins—which many young fans believed were tombstones marking the final resting place of those legendary Yankees. The result was a triple, and Philley scored on a sacrifice fly. But perhaps more importantly, it also seemed to deliver a subtle message to the mighty New Yorkers: history means nothing. This is 1954.

The Yankees rallied to tie it with three unearned runs in the sixth. Perhaps rethinking his decision to start Tom Morgan, Stengel brought on Whitey Ford in relief, and the "Chairman of the Board" held Cleveland scoreless for three innings. Bob Lemon did the same with the Yankees, and the game plunged into extra innings, where the Indians finally pulled away. They loaded the bases with one out in the tenth, and Larry Doby brought two runs home with a single. A Dave Philley RBI made it 7–4, then George Strickland put the nail in the coffin with a two-run triple that sealed a 9–4 Cleveland win. And while Stengel may have regretted his choice in pitchers, it was Ford whom the Indians tapped for the winning rally.

On Saturday afternoon before a national television audience, the Cleveland offense exploded for five runs in the third and four more in the fifth to cruise to an easy 10–2 victory. With nineteen runs in two games at Yankee Stadium, the Indians' bats had come alive. Likewise, Indian pitchers had been effective, surrendering only three earned runs to a potent lineup. The Indians had sent a message to Stengel's boys: don't count us out yet.

The momentum continued with a doubleheader sweep of the Senators in Washington on Sunday, and the Indians had won six straight, catapulting from eighth place to third. This was the kind of baseball Cleveland was used to. And that week, the city picked up yet another victory.

After three decades of debate and deliberation, the U.S. House of Representatives voted to grant the U.S. authority to join Canada in constructing the Great Lakes-St. Lawrence Seaway, a shipping canal covering a 115-mile stretch through Canada and the United States. The notion had been defeated on four separate occasions, but security concerns stemming from the Cold War changed the mood of both Congress and its constituents, and a new view of this liquid highway, which could connect the American Midwest to the rest of the world, was adopted. Embodying this new spirit, a handsome freshman senator from Massachusetts named John Fitzgerald Kennedy led the charge, giving an impassioned speech that propelled the bill's eventual passage in the Senate in January, giving it the momentum it needed to pass in the House. When construction was completed, Cleveland would be accessible by each ocean-going ship on the Atlantic, opening up countless new doors of trade and commerce. Consequently, Cleveland's export volume, already one of the highest in the world, was expected to double to nearly $1 billion per year. Accommodations would have to be made by the city, including one proposal that suggested "moving" Municipal Stadium to make room for a larger port, but Cleveland knew whatever changes were necessary would be worthwhile.

Even Mr. Cleveland saw the Seaway as yet another golden plank in the city's burgeoning national platform. In another of his breathless speeches that week, Louis Seltzer proclaimed that "Cleveland now is poised once more on a new cycle of civic accomplishment that, when tied together with its fabulous industrial growth in recent years and its extraordinary potential . . . will make it one of the most prosperous cities on the American continent." It seemed that everything Cleveland touched turned to gold—a sentiment casually reflected by Al Rosen during a workout at Connie Mack Stadium the following morning: "We're going to win. We'll win and without much trouble." True, the Indians had just taken two of three from the Athletics in Philadelphia to pull within a game-and-a-half of first-place Chicago, but outside of Cleveland, people wondered if such confidence was warranted.

After splitting a pair in Baltimore, the Indians returned home to start a fourteen-game home stand with three against the Yankees, who were in fourth place during their own sluggish start. They arrived in Cleveland on Monday for the stadium's first night game of the season and a special atmosphere filled the lakeside air. In neighborhoods around Cleveland, the sweet scent of blooming lilacs wafted through the streets. As the sun nestled into the horizon, the sky turned purple and soft. Mothers took children for walks along the sidewalks. Fathers sat on front stoops and back porches, enjoying a Chesterfield cigarette or a vodka tonic, perusing that afternoon's *Press* while half-listening to the Indians on a crackling radio set up next to a nearby window. And in backyards and grassy alleys, children played with a new sense of freedom, liberated from their thick winter coats and the onset of pre-dinnertime darkness. Their playful cries and laughter, the eager conversations of mothers taking place over back fences and laundry lines, and the constant hum of the ballgame on the radio all combined to create the pulse of a city celebrating the arrival of spring, which already teetered on the edge of summer. Cleveland's life cycle was gradually revving up once again.

The Yankees' engine also began firing at the outset of this much-anticipated series, plating three runs in the first off Bob Lemon. But the Indians responded with a fifty-two-minute, eight-run assault in the bottom of the frame, highlighted by a grand slam by Dave Philley and the ejections of both Stengel and Yogi Berra—a crippling blow Franklin Lewis likened to "taking onions away from liver." The Yankees continued to creep closer over the remainder of what became a marathon contest, but when the stadium lights were finally turned off just before midnight, the Indians had secured their third straight victory over the Yankees to start the season and moved to within a half-game of first place while keeping New York in fourth, just a game over .500. "Maybe we'll get started when we get out of Cleveland," Stengel quipped afterward.

They needn't wait that long. On Tuesday night, Berra earned revenge for his quick exit the previous day by ripping a two-out, two-run double to break a 3–3 tie in the ninth inning and deliver a much-needed Yankee victory. More painful than surrendering the game-winning hit, the Indians once again were reminded of a glaring weakness in their infield. Al Rosen had done a more than respectable job in the games he'd played since moving to first base, but he still brought very little experience to the position—not something that a pennant contender could afford. This gap showed in the ninth when he failed to cover first after making an initial move to field a grounder between first and second by Joe Collins. Collins reached safely on what should have been the third out, and Berra followed with the game-winning hit. Rosen, who'd delivered a clutch hit in the eighth to tie the game, was still one of the most important players on the team, but in that moment it became clear that the Indians could not contend for a pennant with a makeshift infield. That incident, plus the shaky play of Al Smith, filling in at third for the injured Regalado, was beginning to become conspicuous. Smith, a career outfielder, had committed six errors in his first six games at third base, including one that cost the Tribe a game in Philadelphia. Collins's grounder—combined with Smith's struggles—proved that they needed help, and Hank Greenberg knew it.

As the Indians and Yankees continued their mid-week battle on the lakefront, area housewives were introduced to a bold new era. Outside of Bedford, just south of Libby Road, the dynamic of grocery shopping was turned upside down with the arrival of what was proclaimed as a true "supermarket." With its grand opening that afternoon, Fazio's became the largest retail self-serve food store in Ohio, and one step inside made it clear that the days of the neighborhood grocer were numbered. Though it resembled an airplane hangar from the outside, inside was an environment never seen before. The shiny white floors and walls reflected the chrome and stainless steel surfaces that seemed to stretch over every inch of the 22,000-square-foot facility. But it wasn't just for show—the wide-open spaces were used wisely, giving shoppers more variety and selection than they'd thought possible. It had taken employees three weeks to stock the shelves, which combined to cover more than a mile. The produce counter and dairy case were both forty-six feet long, while the meat case was a whopping seventy-seven feet. Eleven separate frozen food cases were stacked together to form a massive wall. Hanging above this grocery Valhalla were thirteen rows of eight-foot-long fluorescent lights, illuminating the ocean of products below with an efficient, balanced glow.

Anticipating large crowds, Fazio's marked off a massive parking lot that could hold up to 3,000 cars and inside boasted an unheard-of seven checkout lines to eliminate long waits at the register. And unlike most corner grocers, Fazio's encouraged mothers to bring the whole family, since they remained open long after most of the competitors had locked up. Closed Sunday, of course, the store was open until nine p.m. during the week and a startling ten p.m. on Friday and Saturday. In ways that shoppers of 1954 couldn't possibly understand, Fazio's Supermarket marked the arrival of the future.

Yet Fazio's was just the observation deck of a much larger vessel known as Meadowbrook Merchandise Mart, which opened its multiple doors the following week. Just as Fazio's, located within, signaled a change in the dynamic of food purchasing, Meadowbrook displayed the early evolution of what would one day become the modern shopping mall. Cleveland residents were already being drawn to the suburbs to marvel at the spectacle of conveniently located "shopping centers" in which various stores were lined up in long strips at the altar of ample parking. But Meadowbrook was something else again. Inside its 100,000-square-foot emporium, guests entered a new dimension of shopping. Visitors could peruse more than seventy vendors laid out in a county-fair format—a "city of stores" it was called, one that provided "a new kind of shopping!"—separated only by short partitions no higher than eight feet. Between those partitions, they could purchase anything they could imagine: baked goods, poultry, flowers, housewares, or furniture. They could even grab a bite to eat or get their hair cut. "Buy a car or a carrot," Meadowbrook's ads proclaimed. "Buy a diaper or a door. Buy a lock or a lobster. Buy a ham or a house."

Such bold promises certainly caught the attention of Clevelanders, who now didn't have to waste a day hopping from specialty shops to department stores through snarled traffic and miniscule parking lots. For the first time, residents had been provided with a viable option to a trip downtown, a place that was "as friendly as a cracker barrel, as modern as a streamliner."

While the future of retail shopping in Cleveland looked incredibly bright, by the time the Yankees left town, the Indians' future once again looked cloudy. With just over 7,000 in the stands amidst raw and wet weather on Wednesday afternoon, Mike Garcia and Ed Lopat matched one another with five scoreless frames. The Yankees broke through in the sixth and marched to a 5–0 lead, and then held off a furious Indian rally in the eighth to win by one. New York, which had utilized its top three pitchers for this series, left Cleveland holding the same record as the Yankees, 13–10, both two back of the White Sox.

On yet another unseasonably frosty afternoon on Thursday, the Indians were equally cold, trailing the lowly Senators 7–1 in the ninth and only managing one hit over the first eight innings. But everything changed in the ninth as the Tribe rallied to tie, then won on an RBI double by Rosen in the eleventh. It marked Cleveland's eighth late-inning victory of the young season, and Lopez admitted he couldn't remember a team that pulled off more come-from-behind wins to start the year. "They're hard on the nerves," he said, "but I'm not complaining."

The Tribe won easily the next day and then completed the sweep of the Senators on Saturday by scoring two runs in the eighth for a 5–4 triumph. The Indians then took two from Philadelphia on Sunday afternoon as Mike Garcia pitched what he believed was the finest game of his career, allowing just one hit in a complete-game shutout in the nightcap.

The Indians, now tied for first with Chicago, were on a roll.

7 - HARD LUCK

The following Monday, America found out it was still fighting the Civil War.

With the unanimous decision of the U.S. Supreme Court in a case originating from Topeka, Kansas, labeled Brown vs. Board of Education, segregation in schools was deemed unconstitutional, sending much of the nation south of the Mason-Dixon Line into furious hysterics.

And while the debates raged (the term "civil rights" was yet to be coined) on the editorial pages of newspapers from coast to coast, one story continued to dominate Cleveland's sports pages. The red-hot Indians continued their purge of the American League, rallying from three-run deficits on back-to-back nights to beat the Red Sox, then posting another impressive rally two days later to top Baltimore. With more than 24,000 on hand for a Sunday doubleheader with the Orioles, the Tribe put the finishing touches on a nearly perfect home stand. In the opener, the Indians exploded for sixteen hits and fourteen runs in a blowout, giving Bob Feller his 250th career victory. They then changed gears in the second game, prevailing in an old-fashioned pitcher's duel between Bob Turley—who had nearly no-hit the Indians a month before—and Cleveland's Art Houtteman.

"Hard-Luck Houtteman" came into the league with Detroit in 1945, four months shy of his eighteenth birthday, the youngest player to debut in the American League since Bob Feller lit up the circuit at age seventeen nine years before. Naturally, Houtteman struggled at first, and in his first year as a full-time starter in 1948, he lost his first eight decisions and sloshed to a miserable 2–16 record. In the majority of his losses, he didn't pitch that poorly, but either he didn't receive much run support or gave up a big inning at the wrong time. Hence, his unfortunate nickname originated and began to appear in the papers.

But in the years to come, whatever tough breaks he endured on the diamond paled in comparison to the adversity he faced off it. During spring training in 1949, Houtteman was driving back from a dance held at a college in Lakeland, Florida, when his car collided with a fruit truck. Hospitalized with a fractured skull, the early prognosis for his recovery wasn't good. But he pulled through and returned to the team in May. Continuing his rough patch, he lost his first three starts, but then turned things around, finishing the season with a 15–10 record. He was even better in 1950, winning nineteen games, and at twenty-two years old, appeared destined for a promising career. But once again, his life took a series of cruel turns. A few weeks after the 1950 season ended, Houtteman was drafted into the Army. Though he was deemed unfit for active duty because of lingering headaches caused by his accident, he would miss the 1951 season. Things looked up that summer when his wife gave birth to their first child, a daughter they named Sheryl. Seven months later, Houtteman's wife, Shelagh, was driving through the mountains of Tennessee on her way back from visiting her husband during spring training when the car went off the road. It rolled over twice, throwing Sheryl from the car and killing her.

Once again, Houtteman tried to submerge his grief in the magic waters of baseball. He returned later that month to a Tigers team that had lost its first eight games and was essentially already eliminated from the pennant race. He was one out away from immortality on April 26, needing to retire just one more Cleveland batter to secure a no-hitter. Catcher Joe Ginsberg called for a curveball to Indians outfielder Harry Simpson, but Houtteman shook him off and instead threw a fastball. Simpson ripped the pitch for a single, spoiling the no-hitter. It was the beginning of a long year for Art Houtteman.

Suffering from the loss of his daughter and a form of what would later become known as Post-Traumatic Stress Disorder, Houtteman's ERA ballooned almost a full point and he lost twenty games. After losing six of nine starts with an ERA flirting near 6.00 to start 1953, Houtteman was shipped to Cleveland, where Al Lopez, a consummate evaluator of hurlers, saw a spark in the troubled pitcher. "All he needed," Lopez said, "was to regain his confidence." Once again, Mel Harder was called upon to reconstruct a struggling pitcher. Houtteman's incredible bad luck continued in Cleveland as he lost four straight decisions, but he won five of his last six to finish at 7–7 with the Indians with a much more respectable 3.80 ERA. His life outside of baseball also began to heal. Shelagh gave birth to their second daughter, Holly, the following February. After several years of misery, Art Houtteman had finally found a home, one that the specter of misfortune couldn't penetrate.

On that bright Sunday afternoon in May of 1954, as Liberace played a pair of sold-out concerts in Public Music Hall down the street, Houtteman pitched out of jam after jam. The Orioles led off the second and fourth with doubles and the third with a triple—and never scored a run. Another triple in the fifth proved fruitless. Baltimore finally broke through with a run in the seventh and took a 1–0 lead into the ninth. But as he'd done in Baltimore in April, Rosen ruined Bob Turley's day, crushing a game-tying homer to send the contest to extra innings, where Houtteman retired nine straight, then won his own game with a two-out double in the twelfth to score George Strickland from first.

Fans had to wonder: When someone with Houtteman's track record has a day like that, could something special be happening? Even Houtteman had acknowledged the sentiment. During spring training, he'd told reporters that if he could win fifteen games, the Indians would win the pennant. The victory over Baltimore was only his second, but his ERA was 2.83—better than it had ever been in his career. It seemed that Cleveland had reversed the fortunes of "Hard Luck Houtteman."

With Houtteman and the Indians on their way to Chicago for a quick series, back home Clevelanders started making plans for the upcoming Memorial Day weekend. And what better way to start a three-day vacation than with a murder?

On Friday, the Allen Theater debuted the long-anticipated film version of Frederick Knott's successful Broadway play *Dial M for Murder* on its immense panoramic screen. After the play ran on Broadway for eighteen months, there were naturally high expectations for the film, which was directed by Alfred Hitchcock.

Taking place almost entirely in the drawing room of a wealthy London couple, *Dial M for Murder* exploded off the screen with vibrant colors as audiences were introduced to a dashing husband, played by Academy Award-winning actor Ray Milland, cleverly planning to kill his wife, played by an impossibly beautiful twenty-four-year-old Grace Kelly. While critics felt the film adaptation was not as impressive as the play, *Dial M for Murder* was a hit. And while the premise may have seemed far-fetched to some, in a matter of weeks, the subject of a husband trying to kill his wife would be quite real to the people of Cleveland.

Those looking for a little more salsa in their entertainment that weekend could see world-famous singer/dancer Carmen Miranda, who would bring her unique samba style and her trademark hat covered in tropical fruit to the SkyWay Lounge on Rocky River Drive for a nine-day engagement. And after a week that brought both Miranda and Liberace to Cleveland, the city would also welcome Ed Sullivan, host of the popular Sunday-night CBS variety program *Toast of the Town*, who was met by a delegation of dignitaries at the airport, then spoke to a standing-room-only crowd at the Higbee Company Auditorium.

Their fourteen-game home stand now completed with a 12–2 record, the Indians' winning streak ended with back-to-back losses in Chicago. But after flying home for the weekend—marking the team's first-ever round-trip by air—the Big Three rose to the occasion again, holding the Tigers without an earned run over twenty-seven innings in a convincing three-game sweep.

On the eve of Memorial Day, the first symbolic turn of the baseball season, the Indians' sluggish start to the campaign was long forgotten. Now alone in first place with the best record in baseball, holding a one-game lead over the pesky White Sox and three-and-a-half games over New York, Cleveland had won twenty-four of its last thirty games. The Indians had come from behind to win twelve times and had won five after trailing in the eighth or ninth inning. Four members of the starting lineup were hitting better than .300. One of them was Rosen, who had actually improved upon his incredible 1953 statistics and was on pace to challenge the major-league record for RBIs in a season. He'd even come close to tying another major-league record by hitting six home runs in a five-game period.

With Garcia finally untracked, the Big Three were cruising. Bob Lemon was 7–1 with an ERA of 2.25. Early Wynn had already won six, and, as evidenced by the previous Sunday's magnificent double feature against Baltimore, Feller and Houtteman were better than most teams' aces. Everything had come together, and the Indians now looked like the team to beat in the American League. "Given a winner," a *Plain Dealer* editorial stated that spring, "this town still has it in itself to go topsy-turvy with enthusiasm. Let the Tribe take it from there."

That's precisely what would happen. Yet the Indians' success would prove to be just one of several intriguing storylines that would enrapture the city over the next four months.

The most memorable summer in Cleveland history had arrived.

Game 2

AMONG THE MANY OFFERINGS of congratulations Dusty Rhodes received following his "Chinese" home run that won the first game of the 1954 World Series, one that stood out was a telegram from a New York restaurant. "In honor of your game-winning blow," it read, "we invite you to restore your energy with our homer-producing Chinese food."

Witty photographers had Rhodes pose with a Chinese newspaper, as if scanning it for an account of his heroics. Later they paired Rhodes with Vic Wertz, whose 460-foot fly out in the eighth by all rights should have actually won the game. As they snapped their cameras, the photographers brazenly asked Wertz to smile. "What's funny?" Wertz snapped. "I won't smile until we win."

The presumptive theory both in New York and beyond was that Wertz would indeed be smiling by the close of business Thursday afternoon. It had taken an almost biblical string of bad breaks for the Indians to lose the day before. The Giants couldn't possibly expect to receive another such streak of good fortune in Game Two. Plus, the law of averages declared that the Indians were simply too good a team to lose two straight to an inferior ballclub. Reflecting this current of public opinion, President Eisenhower stepped into the press room at his vacation compound in Colorado just before the first pitch and announced, "I'd be willing to bet a golf ball on Cleveland today." The reporters in the room smiled and chuckled, and not surprisingly, no one took the president up on his offer.

The bright sunshine of Wednesday afternoon had dissolved by dinnertime, replaced by a steady autumn rain that lasted through the night and into the morning, and the possibility of Game Two being postponed looked more and more likely as the city awoke. Wednesday's clear blue horizon was now a murky haze beneath an ashen sky that gave the Polo Grounds an eerie, gothic atmosphere. The rain that morning had delayed the start of batting practice for forty-five minutes and forced both teams to cut fifteen minutes off their allotted time. But after the front pushed through and

the fog cleared around lunchtime, the game began on schedule. And so did the Indians' quest to prove that yesterday had been an aberration.

With the sun occasionally peeking out from behind the bloated clouds, New York hurler Johnny Antonelli fired the first pitch of the game, and Al Smith rifled the ball high down the left-field line. Before most fans had even settled into their seats, Smith's blast landed in the upper deck, just a few feet to the right of the foul pole and just short of the roof. Five seconds into the contest, the Indians led, 1–0, and Smith would be the first Indian to receive an electric train set, as promised by the president of the Hobby House back in Cleveland to every Indian player who hit a home run in the Series.

Antonelli recovered to retire the next two batters, but then walked Al Rosen and the forgotten hero of Game One, Vic Wertz. When Wally Westlake followed with a single to center, it appeared the Indians would take a two-run lead in the first inning for the second straight day. But Rosen, with his right leg once again taped heavily to support his throbbing thigh, could only manage to hobble to third rather than sprinting for home as he would have a month before. George Strickland followed by popping out, and the lead remained a single run.

The disappointment of another missed opportunity waned somewhat over the next hour as Early Wynn started the contest ablaze. With the sporadic sunlight broiling away the last of the morning mist and creating a muggy, humid afternoon, Wynn retired the first twelve New York batters, not allowing a hit until the fifth inning. Once he did, however, fate again turned on the Cleveland Indians. Willie Mays led off the frame with a walk, and then took second when Hank Thompson singled to

All smiles on the train ride to New York for the World Series were first baseman Vic Wertz (foreground) and pitcher Early Wynn, along with their wives.

center. Presented his first scoring opportunity, Giants manager Leo Durocher decided it was time to play another hunch. Though just the fifth inning, he pulled back Monte Irvin and sent in Dusty Rhodes to pinch hit. He was greeted with an ovation from the fans, who hoped against the odds that Rhodes could deliver off the bench for the second day in a row.

On the mound, Early Wynn was stewing, the meanness that usually possessed him when he was pitching rising to the surface. Here was the reason none of the Indians had slept well the night before, why the mood in the clubhouse before the game was slightly less sunny than the day before. This goofy-named substitute had tapped a bush-league fly ball to the exact right spot, and he was a hero, for one day anyway overshadowing the magnificence of the 1954 Indians. Wynn's second pitch to Rhodes was high and tight, sending the toast of New York ducking down to his knees in the batter's box. It

was a pitch that seemed to speak, both to Rhodes and everyone else in the ballpark. It said, "Not today."

Ahead one-and-two, Wynn delivered a cutting slider. Rhodes swung and, just as he'd done twenty-three hours earlier, made slight contact off the end of the bat. But this time, the ball floated toward center, not right, where it would fall well before reaching the wall. Yet as Wynn turned, he saw that this was the problem. It wasn't going to go far enough. It carried well over George Strickland's head at shortstop but well short of where Larry Doby was positioned in center. Wynn could see, even as Strickland and Doby sprinted toward each other to catch up with the ball, it was going to land in between them. And, of course, it did.

Mays motored around third to score, and Thompson cruised into third ahead of Doby's throw, which allowed Rhodes to scamper to second as the crowd erupted. The game was tied, and once again Dusty Rhodes was a hero for simply connecting his bat with the ball and letting good luck take care of the rest. Back in Ohio, state auditor James Rhodes was starting to get nervous. The Republican Party's candidate for governor feared that simply by name association, Jim "Dusty" Rhodes was costing him votes in the northeast portion of the state.

Wynn struck out Davey Williams, but then walked Wes Westrum. With the bases loaded, Wynn got Antonelli to ground to second. But rather than coming home with the ball to cut down the potential run, Bobby Avila tried for the double play. He flipped the ball to Strickland covering second for one, and Strickland fired across to Vic Wertz at first. Antonelli just beat the relay, evading the inning-ending double play, and as a result, Thompson came home. The Giants now led, 2–1.

Wynn got out of the fifth without further damage and then pitched out of a potential jam in the sixth when Alvin Dark wound up on second with nobody out after a wild pitch. Rhodes settled into the batter's box to lead off the seventh, and the crowd of nearly 50,000 roared for him. The cheers crescendoed a moment later when Rhodes cut at a "knuckler that didn't knuckle" as Wynn would explain later, and sent it soaring into the upper deck in right field for his second pinch-hit home run of the Series. "There was nothing Chinese about this one," Rhodes would quip afterward. Over the course of a twenty-four-hour period, Dusty Rhodes had etched himself in World Series history.

Yet it was the Indians' offense that bore much of the responsibility for his emerging legend. Had any Cleveland batter come through when necessary, Rhodes would have been a footnote in the box score. Jim Hegan had led off the second with a double, moved to third on a bunt, and was stranded there when Smith struck out and Avila popped out. Wynn nearly helped his own cause in the sixth by blasting a towering fly that glanced off the left-field wall, barely staying in the park. Wynn reached second on the hit but remained there when Smith fouled out.

Avila walked to start the seventh and moved to second on a ground out but got caught in a rundown when he tried to advance to third too quickly on a chopper back to Antonelli. He was tagged out, and another scoring opportunity perished. Then in the ninth, Cleveland put the tying runs on base to start the inning with Doby coming up. With odd-patterned shadows nesting across the infield, Doby swung with every ounce of his being on a two-and-two pitch, hoping to put the Indians on top, but instead missed the ball for strike three. As he regained his balance, Doby tossed the bat into the air and caught the shaft with his right hand in a quick fury, enraged over this third strikeout of the afternoon. Rudy Regalado,

who'd been sent in to run for the hobbling Rosen in the seventh, grounded into a force out, and it would be up to yesterday's hero, Vic Wertz, with two on and two out. This time, with the crowd on its feet, Wertz lifted a fly to deep left center, where it was caught, appropriately, by Dusty Rhodes.

The Indians, who hadn't lost two straight games in more than a month, had now dropped the biggest pair of the season. Afterward, the clubhouse was quiet, holding inside it the stuffy humidity of the afternoon now past. The looks on the faces within were not of anger or shock but simple disbelief. Early Wynn had pitched seven innings and allowed just four hits, but had somehow lost the game. Afterward, he sat on a stool in the clubhouse, his back to teammates and reporters, not speaking to anyone. The Indians had rapped eight hits, twice New York's total, but had scored only one run. For the second straight day, they'd stranded thirteen baserunners, and their count with runners in scoring position in the World Series now stood at an abysmal two-for-twenty-four.

When a reporter spotted Larry Doby in the shower, the outfielder looked dazed. Water streamed off his head and dripped onto the floor as great clouds of steam enveloped him. The reporter's questions were unnecessary. Doby was talking to himself. "I can't come down," he said, raising his hand above his head. "I'm way up here." Then he lowered the hand to his knees. "And I can't get down here. I get up for something like this, a World Series, and I can't come down."

As reporters swarmed around Al Lopez in his stuffy office afterward, the mild-mannered skipper showed signs of strain. He dragged a hand across his weary eyes. "I can't be unhappy with the boys," he said in a monotone, "because they happened to get their hits at the wrong time."

A reporter asked him what was the turning point of the game.

"There wasn't any turning point," Lopez murmured.

"There's got to be a turning point," the reporter persisted. "What was it?"

Lopez's eyes darted to him. "There wasn't any," he said, louder now, his normally gentle voice rising with anger. "I'm telling you."

As if he hadn't heard, the reporter spoke again.

"Was the turning point when Doby couldn't catch that ball Rhodes hit?"

Now Lopez's eyes furrowed, and his face became taut with anger.

"Goddamn it!" he barked. "What are you trying to do? Ask your questions and answer them, too? Goddamn, what are you trying to do?" The subdued chatter of the clubhouse dropped to nothing. "That one was a Woolworth job," Lopez went on, his reddened face glistening with a film of sweat. "A ten-center that nobody could have caught." Then, harking back to yesterday's frustration, he added, "Not even Willie Mays."

Lopez paused to gather himself and was able to continue. "That bloop of Rhodes won it for them," he said, "but the story of the game was obvious: we didn't hit the ball when it counted, and they did.

"We have too good a club for this to be happening to us. We've just got to get out of this park. We'll be all right when we get home."

The players agreed. Once they returned to Cleveland, everything would return to normal. "Hang on, stay in there, keep the faith up—we'll come out on top this 1954 Series," a peppy *Press* editorial predicted. "It's our turn now. Hang on Cleveland— hang on tight, keep the fingers crossed, the mouth corners turned up, and the sights high—high enough to get them over that center-field fence. And we'll win!"

Cleveland settled into its second straight uneasy evening knowing that tomorrow the Series would turn around, and the '54 Indians would once again be compared with the greatest teams ever to play the game of baseball. Such was the magic of the Best Location in the Nation.

PART TWO

THE BEST LOCATION IN THE NATION

AMERICAN LEAGUE STANDINGS ON THE MORNING OF MEMORIAL DAY MONDAY, MAY 31, 1954

	W	L	PCT	GB
CLEVELAND	27	12	.692	—
CHICAGO	27	14	.659	1
NEW YORK	24	16	.600	3½
DETROIT	19	16	.543	6
WASHINGTON	16	22	.421	10½
BOSTON	11	21	.344	12
PHILADELPHIA	14	25	.359	13
BALTIMORE	13	25	.342	13½

8 - BLEED AND BELIEVE

Though scientists and those who clung to persnickety details would protest, summer began on a lazy Monday morning, the last day of May. With a day off from work to honor all the Americans who died protecting their country, many residents of Cleveland enjoyed a leisurely perusal of the *Plain Dealer* before heading off to enjoy one of the multiple Decoration Day (or, as it was unofficially coming to be known, Memorial Day) parades marching through Cleveland's suburbs or the colossal fireworks show at Geauga Lake that evening. With the memories of World War II, and certainly Korea, still vibrant in the American consciousness, Decoration Day was much more meaningful than a mere day off of work or school. It was a day of reflection more than celebration, one of somber thanksgiving rather than the joyous cacophony of the Fourth of July—though this year, after the shocking murder of Marilyn Sheppard in the peaceful suburb of Bay Village on the Fourth, the cacophony would be anything but joyous in Cleveland. With the peonies and coral bells finally opened, children would make small bouquets and accompany their parents to the cemetery to place the flowers beside the gravestones of their ancestors, then spend the morning remembering those who had given their last full measure of devotion for their country.

Still, by mid-afternoon, as thoughts turned to summer and all the activities and chores that came with it, many husbands and wives reopened ongoing discussions over a technical marvel that was already redefining summer in the city: air conditioning.

Two years before, it was still a fad, nothing more than a fanciful—and expensive—conversation piece for people who had more money than they knew what to do with. Besides, the typical working man and the average housewife had doubts that a humming metallic box crammed into an open window could indeed make their lives better. They figured it was nothing more than temporary relief, like standing in front of an open refrigerator on a sweltering afternoon. Barely 4,000 air conditioners were sold in Cleveland in 1952.

But the following year, it went from fad to phenomenon. Over a million were sold nationwide. And the trend continued in 1954, as many houses now were marked by a new symbol of upward mobility—a single-room air-conditioning unit neatly nudged in a window frame. In addition to eliminating the summer nights spent tossing and turning, trying to sleep in a stifling bedroom, air conditioners were seen as a breakthrough in maintaining the home, often called an "ease-for-the-housewife" device. True enough, housewives reported that air conditioning not only made the home more comfortable for cooking and cleaning, but they also saved time. With windows and doors shut, homes with air conditioners were less affected by the dirt and soot that traveled through the air of industrial cities in the summertime, and thereby required less dusting and wall washing.

Air conditioning had put a price tag on comfort, and by 1954, it was relatively low. You could purchase a unit at any department store in Cleveland for between $200 and $300, and the operating costs were roughly $50 a month. Now a new version of air conditioning was beginning to gain traction, a much more elaborate installation in which an entire home could be air-conditioned. York, one of the leading manufacturers, advertised that you could air-condition your house for less than the cost of a good used car, and the standard starting price for such an installation was around $1,500. With winter forgotten, and the prospect of muggy, unbearable days and nights on the horizon, air conditioning was a hot topic in and around Cleveland that Memorial Day amidst the fanfare of picnics, parades, and of course, Indians baseball.

Following the established baseball custom, each American League team would play a doubleheader on Memorial Day afternoon, with the Indians hosting the White Sox in a battle for first place. Despite a forecast for showers, better than 39,000 filed into Municipal Stadium to see the top two teams in the American League launch the season's second quarter. As the holiday sunshine pushed the temperature to the mid-eighties, marking the warmest day yet of 1954, both games went into the eighth inning tied at three. In the opener, the White Sox surged to victory on the strength of a two-run homer by former Indian Minnie Minoso, just entering the prime of a career that would stretch over four decades. The story was reversed in the nightcap when Indians catcher Jim Hegan stepped into the batter's box in the bottom of the eighth inning. Soaked with sweat and weary after catching both games, the thirty-three-year-old Hegan was also having trouble seeing the baseball on its way to the plate as it traveled through the falling shadows. He guessed Harry Dorish would toss him a slider and swung where he thought the ball would be, blasting a homer to left to break the tie and spark a three-run rally. When the long day of action finally concluded just before 7:30 that evening, the top of the American League standings remained the same: Indians on top, Chicago one back.

Though Cleveland didn't play the following day, June 1 would be remembered as one of the watershed moments of the season. That evening, Hank Greenberg made a trade that was ignored by most and questioned by those paying attention. He sent pitcher Bob Chakales to Baltimore for a struggling outfielder named Victor Woodrow Wertz.

Reporters and fans scratched their heads, trying to pinpoint the logic of the move. In previous years, the Indians had a hole in the outfield that a player like Wertz could have filled nicely. But after trading for proven veteran Dave Philley just before spring training began, that hole had been filled. Though Philley was struggling at the plate to start 1954, hitting just .175 through May, he'd become a defensive stalwart in the field and would remain in the starting lineup for the duration of the season. In Wertz, Greenberg saw an asset, even though there wasn't a clear place to put him. But rather than passing on the opportunity to land him, Greenberg trusted his instincts and took a gamble—one that wound up being one of the shrewdest moves in team history.

Wertz appeared to be much older than he actually was. Prematurely bald, he looked forty-nine instead of twenty-nine, and by all appearances seemed better suited for his off-season job as a car salesman in Utica, Michigan, than as a professional athlete. He'd established himself as a potent power hitter in Detroit, clouting ninety-seven home runs in four seasons in the early fifties before the Tigers shipped him to the St. Louis Browns late in 1952. He struggled in '53, then fell off the radar almost completely when the Browns moved to Baltimore. Memorial Stadium's spacious outfield turned many of Wertz's long drives into routine fly balls, and he was mired in a miserable slump in 1954. He struck out in his first six plate appearances and by Memorial Day was hitting .202 with just one home run.

Even while Wertz struggled, Hank Greenberg kept his eye on him. In fact, after the trade, Greenberg said he'd been trying to land Wertz for three years. At first, he didn't consider the possibility that Wertz might be the player who could un-bend the question mark the Cleveland infield had twisted itself into. Knowing his club could use another hitter capable of power, Greenberg saw Wertz as an ideal pinch-hitter and "insurance" player who could fill in when and where necessary. Throughout May, Greenberg negotiated with Baltimore general manager Art Ehlers, trying to swing a deal for Wertz—just as they'd done six months earlier when Ehlers had tried to acquire Larry Doby. Finally, late in the evening on the day after Memorial Day, following an Orioles' loss to Detroit, dropping last-place Baltimore to 14–27, a frustrated Ehlers picked up the phone and called Greenberg. "Let's get together, Hank, or call it all off," barked Ehlers. "I'll give you Wertz for Chakales. Okay?" Greenberg quickly agreed. Bob Chakales was a mediocre hurler the pitching-rich Tribe could easily spare. And so it was that the Indians acquired the final piece to their puzzle.

While both Greenberg and Al Lopez were thrilled to add some pop to the lineup, they never envisioned Wertz being used on a daily basis. "I'm tickled to death to get Vic," Lopez said the next day. "But I don't figure on playing him for the time being." Yet his arrival could not have been timed better. With Al Rosen sidelined for nearly two weeks with an injured finger, light-hitting Bill Glynn took over at first, and while Glynn may have brought a bit more stability defensively, the Indians needed more offensive production. Thus, on June 9 at Griffith Stadium in Washington, Wertz was inserted into the starting lineup at first base—a position he'd never played in his major-league career. "The position wasn't as hard to play as I expected," he said, "because our pitchers didn't let very many men get on base." Using the same glove Al Rosen had borrowed from Detroit's Walt Dropo back in April, Wertz instantly felt at home and brought an energy to the lineup that the Indians had been lacking. With one out in the seventh inning of a scoreless game, Wertz ripped a single to right—Cleveland's first hit of the game—then hustled into third when Dave Philley singled to left. Wertz scored on the next play, a fielder's choice to third, and the Indians won, 1–0. After three months of searching, they'd found their first baseman. Rosen moved back to his home position at third, Wertz handled his new position with aplomb, and the Indians now had All-Stars at four of the five infield positions.

Once Wertz arrived, Lopez noticed that he had unintentionally warped his swing trying to account for the larger outfield in Baltimore and was now straining much too hard to pull the ball. He instructed Wertz to shift his elbows out slightly, and Wertz almost instantly returned to his role as a dependable slugger. After hitting .340 in his first forty-seven at-bats with the Indians, in his first two months in Cleveland, Wertz raised his season batting average sixty points. He would wind up hitting .275 with the Indians in 1954, cracking fourteen home runs. Just as importantly, he found a home in the fifth spot in the lineup, ensuring opposing pitchers knew there would be consequences if they pitched around Rosen.

It was a dramatic change in scenery for Wertz. In May, he'd been floundering at the plate, fighting for playing time on a last-place team. By summer's end, he would be one of the key cogs on one of the finest teams in baseball history. Wertz told reporters he was so excited when he heard he was going to Cleveland that he packed his baseball equipment into his suitcase and stuffed his nice suits in his duffel bag. "For this club," he said, "I'd be happy to be the bat boy."

Wertz joined the Indians in New York the following day and was inserted as a pinch-hitter in one of the team's defining victories of the season. Remembering how they'd been thumped by the Indians on their first trip to Yankee Stadium a month earlier, the Yankees were ready this time. Casey Stengel would pitch Allie Reynolds and Ed Lopat—his Morgan/Miller strategy long forgotten—in an attempt to whittle away New York's three-game deficit. And in the first inning of what would prove to be a long game Wednesday night, the Yankees' offense rocked Early Wynn for four consecutive hits to start the game. Seeing his pitcher didn't have it, Al Lopez replaced him with Don Mossi, but the hole was already dug. When Mossi finally cleaned up the mess, the Yankees had plated seven runs, setting the stage for what appeared would be a rout, particularly with Reynolds on the mound sporting a 1.86 ERA.

But things changed dramatically. Once Mossi stopped the bleeding, from the second inning on, four Indians' pitchers did not allow a hit, providing the Cleveland offense the opportunity to get back into the game. And get back into it they did, starting with a 430-foot, three-run home run by Larry Doby in the third and then another three-run tally in the fourth to make it 7–6. Yet Reynolds managed to settle down and maintain the Yankee lead into the ninth. Three outs from victory, Stengel replaced Reynolds with Johnny Sain, who had been nearly unhittable in his new role as a relief pitcher, allowing only one run in his previous fourteen appearances. Not intimidated by Sain's reputation, Bobby Avila stepped into the batter's box to lead off the ninth and blasted the second pitch out of the park to tie the game, completing an unlikely seven-run comeback against the five-time world champs and raising his season batting average to an astounding .392, the best in baseball.

Ironically, Bobby Avila was one of the few young boys growing up in Veracruz, Mexico, in the 1930s whose first love wasn't baseball. Soccer was his passion, and by the age of fourteen he was playing professionally, earning $50 a month. Gradually, though, Avila's interest drifted to the diamond, where he caught the attention of pro scouts. When the Brooklyn Dodgers passed on an opportunity to sign him in 1948, the Indians swooped in and inked him to a $17,500 contract. After a strong season at Triple-A Baltimore, Avila made a brief appearance in Cleveland at the end of the 1949 season, and then became a handy role player in 1950. He broke into the starting lineup in 1951, hitting .304 and quickly becoming one of the league's best infielders. He hit .300 again in 1952, but dropped to .286 in '53. Now thirty years old and eager to cash in during the prime of his career, Avila worked unusually hard while playing in Mexico over the winter. He hit .408 in forty-five games and reported to spring training with a confidence he'd never had before. Suffering from stomach ailments that turned out to be ulcers, Avila was ordered by doctors to drink plenty of milk, which did the trick, bringing relief to his tortured innards.

Also as 1954 began, Avila felt for the first time like he truly belonged not only in the big leagues but on the team. He'd previously roomed with Mike Garcia, which had inadvertently created a cultural shelter for Avila. The two would often speak Spanish and Avila would use Garcia as a translator when speaking with other players and reporters. Now he roomed with Staten Island native Hank Majeski, who became like a big brother to Avila, helping him open up and become accepted by his teammates. As he broke down the language barrier surrounding him, Avila developed a passion for American movies. If the Indians weren't playing at night, he would often grab dinner after a game, enjoy a thick Cuban cigar, then head to the closest theater to catch a double feature.

As June began, Avila had transformed from a solid hitter to one of the best in the American League. Though he usually didn't start hitting until the weather warmed up in June and July, May concluded with his average spiking between .380 and .390 and he was threatening at making a run at .400—something no one had accomplished over the course of an entire season since Ted Williams thirteen years before. Avila shrugged off the significance of such expectations. "If I ever hit .400," he said in his broken English that the reporters of the day dutifully repeated without corrections, "they make me president of Mexico." Another interesting wrinkle to his batting average's sudden rise is that he'd dethroned Al Rosen as the league's top hitter. If they both kept this up, Avila might cost his teammate the triple crown. "Rosie will be glad to be one-two with me," Avila said with a smile that June. "I be glad to be two-one, with Rosie on top. If we both are high, I think maybe it mean the pennant."

And when Al Smith mirrored Avila's ninth-inning heroics with a home run off Sain in the tenth to give the Indians an improbable 8–7 victory, talk of the pennant now didn't seem so far-fetched. Lopez called it the most important game the Indians ever won in Yankee Stadium. Harry Jones noted in the *Plain Dealer* that "If the Indians win the pennant—and who would like to bet against them winning now?—a person could flip back the pages of his scorebook to a game played in Yankee Stadium on the night of June 2 and say, 'that's the

A quartet of heroes gather after propelling the
Indians to an amazing comeback victory at Yankee
Stadium on June 2 (from left): Al Smith, Larry Doby,
Hal Newhouser, and Bobby Avila.

one that did it.'" If nothing else, Jones contended, the Indians had made believers out of 43,000 Yankee fans "who must now agree the Indians are a team of destiny." On the ride back to the hotel that night, Dave Philley offered a corny quote that suddenly didn't sound so corny. "There is only one way to play this game," he said as the bus steamed through the darkness. "You gotta bleed and believe."

Destiny took a detour the following two days as the Yankees bounced back from Wednesday's stunning loss to beat the Indians twice, again pulling within two games of first place. Friday's defeat knocked the Indians into a tie with Chicago. Though losing two of three in the Bronx was a disappointment, particularly after the stunning start to the series, the Indians had once again delivered a message to the mighty Yankees: even in defeat, they would be no pushover. Once the series was complete, Stengel complained to reporters that the Indians played too rough. "We play hard but fair," he said. "You don't see our guys goin' in with their spikes high. If that's the way they want it, we will too." The Indians shrugged it off. "We don't cry when Yankees hit us," Avila said.

Interestingly, it was the Indians who were the worse for wear following an on-field collision when Hank Bauer slid hard into Avila trying to break up a double play and jammed Avila's right thumb. Like Rosen a week earlier, Avila tried to play through the pain, but after struggling in the next series, he had the thumb examined and discovered he had chipped the bone. He was forced to the bench to let his thumb heal. Rosen, too, had originally refused treatment after hurting his right index finger knocking down a grounder, but once it swelled to twice its normal size and his batting average dropped forty points, he had it looked at.

Even with their top two hitters now nursing throbbing digits, the Indians kept winning. When spring-training phenom Rudy Regalado slumped and was benched, Al Smith moved back to third and journeyman Wally Westlake filled in capably in left as Lopez cunningly plugged another temporary hole in the dike. It seemed everything the Indians tried, worked. When their eastern swing continued in Philadelphia, Cleveland's veteran outfielder Dale Mitchell, who'd played a vital role in the team's successful pennant drive six years before, flopped down next to a reporter sitting on the dugout bench in Connie Mack Stadium before the first game of the series.

"How much you think we'll win by?" Mitchell asked, referring to the pennant.

The reporter raised his eyebrows at this unbidden display of confidence. If the Indians' infield play didn't improve, he told Mitchell, he didn't think they'd win the pennant at all.

Mitchell smiled and shook his head. "We'll win it all right," he replied. "The only question is how much we'll win by. Two games, ten games—but we'll win."

The reporter, who'd been covering baseball for more than two decades, couldn't remember when a player had spoken to him with such assurance. Mitchell went on to say, "We've just got so much more stuff than any of those other clubs." Asked if he felt the 1954 Indians were a team of destiny, Mitchell snorted, "Destiny? Naw, I don't think we're a team of destiny, whatever that is. I just think we're the best ball club in the league, with something to spare."

In the years to come, such bravado from a Cleveland athlete would be akin to standing in an open field and holding a fork in the air during a thunderstorm. But the team backed up Mitchell's bold words. That afternoon, Mike Garcia held the Athletics to just two hits over eleven innings—the opening salvo in a three-game sweep that the Indians accomplished without their best offensive player and using only one of the Big Three. The romp in Philly was followed by a domination of the Red Sox in Fenway Park. "It must have been like that with the Yankees when they were winning all the time," Rosen noted. "We're going to take it all and we know it. Not just me and a couple of other guys, but everybody."

As the Indians wrapped up the only five-game sweep in franchise history with a pair of victories in Boston on Sunday afternoon, a woman from Painesville, Ohio, relaxing at the beach in Fairport Harbor, just east of Cleveland, fell into a casual conversation with a woman she'd never met before. After chatting about various topics, the Painesville woman listened intently as her new friend—Marilyn, she thought her name had been—mentioned that she'd tried to divorce her husband while they were living in California a few years before, but his family had talked her out of it. The Painesville woman would remember this chance encounter, and two fortnights hence she would recount it to the Cleveland Police, after hearing that her friend Marilyn had been murdered.

When the Indians returned home June 15, they'd completed a fourteen-game eastern swing with a 10–4 record, and after briefly falling behind Chicago, had moved back atop the standings. During the ensuing home stand, the stadium organist filled the between-inning breaks with a little tune called "There's No Place Like First Place."

Following that sentiment, the Indians would remain there for the rest of 1954.

9 - TWO AGING ACES

Back in Cleveland, summer had begun with unusually cool temperatures. The crocuses, daffodils, and tulips traditionally bloomed mid-May but were late this year. Afternoon highs only reached the mid-sixties, and people used to sleeping with their windows open throughout late May either tossed an extra blanket on the bed or slid the windows closed. All those new air conditioners that had been installed were getting no use.

But another household appliance was plenty busy that June, thanks to the owners of a chain of restaurants that were among Cleveland's most popular dining spots. Patrons loved the food so much, the restaurants began receiving unusual requests: customers asked if they could have their meals frozen so they could be picked up, survive the drive home, and then be re-heated for the entire family to enjoy. The restaurants were happy to accommodate their patrons until the requests became overwhelming. Management knew something had to be done.

On the day the Indians rallied from a seven-run deficit in New York to beat the Yankees, the family that owned the restaurant chain announced the opening of a plant that would produce frozen meals that could be purchased at their restaurants. The same recipes would be used on the same popular dishes: baked ham loaf, chicken chow mein, chicken noodle casserole, and of course, macaroni and cheese. The company president declared that these frozen meals would be of the same quality as the ones served in their restaurants—in essence, it would be like going out to dinner without leaving your home. Soon these frozen meals would be available in grocery stores around northeast Ohio and eventually across the country. An even larger production plant had to be built in Solon to keep up with the demand. Ironically, the little chain of restaurants was quickly forgotten, but its name would live on. In 1954, frozen dinners were nothing more than an improvised shortcut to meal preparation, but over the following decades, aided by the introduction of the microwave, frozen food would become an essential part of the American kitchen. And Stouffer's would become the most recognizable name in the industry.

As the first Stouffer's frozen meals rolled off the assembly line, the Indians' winning streak hit nine following a three-game sweep of Washington and a four-hit shutout victory by Mike Garcia over Boston. They had now assumed a four-game lead over both the Yankees and White Sox, and even better, Rosen and Avila were ready to return to action. With their potent bats in the lineup, plus the addition of Vic Wertz's steadily rising batting average, the Cleveland offense was poised to get back into the swing of things. And the timing was perfect, since the Indians' starting pitchers had burned quite a bit of energy maintaining the club's winning ways when injuries pecked at the lineup. With more than three months of the season remaining, the Big Three needed a break if they were going to be effective down the stretch. The time had come for the final quest of a legendary Cleveland hero.

By 1954, Bob Feller was no longer the gun-slinging "Rapid Robert" he'd been in the 1930s and 1940s. He was thirty-five and in the twilight of a career that included 250 victories, 2,500 strikeouts, three no-hitters, and fourteen one-hitters. His last "Feller-esque" season had come in 1951, when he posted his final twenty-win campaign. Over the next two seasons, he went 19–20, racking up more walks than strikeouts for the first time in his storied career. Feller began to realize he couldn't rely solely on his legendary fastball to get hitters out, and he couldn't try to collect strikeouts like firewood as he once did. While his fastball was still viable (it had "slowed" to ninety-five miles per hour), Feller sharpened his control to get batters to hit the ball where he wanted. He added a good slider and sinker to his already effective curve and was even developing a knuckleball. After giving up more walks than any pitcher in American League history throughout his career, Feller's emphasis on control for 1954 resulted in a dramatic decrease in bases on balls—just seventeen in his first seventy-five innings of the season. In a shutout victory in Philadelphia, he threw ninety-seven pitches, eighty of them for strikes. With this new approach, Feller felt better physically than he had in years. He even returned to the same conditioning schedule he'd used when he was twenty, a system he'd abandoned as he got older to rest his arm between starts.

Now, with Cleveland's Big Three needing whatever respite possible, Feller once again stepped to the forefront. And though his prime was well past him, 1954 may have been his finest hour. Starting with a masterful performance in a 2–1 win over the Athletics on June 6, over the next six weeks, Feller won seven consecutive starts—five of which were complete games—while posting a spectacular ERA of 1.51.

Following a five-hit Feller victory over the Red Sox on June 20, the Indians were 44–18 and had won eleven of their last thirteen. Firing on all cylinders, the Tribe would host the Yankees for three games the last weekend of June with a chance to deliver a body blow to New York's hopes for its sixth straight pennant. Already trailing Cleveland by four games, the Yankees needed to make a statement like the one the Indians had already made twice in New York. All memories of the last three Septembers aside, with the way the Indians were playing, Casey Stengel knew his club could ill-afford to go into July five or more games off the pace.

Still, the Yankees came to town with that New York swagger embodied in its fans and certainly in its beat writers. From the Municipal Stadium press box, the Yankee reporters snickered Friday and Saturday nights as they witnessed the Indians' latest marketing initiative. Before night games, fans were invited to enjoy a picnic in the narrow canyon between the outfield fence and the center-field bleachers. For between $2.50 and $4.50, each fan would get a picnic dinner and a grandstand seat for that evening's game. Plus, Indians players would stop by to mingle with the picnic-goers and sign autographs. The visiting New York writers teased their Cleveland counterparts about it, calling it a "bush-league" idea. "Call it anything you like," Nate Dolin, Director of Stadium Operations, replied, "but those things bring fans closer to the club." The New Yorkers rolled their eyes and stuck to their opinions.

True, the picnic-in-the-park idea smacked of small-town nostalgia. But the New Yorkers had no license to criticize pre-game entertainment. During the Indians' last trip to New York, fans who arrived early at Yankee Stadium were treated to an elementary-school atmosphere as Indians and Yankees players competed in comical field events. Ray Narleski topped his competition in a fungo-hitting contest, while Don Mossi triumphed in a blindfolded relay race. The Yankees won the four-man relay, and Ralph Houk and Bill Skowron upset Bob Feller and Hal

Newhouser in the much-anticipated egg-throwing contest. Clearly, the Yankees would never stoop to bush-league promotional tactics.

Once the picnics were wrapped up Friday and Saturday nights and the largest crowds of the season filed into Municipal Stadium (better than 46,000 for both games), the Yankees made it clear that there would be no cakewalk to the pennant. They blasted Mike Garcia for six runs in just over two innings in the opener, and Allie Reynolds handcuffed the Indians' bats in an 11–0 thumping. Cleveland pitching was ravaged in the second game as well, with Early Wynn taking the loss in an 11–9 slugfest—the first Indians-Yankees game ever played on a Saturday night. In two games against the Yankees, the Indians had allowed more runs than they'd permitted in the previous seven games combined. "We are the champions," Stengel said, "and I guess we showed them." He went on to add that the Indians seemed to have lost something, and that the Yankees felt they were still better than both the Tribe and the White Sox. Both could be surpassed after the All-Star break, Stengel predicted. Cleveland's four-game lead was down to two, and with Whitey Ford toeing the rubber for New York on Sunday, the prospect of a Yankee sweep hung over the stadium like storm clouds over a parade. The sunny optimism of 1954 was ready to evaporate. For as good as the Indians had looked for much of the early part of the season, to lose three straight in their home park to the Yankees likely would be enough to both crush Cleveland's spirit and give New York enough momentum to not only vault past the Tribe in the standings but also coast to yet another pennant. And with the prospect of a devastating sweep looming, the Indians would be forced to hand the baseball to a man who, six months earlier, had decided his playing days were over.

Bob Lemon started and, like the other two members of the Big Three in this series, was scored upon early as New York grabbed a 1–0 lead in the first on a Mickey Mantle RBI. Things looked even grimmer going into the third when Lemon left the game after straining muscles in his ribs. With each member of the Big Three now having come up empty in the most critical series of the year, Al Lopez in desperation, called on veteran Hal Newhouser, who just one year before had hung up the cleats, apparently for good.

It may have ended unceremoniously, but Hal Newhouser's career had been great. In fifteen seasons with the Detroit Tigers, Newhouser had become arguably the most dominant pitcher in the game, winning 200 games, playing in seven All-Star Games, and twice being named league MVP. He won two games in the Tigers' World Series triumph over the Chicago Cubs in 1945 and led the American League in victories on four separate occasions. Interestingly, it was a crucial game in Cleveland at the peak of his career that led to his downfall. Though the Tigers were well out of the pennant race, Newhouser was tapped to pitch the 1948 season finale against the Indians, who were one win away from the World Series. Newhouser handcuffed the Tribe that day, forcing a one-game playoff with the Red Sox the next, but the victory was costly. The extra wear marked the beginning of a bout with arm troubles that would plague him over the next five years. With each successive season, his victory total shrank while his ERA grew. After being bashed around in his first seven appearances in 1953, Newhouser was released. Hank Greenberg quickly got in touch with his old teammate and asked him to sign with the Indians, who would find a way to use him. But Newhouser, fatigued and frustrated by the years of struggle, turned him down. He retreated to his home in Detroit to begin his retirement.

He didn't touch a baseball for the rest of that summer. Then on a snowy afternoon in December, he was fooling around in his basement and started tossing baseballs against the cement wall. For the first time in five years, his arm didn't creak with pain. After giving it some thought over the holidays, Newhouser decided he might still have enough left in his arm for one last mission. He called Greenberg, who invited him to Tucson for spring training and offered him a contract. Newhouser agreed to come to camp, but turned down the contract. He didn't want to sign anything, he said, until he was sure he could help the team. "It's

Though his career apparently had ended a few months before, pitcher Hal Newhouser (right) joined the '54 Indians. GM Hank Greenberg (left) looks on as Newhouser calls home with the news that he was back in baseball.

up to me to show how much I'm worth," he told reporters in February. The Indians eased him into action in spring games, and when he was hit hard in his first outing, Newhouser wasn't concerned. He remained pain-free and knew it was just a matter of getting his sharpness back. He made the team and signed a contract. The Indians front office knew that if Newhouser could deliver just one win over the Yankees, he'd be worth every penny.

He made his Indian debut in his hometown of Detroit in April, where he was greeted by a mixture of cheers and boos from the Tiger faithful, then was roughed up by his former teammates in defeat. It would turn out to be the last start of his illustrious career, as Newhouser would spend the rest of the summer filling a crucial niche in the bullpen. His first relief appearance on May 2 had an historical flavor to it: the contest was started by Bob Feller, then finished by Newhouser. The two longtime rivals, who had dueled in a handful of classic games over the past two decades, now had combined their forces—along with their 449 career victories. Newhouser captured his first triumph in an Indians' uniform by pitching two shutout innings in their wild win over Washington in mid-May in which they scored six runs in the ninth to force extra innings. Newhouser, whose career had been complete the previous winter, had found a new home. And the 1954 Indians' pitching staff now had its fourth future Hall of Famer.

But now, with the Yankees looking to pull within a single game of Cleveland and the pennant race already reaching a nexus, Newhouser rode to the rescue after Lemon left the game. Despite having pitched in relief the night before, he found enough gas in the tank to wiggle out of jams in the third and fourth. After Dave Philley tied the game with a homer, Newhouser started to cruise, retiring nine of ten batters to give the Cleveland bats a chance to warm up. And, after the stretch the Indians were enjoying, it seemed only appropriate that a journeyman outfielder named Wally Westlake would give the Tribe the lead for good.

In his efforts to land Vic Wertz over the previous few weeks, Hank Greenberg had very nearly dealt Wally Westlake to Baltimore. While being traded would have been nothing new to the veteran outfielder, keeping Westlake turned out to be almost as wise a decision as acquiring Wertz. With the physical appearance of a heavyweight fighter and a name reminiscent of a cartoon character, Wally Westlake had already been traded four times before Cleveland purchased him from Cincinnati late in the 1952 season. He'd enjoyed modest success in four years with Pittsburgh, then slumped after he was traded to St. Louis and continued his slide in Cincinnati. When the Indians purchased his contract, Westlake was more relieved than stunned. "I was surprised somebody did want me," he said. "I was darn grateful." Still, after hitting just .232 in the final month of 1952, then struggling again to start the following year, Westlake feared his days were numbered.

Finally, in early July, as he got dressed before a game at the stadium, a clubhouse boy found Westlake and told him Hank Greenberg wanted to see him. Naturally, as he marched slowly up the long, narrow concourses toward the stadium offices, Westlake expected the worst. It had taken him seven years to break into the majors, and now, after six full seasons, it appeared his journey was at an end. Like a death row inmate mounting the gallows, Westlake reached the general manager's office and opened the door. Inside sat Greenberg and Al Lopez, and between them was something that seemed quite out of place in a ballpark—a film projector.

"Sit down, Wally," Greenberg said in a friendly tone that slightly eased Westlake's nerves. "We would like to show you some films." Westlake, who'd known and respected Greenberg from the short time they were teammates in Pittsburgh during his first year and Greenberg's last, sat beside his bosses and they switched on the projector. They watched the flickering light display one of Westlake's recent at-bats, captured through the lens of a camera operated by a motion picture photographer who recorded all of the Cleveland Browns' games for study by the coaches and players. As they watched, Lopez and Greenberg showed Westlake how the stride of his swing was both too quick and too long, and that was the reason for his struggles at the plate. Like a scientist peering through a microscope for the first time, Westlake felt both enlightened and empowered.

Over the next few weeks, Lopez worked with Westlake on his swing, and the results were dramatic. He hit a career-best .330 in 1953 and had gone from a washed-up benchwarmer to a key component of Lopez's arsenal. Now thirty-three years old, he knew each day of his career from this point forward was made possible only by the revolutionary concept of using technology in performance analysis in baseball. "Movies are an important tool in football," Lopez said, "and I think they could be used more in baseball, too."

Now a regular starter in the outfield, Westlake pounded a two-run home run off Whitey Ford to give the Indians a 3–1 lead, and a two-out single by Al Smith made it 4–1. Newhouser held off the Yankees through the eighth, dodging a handful of potential landmines to maintain a 4–3 lead. In the ninth, Garcia was called on to make amends for the mess he'd made Friday night, and he quickly retired New York in order to preserve a season-saving triumph before 47,000 relieved fans. "It gives us a chance to pull ourselves together," Lopez admitted afterward. "We're going to be all right." In one afternoon, as predicted, Hal Newhouser had earned every cent of his 1954 salary.

Afterward, he eased slowly onto a stool in front of his locker and sat there for a long time. His six-inning stint had been Newhouser's longest appearance in two years, and his body throbbed in protest. "A terrific win for us," he said to no one in particular as he gave his weary muscles a break for the first time that day. Too tired to carry on a conversation with either his teammates or the reporters buzzing around the triumphant locker room, Newhouser simply slouched on the stool, waiting to gather enough energy to stand up again. His eyes were vacant and glassy, staring across the room but seeing nothing. Finally, after many of his teammates had already left, he lifted his aching bones off the stool. "A terrific win," he repeated again, as he slowly trudged toward the showers.

Lemon, now out of uniform and fully dressed, watched him go. Then he turned to Mel Harder and shook his head in disbelief. "What a guy to have on our side," he said.

10-SEVEN MINUTES OF SILENCE

he words crackled across the air defense system: "Strong movement of unidentified aircraft penetrated United States–Canadian border, heading south."

In all, 425 planes had invaded American airspace with explosives and chemical and biological weapons to be showered upon more than forty cities. The primary payload was an atomic bomb five times more powerful than the one dropped on Hiroshima. Its target was Washington, D.C.

At 2:30 p.m. on an otherwise ordinary Monday afternoon in June, Cuyahoga County's 100 air raid sirens screamed to life and more than one million people sprang into action. Cars pulled over and passengers raced out, seeking the nearest bomb shelter. At Hopkins Airport, all flights were grounded. Factories and businesses, including the Cleveland Stock Exchange, came to a standstill. For three minutes, the sirens wailed their warnings across the entire county, and people scurried for shelters. Three American fighter jets ripped across the sky, leaving a roar echoing in the quickly emptying streets and alleys.

Once the streets of downtown Cleveland were clear, the only sign of life was the constant throbbing of the sirens. Abandoned automobiles were parked helter-skelter along the curbs. Traffic signals cycled through their rotations with no response. The grind of Cleveland's industry hushed to a whisper. Then, as suddenly as the sirens had begun, they fell silent. But the streets remained empty. For the next seven minutes, people remained in their shelters, which swelled with heat and the smells of sweat, cigarette smoke, aftershave, and perfume.

Seven minutes.

At 2:40, the sirens sounded again, but this time in three steady blasts, each lasting one minute, separated by two minutes of silence. People departed the shelters, returned to their cars or places of business, and resumed their day. Operation Alert—the most intensive civil defense test in American history and the first nationwide atomic-age exercise—was completed.

"Practice Today Will Save Lives Tomorrow" was the catchy motto of the test, and across the nation local governments had spent weeks educating the public on the details. In Cleveland, Boy Scouts spent that morning distributing printed instructions for not only the drill but what to do if it weren't a test. Air raid wardens visited suburban homes to provide instructions and answer questions. They suggested that the atomic bomb casualties in Japan could have been reduced by 50 percent had the population taken shelter quicker.

Cities went through their elaborate exercises at various times according to a schedule. Even President Eisenhower participated, as he and his staff evacuated their offices in the White House to take shelter. But, perhaps symbolically, Congress was exempt from the exercise. With its citizens dutifully preparing for the end of the world, both the House of Representatives and the Senate went about their usual business.

The results were mixed. Theoretically, authorities reported, five million people would have been killed in the attack, proving that

America still had a long way to go to meet the desired level of readiness. But in general, the test was considered a success. Cleveland's scenario was an atomic bomb being detonated downtown, which included every bridge over the Cuyahoga River being "blasted to smithereens" as the *Press* gracefully described it. In response, downtown Cleveland's streets were cleared in one minute and fifteen seconds—all traffic was stopped and all pedestrians moved into shelters. "If we do that well when a bomb drops," a police inspector proclaimed, "the damage will be slight."

Now fully prepared for the end the world, Clevelanders turned back to the ebb and flow of everyday life. And the one thing that connected everyone that week was the oppressive heat that covered the city like a wool blanket. After highs in the low 90s over the weekend, thermometers reached 97 in the late afternoon on Tuesday, setting a new record. The wives who had talked their husbands into purchasing air conditioners slept soundly that night, even as a wave of thunderstorms swept through, with bolts of lightning illuminating the heat-seared landscape and strong winds jerking tree branches back and forth. Little did the drenched populace know that this storm would be the last of its kind to steam across northeast Ohio for almost two parched months.

Somehow, the storm front managed to evade downtown that night, and the Indians-Senators game went on as scheduled after a ten-minute delay during a light shower. Al Rosen cracked a pinch-hit double to break the game open in the eighth and Cleveland cruised to another victory. Rosen returned to the lineup at first base five days later, and, a week after that, once his finger was healed enough to make the long throw across the infield, he moved back to third base. Taking Rosen's place at first was Vic Wertz, and there he would remain for the rest of the season. Al Lopez had taken a spare part that some in the press had deemed unnecessary and turned it into the perfect complement to his infield. With Rosen and Avila both back, Wertz continuing his Cleveland resurgence, and the Indians' pitching smothering the opposition, Lopez was finally getting some of the attention that had evaded him.

"In running a team, he uses his tongue less than his head and eyes," Hank Greenberg said of his manager, "which are black and sharp and not afraid to look at you." To those who followed the Indians, it came as no surprise that this team was patterned after its skipper—who'd earned the nickname "El Señor"—both in temperament and professionalism. The Indians front office wanted him to be more fiery or demonstrative—like Casey Stengel or Leo Durocher—but Lopez always shrugged off the idea. "I can't do something I don't feel," he said. "I don't believe in that kind of managing. In football, pep talks might be valuable to key up the players for a certain game. In baseball we play every day, 154 times a year. You play better when you're relaxed. If I tried to be mean and nasty, it would be an act. It wouldn't be me." Nor would it be the Indians. Or Cleveland.

Born in Tampa to Spanish immigrants, he was considered one of the nicest men in the game, even though he didn't fit the profile of a typical baseball man of the era. He didn't smoke. He didn't drink. Prone to a nervous stomach, he refrained from eating spicy foods and ice cream. Lopez would hold one team meeting a year, and that would be in the first week to go over the team rules. To call meetings anytime the team went into a slump, he felt, would either be self-serving or melodramatic. When a player made a mistake in a game, no matter how crucial or senseless, Lopez would wait until the next day to discuss it. Some interpreted this self-control as a lack of competitiveness, but in fact the opposite was true. Lopez was as fierce a competitor as anyone in baseball, and he expected to win every single game. "Worse than losing is to look at Lopez after the game," Bob Lemon once said. "Sometimes he'll come in the clubhouse instead of going direct to his office and it kills us to see the look on his face."

Lopez maintained the same quiet intensity throughout his nineteen-year playing career, compiling a solid .261 lifetime batting average and earning two All-Star bids as he became one of the most respected catchers in the National League. Not surprisingly, over those two decades, he became quite adept at handling pitchers, knowing and appreciating how they think and how to best use their strengths. This lifelong study of hurlers began as a teenager in Tampa, when Lopez

Indians manager, Al Lopez (left) helped develop the greatest pitching staff in baseball history, anchored by future Hall of Famer Bob Lemon (right).

earned five dollars a week catching the legendary Walter Johnson during spring training.

Even as a rookie, Lopez was already demonstrating the cautious approach to the game that would define his career. Then, after breaking in with four solid seasons with the woeful Brooklyn Dodgers in the early 1930s, he was introduced to an entirely different type of personality when a quirky character named Casey Stengel became his manager.

Despite their differences, Lopez and Stengel became good friends—the young player respecting Stengel's spontaneity, the grizzled manager admiring Lopez's diligence. The following year, Stengel named Lopez captain of the Dodgers, and he adopted similar leadership on the field. Stengel trusted Lopez implicitly behind the plate, allowing him to call his own pitches and maneuver the defense as he saw fit. With Lopez on the field, Stengel once said, "I could sit back and take a nap."

When Stengel was forced to trade Lopez to the Boston Bees (soon to revert back to its previous nickname of "Braves") in 1935 so the ramshackle Brooklyn franchise could make ends meet, the manager was crestfallen. Lopez saw how much it upset Stengel to break the news, and both of them realized they'd developed much more than a typical player-manager relationship. The pair was reunited in Boston when Stengel became the Bees' manager in 1938, and ironically, Stengel was once again forced to trade his good friend and protégé, this time to Pittsburgh in 1940. After seven solid seasons with the Pirates, Lopez landed in Cleveland primarily as a backup in 1947, a season defined by the arrival of new teammate Larry Doby. Despite limited playing time, Lopez caught the attention of flamboyant owner Bill Veeck, who recognized Lopez's natural abilities as a leader and saw the glimmer of potential that would take Lopez to Cooperstown.

At the 1947 World Series, where Veeck took Hank Greenberg under his wing, he also floated the notion of trading his player/ manager, Lou Boudreau. Veeck took Lopez aside and told him of his plan, asking if he'd be willing to take over as Tribe manager. Lopez was stunned. Though his future hung before him like a carrot tied to a stick, his moral center wouldn't allow him to take a bite. Lopez feared people would think he'd been maneuvering for the job while playing for Boudreau. He turned Veeck down, telling him he couldn't take the job of the man he'd played for. Thus, Boudreau stayed in Cleveland and managed the Indians to a championship in 1948. Lopez, meanwhile, took over as manager of Indianapolis in the American Association and guided the team to 100 victories and the pennant in his first season.

After two strong finishes in Indy the next two years, Lopez got the chance he'd been waiting for when Hank Greenberg came calling. Fed up with the Indians' sloppy finishes of the previous two seasons, Greenberg cleaned house after 1950, firing Boudreau in November and ushering in a new era of Cleveland baseball by bringing in the forty-two-year-old Lopez as the first full-time Hispanic skipper. In his first three years, he led the Indians to a trio of the finest finishes in franchise history—back-to-back ninety-three-win seasons followed by a ninety-two-win campaign. It was the beginning of a string of five consecutive ninety-win seasons—still the best five-year period in Cleveland history. Yet each time Lopez couldn't quite dethrone his old mentor, Casey Stengel.

And the near-misses had taken their toll. Lopez slept poorly in the final weeks of the previous two seasons, and after the strong finish in 1953 proved fruitless, he felt more impotent than ever. He wondered if perhaps he'd done all he could, had taken this team as far as it could go under his leadership. It was just a matter of time, he knew, before he would begin to bear the brunt of frustration from the fans and front office. One more second-place finish might seal his fate. So when the Cincinnati Reds quietly approached him after the 1953 season and offered him their managerial job, Lopez seriously considered it. Showing due diligence, he talked it over with Hank Greenberg, who understood Lopez's position and faced much of the same doubt and public pressure. They went round and round the issue until finally Lopez shrugged and said, "If you want me back, I'll be back." Greenberg did want him back, and Lopez returned for 1954.

Though Lopez's fears were valid, his natural abilities to lead a baseball team were clearly defined and proven. All that kept Lopez from receiving consideration as the best manager in the game was Casey Stengel and his mighty Yankees.

And, as expected, here they came. On the Friday that opened the Fourth of July weekend, New York overtook the White Sox to claim second place, four and a half games behind Cleveland. From that point forward, for the remainder of the season, the pennant race would be strictly a two-team affair.

In retrospect, that summer is remembered like a warm postcard from a place so idyllic it bordered on fictional. In Cleveland, it was a summer of pride, a season of bountiful promise and prosperity that felt like a reward passed down to this generation from all those who had come before. Mostly, though, it was a golden summer for children.

They would leave the house in the morning when their fathers left for work. After baseball games or bike rides, they'd return home for lunch, then would be shooed back outside for the afternoon, not to return until dinnertime. There would be trips to Lawson's for a soda pop

With mighty Municipal Stadium nestled on the shore of
Lake Erie and the Terminal Tower lighting up the sky,
Cleveland looked like The Best Location in the Nation.

or to the local pharmacy for a chocolate phosphate. Debates were held

over the ideal place to build a bomb shelter and what games and toys

should be brought when the time came to use it. If the day were rainy

or unusually hot, kids would traipse down into cool, often unfinished

basements, where board games like Monopoly and Risk and card games

like Canasta and Tripoli were the entertainment of choice. The family

would reunite for dinner, then, as dusk settled over the city, would

spend the evening together—the parents sipping iced tea and smoking

on the back porch while the kids chased fireflies or played shadow tag

with flashlights. Or the entire crew would hop in dad's car for a trip for

ice cream or sweet corn or just a drive around the neighborhood.

As dusk became evening, the children would be rounded up and

herded into their rooms for the night. But if the Indians were playing, the night was just beginning. A youngster lucky enough to have a small radio or resourceful enough to construct a crystal radio in his or her room could tune in to WERE and listen to Jimmy Dudley paint a portrait of that night's game. Dudley's friendly cadence and the ebb and flow of the ballpark crackling in the background would carry the listener into a satisfying cocoon. Outside the open window, the backyard was now dark, lit solely by moonlight and the flicker of lightning bugs. Only the drone of crickets and the soft whisper of leaves in the wind gave evidence that life carried on. As they sought sleep in the humid night, children could lay their heads beside their windows and try to guess the model of the next car that came down their road by the distinctive sound of its engine.

The summer was at its apex, its promise of freedom at its most enticing. The beginning of school was so far away as to be inconsequential. The days were bright and hot, the nights breezy and long. The Indians were in first place. There were television programs like *The Pinky Lee Show* and *Howdy Doody* on weekday afternoons and double features at the local movie theater for a quarter on Saturdays. The entire landscape contained not only a clear sense of right and wrong but of purpose and design. Whether the topic was Cleveland or the nation as a whole, there was a feeling that everyone was in it together, a friendly—if not unrealistic—residue remaining from the world war that had concluded less than a decade before. From one house to the next, it seemed, all was right in the Best Location in the Nation.

And on one of these succulent June evenings, shouts for help drifted on the breeze through the windows of the Sheppard house on the lake in Bay Village. They woke Marilyn Sheppard, an auburn-haired beauty who'd married her high school sweetheart, Sam, now an ambitious doctor with a bright future. Three months pregnant with their second child, she leaned over to the bed beside hers and tried to wake Sam, who she knew was an unusually deep sleeper. She called his name several times before lightly shaking him, but Sam remained asleep. Finally, she grasped him with both hands and grappled with him until he grudgingly re-entered consciousness. She told him of the cries she heard on the lake, and the two of them walked out of the house and down to the shore to investigate. Not far offshore, a fishing boat had tipped, spilling its passengers into the water. Sam, who likely would have slept through the entire affair had Marilyn not wakened him, boarded his own boat and sped out to offer assistance.

A month later, this story would take on added meaning and importance, albeit in a context unimaginable on this tranquil night. But for now, it served as yet another instance of Cleveland's burgeoning sense of community—a reflection of heroism not uncommon in a magnificent city enjoying a majestic summer.

Yet beneath this shiny veneer, the summer, like any in a big city, had its share of sinister happenings, including a rash of arsons in Negro neighborhoods and the usual liquor store hold-ups and robberies. And on the first day of summer, at 1:45 a.m., a twenty-year-old pregnant woman slept peacefully in her East Side home until she awakened to a shadowy form looming over her. As she started to scream, a hand covered her mouth and the shape overtook her. With her husband out driving his cab that night, she was raped in her own bed before the figure slipped through the window and into the night.

Fifteen minutes later, three blocks away, another woman awoke to see the silhouette of a man's head and shoulders through her own bedroom window. She screamed, and the man ran away. The woman later told police that the same thing had happened two weeks earlier. A half-hour after that, a woman woke to see a man crawling on the bedroom floor toward her. She screamed, waking her husband, and the figure dashed out the window. Roughly an hour later, a figure was spotted by a fourth woman peering through her bedroom window. And as police tried to piece together all the incidents and determine if the intruder was in fact the same person, or if he was the same man who had been responsible for similar incidents over the previous few weeks, they learned of a fourteen-year-old girl who had been grabbed by a man who'd climbed through her window at 1:30—fifteen minutes before the attack on the pregnant woman. The girl's screams sent the figure scurrying back through the window, but her story combined with the others seemed to verify that the same man was connected to more than one—if not all—of these intrusions.

The Cleveland police made an arrest that night but soon realized their suspect wasn't the perpetrator and released him. Ultimately, they were unable to identify the intruder.

11 - THE SPHINX AND THE HOWITZER

Golf fans in Cleveland were both proud and disappointed—as if they'd been forced to share a wonderful secret with the rest of the world.

With the annual Plain Dealer Cup coming up, they hoped for another chance to see a twenty-four-year-old amateur named Arnold Palmer, whom Cleveland had claimed as an adopted son. While in the Coast Guard, Palmer, a native of Latrobe, Pennsylvania, had been sent to Cleveland for PR work and remained there once his duties were complete. He got an account job with a paint manufacturer and spent every free moment playing golf at Pine Ridge Country Club in Wickliffe.

He'd put on a record-breaking performance at the tournament the year before and would win the Cleveland Amateur and Ohio Amateur titles in 1953 and 1954—the first person ever to win back-to-back Ohio Amateurs. But on the first Monday in June at the Canterbury Club in Cleveland, Palmer qualified for what was then informally referred to as the "national open"—officially called the U.S. Open. It would be Palmer's second straight trip, though he regretted what he'd have to give up in order to make it. "I wanted very much to play in the Plain Dealer Cup again," he said, "but naturally I can't pass up the Open."

As in 1953, Palmer failed to make the cut at the national tournament, but his 1954 success symbolized a watershed moment. After he won the U.S. Amateur Golf Championship in Detroit that August, the *Press* stated that he was "born to be a great golf champion," while the *Plain Dealer* remarked that the '54 U.S. Amateur had witnessed the birth of "a new super champion." He officially turned pro that November, signed a lucrative contract with Wilson Sporting Goods, and over the next ten years would win seven major championships—a run of success that would go unmatched for more than thirty-five years until Tiger Woods came along. Palmer would call the summer of 1954 the turning point of his life. Though he was officially from out of state, Cleveland had made him one of its own. Another champion for a championship city.

Clevelanders were getting used to the notion of the Indians on top of the Yankees in the standings instead of the other way around. Attendance was gradually increasing—albeit not as much as the front office wanted—and the players were becoming more in demand. Basch's jewelry store hosted "Cleveland Indians Day" on a Monday off-day, during which it invited customers to let Bobby Avila show them the new Zenith three-way portable radio or have Dave Philley talk about the Norelco Electric Shaver.

More than just winning, the Indians were doing amazing things on an individual level. Pitcher Don Mossi, nicknamed "The Sphinx" because of his dark complexion and large ears, retired twenty-eight consecutive batters over eight appearances, exceeding the equivalent of a perfect game. The *Press* mused that Mossi's "heart must be as big as his ears." Born with a left arm so crooked he couldn't completely straighten it, Mossi turned his defect into an advantage, developing a unique and effective curveball. After five years in the minors, he broke in with the Indians in '54, and he and Ray Narleski became the first true relief pitchers in Cleveland baseball history. In 1954, the youngsters would combine for twenty "saves" (the term would not become an official statistic for another fifteen years), with Narleski posting an ERA of 2.22 and Mossi 1.94.

Adding to the rosy condition of the Indians was an incredibly bright beacon of potential shining from Indianapolis, Indiana. By this time, most baseball fans wondered if the Indians had made some sort of deal with the devil that allowed them to find little-known pitching prospects in obscure locations, then mold these youngsters into players capable of dominance. Cy Slapnicka, the scout who'd taken on the status of legend after having found Bob Feller amidst the Iowa cornfields in 1935, was vacationing in Florida when he wandered through a tiny town midway between Boca Raton and West Palm Beach called Lake Worth. A policeman recommended he check out a pitcher at the local high school who was supposed to be pretty good. Slapnicka followed the lead. "One look was all I needed," Slapnicka said. "You didn't have to be an expert to see this kid had it." Once the young man graduated, Slapnicka signed Herbert Jude Score to a contract on his nineteenth birthday.

In some ways, it was amazing Score's baseball career was still going at the age of nineteen. His mother, a devout Catholic desperately hoping her first child would be a boy, prayed to St. Jude to grant her wish. She then gave Herb the middle name of Jude after the holy figure considered to be the patron saint of lost causes. Score wore a St. Jude medal around his neck but didn't need to be reminded of the adversity he'd already overcome.

When he was three, Score's legs were shattered when he was hit by a bakery truck. His youth was later shrouded by bouts with pneumonia and rheumatic fever, then a sudden attack of appendicitis in high school. By then, his father, a New York police officer, had abandoned the family and Score had moved from Queens to Lake Worth with his mother and sickly younger sister. Score's bad luck continued even after he signed with the Indians. He tripped in the outfield chasing fungos in his second minor-league season and dislocated his shoulder, which forced him to miss half the year.

Not only had the team landed a good prospect, but for the first time in memory, the Indians had beaten the Yankees at their own game. New York had actually spotted Score first, and a scout had recommended to owner George Weiss that the team should offer him a big bonus to sign. Weiss was intrigued by Score's potential but told the scout to offer nothing more than $4,000. The Indians swooped in and offered $60,000. Yet the young pitcher had two higher offers on the table from other teams. He turned them down. "I knew Cleveland had a big park," he explained, "good to pitch in, and I knew they needed left-handed pitching. But mainly it was Slap. I was sold on him as a person."

Score's personality was reflected in how he handled his sudden wealth. He handed over a large chunk of it as a down payment on a house for his mother and then bought himself a record player. Listening to music, after all, was one of the only things that could relax his competitive nature and calm his jittery nerves.

It didn't take long for the comparisons to start between Score and Feller, though as a southpaw, Score was even more appealing. Like Feller, Score had a wicked fastball that led to occasional control problems; he walked 187 batters in his first 160 minor-league innings. When warming up prior to a game, he'd thrown a pitch so hard it sailed over the catcher, off the field, and dented the fender of a car being given away that night. One minor-league manager nicknamed him "The Howitzer."

"There are pitchers bigger and stronger than I am," Score said, "but the Lord gave me the gift of speed. Actually, it's really not in the arm itself, but in the coordination of my throw."

After going 2–5 in his first minor league season in 1952, he improved to 7–3 with Reading in his injury-shortened 1953 season, twice taking a no-hitter into the ninth inning. Still struggling with his control, in the spring of 1954, Score was turned over to Ted Wilks, the Indianapolis pitching coach, and just as Mel Harder had done with Bob Lemon and Early Wynn, Wilks turned Score from a bazooka to a high-powered rifle. He taught Score to slow down his delivery and showed him that he was kicking his leg too high and tossing his head back too much. He also sharpened Score's curveball and helped him develop a nice changeup. After an intense spring training, the lights came on for Herb Score in 1954. In his first sixteen starts, he went 12–2 with nine complete games and had clearly established himself as the finest pitcher in the American Association, leading the league in votes for its all-star game. He was bound for greatness. "Provided," Hank Greenberg added as a caveat, "nothing happens to him." With Score getting better with every start, the Indians' future might have been even brighter than that of the city they called home.

And with the White Sox rolling into town for a four-game series over the Fourth of July weekend, the Indians were in a position to make their immediate future look even better. Though the Yankees nipped at their heels, the Indians knew the Sox were even closer. But on Friday afternoon, Chicago's modest hopes for the weekend were

Cherub-faced Herb Score receives the 1954
minor league player of the year award.

derailed. With better than 48,000 in attendance, the Tribe swept a
doubleheader, their seventh doubleheader sweep of the season in eight
tries. With Bob Feller handcuffing the Sox offense in another complete-
game performance, the Indians pulled ahead in the eighth and won,
3–2. The nightcap was nearly identical: Chicago led early until a three-
run homer by Doby in the fifth gave Cleveland and Early Wynn a lead
they would not relinquish. In five hours, the Indians had put two more
games between themselves and Chicago and the Yankees leapfrogged
the White Sox in the standings.

The most infamous holiday weekend in Cleveland history had
begun.

rom the outset, July 3, 1954, was a strange day.

It began with a news bulletin that stunned Cleveland radio listeners. Alan Freed, their beloved Moondog, would be leaving WJW that fall to take a job with WINS in New York for a whopping $75,000 a year. It marked the first time that a disc jockey moving from one city to another, not an infrequent occurrence, was national news. Ironically, Freed's achievement eventually led to his demise when he accepted bribes from record companies to play specific songs on the air. He lost his New York job and spent the final years of his career in smaller markets, no longer an icon of the industry. A heavy smoker, he became an alcoholic and died of uremia and cirrhosis in 1965 at the age of forty-three. Alan Freed would ultimately return to Cleveland when his ashes were donated to the Rock and Roll Hall of Fame.

On that same Saturday, just after sunset in a quiet Lakewood neighborhood, a stargazer noticed something peculiar streaking across the sky through a pair of binoculars. Against the growing darkness, he saw a crescent-shaped object with what appeared to be portholes on one side. It hovered a hundred yards above the ground for several seconds before making a sharp turn to the southeast and vanishing into the falling night. It was the second reported UFO sighting in the Cleveland area in 1954, with four more to follow before the calendar turned.

For many families around Cleveland, that Saturday was hectic and harried as households prepared for the Fourth of July barbeques and parties that would take place the following day. But at the Sheppard home, a nice but modest four-bedroom, two-story Dutch Colonial in the small, affluent suburb of Bay Village, that day was calm. Though the house would host a large get-together on Sunday for all the interns who worked with Dr. Sam Sheppard at nearby Bay View Hospital, there was a relaxed atmosphere around the home. Sam and Marilyn planned to spend much of the day in the shady yard and down on the beach, which could be reached by a long wooden staircase just across from the back door. It was already a weekend of celebration, as Marilyn had publicly announced her pregnancy at a party at Sam's brother Stephen's home the night before. Word would trickle out later that Sam may not have been quite as enthusiastic about the prospect of a second child, but for now, he played the role of proud father-to-be.

On this fateful Saturday, with their refrigerator full of hot dogs for the next day's party, they played with their seven-year-old son Sam Jr., nicknamed "Chip," and visited with their neighbors, Don and Nancy Ahern. With them for much of that day was an old friend of Sam's, a doctor named Les Hoversten, who had been visiting as he looked for a job. Though Marilyn couldn't stand Hoversten and he'd encouraged Sam to leave his wife, these unfortunate details mattered not on July 3. And Hoversten's sudden decision to borrow Sam's car and drive to Kent to spend the night with friends drew no suspicion that afternoon.

As is often the case with doctors, Sam's day off was interrupted by three trips to the hospital. The longest was a call that afternoon to attend to a boy hit by a truck. Despite Sam's best efforts, including manually massaging the boy's heart with his fingers, the boy died. Sam returned home just a few minutes after five o'clock, greeted by his son, the family dog, Kokie, and Marilyn, brushing the flour off her hands from making a blueberry pie for dessert that night. Sam had wanted to mow the lawn before the party the next day but now realized he wouldn't have time. They were expected at the Aherns' for cocktails before hosting dinner at their own home. Sam quickly got dressed and accompanied his family down the street.

The day's last call to the hospital came just after the Sheppards had arrived at six. With the families' three young boys playing around them and drinks in hand, the Sheppards and Aherns discussed the

In 1948, Dr. Richard Sheppard Sr. launched a family medical legacy with the opening of Bay View Hospital.

usual topics that were on everyone's minds that summer: the Army-McCarthy hearings, Operation Alert, the impending construction of the St. Lawrence Seaway, and of course, the first-place Indians. Sam, a big baseball fan, was sipping a martini when he received a call to come to the hospital to treat a young boy with a broken thighbone.

As he drove the short distance down Lake Road, many Indians players began arriving at the stadium for that night's big game with Chicago. Despite the many holiday happenings taking place in the area that night, another good crowd of 27,000-plus would attend, and they would get more than their money's worth.

By the time Sam was finished at the hospital, it was past eight, and he returned home just in time for dinner. As the food was being placed on the table, the Indians grabbed an early lead on a first-inning sacrifice fly by Al Rosen. And with Art Houtteman cruising, it appeared the tone had been set for a third straight Cleveland triumph over the White Sox. As the Aherns and the Sheppards sat down to eat, Larry Doby blasted his fourteenth home run of the year to make it 2–0 in the third.

Marilyn's dinner was perfect. While the children ate inside, the adults gathered on the screened-in porch overlooking the lake, where they enjoyed cottage ham, tossed salad, string beans, applesauce, and potatoes as the sun went down, laying a long golden track across the water. A breeze sashayed up the beach and brought with it a surprising coolness for a mid-summer night. At one point, Sam got up from the table to put a brown corduroy sport coat on over his t-shirt to stay warm. For dessert, Marilyn brought out her blueberry pie, Sam's favorite.

As they finished dinner and the women cleared the dishes, the Ahren boys returned home and the Indians' cruise to victory hit rough waters. Back-to-back home runs by Nellie Fox and Minnie Minoso in the sixth gave Chicago a 3–2 lead. White Sox pitcher Sandy Consuerga, in the middle of the only All-Star season of his career, hit his stride and pitched four consecutive scoreless innings.

As Consuerga mowed down the Indians, the peculiar flavor of the day once again intruded. Up in the stands, forty-four-year-old Joseph Knable, a used-car dealer from Youngstown, felt a tightening sensation in his chest. His wife, Bessie, helped him to the stadium's first-aid room, but they discovered that the doctor had already left for the night and the on-duty nurse was intoxicated. As her husband's condition worsened, Mrs. Knable notified a police officer, and Joseph was transported by ambulance to Lutheran Hospital, where he was declared dead on arrival. Two months later, the grieving widow would sue the Indians for $100,000.

Still, the majesty of the evening persevered. In Edgewater Park, located perfectly in between the game and the dinner party, a crowd of better than 125,000 gathered for the Festival of Freedom fireworks display, a thirty-five-minute show that launched at 9:30. The rockets painted the night sky, the bright colors reflecting beautifully in the lake below. Back in Bay Village, several residents of Lake Road stepped out onto the beach, where they could enjoy an ideal view of the sulfuric sensations just a few miles away.

After the dinner dishes had been cleared and the fireworks had ceased, Marilyn took young Chip upstairs to his room. They said Chip's evening prayers together, and then she tucked him into bed. Downstairs, Don Ahern flipped on a portable radio and sat in a corner, listening to the Indians game. Marilyn returned and joined the others in the living room, turning on the television to watch a movie on Channel 3. Written and directed by longtime suspense radio icon Arch Obler, *Strange Holiday*

Marilyn and Sam Sheppard led what appeared
to be an ideal life along the Lake Erie shore.

was the story of a man, played by Claude Raines, who returns from a
camping trip to discover that the United States was now operating under
a dictatorship, having been taken over by fascists. He's thrown in prison
while trying to understand this new world. The scenario did not seem at
all ironic to the Sheppards or Aherns on the night of July 3.

Four outs away from defeat, the Indians found new life when
Wally Westlake blasted a home run in the eighth to tie the game. Don
Ahern excitedly shared the news with the others, but they were more
interested in the movie. At the end of a long, busy day, Sam kept
nodding off in a large overstuffed chair. At one point Marilyn nudged
him and told him to wake up and pay attention—they were just getting
to the good part. Sam sat up as Marilyn moved over to him. She sat

on his lap and they snuggled together, looking like the young, happy couple everyone assumed they were. Smiling, Nancy Ahern called her husband over to her and they also nestled. "You're not the only ones who can be loving," Nancy said teasingly.

Thirteen miles to the east, Don Mossi got the Indians through the ninth, and the game spilled into extra innings. Hal Newhouser took over in the tenth and began a pitching duel with Chicago reliever Jack Harshman. After the White Sox got a runner to second with two out in the tenth, neither team threatened to score over the next four innings as the game toiled endlessly into the night. Finally, in the fifteenth inning, the White Sox broke the stalemate on a two-out RBI single by Johnny Groth. With clocks now inching past midnight, the Indians marked the arrival of Independence Day with a rally. Doby opened the bottom of the fifteenth with a walk, followed by a single to left by Rosen. Pinch-hitter Sam Dente laid a perfect bunt down the third-base line that Minoso couldn't get to in time and the bases were loaded. Al Lopez then called on another pinch-hitter, Hank Majeski, who rifled a base hit to left on the first pitch to score Doby and Rosen and end the four-hour marathon. The Indians had won, 5–4, their twenty-eighth come-from-behind win of the season, and with a game still to play Sunday, they had secured a victory in one of the biggest series of the year.

Don Ahern flipped the radio off and, seeing both Marilyn dozing in the overstuffed chair and Sam asleep on a daybed near the staircase, he and Nancy tried to slip out without waking them. Nancy closed and bolted the door to the back porch. But on their way out the front door, Marilyn got up to see them out, thanking them for a wonderful evening. Sam, a deep sleeper, didn't move. Marilyn said good-bye and closed the door after the Aherns left. Nancy didn't notice whether or not Marilyn locked the door behind them.

As the Indians returned to the clubhouse triumphant after yet another satisfying victory, Marilyn Sheppard turned off all the lights on the first floor and began her way up to bed. Sam Sheppard would vaguely remember her gently shaking him on the daybed and telling him she was going upstairs.

He would never see her alive again.

Game 3

J UST BEFORE NOON, seventy-five-year-old Walter Smyth
settled into his seat at Municipal Stadium for an afternoon
of championship-caliber baseball on this cool first day of October,
fully anticipating that his Indians would turn things around after a
disappointing start to the 1954 World Series back in New York. A retired
sales executive from Rocky River and longtime Tribe fan, Smyth had seen
the Indians win two world championships and knew, as did most fans,
that this pennant-winning team was better than both of its predecessors.
Though the skies were dark and threatening, today would be a bright day,
he was certain, one that would see the Indians return to their winning
ways and Cleveland find its groove again.

Before he could even lean back in his seat and take in the
autumn afternoon, Smyth felt a burning pain in his chest. It seized him
completely, curling his face into a wince, and he toppled out of his seat
onto the concrete floor. Other fans just arriving saw Smyth collapse
and quickly summoned an usher, who in turn found a physician there
to watch the game as well. After a cursory examination, the doctor
knew what had happened and knew there was nothing he could do. He

pronounced Smyth dead of a heart attack—marking the third time this season death had visited Municipal Stadium.

Less than an hour later, with a funereal aura still hanging over the ballpark—not unlike the murder mystery that had hovered above the city for much of the summer—the Indians took the field for Game Three of the 1954 World Series.

And if the team looked more sluggish than its opponent as the one p.m. game time drew near, there was good reason. Not only had the New York Giants had the better of the Indians in the first two games of the World Series, but they also beat them soundly on the ensuing trip to Cleveland.

Over an hour after wrapping up their Game Three victory Thursday afternoon, the Giants boarded a plane and took off for Ohio. After circling over Chagrin Falls and Brecksville for fifteen minutes as it awaited landing clearance through a passing thundershower, the plane landed at Hopkins Airport just before eight p.m. The Giants, upbeat from the day's triumph and satiated from the steak dinner they'd enjoyed on the plane, trekked to the Manger Hotel for a good night's sleep. Eleven hours later, as the Giants were rolling out of some of the finest hotel beds in Cleveland to start the day, the Indians' train pulled into Union Terminal, and the bleary-eyed players disbanded for a few hours of recovery at home before gathering at Municipal Stadium later that morning to prepare for Game Three. Hoping to change the team's luck, station officials took action when they noticed that the Indians' train was set to arrive on the same track it departed upon—number thirteen. At the last moment, the train's destination was changed to track eleven.

Even if its ballclub was weary from the long train ride and two heartbreaking defeats, Cleveland was set for the return of the World Series. Preparations had been under way for weeks, and Mayor Anthony Celebrezze oversaw a plan to ensure Cleveland would be both clean and appealing for its visitors. Police officers were encouraged to be courteous to their guests and were instructed to make sure their uniforms were in good condition. Celebrezze ordered a stop to all road construction for the weekend and wanted cab drivers to be schooled in common courtesy. On Thursday night, as both teams traveled west beneath the autumn moon via their differing modes of transportation, the Cleveland Fire Department hosed down prominent sidewalks like a humming housewife vacuuming the living room with company on the way. Police chief Frank Story, his already busy days now filled with the preparations for the nation's most anticipated murder trial, met with his subordinates to solidify plans for handling the incoming crowds.

Ironically, one of the primary issues that concerned city officials was where to put all the people who would be swarming into town. Even before the Yankee Doubleheader, hotels had been flooded with room requests, and once the clinch was official, the calls increased threefold, coming in from all over the country. Yet with an iron and steel engineers convention already scheduled for that first weekend in October, hotel rooms were at a premium. The Manger Hotel nearly filled every room when an alert clerk remembered that they had to save some for the Giants, who'd already booked them. When legendary former Yankee Joe DiMaggio, covering the Series as a guest reporter for a New York paper, requested a room at the Manger, he was politely informed there weren't any. He was also casually asked if his new wife, Marilyn Monroe, would be joining him. Unfortunately, she was still busy filming a new movie, *The Seven Year Itch*. Had she accompanied her husband to Cleveland, one of the Manger's staffers jokingly suggested they would have sped up the remodeling of the hotel and quickly created another room. Little did he know that the fairy-tale marriage of the sultry actress and the swashbuckling athlete was already crumbling.

Nearby, the Hotel Hollendon was busy preparing for its role as "World Series Headquarters," housing better than 750 reporters. In the sparkling lobbies of these grand hotels, Cleveland's police officers would go to work. An extra twenty-five detectives were assigned to the fourteen-man hotel, check, pawn, and pickpocket detail, several of whom would go undercover in lobbies to watch for sharpies setting up crap games or other illegal activities such as prostitution. Another twenty detectives would be posted at the ramps and entrances at Municipal Stadium watching for pickpockets and ticket scalpers, and yet another group was stationed on the roof of the ballpark with a

new technological wonder called a "walkie-talkie" to watch the nearby parking lots for vandals and thieves and radio down to their colleagues with the precise location of an offense.

Smaller hotels and inns in Mansfield, Akron, and Toledo began fielding calls and organized extra train or bus dispatches to Cleveland for each day the Series would be in town. The Red Cross provided blankets and cots so that visitors could sleep in Public Hall or Cleveland Arena. The Convention and Trade Show Bureau put out a call for any citizens wishing to rent rooms in their private homes. By the time the World Series arrived, more than 2,500 homes would be used by out-of-town renters. Officials even entertained the idea of docking two colossal passenger ships along the lakeshore near Burke Airport and using them as makeshift hotels, but the logistics proved too complicated.

Just as in New York, local businesses smelled the money

coming like the metallic tang of an approaching thunderstorm on a hot summer day. Prices spiked all over town, one lunch counter raising the cost of a cup of coffee from ten to twenty cents. Restaurants also introduced new menus with considerably higher prices, but waitresses, seeing the astonished looks on the faces of their regular customers, whispered that they could just pay the regular price. Owners of burlesque theaters sent barkers into the street to lure in new customers, and the SkyWay Lounge had the good fortune of having landed singer Harry Belafonte for this most important weekend. The Alpine Village Club had already begun promoting a massive victory party for Sunday evening, originally scheduled with the notion that the Indians would be wrapping up the Series that afternoon. Even though at best the hometown team would still be one win short of the championship come Sunday night, the party was still set.

Municipal Stadium itself was undergoing some housekeeping, from the hanging of the traditional red, white, and blue bunting around the park to the installation of two new photographer slings from the upper deck to account for the dozens of additional cameramen on their way into town. New telephones were installed in the press box, which for the first time would admit females among the better than 600 writers and photographers expected. Groundskeepers, noticing a few dead patches in the outfield grass, touched them up with green paint.

Though they wouldn't get to see or appreciate the work being done to the ballpark, the thousands of fans who didn't have the good fortune to land Series tickets became golden geese for Cleveland's advertising executives. "Life can be beautiful," announced an ad for radio station WTAM, "if you have World Series tickets. If not, let these radio programs calm your nerves . . ." With stores promising delivery before the start of the Series, television sales boomed. Many Cleveland schools dismissed their pupils at noon that Friday. And in Bay Village, the city's embattled mayor, whose life had been utterly ravaged over the past three months, was given special leave from the hospital, where he was being treated for horrible stomach pains, to attend the World Series.

With the new television sets tuned to WNBK and better than 70,000 fans—most carrying umbrellas and raincoats—crammed into the stadium, the stage was set for the Indians to claw their way back into the World Series. But that's not at all what happened. Beneath foreboding, gray skies that threatened to burst with rainfall at any moment, the Indians played as if enduring their own delay, numbing the once-optimistic gathering of fans into grim lethargy. "They went to see a rejuvenation," the *Plain Dealer*

stated, "but found a wake."

The first bad sign came when the starting lineups were announced. Al Rosen was not included. Seeing how Rosen's tattered thigh had crippled scoring opportunities in the first two games, Al Lopez left him in the dugout. When Hank Majeski's name was announced over the loudspeakers as Cleveland's starting third baseman, gasps and groans rippled through Municipal Stadium. Less of a surprise was Lopez's decision to send Mike Garcia to the mound, eschewing his original plan to start Bob Feller in Game Three and save Garcia for Game Four. Though Garcia had pitched twelve innings in a desperate attempt to earn his twentieth victory in the season finale five days before, Lopez felt he had no choice. He had more confidence in Garcia in a game of this magnitude.

If Garcia came through, and the Indians narrowed the lead to one game, Lopez would come back with Feller on Saturday and Bob

Lemon on Sunday. If he didn't, Lopez had no choice but to bump Lemon, his ace, up to Saturday. Rapid Robert's final quest to win a World Series game would hinge upon the Bear's tired arm.

The Giants lit up the scoreboard early. Willie Mays delivered his first hit of the Series, a two-out single in the first to score Don Mueller from second. And since Mueller had only reached second because of a throwing error by George Strickland, and Mike Garcia had struggled in the opening frame, allowing three baserunners, panic began to creep into Municipal Stadium. For the first time all year, it was warranted.

By the time the Indians collected their first hit, the Giants led 4–0 and Garcia was in the showers. The gloom began gathering in the third when New York put runners on the corners with nobody out. The Indians caught a break when Alvin Dark got caught in a rundown on a Mays grounder to third, but even

when faced with trouble, the Giants turned it into a positive. Dark danced along the baseline long enough to allow Mueller to move from first to third and Mays to take second. After an intentional walk to Hank Thompson loaded the bases with one out, Leo Durocher chose to trust another unorthodox hunch. Though just the third inning, he sent out the game's first pinch-hitter—none other than Dusty Rhodes—in place of Monte Irvin. The crowd "oohed" in surprise when the move was announced over the public-address system, then passionately booed their nemesis. As he'd done in the previous two days, Rhodes delivered, slapping a weak bouncer between first and second on the first pitch to score both Mueller and Mays. In his four at-bats in the Series, Rhodes now had collected four hits and knocked in seven runs. By contrast, the entire Indians lineup had only managed to score three runs.

New York tacked on another run on a squeeze play moments later, and making matters worse, Garcia's throw to first went awry. The crowd realized there would be no comeback. The Indians were flat and listless, impotent at the plate and now even their magnificent pitching was failing them. Art Houtteman relieved Garcia and permitted another run before Ray Narleski took over in the sixth and promptly gave up one more. It was 6–0 before an Indian touched second base—in the seventh inning. Vic Wertz, the only Indian hitting his weight, blasted a home run to right center, symbolically sailing over the head of Willie Mays.

For much of the afternoon, Municipal Stadium was silent. The only noise was the irritating buzz of a quartet of small airplanes circling over the stadium "like buzzards over a corpse," the *Plain Dealer* noted. Apathy swept through the park like a low-grade fever, and fans started scanning the box seats to see what celebrities were on hand and what they were doing. Earl Warren, Chief Justice of the U.S. Supreme Court, still under fire south of the Mason-Dixon line for his role in the controversial Brown vs. Board of Education decision five months before, sat nobly near one dugout, not far from Clark Gable and Danny Kaye, who'd sung the national anthem, and silently suffering Indian fans Abbott and Costello, who'd followed the club from New York. And of course, nearby sat Cleveland's own Bob Hope, glum and sulking along with the fans around him. Yet even in this bleak atmosphere, Hope's sense of humor persevered. "You'd better sell all your stock in the Indians!" a heckling fan called out. Hope turned to him and shouted, "Communist!" It brought a round of laughter from the entire section of the stadium, one of the few moments of levity any of the fans experienced all day. The only real cheers of the game came when Narleski struck out Rhodes on three straight pitches to start the seventh, then when Mossi fanned Rhodes again in the ninth.

When Cleveland finally did show a glimmer of life in the eighth, scratching out a run and loading the bases with only one out and the heart of the lineup coming up, Durocher called on a young reliever named Hoyt Wilhelm, just completing the third of what would become a twenty-one-season, Hall of Fame career. Using a knuckleball, Wilhelm retired the final five batters on just thirteen pitches, mercifully ending a miserable afternoon. Bob Lemon would start on Saturday. Bob Feller would watch.

Hal Lebovitz wrote that the Indians "were like an old man trying to run up a steep hill while carrying a ton on his back, chasing a grinning youth." Afterward, the Cleveland clubhouse matched the grim flavor of the ballpark. Players, looking as old and tired as they did on the field, quietly went through the motions of removing their uniforms, which seemed to have lost some of their ivory sheen. Instead of vibrant white, the brand-new wool jerseys now looked the color of dirty dishwater. The "Indians" script across them, once a bright red, now resembled dried blood.

The anger and frustration that had pervaded the players after the two games in New York was replaced by a sullen, defeated acceptance. "I thought it might be a close series, but I never thought we'd lose three straight," Al Smith muttered as he sat in front of his locker. The sentiment was echoed by hundreds of fans over hundreds of drinks poured as autumn dusk fell over the city. Downtown Cleveland's bars and restaurants were packed to the brim that Friday night, but the mood was anything but celebratory.

Any attempts at optimism soured on the vine. "So nobody's won the Series after losing the first three," Vic Wertz announced defiantly in the somber clubhouse. "Well, nobody in the

American League ever won 111 games, either. Maybe we're due for another first."

None of his teammates seconded his enthusiasm. All the achievements of the magical summer were now slipping away like the leaves just beginning to fall off the deciduous trees and whisked off by the October breeze. After winning more games than any team in American League history, the 1954 Cleveland Indians now looked like they couldn't win a game if their lives depended on it. The mass celebration that revolved around the World Series returning to northeast Ohio had ended almost as quickly as it had begun. The jovial mood had turned sour, the ticketholders becoming mourners rather than fans.

In a realization that formed an eerie parallel to the summer just past, they were watching their beloved Indians be beaten to death in their own home.

PART THREE

MURDER ON THE LAKE

AMERICAN LEAGUE STANDINGS ON THE MORNING OF SUNDAY, JULY 4, 1954

	W	L	PCT	GB
CLEVELAND	51	22	.699	—
NEW YORK	48	28	.632	4 1/2
CHICAGO	46	29	.613	6
DETROIT	31	39	.443	18 1/2
WASHINGTON	30	42	.417	20 1/2
PHILADELPHIA	29	42	.408	21
BALTIMORE	29	44	.397	22
BOSTON	26	44	.372	23 1/2

13-THEY'VE KILLED MARILYN

S am awoke to screaming.

He groggily pulled himself off the daybed and moved as quickly as he could up the stairs, from where he'd heard Marilyn yell his name. As a doctor, he was used to reacting quickly out of sleep, and his mind began whirling, trying to anticipate what was happening. His first estimation was that Marilyn was having the same kind of convulsions she'd suffered through during her first pregnancy. With the fuzz of his slumber just beginning to clear as he reached the top of the stairs, Sam could see into the guest bedroom, which he and Marilyn used in the summer to enjoy the cool night breeze off the lake.

What he saw next was visible only by the light emitted from the dim light bulb in the adjoining dressing room Marilyn had left on in case Sam came up to bed in the middle of the night. Just above his wife's bed, to the left of his own, he could make out an indefinable shape. He was unsure whether it was a man or a woman, or even if it were a person. All he noticed was its color—a bright white that seemed to glow in the surrounding darkness—and a guttural, bubbling sound coming from beneath the shape. Before he could move any closer to determine what his sluggish senses were reporting, Sam felt a powerful blow to the back of his neck and his world went a shrill red. Then completely black.

When Sam slowly returned to consciousness, he was lying on his stomach on the floor just outside the bedroom. On the floor in front of him, he could see his wallet. Somewhere in the back of his mind, he knew this wasn't right, and that something else, something much more important, was horribly wrong. He sat up slowly, ignoring the ache that flared in his neck, and then carefully lifted himself to his feet. What he saw was unimaginable horror.

There was blood everywhere—on the floor, splattered on the walls, even collecting in small pools on the bed that had soaked through the sheets and into the mattress. And in the center of this crimson ocean lay Marilyn. Her hair was torn and matted, her face buried and indistinguishable beneath a mask of blood. Sam rushed to her side and his fingers flashed to her neck, searching for a pulse. He found none. Again acting purely on panicked reflex, he started toward Chip's room, not yet allowing this information he'd just gathered to fully process. He walked down the hallway and quietly opened Chip's door. Illuminated by the sliver of hall light, his seven-year-old son slept peacefully in his bed, unaware that his mother lay lifeless just a few feet away. Sam closed the door.

On his way back across the hallway, he heard a shuffling downstairs. Sam stopped and turned, peering down the staircase. He saw a long shadow creep across the living room floor toward the back porch, where just a few hours before the Sheppards and Aherns had enjoyed a pre-holiday dinner. Sam moved swiftly down the stairs after the shadow, but when he reached the landing, he saw no one. He glided to the back door of the house leading to the porch and looked out. Several yards away he could make out a silhouette beginning to climb down the long wooden staircase that led from the Sheppards' narrow backyard to the beach. Sam bounded out into the yard to the staircase and frantically started down the two sets of stairs, the roaring blood in his head drowning out the crash of the waves below. Halfway down, he realized he'd lost sight of the shadowy figure and had no idea which direction he should go. Then, just as he reached the beach, Sam found it again, a moving black shape against the lighter slate of sand.

A successful athlete in high school, Sam sprinted toward the figure and threw himself at it as if making a flying tackle on the football field. The two toppled to the beach, sending sand spiraling into the night. Before Sam could try to contain the shape, its strength and force overwhelmed him. They rolled in the sand in a vicious struggle, the waves thrashing and the seeping water foaming up around them. They were almost completely surrounded by darkness, isolated on this narrow stretch of beach beside the unusually vicious water of Lake Erie, which stretched into the horizon. What little light there was came from the distant glow of the Cleveland skyline, which sat like an oracle overlooking the beach and this conflict.

In the darkness, Sam was unable to tell who he was fighting, and only later was he able to process what few details he could gather: white, tall, large head, and, most notably, thick, bushy hair. But all of this information faded as the figure began to overpower Sam. He could feel his own strength begin to evaporate as he became aware of a choking sensation. And then, once again, the world faded away.

This time, it was the water that awoke him, rushing over and beneath his legs as the tide smoothly sifted in and out. His legs in the current, Sam was lying on his belly in the sand, vaguely aware that he wasn't wearing a shirt. When he started to move, his neck screamed in protest, sharp pinpricks of pain tumbling halfway down his spine.

Again trying to understand the chain of events that had just occurred, Sam eased himself up out of the sand, now realizing that the sky was no longer pitch dark and that the sun would soon be rising behind the Cleveland skyline in the distance. He eased back up the fifty-two steps and into the house, which he now realized was a mess. Drawers had been pulled out in the living room, his medical bag lay on the floor upturned and rooted through, and his den had been ransacked, with old athletic trophies mangled and left destroyed. The only thing that looked in place was the brown corduroy jacket Sam had slipped into over his t-shirt the night before, folded neatly on the daybed where he'd been sleeping. He quickly moved past the jacket and climbed the stairs back to the bedroom, where the mutilated corpse of his once-beautiful wife lay on the bed, gone forever along with the unborn child sleeping deep inside her.

Her pulverized face angled to the side, her pajama top had been rifled up, exposing her breasts. The pajama bottoms and underwear had been pulled down. Her legs dangled off the end of the bed, just beneath a decorative wooden bar. Sam somberly covered Marilyn's legs and genitals with a sheet. Then he went downstairs. His mind whirling, he picked up the phone, knowing someone should be contacted. Still acting without much regard for logic, Sam dialed the first number that floated across his clouded mind: for some reason, that of his neighbor, the mayor of Bay Village.

Spencer Houk's telephone rang at 5:45 a.m. The voice on the line was shrill and panicked, but Spencer recognized it immediately. "For God's sake, Spen, come quick!" Sam cried. "I think they've killed Marilyn!"

This was Sam Sheppard's story.

Though it would be questioned, criticized, and doubted for years, its principal elements—those that made sense and those that didn't—never changed.

Spencer turned to his wife, Esther. "Come quick," he said, repeating Sam's request in a frantic voice that immediately frightened his wife. "Sam says somebody tried to murder Marilyn!" Esther vaulted out of bed, threw on a pair of slacks and a t-shirt, and raced downstairs to meet Spencer. She asked if they should walk or drive the roughly 100 yards to the Sheppard home three houses down from their own. Spencer decided they'd drive. And thus began the series of details unrelated to Sam that would keep amateur sleuths talking for years—why did they drive? True, Spencer had a bad knee, and maybe this was the sole reason, yet the distance was so short that a direct route on foot would have gotten them there just as quickly. To drive rather than sprint headlong to the house suggested a calmness about the Houks, that they were not fueled by panic. Yet if this was the case, why didn't they call the police or an ambulance before leaving their own house? Where did rational thought begin and where did it end?

They arrived at 5:50 and approached the front door, which was closed. But when Spencer reached for the doorknob, it turned easily and they rushed in. This detail, which neither Spencer nor Esther truly paid attention to at the time, would later become much more significant. As the early morning light spread across the living room, the first thing Spencer saw was Sam's medical bag overturned on the floor, with its contents on the carpet. As his eyes swept across the large room, he also noticed that the door on the opposite end of the house leading to the back porch hung open. They found Sam in his ransacked den, just off the living room, sitting in a leather chair. Holding his neck, he was bare-chested, wearing only tan trousers, socks, and a pair of loafers—all of which were wet. His face had begun to puff with fresh bruises. There were clumps of sand in the cuffs and pockets of his trousers, but none in his hair. Spencer knelt down beside Sam and asked what had happened.

"I don't know exactly," Sam replied groggily, "but somebody ought to do something for Marilyn."

Spencer couldn't process this strange comment. "Sam," he said as calmly as he could, "get hold of yourself and tell me what happened." But Esther understood. She charged up the stairs to the bedroom— raising the question of how she knew where to go without being told, particularly since she later admitted she'd never been on the second floor of the Sheppard home before. On the way up, she noticed water on the steps. When questioned, Esther would also note that she had seen Kokie, the Sheppard's Irish Setter, inside the house when they arrived. But later, she said she hadn't seen her. The whereabouts of the dog on this morning would become one of the lasting mysteries of the summer.

Esther reached the top of the stairs and gasped as she looked into the bedroom. Her first thought was that it wasn't real, that it looked like some elaborate, distasteful wax museum display. Something like this couldn't happen in Bay Village, certainly not a football field away from her own house. With trembling fingers, she instinctively felt for her neighbor's pulse and could find none.

She raced back down the stairs, calling wildly to her husband, "Call the police! Call the ambulance! Call everybody!" Without questioning it or examining whatever his wife had seen, Spencer called the Bay Village police. It was 5:57 a.m.—the precise moment of sunrise on this Fourth of July.

The first police officer, Fred Drenkhan, arrived four minutes later—making the trip from the police department more quickly than the Houks had from three houses away. Drenkhan quickly examined the scene upstairs and returned to Sam in the den. They knew each other and had worked together before at crime scenes and accidents. As Drenkhan and the Houks listened, Sam told his story for the first time. As he did, Drenkhan noticed that the right side of Sam's face was now clearly swollen, and he could make out small cuts on his inner lip. After Sam finished his story, Drenkhan glanced around the house once more and came to an obvious conclusion: whatever had happened, it was too big for the Bay Village police, which had never before been in charge of investigating a murder. This was, after all, the first homicide to occur in Bay Village in eleven years. He suggested to Spencer that as mayor, he contact the Cleveland police for assistance. He did. And shortly thereafter, in another defining moment of the investigation, the Cuyahoga County coroner was alerted of the incident.

Meanwhile, unaware of the machinations that had been set in place around him or the waves of officers and authorities who now swarmed the house, Sam wandered through the kitchen, repeatedly muttering, "I've got to think." Esther offered Sam a drink to calm him, but he refused, knowing it would only further cloud his mind. Spencer phoned Sam's brother, Dr. Richard Sheppard Jr., who worked with Sam and their father, Richard, at Bay View Hospital. When Richard arrived at 6:10, Sam was laying flat on the floor of the den, trying to ease the pain in his neck and back. Richard, possessing the same doctoral instinct as his brother, raced upstairs to assess the situation and see if Marilyn needed assistance. He came back down the stairs slowly and stepped back into the den.

"Sam," he said quietly, "she's gone."

Sam's face twisted into further agony. "Oh, God, no!" he yelled and writhed on the floor. Richard told the others his preliminary guess was that Marilyn had been dead anywhere between twenty minutes and two hours.

Spencer Houk claimed that Richard then confronted his suffering brother. Gazing directly into Sam's eyes, Richard firmly asked his brother, "Did you do this?"

Sam angrily replied, "Hell, no!" Both Richard and Sam would deny this exchange took place.

Through it all, young Chip slept. Beside the fact that there were two closets cushioned between his room and the guest room, he was as deep a sleeper as his father. Just before 6:30, his uncle Richard woke the boy and carried him downstairs, then out the door and to his car. Chip would never live in the house again. When the time came to explain what had happened, his uncle told Chip that God had needed someone to watch over an infant in heaven and had picked Chip's mother because she'd done such a wonderful job raising him.

Soon after, Sam's other brother, Dr. Stephen Sheppard, arrived. He examined Sam and determined he needed to be taken to the hospital for further examination. He helped Sam dress and led him outside toward his car. On the way, they stopped and Stephen told Bay Village Police Chief John Eaton that he wanted to take Sam to the hospital to be treated for his injuries. Eaton allowed them to go. As they made the two-mile trip to Bay View Hospital, Sam sat stunned, as if trying to absorb the magnitude of what he'd witnessed. Stephen would later recall Sam crying out, "My God, how could this happen? Marilyn is dead. Why couldn't it have been me?" At Bay View, x-rays were taken.

Sam's reflexes were noticeably weak and he received a shot of Demerol to help ease his pain.

Twenty minutes after Drenkhan's arrival, the first reporters appeared out of the dawn mist. And when the nearby residents of Lake Road began to rise on this holiday Sunday morning, they noticed something was awry at the Sheppards'. Many gathered on the lawn and driveway, trying to piece together what had happened on their quiet little street.

Otto Graham, the star quarterback of the Cleveland Browns and a Bay Village resident, was driving down Lake Road to pick up a copy of the Sunday *Plain Dealer* when he noticed all the police cars and bystanders at the Sheppards' home. Graham and his wife would often go bowling with the Sheppards and Houks on Sunday nights and the couples would visit each other's homes. Graham pulled over and walked up to the house to find out if, as he assumed, someone had drowned in the lake. With the house not at all secured, Graham simply walked in as he'd done as a guest on several other occasions. He was shocked when officers inside told him what had happened and showed him the murder room. Seeing the battered body of sweet Marilyn, Graham immediately formed the opinion that whoever did such a thing must have been utterly crazy. It matched the view of both Eaton and Drenkhan, who felt that the murderer had likely been a drug addict who had broken into the doctor's home looking for narcotics. And indeed, Sam noted that a bottle of Demerol had been taken from his upturned medical bag. There were also signs of a bungled robbery—five of which had occurred in Bay Village in a one-month stretch the previous winter. Marilyn's watch was found on the floor of Sam's study, with blood stains visible on the band. It had stopped at 3:10. Her wallet was also found in the kitchen, emptied of the fifty dollars in cash it had contained. Likewise, seventy dollars in the billfold section of Sam's wallet was gone, but sixty-three remained in a small hidden pocket of the wallet. Stephen also reported seeing a cigarette butt floating in the toilet of the upstairs bathroom soon after he arrived—which was peculiar since Marilyn hadn't been smoking during her pregnancy and Sam smoked a pipe. The cigarette butt was never entered into evidence, but it seemed to serve as another suggestion that a third party had been in the house at some point during the night. Whatever logic flickering within these theories was about to be snuffed out like a candle in a windstorm. At 7:50, the Cuyahoga County coroner, Dr. Samuel Gerber, arrived.

He stepped out of his car cool and calm, and of course, in control. As always, his suit and shoes were crisp, his gray hair slicked to the side under a stylish white hat whose brim shadowed his pallid complexion. The slender, dapper Gerber entered the house confident that he was needed. What little he knew of the situation so far added up to one thing: it demanded his command and experience. He found Eaton and matter-of-factly informed him, "You're going to need some help on this case." From that point forward, Samuel Gerber was the face of the investigation.

Like Louis Seltzer, it was difficult to imagine Cleveland without Samuel Gerber. He'd been elected coroner in a stunning upset over the incumbent in 1936, and quickly made himself a celebrity by presiding over the investigations of six of the thirteen slayings among the grizzly Cleveland Torso Murders, combining forces with Eliot Ness, Cleveland's dashing public safety director. Gerber's work on the case—though it never led to the apprehension of the killer—made him a household name both in Cleveland and across the country. He gave lectures all over the world and had even been summoned to assist Scotland Yard. Not only was this rise to prominence unusual for a coroner but completely outside the parameters of his position. The job of county coroners across the country was to examine the murder scene and victim to determine the cause of death and provide the district attorney with forensic evidence to use in court. But in Cuyahoga County, things were considerably different. Both a practicing physician and a licensed attorney, Samuel Gerber may well have been the most powerful figure in Cleveland's criminal justice system.

For nearly an hour, Gerber surveyed the scene. He made a cursory examination of Marilyn's body before it was removed and taken to the morgue. When her body was lifted, two fragments of teeth were

At the apex of his career in 1954,
Cuyahoga County Coroner Dr. Samuel Gerber
wielded incredible political power.

The beach behind the Sheppard home, where Sam
claims to have fought with the bushy-haired
intruder who killed Marilyn.

found on the bed beneath her, along with a mysterious red fragment
that appeared to be either paint or toenail polish. Marilyn's hands were
slivered with small cuts, and the fingernail on her left fourth finger had
been completely torn off. Gerber calculated the time of death between
three and four a.m. The official autopsy findings would provide a
much larger window of 3:30-5:30, but by then, Dr. Gerber's opinion had
already been printed in the newspapers.

He walked down to the beach where Sam had supposedly battled with the murderer. But there was no sign of a struggle. Nor was there any sign of the t-shirt Sam had fallen asleep wearing the night before. Sam vaguely recalled awaking during the night and removing his brown jacket, which still lay neatly folded on the daybed by the stairs as police (and others) traversed through the house, but he had no memory of ever removing his t-shirt. He'd awakened on the beach bare-chested, the t-shirt gone. If Sam's story was true, why would the killer take the time to remove Sam's t-shirt and either destroy it, hide it, or take it with him? And if Sam's story weren't true, was finding a blood-soaked t-shirt the key to proving his guilt? Never in the history of Cleveland would one item of clothing become so important.

Nurturing his reputation with the media, Gerber accompanied a *Press* reporter and photographer, along with a *Plain Dealer* reporter, on a tour of the house. Along the way, the reporters spotted some photo albums and "borrowed" a few family pictures. Ironically, getting access to the murder scene wasn't that much of a scoop, since by that time, much of Bay Village had already been through the house. Not sealed by the police, anyone—whether the Browns' starting quarterback or a seven-year-old neighbor who came through looking for his pet turtle— could and, for the most part did, traipse into the Sheppard home. An unnaturally small number of fingerprints were found, as if the surfaces of the entire house had been wiped down. The few that were found were indistinguishable. But what the scene lacked in fingerprints, it made up for in small drops of blood, which were found trailed all over the house, including on the back porch and on the stairs leading to the murder room. But even these weren't considered viable since it was soon discovered that Kokie was in heat and had recently dripped blood through the house. And since the droplets couldn't be distinguished as either human or animal blood, they proved of little value other than to serve various hypotheses.

And where was Kokie during this entire episode? The dog would often spend summer nights outdoors, but neither Sam nor the Aherns could remember if she had been inside or out on the night in question. The answer seemed to hinge on whether or not Esther Houk had indeed seen Kokie on her way up the stairs when she first arrived at the house. The first arriving police officers noticed the dog running around the outside of the house—and that it was favoring its right rear leg, as if it had been struck. Had Kokie slipped out during the confusion of the Houks' arrival, or had she been outside the entire time? And if the dog had been in the house all night, why didn't it bark when an intruder entered? A neighbor told police that Kokie's barking woke him almost every morning. But Kokie was also gentle and timid (not a barking dog, as Sam would say) and would cower when threatened and retreat when kicked or hit. Either way, it mimicked all too familiar the Sherlock Holmes story "Silver Blaze," in which a horse is stolen from a stable and its trainer murdered. Holmes mentions to another detective that the key to the case centered on "the curious incident of the dog in the night-time." When the detective replied that the dog had done nothing, Holmes acknowledged that this was the curious incident. He cracked the case following the logic that the midnight visitor was "someone whom the dog knew well."

Gerber, Cleveland's own Sherlock Holmes, was stunned to discover that Sam wasn't at the house when he arrived. When informed he'd been taken to the hospital to be treated for injuries, Gerber became visibly upset. To Gerber, it appeared that the suspect had been spirited away from the crime scene by his brothers to the family hospital before he could be questioned by police. Perturbed at the inconvenience, Gerber traveled the two miles to Bay View to confront his suspect. In time, some would wonder if Gerber were inclined to dislike Sam Sheppard even before he arrived at the scene. Medical doctors often looked down on osteopathic surgeons such as Sam, not considering them "real" physicians. Yet by the 1950s, osteopathic medicine was becoming more popular and more accepted by the medical community. As a result, osteopaths like the Sheppards and hospitals like Bay View prospered—and some of the old guard silently stewed. An unspoken rivalry had developed between medical doctors and osteopaths, raising the question of whether Gerber had an ax to grind when he was called to the Sheppard murder scene.

When Gerber arrived at the hospital just after nine a.m., he was shown into Sam's room by his brother. Sam Sheppard lay there, his eyes now a bluish purple and nearly swollen shut, Demerol coursing through his veins. Even in this state, he would have recognized Samuel Gerber and, consequently, realized how important this incident had become. The door was closed, and Samuel Gerber and Sam Sheppard were alone in the tiny room that smelled of fresh bandages and medicine. They faced one another like fighters in an arena, not knowing that they were about to become adversaries in a war of public opinion that would not only last the entire summer but echo through the coming decades.

Gerber approached Sam with a smile, which Sam remembered as odd. Whether it was just an attempt by Gerber to put Sam at ease or an exaggeration caused by the Demerol, that smile made Sam very uncomfortable. Gerber politely offered his condolences and asked Sam to explain what happened. And once again, Sam told his story. Gerber listened patiently and then followed with a series of basic questions in a flat monotone, which Sam answered. The interview lasted thirty minutes. On his way out, Gerber requested that all of the clothes Sam had been wearing that morning be turned over to him. Aside from one splotch of blood on the trousers, which Sam said got there when he leaned over Marilyn to examine her, there was no blood on any of Sam's clothing.

Sam was originally diagnosed as having a spinal cord contusion and a concussion, which together had combined to cause a malfunction in the nervous system. When he arrived, his body temperature was a startling 94 degrees—a sign of shock—and the skin on his feet and toes was wrinkled and shrunken, indicative of a long duration submerged in water. Unconvinced by this analysis, Gerber summoned another physician to examine Sam—one who wasn't an osteopath and didn't work at Bay View Hospital. He disagreed with the Sheppards' diagnosis of the injuries, adding that he felt Sam's wounds were not only superficial but possibly self-inflicted. Brother Stephen disagreed wholeheartedly, noting that it would be impossible for Sam to fake such injuries.

Shortly after Gerber's initial interview, Marilyn Sheppard's body underwent an autopsy. She was found to have a total of thirty-five injuries, including twenty-seven to the head, any one of which could have killed her. It was, as Gerber said later, "definitely a murder of anger." But Marilyn had not died immediately. Gerber would later reveal that she may have remained alive for as much as a half-hour after the first lethal blow was struck. A vaginal exam showed no "traditional" sexual activity in the previous twelve hours, but a further investigation was not conducted to see if she had been raped. Perhaps most heartbreaking, the unborn child that had died along with her was determined to have been a boy. Later it was revealed the child would have been named Stephen, after Sam's brother.

During the autopsy, the chief pathologist washed off Marilyn's face with water to better see the wounds, rinsing away the caked blood—and perhaps any fibers, splinters, or other foreign particles that could have been used to further determine what had happened.

It had now been several hours since the police had arrived and begun investigating the scene of the crime. In that time, things only became more snarled. Five separate jurisdictions wound up conducting overlapping yet separate investigations: the Bay Village police, the Cleveland police, the county sheriff, the county prosecutor, and of course, the county coroner. There was no clear chain of command, no specific direction given, no central repository for whatever each unit discovered. Yet for all the work being done, there was little to show for it. There was no motive, no murder weapon, no clear evidence, and no witnesses.

Yet for Samuel Gerber, it was an open-and-shut case. He simply didn't believe Sheppard's story. He wrote this in his initial report, along with his opinion that Sam was the murderer. It goes without saying that this was outside the charge of the county coroner.

After returning from the hospital to the house, Gerber met with a handful of the officers on the scene. One of them later claimed Gerber told the group, "I think Sam Sheppard did this. Let's go get him, boys." Gerber denied saying this, and considering his experience and position, there's little to suggest that these words were actually uttered—except, perhaps, that over the next five months, Gerber would make it his mission to "get" Dr. Sam Sheppard. For the next two weeks, Gerber set up a makeshift office on Lake Road, continually visiting the Sheppard house to compare evidence and statements. His center of command was the Houks' living room three doors down, where Esther often served him his meals.

Eager to conduct a more extensive search, the police did what any law-enforcement officials would do when investigating a brutal homicide: they rounded up a bunch of teenage boys from the neighborhood and asked them to find the murder weapon. One group put on bathing suits and dragged the bottom of the lake while another cut down the thick underbrush along the bluff between the house and the beach. (Later would come the revelation that some bystanders at the scene remembered seeing a visible swath beaten through the brush, as if someone had recently walked through it. But by then, almost all of the brush had been cut down.) At 1:30 that afternoon, one of the boys—the sixteen-year-old son of Spencer and Esther Houk, as it happened—spotted something tangled deep in the brush. Sam would have recognized it at once. It was the green bag in which he'd kept the tools to his motorboat, usually in the desk in his den. But now the tools were gone and inside the bag were three items Sam later said had been in his pants pockets: his college fraternity ring, his keychain, and his missing watch, which had water beneath the crystal and blood on the band. Sam would explain the blood had been transferred to the watch when he was searching for Marilyn's pulse. Most interesting of all, the watch had stopped at 4:15.

As Gerber questioned Sheppard, Cleveland homicide detectives Robert Schottke and Patrick Gareau arrived at the house on Lake Road. There wasn't much they could do that either hadn't already been done or couldn't be done. Since so many people had been in the house,

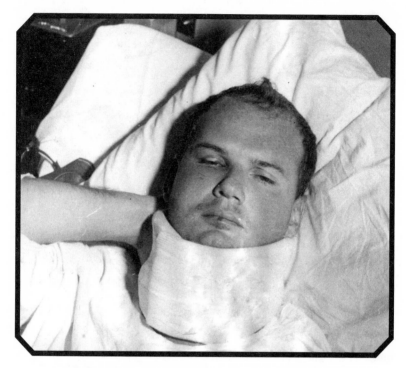

Sam Sheppard, dazed and heavily medicated at
Bay View Hospital, recovers from his alleged
encounter with Marilyn's killer.

whatever fingerprints or other evidence collected now were almost
entirely useless. What they did see, however, made them doubt Sam's
story. There was no sign of a struggle on the beach, and the mess inside
the house seemed a bit too organized, as if it had been staged. The
deputy inspector of the Cleveland Detective Bureau would later call
Sam's version of the intruder "the neatest burglar ever." That afternoon,
Schottke and Gareau made the two-mile trip to Bay View, where Sam
once again told his story and answered questions.

Just when the session was nearing its conclusion, Schottke and
Gareau glanced at one another and exchanged the knowing look that

veteran law-enforcement officials often share. Schottke turned back to Sam and mentioned the possibility of his taking a lie-detector test to verify his story. Sam was nonplussed. He thought this sounded like a waste of time, that instead of sitting here fiddling around with him, the detectives should be back at the house collecting evidence and clues— "clews" as it was written at the time.

Schottke shrugged. "Why should we look for any clues when we have everything we need right here?"

Like a stray cat sensing danger, Sam's skin tightened. "What do you mean?" he asked, trying not to let panic creep into his voice.

"What do you think I mean?" Schottke responded casually. "I don't know what my partner thinks," he said, nodding toward Gareau, "but I think you're the one who killed your wife."

The silence that followed was sharp and chilling. The detectives claimed that Sam made no response. He said he cried out, "Don't be ridiculous! I have devoted my life to saving lives. I love my wife!" Sam called for a nurse, who retrieved Sam's father. Sam explained what the detectives had just said. Richard Sr. turned to them, whatever politeness and cooperation that had existed before now gone. His eyes narrowed and he yelled, "Get the hell out!" The detectives did, and the brothers entered the room where their father was trying to console Sam, who had begun crying. "Those policemen think I killed Marilyn," he sobbed.

Sam's brothers and father looked at one another and knew what needed to be done. It was risky, since in the America of the 1950s it would all but admit his guilt. But they knew they had no choice.

Sam Sheppard needed a lawyer.

14 - THE LOST WEEKEND

As authorities scurried around the Sheppard house and shuttled back and forth to Bay View Hospital that Sunday afternoon, down the shore, the Indians put the finishing touches on a masterful Fourth of July weekend, completing a resounding four-game sweep of Chicago with a splendidly pitched 2–1 victory.

History was now on Cleveland's side. Since 1900, the majority of each league's pennant winners held control of first place on Independence Day. Only eighteen times in fifty-three seasons had the team in first on the Fourth not won the American League championship. Yet since six of those eighteen occasions saw the Indians tumble out of first in the second half of the season and lose the pennant, longtime Cleveland fans weren't comforted, even when the winning streak reached eight games with a pounding of Detroit behind three home runs by substitute infielder Bill Glynn, who'd collected only six home runs in his career going into the contest. Two days later at home against Baltimore, the Cleveland offense caught fire again. Glynn's surprising power surge continued when he led off the bottom of the first with a homer, beginning a string of ten consecutive Indian batters to reach base to start the game. When the first inning was complete, the Indians had plated eleven runs and coasted to another easy victory, starting another sweep of the Orioles.

The good news just kept coming that week when the results of the All-Star Game fan balloting were announced. Al Rosen received more votes than any player in the American League and would start—albeit at first base—along with Bobby Avila at second. Two days later, Casey Stengel, manager of the AL team, filled out the rest of the roster with three more Indians: Mike Garcia, Bob Lemon, and Larry Doby. With the game to be played at Municipal Stadium, such a large caucus of hometown players only seemed appropriate. Both fans and reporters felt the Indians were finally beginning to get the recognition that had evaded them. After one quick weekend trip to Chicago, the Indians could return home and welcome the dignitaries of baseball as the city of Cleveland would set out to prove it was as excellent as its baseball team.

Winners of eleven of their last twelve, the Indians had no reason to anticipate this four-game series with the White Sox going much differently than the one the previous weekend in Cleveland, especially when the Tribe grabbed an early 2–0 lead on Friday afternoon, then broke a tie in the seventh to surge ahead 3–2. But then the unexpected happened. After starting pitcher Art Houtteman gave up a leadoff single in the bottom of the seventh, he was replaced by Hal Newhouser, who had already ridden to the rescue several times for the Indians. Yet this time, he reverted to a pitcher who looked like he should hang up the cleats. He walked the only two batters he faced to load the bases, setting the table for a four-run Chicago rally that clinched an 8–3 triumph.

Things only got worse the next two days as the Indians played twenty-six consecutive innings without scoring a run. The White Sox scored back-to-back 3–0 shutout victories, then roared to an 8–0 lead in the second game of Sunday's doubleheader before Cleveland scored two meaningless runs in the ninth to halt their drought. Not only had the Indians' normally stellar pitching been sub-par, but their offense had vanished. Each still nursing his own sore finger, Al Rosen and Bobby Avila combined to hit just .111 in the four-game set. As two of their top sluggers slumped, so too did the Indians, who had been shut out three times in a week after being shut out only once in the previous three months. When the curtain closed on a miserable weekend, the White Sox had atoned for their four-game sweep in Cleveland by delivering one of their own, and after New York completed a sweep of the Senators, the Indians' comfortable four-game lead over the Yankees had been whittled down to a mere half-game.

Here it was, then. Writers and the more cynical fans had patiently waited through June, anticipating the usual Tribe collapse and wondering how it would arrive this time. Granted, it had come a bit earlier than usual, but most saw the four-game meltdown in Chicago as proof that the '54 Indians were indeed no different than their predecessors.

Lopez saw it coming but couldn't help but become irritated at the natural questions and assumptions that his team had folded under pressure. "For anybody to make the charge that the Cleveland club has played anything but game and courageous ball, at all times, against all opposition, is a downright lie," he barked at one point. Chicago manager Paul Richards, whose club had lit the first match in this bonfire of doubt, came to Lopez's defense. "Most of that 'fold' guff comes out of New York," he grumbled. "It should be stopped. It certainly is no compliment to the Yankees to say they succeeded because Cleveland choked. It's libel, it's phony, and it's plain trash."

"What we need is a little vacation," Lopez added optimistically. "The All-Star Game couldn't come at a better time."

After three months of nearly perfect baseball, everything had gone wrong at once for the Indians and they'd lost four straight games for the first time all season.

It wouldn't be the last time.

15 - THE STRONG ARM OF THE LAW

With the All-Star Game approaching, all of Cleveland buzzed with anticipation of the entire baseball world focusing its sights on the Best Location in the Nation. But the glimmer that would be expected from hosting such an event was dulled somewhat by the drama playing out in Cleveland's own backyard. With each edition of Cleveland's three newspapers, Marilyn Sheppard's murder was evolving from a tragic criminal act to something far more sinister.

Samuel Gerber's belief in Sam's guilt began to slither between the long black lines of newspaper type. He told reporters that the case hinged on three key elements: a motive, the murder weapon, and the missing t-shirt. Find one, Gerber declared, and you could unlock the mystery.

Meanwhile, the Sheppards added fuel to the growing flame of doubt. For one, they'd brought well-known criminal defense and labor lawyer William Corrigan into the picture. Referred by Arthur Petersilge, the Sheppards' family lawyer, Corrigan, a gaunt man with a droopy face and sunken eyes, met with the family at Bay View. But he was quick to point out to reporters that he had not been commissioned by the family. "The family recognized that a crime had been committed," Stephen Sheppard explained, "and felt it would possibly affect Bay View Hospital, as well as the family. We felt we needed professional advice."

Meanwhile, on Monday in University Heights, Marilyn's father, Thomas Reese, received two strange phone calls from an FBI agent named Tom Dixon, who said he had information on Marilyn's death he wanted to share with Reese. They arranged a meeting, but just before leaving, Reese decided to double-check the agent's background. He called the Cleveland FBI office and was informed that there was no one named "Tom Dixon" who worked for the FBI. It was just one of several encounters the Reeses had with crazed or cruel individuals that week, some of whom walked right up to their front door to attempt to involve themselves in the case. Stephen Sheppard received crank phone calls at all hours. All around Cleveland, amateur sleuths were

Marilyn Sheppard

trying to solve the mystery on their own. "It would seem," a *Plain Dealer* editorial stated, "as though the entire population of northern Ohio had suddenly turned detective and was engaged in weighing the evidence and evaluating the clews."

The story was now drawing national attention. Papers in New York and Chicago covered the developments with stories each day. But all media representatives, both local and national, were trumped by the *Press*, which set the tone for its coverage of the investigation with its first issue. Beneath the front-page banner headline "Bay Village Doctor's Wife Murdered" and related articles and photographs was a glowing profile of *Press* editor Louis Seltzer. It would not be the last time Seltzer would appear to be a part of the story.

Though police and reporters swarmed Bay View Hospital and Sam's room was under constant guard, Stephen determined that his brother was in no condition to undergo any more questioning. That Corrigan was allowed to speak with Sam while he himself was not further inflamed Gerber. Sam remained isolated in his hospital room all day Monday. Then all day Tuesday. If an intruder had indeed murdered his wife, it appeared Sam and his family were allowing the killer's trail to get cold. Marilyn's funeral was scheduled for Wednesday afternoon, and Sam was permitted to attend so long as he used a wheelchair and wore a thick neck brace. Gerber felt this permission indicated that, come Wednesday, Sam would also be well enough to answer more questions. At an impromptu conference between authorities and members of the Sheppard family at Bay Village City Hall on Tuesday night, Gerber relayed his frustration at Sam's inaccessibility. If he was not permitted to speak to the doctor, Gerber said, it would be necessary to hold either a public hearing or a coroner's inquest, at which Sam would be forced to testify under subpoena. "I'll subpoena the whole family if necessary," Gerber announced to reporters. Still, his brothers and father insisted that Sam was not in a condition to answer any questions. Gerber left the conference stewing, and the family continued to prepare for the funeral the following afternoon.

Wednesday's weather matched the mood that had settled over the city. Dark clouds blanketed Cleveland all morning, keeping the temperature in the mid-60s, unusually cool for early July, particularly after June's heat wave. As light rain spickle-spackled against the window of his hospital room, Sam Sheppard lay quietly, his eyes closed, listening to the soothing pulse of classical music from a small record player beside the bed. Though relaxing, the music also made Sam think of Marilyn, and how much she loved to listen to classical orchestras and symphonies. A drizzle fell as the Sheppard and Reese families somberly arrived at Knollwood Cemetery in Mayfield Heights to honor Marilyn. They gathered in a narrow, dark crypt, which was lit only by candles that cast long shadows on the gray stone floor. Sam was one of the last to arrive, escorted into the mausoleum from an ambulance in a wheelchair. It was his first public appearance in the thick, leather neck brace that would define him for the rest of his life.

As the service began, the lights in the Sheppard house on Lake Road blazed through the dark afternoon. Inside, Samuel Gerber once again examined the scene of the crime and toured the home, this time accompanied by a pair of county prosecutors. Meanwhile, a mile west of the Sheppard house, another Bay Village home was broken into. A $500 diamond ring and watch were taken. Police vowed to search for a connection between this break-in and the murder of Marilyn Sheppard.

Her service was brief, with no music or dramatic eulogies. By the time it ended at three p.m., a light rain had once again begun to fall. Sam, whose head throbbed with pain, returned to Bay View. When he arrived, he was once again sedated, and Stephen told deputy sheriff Carl Rossbach that Sam couldn't be questioned. Rossbach left disappointed and informed Gerber that they'd once again been stymied. "Here is a witness," Gerber pontificated to the *Press*, "surrounded and shielded by his own family of doctors. It's a situation that's got to be straightened out immediately.

"We have tried to be humane in this inquiry," he went on. "We expected cooperation from the family but don't seem to be getting it. We'll now have to use the strong arm of the law."

Rossbach would have been even more frustrated to discover that shortly after he left, a *Plain Dealer* reporter and photographer were permitted into Sam's room. Still wearing the neck brace, the exhausted doctor lay flat on the bed. The photographer snapped a picture that would appear on the front page the following morning. When the reporter asked Sam if he would cooperate in the investigation, he replied, "Heavens, yes!" as if there was no reason that he wouldn't. Did he feel well enough to be questioned, he was asked. "My doctors tell me that I'm not in shape yet," was the reply. To investigators, this made no difference. The deputy inspector of Cleveland's Detective Bureau noted that if a witness is injured by the suspect, it's even more important to question him right away. For example, he noted the recent assault on a four-year-old boy left for dead (through which an eyewitness earned a very large check from Louis Seltzer for helping catch the culprit). Though the boy was badly beaten and very scared, he was questioned right away, and it helped lead to the quick arrest of the suspect.

For Samuel Gerber, Thursday morning was high noon in what had become a very public showdown with the Sheppard family. Joined by Rossbach and homicide detectives Patrick Gareau and Robert Schottke, he marched into Bay View once again to question Sam and this time was admitted to his room. Five minutes later, Arthur Petersilge and William Corrigan entered. Ten minutes after that, Gerber and his entourage left the room, and the coroner spent much of the morning sparring with Corrigan, who by now had officially been retained by the Sheppard family.

As the two argued legalities in the hallway, inside Sam's room, the patient and his brothers and father composed a short written statement to be released to the press still gathered outside. In it, Sam said he was not refusing to talk to the authorities but that he already had provided everything he knew. The statement also announced a reward of $10,000 to anyone who provided information leading to the "arrest and conviction of the murderer of my wife."

After his conference with Corrigan, Gerber was visibly angry. He pulled out a piece of paper and, handing it to Rossbach while motioning to Sam's room, snarled, "Forthwith." It was, as Gerber had promised two days before, a subpoena calling for Sam to appear at a coroner's inquest. Rossbach entered the room to deliver it, demanding that Sam be transported to the county morgue for an inquest. "Absolutely not!" Corrigan barked. "This man is sick. He is in a hospital. He cannot be moved." In the discussion that followed, an unorthodox agreement was made. Gerber wouldn't question Sam, instead yielding to Rossbach, but neither of Sam's attorneys would be present during the questioning. Sam just wanted a third party there, someone he knew. They settled on Fred Drenkhan, the Bay Village officer who knew Sam well and was the first to arrive at the scene Sunday morning.

Rossbach got right down to business. "You're a suspect in your wife's murder," he said, almost casually. As he had when Schottke and Gareau had made a similar statement, Sam responded with shock. "You don't think I killed her, do you?" he said. "My God, do you think I would do that when we were expecting our baby?" For the next three hours, Rossbach questioned Sam. Several times during the interview, Sam broke down and cried, but throughout he gave his answers freely and clearly. Finally, when the long-awaited questioning ended, Rossbach left the room and again faced the gaggle of reporters in the hospital lobby. He shook his head slowly and muttered, "We're as much in the dark as we were before."

Two miles away, as a constant line of cars motored past the Sheppard house and boats crept up to the shore behind it to get a closer peek at what literally overnight had become a tourist attraction, there was a sudden flurry of activity. Police found a human skull with bits of flesh still clinging to it wrapped in newspaper in the Sheppard garage. Also found were portions of four other skulls. But Gerber extinguished any rumors before they could ignite. The skulls were anatomical specimens used for research, not previous victims. For one horrifying moment, Gerber must have recalled the thirteen decapitated heads discovered during the grizzly Torso Murders of two decades before. The last thing he needed now was a public reminder of the most infamous string of murders in Cleveland history—and that the killer was never caught.

That afternoon, Sam Sheppard was released from Bay View and driven to his father's house (both the *Plain Dealer* and *Press* dutifully printed the address). The following day he would be allowed back into his own house for the first time for a police-supervised reenactment of the events of the night of the murder, including the struggle with the intruder at the top of the stairs and then on the beach. Publicized in the media like a circus, the reenactment drew hundreds of reporters and curious spectators to the Sheppard home. Cars were parked all over the front lawn and visitors moseyed through the premises trying to get a look at Sam. Carrying three daisies picked by Chip, Sam entered the house for the first time since discovering Marilyn's body.

When he arrived, Corrigan pulled Sam aside and spelled out what he felt was the reality of the situation. "You're being accused of murdering your wife," he said. "These men are here to get a confession." Just as he had when originally confronted with the notion of being a suspect, Sam became highly emotional. "I didn't do anything to Marilyn!" he shouted, as tears spilled down his face. Shortly afterward, Rossbach approached Sam to ask the question he'd been trying to ask for four days. "Under your constitutional rights, you don't have to answer this question," he began carefully, "but did you kill your wife?" Again Sam emphatically denied it, this time adding, "She was the only girl I ever loved and ever will love." In the coming days, this comment would receive much more scrutiny.

Before Rossbach's questioning could continue, Corrigan stepped forward to inform Sam, "Don't say a word. I'm your lawyer." As if on cue, out of the pack of police and investigators emerged Samuel Gerber, who had almost blended into the background. Once again, he and Corrigan engaged in a bitter argument. When the debate reached a standstill, Sam felt obligated to say something. He turned to Stephen, who, even more than Corrigan, had become his trusted advisor.

"What should I do?" Sam asked meekly. Stephen, perhaps exhausted from the ugliness of the situation and growing weary from the phone calls and unwanted visitors and the weight of public opinion that was beginning to gather on the family's shoulders, had no more advice to offer.

"Look," he said with a shrug of his shoulders, "you're over twenty-one. Make up your own mind."

Sam mulled over the comment, and perhaps the irritated tone of his older brother, turned to Gerber and Rossbach and finally said, "I'll talk."

He answered questions over and over as he guided police through the events of the early morning hours of July 4, though they didn't force him to enter the murder room, which was still stained and splattered with Marilyn's blood. When he saw the county fair atmosphere that had developed out front, Sam became furious. He angrily declared, "They're all over the lawn. I want them off my property." Then, with a lump in his throat, he added, "Marilyn wouldn't like it." Police cleared the lawn of all people and cars. Even Gerber was gracious enough to move his own car to the driveway from its prime spot near the front door.

For the police, nothing was gleaned from the reenactment exercise. But the Cleveland papers got exactly what they wanted: new material for fresh ink. In the middle of its front-page story on the reenactment, the *Press* dropped in a partial list of the paperback mystery novels on the Sheppard bookshelf: *Blood in Your Eye*, *Blood on My Hands*, and best of all, a tale titled *I Killed My Wife*. Inside, the *Press* ran the first in what would become an historic line of editorials concerning the investigation. Under the title "Too Much Time Lost," the *Press* began, "Within

He dozed off on downstairs couch and was awakened by Marilyn's cry for help.

He went downstairs again, walked around and paced and then thought of a telephone number. It was that of Mayor J. Spencer Houk of Bay Village. Houk and his wife responded quickly, found him sitting in his den, holding the back of his neck.

He rushed upstairs to her bedroom. He "tried to go to Marilyn but I was intercepted. I was struck from behind" and knocked out.

He went into Marilyn's room, saw that she had been terribly beaten and "felt that maybe I'd wake up. That maybe this was all a terrible nightmare or dream."

After a short, fierce struggle there he was again knocked out. He came to later, lying in the water. He struggled up and back into house.

He came to on the floor. He heard a noise and dashed downstairs, chasing the figure out on to the Lake Erie beach.

Sam Sheppard's bizarre account
of the morning of July 4, 1954.

memory no murder case in this part of the country has prompted so much discussion or speculation as that of Mrs. Sheppard." It went on to criticize the police while simultaneously questioning the Sheppards' motives: "the investigative authorities were slow in getting started, fumbling when they did, awkward in breaking through the protective barriers of the family, and far less aggressive than they should have been . . . ." Considering the proclamations and accusations veiled as editorials that the *Press* would deliver over the next three weeks, its opening salvo was quite tame.

On Saturday, July 10, wearing the neck brace and now dark sunglasses because he said bright light hurt his eyes, Sam spent nine hours in the county prosecutor's office again answering questions from Rossbach, Gareau, Schottke, and a handful of others. He was asked to take a lie-detector test but refused on the grounds that in his emotional state, the results would be unreliable—again adding a sprinkle of suspicion in the mind of John Q. Public. Prosecutor John Mahon pointed out the general view of the era: anyone telling the truth should have nothing to fear from a lie-detector test. Few new details were revealed in the session, but two caught reporters' attention. They discovered Sam was now carrying a .38 revolver—for his own protection, he stated. And there were whispers of a "mystery woman," who derived from a question posed to Sam as to whether he and Marilyn had recently gone through any quarrels or conflict. The only incident he could remember was a misunderstanding over a watch he had purchased for another woman during a trip to California four months earlier. No further details or names were revealed, but reporters and readers could sense there was more to this subplot. Indeed there was.

In the meantime, in the wake of the Sheppards' reward offer came three eyewitness reports that, though mutually exclusive, supported Sam's theory of the events of that night. The first came from a family, the Benders, who drove past the Sheppard home at 2:15 a.m. and noticed two lights on—one upstairs and one downstairs. The upstairs light was the dim changing-room bulb that Marilyn always left on when Sam was asleep downstairs. But the downstairs light is what made the account important. According to the Benders, there was a light on in Sam's study some two hours after the Aherns had left and Marilyn had gone to bed. Nancy Ahern remembered the study light being on when they left, but since it was likely Marilyn would have turned off all the downstairs lights before retiring, this suggested that someone had turned the light on again. Gerber turned the idea on its side, noting that it was unlikely a burglar would enter a house in which a light was on. On the contrary, a Lake Road neighbor reported he'd been outside at 3 a.m. and hadn't seen any lights on in the Sheppard home.

Leo Stawicki, a steelworker who was returning home from a fishing trip on the night of the murder, came forward and said that between two and 2:30 a.m., he was driving along Lake Road when he noticed a bushy-haired man in a white shirt walking along the side of the road just ahead. Another man, factory worker Richard Knitter, stated he was driving with his wife on Lake Road on the way back from seeing *Gone with the Wind*, showing continuously all weekend at the State Theater in Euclid. They'd stopped for a late dinner at a restaurant in Rocky River and were passing the area of the Sheppard home at 3:50 a.m. when they also saw an ugly, bushy-haired man trudging along the road beside Lakeside Cemetery, about two hundred yards from the Sheppard house. He looked so ominous that Knitter commented to his wife, "How would you like to meet that guy in the dark?"

In retrospect, they wondered if perhaps Marilyn Sheppard had.

16 - THE CLEVELAND SPECTACLE

S tarting that Monday, for three days, Cleveland was the center of the baseball universe.

By car, bus, train, and plane, fans poured into the city from all over Ohio as well as neighboring states. Those who arrived without hotel reservations were in for an inconvenient stay. All downtown hotels had been booked for a month, sending some visitors scurrying out of town to secure accommodations. Even those who didn't make the trip could enjoy one of the great annual spectacles of an American summer. The Mutual Broadcasting System would deliver the game across 560 radio stations, while Gillette sponsored NBC's national telecast.

Better than 68,000 fans would pack into the ballpark on the lake on this Tuesday afternoon, slightly short of expectations that called for a crowd of better than 70,000, which would have set a new All-Star Game attendance record. As it happened, the mark of 69,812 from the first time Municipal Stadium hosted the event in 1935 was still number one and would remain atop the list for another twenty-seven years—until the third time Cleveland hosted the All-Star Game. Hank Greenberg welcomed the entourage of reporters and baseball dignitaries like a proud father at his daughter's wedding reception. After years of struggle and being second-guessed as GM, Greenberg and his decisions had been verified by the Indians' strong first half. Now he hoped to continue the trend. Fueled by newfound confidence, he pointed to the mammoth crowd as proof that his radical interleague-play concept could work. "I proposed it because I think it's good for baseball," he said. "If it's turned down, I won't be distressed—it's experimental. It may work, it may not. But we won't know unless we try."

A full-page ad in that week's *Sporting News* depicted a cartoon of Chief Wahoo standing outside Municipal Stadium holding a key to the city. "Your 1954 All-Star Host, the Cleveland Indians," the headline declared. The text below shifted into Hollywood "Indian" diction: "Heap Big Welcome to Honored Players—Distinguished Officials—Loyal Fans." Included among these loyal fans were thousands of Tribe rooters who saw this three-day festival as an appetizer for later delicacies. "No doubt many of them considered the big day a forerunner of others to come—in October," *Sporting News* conjectured. "The Indians passed the traditional July 4 milestone in first place. Pennant fever once again beads the brows of Uncle Moses' children."

Northeast Ohio fans were also eager to get a first-hand look at the almost-mythical players from the far-off land of the National League. Likewise, many National League All-Stars, including Stan Musial of St. Louis, would get their first look at iconic Municipal Stadium. In an interview just after arriving in Cleveland on Monday, the Giants' Willie Mays insisted that he knew all about Municipal Stadium and was looking forward to seeing what he could do with the short right field and tall right-field wall. The reporter looked at Mays questioningly. Brooklyn catcher Roy Campanella overheard the comment and burst out laughing. "Not that park!" he cried. "This is the big stadium down by the lake, the biggest baseball park in the country." The Say Hey Kid had been thinking of the Indians' old home, League Park, which they'd abandoned eight years before and Mays had encountered during his brief tenure in the Negro Leagues. "You could put League Park inside the stadium!" Campanella pointed out.

Any other time of year, the image of a Giant and a Dodger not only joking side-by-side but preparing to join forces would seem utterly displaced. Each July, the All-Star Game served as a peaceful armistice, a welcome three-day interruption to often-heated pennant races. Rivals became teammates and their objectives became much broader. Just as the ten participating Giants and Dodgers temporarily forgot their disdain for each other's ballclubs, the nine Indians and Yankees could put aside their partisanship and focus on underlining their league as the superior circuit.

Though many talented players gathered at Municipal Stadium for the 1954 All-Star Game, Al Rosen (far left) shone brighter than legendary stars like (from left) Ted Williams, Mickey Vernon, and Mickey Mantle.

Yet for all the good-natured ribbing and congenial reunions, there was also a detectable level of tension. Some players appearing for the first time were apprehensive about making fools of themselves on such a grand stage. Though Al Rosen had played in the previous two All-Star Games, he became more and more uneasy as Tuesday approached. On Sunday, as the Indians finished their disastrous trip to Chicago, he asked Al Lopez to call Casey Stengel on his behalf. Though he would undergo x-rays on Monday and would learn that the finger was healing nicely, Rosen's grip on the bat, and consequently his swing, was still compromised. He wasn't afraid he would worsen the injury by playing in the All-Star Game but that he would hurt the American League's chances for victory. He, like the players and managers on both sides, wanted very badly to win. In the years to come, the All-Star Game (and all subsequent versions in other sports) would serve as little more than a showcase for individual achievement. The outcome of the "game" itself matters little, if at all. But in 1954, as in the twenty All-Star Games that came before it, the Midsummer Classic was a serious competition, a prime opportunity for each league to prove it was better than the other. Casey Stengel selected his players not to fulfill quotas or massage egos but to construct a team capable of winning. Though he'd won five World Series, Stengel had failed in four attempts to captain the American League to victory in an All-Star Game. And he wanted very badly to do so.

Lopez eased Rosen's concerns but didn't relay the message to Stengel, who didn't learn about Rosen's hesitancy until he told the manager just before the game. After getting little sleep on Monday night, Rosen awoke Tuesday morning with a finger throbbing worse than ever. "I probably won't do your club any good," Rosen explained, "because I haven't helped my own club lately." True enough, Rosen's batting average had dropped sixty points since he'd injured his finger in May, and he'd only hit one home run in the previous six weeks. Stengel respected his intentions, but thought even an injured Rosen could help the team. Plus, all starters were required to play at least the first three innings. After discussing the matter with baseball commissioner Ford Frick and receiving permission, the wily manager made a deal. Bat once, he said, and if Rosen wanted him to take him out of the game, he would.

The tone for the afternoon was set before the first pitch, when the world-renowned Cleveland Orchestra presented a one-hour concert. As music echoed through the park on a sunny summer afternoon, the temperature continued to climb. The drought that had parched the city entered its second month. At game time, thermometers outside of Cleveland swelled to 93 degrees, though the steady lake breeze coursing through the stadium kept it much more tolerable, hovering in the low eighties. All downtown streets leading to the ballpark were jammed by noon, ninety minutes before game time. Air traffic swarmed around Burke Lakefront Airport, with private planes landing by the minute carrying passengers heading for the game.

Whitey Ford, the American League's starting pitcher, cruised through the top of the first, but after Minnie Minoso flied out to open the bottom of the frame, Bobby Avila gave the hometown crowd something to cheer about by lacing a single to left off Philadelphia's Robin Roberts. Mickey Mantle flied out and Yogi Berra walked, moving Avila into scoring position. With a chance to further energize the crowd by bringing his teammate home and giving his team the lead, Al Rosen struck out to end the inning. If he'd been retired any other way, Rosen likely would have taken himself out of the lineup. But striking out in front of a huge crowd in his own ballpark ignited Rosen's pride. For the first time in weeks, he forgot about his aching finger. When Stengel approached him, he said he wanted to stay in the game.

When Rosen returned to the dugout after the National League batted in the second inning, Boston great Ted Williams slid over on the bench beside him and started talking about what had happened in Rosen's first at-bat. When you're facing a pitcher you don't think you can get the bat around quickly enough against, Williams said, make sure you choke up on the bat. He illustrated his point with a nearby bat and, through the remainder of the inning, he and Rosen discussed how to improve his swing.

With the game still scoreless in the third, the American League threatened once again with a leadoff walk to Minoso and another single by Avila. But Mickey Mantle was retired and Berra grounded out to advance the runners. Just as he had two innings before, Al Rosen stepped to the plate with two on and two out. But this time, choking up on the bat ever so slightly and lifting his mangled right index finger off the handle, he crushed a Roberts pitch over the outfield wall in left center field for a three-run home run. The colossal crowd howled in delight. After crossing home plate, Rosen was swarmed by his teammates in the dugout, including Williams, who beamed like a proud father.

After the Tigers' Ray Boone followed with another home run seconds later, the AL led 4–0 and appeared poised to coast to victory. But in the fourth, Stengel replaced Whitey Ford with Chicago's Sandy Consuegra, who was promptly bombed for five hits and five runs to put the National League on top. The Municipal Stadium throng roared again when Stengel called on Bob Lemon, who cleaned up the mess and got out of the inning. Despite Lemon's effectiveness, one of the great slugfests in All-Star Game history had begun.

Though hampered by a mangled right index finger
that nearly forced him out of the lineup, Al Rosen
smashed two home runs in the 1954 All-Star Game
using an unorthodox grip.

With most of Cleveland—and much of the nation—spellbound with the game at Municipal Stadium, the wheels of the Marilyn Sheppard murder investigation kept turning. As the world's greatest baseball players put on a show just a few miles away from the site of the killing, on the other side of the continent, the district attorney of Los Angeles called a pretty young woman to his office for questioning. She was asked about her relationship with Dr. Sam Sheppard, a wedding she'd attended with him, and a watch she'd lost. In the days to come, this brown-eyed beauty's story would blow the doors off the Sheppard case. But the intrigue surrounding this mystery would have to wait until tomorrow. For now, Clevelanders were tuned in to what was later called the greatest All-Star Game ever played.

The National League's sudden lead only lasted a few minutes. Bobby Avila's third at-bat of the afternoon proved even more valuable than his first two, as he lifted a sacrifice fly to score Chico Carrasquel to knot the score at five apiece. Cincinnati's powerful slugger Ted Kluszewski ripped the third home run of the game in the fifth, a two-run blast to make it 7–5. But once again, the National League's advantage was short-lived. Yogi Berra led off the bottom of the inning with a single, and Rosen mirrored the heroics of his previous at-bat by crushing another home run, this one soaring over Jackie Robinson's head in left, to knot the score. It only seemed appropriate that in their own park in the middle of their season of destiny, the Indians were dominating the Midsummer Classic. And they weren't finished yet.

Ted Williams, inserted in the fourth, led off the bottom of the sixth with a walk and moved to third on a Minoso single. Up stepped Bobby Avila, who'd already put forth one of the greatest All-Star displays in Cleveland history, collecting two hits while scoring one run and knocking in another. This time he laced another single to left, scoring Williams. Avila was showered with applause as the American League took back the lead. But they would need the heroics of one more Indian to secure victory. In the top of the eighth, pinch-hitter Gus Bell of the Reds hit a two-out, two-run homer to make it 9–8, NL. The Nationals then attempted to add to the lead but Red Schoendienst was caught stealing home to end the inning in what would prove to be the most controversial play of the game.

Milwaukee's Gene Conley was called on to close out the victory, and he started the bottom of the eighth by enticing Minoso to ground out. Down to his last five outs, Stengel called for Larry Doby to pinch-hit. As if following a script, Doby rifled the sixth and final home run of the contest over the left field wall to tie the score once again. It continued to be an Indian afternoon at the zenith of an Indian summer.

After Mantle and Berra coat-tailed Doby's momentum with back-to-back singles, Rosen reached base for the fourth time with a walk. It allowed Mantle and Berra to score moments later on a two-out bloop single by Chicago's Nellie Fox, giving the American League its final runs of the afternoon. When Virgil Trucks coolly retired the side in the ninth, the AL had captured its first All-Star Game victory in five years—thanks almost entirely to the participating Cleveland Indians. "Now they see what I'm up against in this American League," Stengel told Cleveland reporters afterward. "Your Cleveland guys sure did a job." In eight at-bats, Avila, Doby, and Rosen combined for seven hits and knocked in eight of the team's eleven runs. Rosen, who hadn't wanted to play, collected three hits and five RBIs and was one of just six players who played the entire game. "That Rosen," Stengel said, "was really something."

Even beyond Cleveland, it was a game to remember. Five records were broken, including most combined runs and most combined hits. Arch Ward, sports editor of the *Chicago Tribune* and the founder of the All-Star Game, called it the best he'd ever seen. "Baseball reached one of its finest hours," stated *Sporting News*, "made its old friends happiest and won new friends literally by the millions—as a result of the game played on the field.

"The Cleveland Spectacle proved that the old game has so much to offer."

Perhaps the most notable mark to fall, *Sporting News* suggested, was Casey Stengel's All-Star losing streak, and for this victory, he was visibly grateful. "Listen, you men," he called out in the celebratory clubhouse after the game. "I want to thank every player here for winning today, not only for myself and themselves, but for the American League." A good-natured cheer trickled through the room as the players acknowledged the service they'd rendered their circuit.

"Don't ever forget it," Stengel went on. "It's the best league, and if you weren't good players, you wouldn't be in it."

The players broke into a round of applause, joined by Stengel. As the cheers echoed across the room in the bowels of the ballpark, high above them in the press box, sixty-three-year-old Elmer Stilwell, a longtime Western Union telegraph operator, collapsed as he sent the game story to United Press International in New York. Minutes later, he was pronounced dead of a heart attack.

Unaware that the angel of death had once again visited Municipal Stadium, the American League players and coaches basked in their accomplishment. But the revelry didn't last long. The Old Perfessor soon held up his arms like a teacher dismissing a class at the end of a school day. "Now I got to go to work on that half-game Cleveland's got us by," he said, drawing more laughter.

With that, the truce was over. The pennant race would now resume.

17 - MR. CLEVELAND TO THE RESCUE

For the Sheppards, it only seemed symbolic that the summer heat that had scorched Cleveland in June returned just as investigators began to intensify their focus on Dr. Sam. The cool and calm that had settled over the city and Sam Sheppard in the days after the murder were gone, seared by blazing temperatures and accusatory questions. "There's one suspect so far," Carl Rossbach said, "and that's Dr. Sheppard. Until something turns up, we'll have to keep questioning him until he gives us something to go on."

A wave of interest rose on Wednesday the fourteenth over the discovery of a t-shirt snarled into a wire behind a neighboring house. The t-shirt was ripped from top to bottom and had small dark stains on it, but tests couldn't decipher the stains as blood—more likely, they were from the rusted wire. Two details though, suggested that the t-shirt was not Sam's. For one, it was a large size, while Sam generally wore medium. Also, the brand didn't match. Sam never paid attention to the brand of his t-shirts, but the one found was a Jockey. All his others were Hanes.

As the investigation continued, Sam returned to work, still wearing the leather collar around his neck and the dark glasses over his eyes. He saw patients, who were generally soothing and understanding, knowing exactly what had and what was happening. It was as close to

Sam Sheppard emerged into the public eye in the days following the murder in peculiar fashion— wearing dark sunglasses and a neck brace, an image that would define him for the rest of his life.

his normal life as Sam had come since the Fourth of July. But as the month progressed and the oppressive heat continued, Sam's small dose of normalcy proved short-lived.

"I'm convinced that the killer is still in Greater Cleveland," Samuel Gerber announced on July 19, "reading every newspaper account of the investigation and chuckling over his shrewdness." He then paused and added as an afterthought, "If he remembers that he committed the crime." In the same breath as suggesting the killer may be a raving lunatic, Gerber called him "the most brilliant murderer in the annals of Greater Cleveland crime" for his ability to cover up and dispose of critical evidence.

Despite Gerber's confidence and frankness, he was beginning to find himself jammed into the vice of community pressure, the handle turning a little more with each passing day. Every idea, every lead resulted in a dead end. Sam provided a list of patients who may have held a grudge, which led nowhere. Ohio Bell was asked to trace all phone calls coming into or out of the Sheppard home that night but reported that such a search was impossible. Every incinerator and fire pit near the Sheppard home was checked, but no trace of either a potential murder weapon or clothing was found. "It's the most baffling mystery I've ever encountered in my nineteen years as Cuyahoga County coroner," Gerber admitted as July droned on. "It's prevented me from eating or sleeping regularly for the past three weeks."

A *Plain Dealer* editorial on the eighteenth mirrored the one launched by the *Press* nine days before. It ticked off a number of procedural mistakes made over the previous two weeks, including the confused tangle of authority and the long delay before Sam Sheppard was officially questioned, concluding that the entire investigation had been bungled. Just as the heat was on Sheppard, after developing no solid leads or evidence for two solid weeks, Dr. Gerber and the Cleveland police—still unofficially assisting Bay Village—were also facing serious pressure. Though the search continued, and had included assistance from Army experts with a magnetic mine detector, the murder weapon had yet to be found.

William Corrigan, tiring of the constant speculation and questions, announced that from that point forward, the Sheppards would only speak to the county sheriff or proper police authorities. In other words, he said between the lines, no more interrogations from Dr. Samuel Gerber. Naturally, Gerber was outraged. "Corrigan should not try to tell city or county officials what they should or should not do," he snapped to reporters. "We know what we can do and must do under the statues, and we are doing it. We are not going to let Corrigan run this investigation." It had been a shot across the bow, and Gerber wasn't going to stand for it.

Leads, even confessions, were coming in from all over Cleveland. Very few amounted to anything, but the papers happily printed anything they could dig up, including the story of a Painesville woman who believed Marilyn Sheppard had revealed her desire to divorce her husband on a chance encounter on a Fairport Harbor beach in June. Random as this anecdote was, there was evidence to support it. Found among Marilyn's possessions—and subsequently printed in the papers—were letters from years before in which family members encouraged Marilyn to fight through a difficult period with her husband and keep her family together.

And as if summoned on cue from distant California, the "mystery woman" of the case emerged—enter Susan Hayes, stage left.

She was a slender, freckle-faced, twenty-four-year-old with light-brown hair and dark brown eyes. Even in the emotionless photographs taken during the investigation, her prettiness shone through. Her name had first entered the arena during Sam Sheppard's nine-hour tumble with the county prosecutor, and Cleveland police began digging, not quite sure what they'd find. To start, all they knew was that Miss Hayes had been a medical technician at Bay View for three years before moving to Los Angeles that February. While at Bay View, she had been an acquaintance of Sam's, and when Sam had traveled to California for a medical convention in March, he met her there and they attended a wedding in San Diego together. At the wedding, she lost her purse, which contained a valuable watch. After a fruitless search for the purse that night, Sam bought her a new watch to replace it and had it sent to her. The original watch had turned up in a gas station bathroom and the proprietor had mailed it back to Sam in Ohio, since he'd left his name and address at several locations during the search. Sam forwarded the watch to Susan's parents in Rocky River, who then shipped it to Susan. Sam said Marilyn knew about his purchase of the watch and admitted she was upset when she learned the details. But he hadn't kept it a secret from her. Both he and Susan Hayes denied having anything but a casual relationship. But investigators felt there was something more to this story than a mere watch. They were right.

Little by little, further details emerged. Rossbach questioned Susan's parents, who revealed that Sam often drove her home from Bay

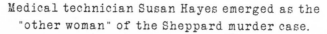

Medical technician Susan Hayes emerged as the "other woman" of the Sheppard murder case.

View Hospital. Susan mentioned that during her tenure at Bay View, she had been engaged to another doctor, Robert Stevenson, before the couple decided not to get married. For those fully engrossed in the drama of the investigation, the doctor's name instantly rang a bell. Dr. Stevenson lived in Kent, and it was his house that Sam's guest, Dr. Lester Hoversten, had abruptly decided to visit on the afternoon before the murder. People wondered—was the world truly such a small place?

While the Susan Hayes subplot added freshness to the story as it entered its third week, Mr. Cleveland didn't like what he was seeing. Louis Seltzer felt that the dry spell of this investigation had gone on far too long. No murder—particularly such a well-publicized one— should go unsolved in his city. And now that the rest of the country was watching, he wasn't about to allow some bungling police officers and prosecutors give Cleveland a bad reputation. Even worse, he saw that the other Cleveland papers were beginning to tire of the case, as evidenced by a *News* headline proclaiming "Murder Probe Hits Blank Wall." He could feel it slowly fading into the background. "The newspapers began to lose interest—except one . . ." Seltzer would write in his autobiography. "The *Press* kept the Sheppard murder case in top position on page one."

Seltzer was convinced that a conspiracy was taking place among the law-enforcement and legal machinery of his city. As Cleveland's self-appointed watchdog, he was outraged, and he certainly wasn't about to let the *Press* play along. "It kept steadily prying into the case," he would write, "asking questions, trying to break through the wall around Dr. Sam." By the third week of July, Louis Seltzer decided it was time to personally jump start this investigation and make sure justice was served. And maybe sell a few newspapers in the process.

On July 15, Seltzer revved into action. His first order of business, as always, was to cut through the red tape and bureaucracy of the investigation and go straight to the horse's mouth. He personally wrote a note to Arthur Petersilge, the Sheppard's family lawyer, offering Sam a way to improve his reputation:

> Dear Mr. Petersilge,
>
> Nothing in recent years has so gripped the attention of the community as the murder of Mrs. Marilyn Sheppard.
>
> As you know, newspapers not only around this area but across the country have devoted much space to developments in the mystery.
>
> Of necessity, Dr. Samuel H. Sheppard has become a central figure in the investigation. This is true because he is the only person other than his wife and son known to have been in their home that morning. Because the case seems stalemated, Dr. Sheppard has become a mystery man. Much of the whispering and rumor-spreading can disappear, I feel sure, with a complete expression from Dr. Sheppard himself.
>
> It is with this thought in mind that the following questions are submitted to Dr. Sheppard through you as his counsel. The columns of *The Press* are open to both of you for your replies to these queries and any other matters you may deem pertinent to the case.
>
> An early reply will be appreciated.
>
> > Respectfully,
> > Louis B. Seltzer

Included was a list of eleven questions ranging from as general as asking Sam's recollection of the night of the murder to his thoughts of how the police had handled the investigation and how he felt he'd been treated by the media. Understanding the importance of public opinion, both Petersilge and Corrigan advised Sam to respond to Seltzer's questions and helped him craft his answers. Though the replies were generally benign and non-critical, Sam and his lawyers still managed to illustrate their portrait of the killer (a psychotic or someone under the influence of narcotics or alcohol,) while slipping in subtle jabs at the police (". . . there is no justification for release or publication of confidential information which the authorities may obtain . . .") and newspapers ("There has been a great deal of misinformation published.")

Their reply was indeed made promptly, and Seltzer showed his appreciation by publishing the questions and answers on the front page of the *Press* two days later. On the day in between, the *Press*'s editorial page included a piece titled "Finger of Suspicion." Slightly more inflammatory than the editorial of a week earlier, this one shifted gears from not only spotlighting faulty police work to questioning the intentions of Sam Sheppard and his family. It suggested Sam was receiving special treatment because of his family's legal and government connections and also claimed that the Bay Village police were hostile to outsiders and refused help from the Cleveland police—allegations that had never been mentioned before. "Every further moment of fumbling," the editorial stated, "is helping a murderer escape."

Clearly not impressed with the responses Sam had submitted to his questions, Louis Seltzer prepared to take his game to the next level. In so doing, he would shatter the framework of journalism itself. He pledged to launch all of the paper's "editorial artillery" at the case in an effort "to bring the wall down."

"There were risks both ways," he later wrote. "One represented a risk to the community. The other was a risk to the *Press*. We chose the risk to ourselves." On July 20, the first round of Seltzer's artillery hit newsstands. The *Press* published a new editorial, this one even more dramatic and accusatory than either of the previous two, under the title "Somebody is Getting Away With Murder." Seltzer would later admit to writing this editorial himself, not wanting any of his writers to have to take the risk. Though the article didn't straight out say that Sam Sheppard was the "somebody" in question, it stated in no uncertain terms that the police were treating him far too kindly, and that it was holding up the entire investigation. "What's the matter with us in Cuyahoga County?" the editorial asked, maintaining the "we're-in-this-together" theme of Seltzer's beloved paper. "Who are we afraid of? Why do we have to kow-tow to a set of circumstances where a murder has been committed?"

"It may not have been a good editorial," Seltzer wrote in his memoirs, "but it was a hard-hitting editorial. It was intended to be." But the language it contained was less notable than where it was located—Seltzer had printed it across the front page of the paper, defying generations of journalistic standards, both past and future.

Like any effective artillery attack, that afternoon's *Press* rattled Cleveland to its core. The factory worker reading it at his kitchen table after a long, sweaty shift on a hot July day grunted in agreement: *Why was this slick doctor getting special treatment just because he was rich? I've been breaking my back all day to put food on the table for my kids. If I get in trouble, I face the consequences. Why doesn't this guy?*

The column was read up the chain of civic government. Cleveland's power brokers saw that, right or wrong, Louie had his wind up. And no one could predict where he would aim his next artillery blast. This may have started out as a problem for the Bay Village police, but now it had enveloped the entire county, covering Samuel Gerber and even with the minimal role it had played thus far, the Cleveland Police Department. Louis Seltzer was on a tear, and the shock waves this notion sent through the corridors of power in Cleveland set the wheels of progress into rapid motion.

That evening, at its regularly scheduled monthly meeting, the Bay Village City Council discussed and debated Resolution 54-124, which would instruct Mayor Spencer Houk to go to Cleveland Mayor Anthony Celebrezze to request that the Cleveland Police Department officially take over the investigation of Marilyn Sheppard's murder, with Bay Village agreeing to reimburse the additional costs the department would incur. Before the vote, Houk informed the council that the Bay Village police had done everything they could in this case, and—as opposed to what Louis Seltzer and the *Press* believed—had cooperated fully with every other law-enforcement department that had been part of the investigation thus far. The council approved the resolution by a six-to-one vote, and Celebrezze gladly accepted the challenge.

With the spotlight now shining on him and his subordinates, Cleveland Police Chief Frank Story rose to the occasion. He told the *Press* he "was convinced of the identity of the murderer" and there would be no more dilly-dallying. He would launch a round-the-clock effort to bring the killer to justice, starting with the appointment to the case of every available homicide detective. He notified Captain David Kerr, the head of the homicide department who had earned a national reputation for cracking tough cases, to cut short his family vacation to Cuba and return to Cleveland.

It was game time.

18 - STEAMED UP

This was Hank Greenberg's last chance. And he knew it.

As the second half of the 1954 season began, the Indians' general manager knew that the next three months would not only define his career but also potentially alter the course of his life. For all the good he'd done, for all the foresight he'd brought to the franchise in restructuring its farm system, another late-season collapse that resulted in another Yankee pennant would be catastrophic. The stakes were higher for Hank Greenberg than for any of the players or even Al Lopez. If the Indians couldn't capture the flag this time, the frenzy of a frustrated fan base would demand his removal as general manager, and the board of directors would have no choice but to comply. He also knew, despite the success the Indians had enjoyed under his leadership, that between his perceived aloof, almost pompous personality and the often-unspoken anti-Semitism that still clouded the sport, other job offers would not be forthcoming. Cleveland was his first—and last—chance to succeed as a general manager. And if the 1954 team couldn't bring home the pennant, Greenberg was finished. His entire legacy would hang in the balance each remaining day of what had become a sweltering summer.

On the afternoon following the All-Star Game, the temperature in Cleveland reached a blazing 99 degrees. Then, over the next two hours, a cold front swept through and dropped the temperature eleven degrees, which Clevelanders found not at all unusual. Still, there was no rain to provide even temporary relief.

As window air conditioners buzzed and residents flopped into lawn chairs and fanned themselves with newspapers, the Indians held a spirited workout at Municipal Stadium. From the attitude and energy they displayed, Al Lopez could see the debacle in Chicago just before the break would have no lingering effects on his club. As he'd predicted, the All-Star Game could not have come at a better time, and the squad's incredible showing in the contest seemed to have reignited the team's pilot light. The Indians began the second half of their season in Philadelphia, where Early Wynn pitched a three-hit shutout on Thursday and Bob Feller pitched a two-hit shutout on Saturday, bookending an almost effortless sweep of the staggering Athletics amidst the heat wave that had followed the Indians east. Weary from the sweltering conditions, the players would huddle between innings in the cool darkness of the tunnel connecting the dugout to the clubhouse before being forced to take the field again.

Despite success in Philadelphia, Cleveland's lead remained a meager half-game because the Yankees simply would not lose. Following a sweep of the Orioles after the break, New York's winning streak reached twelve and then stretched to thirteen after the first game of a doubleheader in Detroit on Sunday afternoon. Meanwhile, after the Indians dropped the first game of their double feature with the Senators in D.C., for the first time in seven weeks the Tribe tumbled out of first place. But New York's perch lasted less than three hours, as the Indians came back to win the nightcap while the Yankees lost, ending their long winning streak and dropping them a half-game back again.

The Cleveland express then steamed into Boston, where the Indians picked up a pair of victories to improve to 8–0 in Fenway Park in 1954. Meanwhile, in Chicago the Yankees swept a doubleheader over the White Sox and remained a half-game back. The Indians then rode the rails south into New York for a weekend series that would represent a battle for first place with the surging Yankees.

While the Indians felt confident, back in Cleveland, longtime followers of the team once again braced for the worst. "Why get steamed up about the Indians?" a cab driver ruminated to a *Look* magazine reporter dispatched to Cleveland to write a story about the Indians' fast start to the season. "They can never beat the Yankees in the big ones. Especially in New York. They'll blow it again down the stretch, Mister."

Friday's game matched Early Wynn against Ed Lopat, and Wynn wobbled in the early going as New York crept to a 2–0 lead in the fourth. The electric Yankee Stadium crowd of 61,000-plus began to taste the appetizer of a big weekend for the Bronx Bombers. But the tide began to turn in the sixth when Larry Doby blasted a solo homer off Lopat. Cleveland shortstop George Strickland tied the contest an inning later with a two-out RBI single, then Al Smith opened the floodgates with a three-run home run. Doby added another home run in the eighth and Smith knocked in another pair in the ninth as the Tribe delivered one of the most important victories of the season.

Yet the triumph was costly. Trying to advance on a bunt in the ninth inning, Strickland was drilled in the face with a thrown ball that cracked his jaw in two places, knocked out a denture, and caused severe bleeding and swelling inside his mouth, which would be temporarily wired shut with rubber bands. Strickland would be sidelined for the next three weeks.

The following afternoon, with journeyman Sam Dente filling in at short, the Indians surged to a 3–0 lead behind the steady pitching of Don Mossi, making a rare start in place of Bob Lemon, still bothered by a nagging rib injury. Mossi was masterful until the seventh, when a pair of walks sparked a New York rally to tie the contest. Sore but still effective, Lemon relieved Mossi and shut down the Yankees in the eighth and ninth to send the game to extra innings. Leading off the tenth, Lemon singled, then came home on a dramatic two-out home run into the right-field stands by Larry Doby—his third of the series and twentieth of the season. New York fought back in the tenth as Mickey Mantle doubled and scored on a single by Yogi Berra to make it 5–4. Ray Narleski came in and thwarted the rally to secure another huge victory for the Indians, pushing their lead up to two and a half games in what the *Press* called "a baseball drama of the celluloid variety."

Sunday afternoon's finale pitted Mike Garcia against Whitey Ford before 57,000 at Yankee Stadium, which had seen better than 150,000 fans pass through the turnstiles for the series. Garcia kept New York at bay, and when Vic Wertz came through with a two-out, two-run single in the sixth to break a 1–1 tie, the Indians were within reach of the seemingly impossible: a sweep of the Yankees in New York. But in the seventh, former Indian Eddie Robinson, a key component of the 1948 pennant drive, ripped a bases-loaded double to tie the game, and once again the two rivals delved into extra innings. New York prevented the sweep when third baseman Andy Carey rolled a single past Avila with the bases loaded in the eleventh. The Tribe's lead was back down to a game and a half, but they'd delivered another statement in the Bronx. The expectation for disaster heading into the series—reflected by the cab driver back in Cleveland—had once again been allayed.

When the players arrived back in Cleveland at ten that evening, they were greeted by 8,000 fans at Hopkins Airport, appreciative of what writers conjectured was the best eastern swing in franchise history. In an eleven-game trip, the Indians won nine, including a pair of huge decisions in New York, to hold on to first place. Now the team would return home and play twenty-two of its next twenty-five games at Municipal Stadium.

The strong showing prompted a glowing editorial in Monday's *Press*. "Even the most grudging of our New York journalistic contemporaries," it said, "must now be acknowledging they better take a new look at the Cleveland Indians."

It was the beginning of a busy week for the editorial staff of the *Press*. By Friday, it would put aside all other civic issues and debates and settle on one clear mission: sending Sam Sheppard to jail.

19-GET THAT KILLER

Louis Seltzer still wasn't happy.

Pleased that Bay Village officials and the Cleveland Police Department had quickly followed his instructions, he wanted to make sure the fire he'd lit wasn't snuffed out. And the only way to do that was to prod the unofficial patriarch of the investigation with Louis Seltzer's version of a big stick: bold type on the front page of the *Press*.

The headline of the July 21 edition was essentially a personal note from one of the most powerful men in Cleveland to another—one that would be read by the entire city:

"Why No Inquest? Do It Now, Dr. Gerber"

Again splashing an opinion piece just beneath the banner, Seltzer now focused his editorial crosshairs on Samuel Gerber. He began: "Why hasn't county coroner Sam Gerber called an inquest into the Sheppard murder case? What restrains him? Is the Sheppard murder case any different from the countless other murder mysteries where the coroner has turned to this traditional method of investigation?" Once again, the *Press* was subtly telling its readers that Sam Sheppard was receiving special treatment because of his financial and career status—and by deduction, that any regular Clevelander would have been treated differently.

"The murder of Marilyn Sheppard is a baffling crime," the editorial stated as it came in for a landing. "It may never be solved. But, this community can never have a clear conscience until every possible method is applied to its solution.

"What, Coroner Gerber, is the answer to the question—why don't you call an inquest into this murder?"

For the second straight day, Louis Seltzer's dramatic words rattled Cleveland, prompting astonished conversation over dinner tables and back fences. And also for the second straight day, Seltzer achieved exactly what he set out to do. That evening, dutifully following Seltzer's instruction, Samuel Gerber announced an inquest would commence the following morning in the gymnasium of Bay Village's Normandy Elementary School, two miles from the scene of the murder. Why such a large venue was selected rather than a conference room at the coroner's office was simply explained: much like the Indians preparing the stadium for the All-Star Game the week before, Gerber anticipated a big crowd. And, not surprisingly, he got one.

As Bay Village residents awoke on that sunny Thursday morning, they discovered their small lake town had become center stage. Though the inquest wasn't scheduled to begin until nine a.m., spectators began arriving at the school hours earlier. When reporters showed up, they discovered the parking lot was already filled and were forced to find parking along the narrow streets. Inside the bright auditorium that smelled of disinfectant and the stale air of a school in summer, dozens of folding chairs had been arranged in rows facing two tables angled to form a "V." The chairs were filled with breathless spectators, primarily housewives wearing sundresses and carefully designed hairstyles. This was no parent-teacher conference but rather a social occasion at which to be seen. The routine of everyday summer life was set aside. "Many a dish went unwashed and many dinners were late," the *Plain Dealer* noted. Several spectators dragged along their children, who were either sent outside to play in the schoolyard or wander through the hallways of the school while their mothers watched the proceedings. Some resourceful pre-teens brought stacks of comic books, which under other circumstances may have prompted another round of the civic debate over their effect on the minds of young people. But such topics could wait for another day. Today, there was a murder to solve, and Samuel Gerber meant to do just that.

As if serving as a cheerleader, the *Plain Dealer* that morning published an editorial under the rah-rah title "Get That Killer." Though the headline hinted that the opinion beneath would be as inflammatory and dramatic as those of Louis Seltzer and the *Press*, an eye-catching title was as close to its competition as it would get. As if unable to go through with a Seltzer-like attack, the editorial writers succinctly and professionally suggested that more action was needed and stopped short of accusations or assumptions. The *Cleveland News* followed suit with an even more thoughtful editorial titled "Time to Bring Bay Slaying Into Open." Needless to say, neither of these pieces garnered much attention.

The witnesses called to the inquest were required to testify, unless they chose to plead the Fifth Amendment. Further, Gerber made it clear there would be no meddling by William Corrigan or any other defense attorneys who attempted to intervene. After all, Gerber insisted, this was not a trial. Both Corrigan and William Petersilge were permitted to attend the inquest but solely as spectators. They could offer no counsel to any witness, ask no questions, nor object to any questions asked. For practical reasons, even if Corrigan wanted to object to anything, there was no one to object to. While this event had certainly taken on the stage dressing of a trial, there was no impartial official overseeing the proceedings. Though Gerber received some legal assistance from assistant county prosecutor Saul Danaceau, who sat beside him during the inquest, the illustrious coroner would serve as judge, prosecutor, and medical expert. It was a one-man show, and Samuel Gerber was the star.

Once the crowd had settled in and all the reporters and photographers were in place, the show began. The first witnesses were the Houks, who recounted their version of the story starting with Sam's frantic phone call. After a break for lunch, the Houks finished their testimony, along with Bay Village police officer Fred Drenkhan. At just past three p.m., Gerber called Sam Sheppard to testify.

Sam had been in a designated waiting room, lying flat on the floor to alleviate the nagging pain in his back with his neck brace resting

Like gunslingers in a shootout, Samuel Gerber (left)
and Sam Sheppard faced off in a tense,
verbal battle during the inquest.

on a chair. Crackling through the speaker of a small portable radio nearby, Jimmy Dudley's soothing voice temporarily lifted Sam out of this nightmare, taking him to Fenway Park, where Vic Wertz had just tomahawked a first-inning home run to give the Indians a 3–0 lead over the Red Sox. But Sam was soon forced to leave his comforting shelter when a knock on the door notified him that the time had come. He carefully lifted himself off the dark floor and replaced the neck brace. He also slipped on the large dark sunglasses to protect his wincing eyes from the bright light that still irritated him. He slowly shuffled down the corridor to the gymnasium and entered, as every head inside turned to see the face of the man they'd heard so much about.

He could feel their gaze creeping over every inch of him, judging him, trying to determine if in fact he had killed his wife. Though he was wearing a sleek black suit and was still the same handsome young doctor he'd been three weeks earlier, now he looked dramatically different. Between the neck brace, the sunglasses, and the stiff manner in which he moved, he no longer looked like the friendly caregiver his patients called "Dr. Sam." Now, as he made his way across the room to the makeshift witness stand, he looked inhuman, almost robotic. Adding to this perception, when he reached the front of the auditorium, Gerber motioned to a police officer, who approached Sam and gently ran his hands around his chest and over his pockets, searching for any weapons he might be carrying.

Sam propped himself uncomfortably in a folding chair behind the designated table, crossing his legs but still appearing stiff and awkward. Through the dark tint of the sunglasses, he saw the tall, slender form of Samuel Gerber sitting at the other table. Gerber sat patiently, staring at Sam Sheppard with the same polite, accommodating expression he wore during their first encounter in the small hospital room at Bay View. This time, however, as he began his questioning, Gerber's conviction of Sam's guilt was much stronger. And now he had an audience.

Once again, Sam described the events of that night, peppered by rapid follow-up questions from Gerber along the way. Spectators and reporters tried to count how many times the doctor answered "I don't know" or "I cannot say." Most lost count. It seemed that this was how he replied to every other question.

Sam showed his first indication of emotion when Gerber queried about what he did when he discovered his wife's body. "She was uncovered," Sam answered, "so I covered her up."

"Where was she uncovered?" Gerber asked.

Sam's lips pursed as he thought of Marilyn—her head pulverized and covered with blood, her pajama top wrinkled up past her breasts, and her pants pulled down past her knees. His eyes welled with tears. He removed the sunglasses and rubbed his eyes as he choked back a sob.

But Gerber still wanted an answer. "Where was the sheet?" he asked, rephrasing the same question.

Now Sam reached into his jacket pocket and pulled out a handkerchief. He blotted his cheeks and rubbed his nose before offering his all-too-familiar response: "I don't know." He provided the same answer when Gerber asked about the location of a light switch on the stairwell. "Do you mean you've been living in that home three years and don't know where that light switch is?" the coroner snorted.

It didn't take long for the festering tension between the two doctors to rise to the surface. As Sam described the moment of first discovering the figure looming over his wife, then getting hit from behind, Gerber chimed in, "You said you saw a form ahead of you, and now you want me to think someone followed you up the stairs?"

"Doctor, you're saying that," Sam replied coolly.

"I'm only trying to straighten you out," the coroner snapped back.

"But you are telling me."

Sam landed a subtle jab after Gerber asked what the intruder was wearing. "I tried to answer that for you a couple of times and you interrupted," he replied.

Gerber, stewing at what he took as Sam's arrogance and lack of respect, struck back moments later when asking about the pants Sam was wearing that morning.

"What color are they?" Gerber asked.

"I have two pairs," Sam responded, "a blue pair and a brown pair. The blue pair is all right, so they must be the brown ones."

"Were they new or old?"

"I bought them last summer."

"Were they in good condition?"

"Fairly good."

"Were they whole?"

Sam flinched slightly, not understanding. He asked, "What?"

"Were they whole?" Gerber repeated slowly, as if speaking to a child. Then, for good measure, he spelled out the word. "W-h-o-l-e." A few giggles escaped from the crowd.

"As far as I know," Sam replied, now visibly irritated.

His frustration mounted in another question about the whereabouts of Kokie after the Houks arrived. "Where was the dog at the time?" Gerber asked.

"I do not know," Sam answered once again.

As if he hadn't heard the reply, Gerber fired back, "Was the dog in the kitchen?"

Sam glared at the coroner and answered again, but this time louder and more forcefully, "I—don't—know."

For some reason, Gerber then began a line of questioning about Marilyn's funeral.

"Who was in charge of arrangements for the funeral?" he queried.

Once again, Sam replied, "I do not know." He paused for a moment, letting the question sink in, and then he asked one of his own. "Is that important at this time, Doctor?"

Gerber straightened behind his own table and said, "Anything is important, Dr. Sheppard."

The coroner then probed the theory that Sam had washed himself off in the lake. With no defense attorney to object and no judge to sustain, Gerber kept repeating the same question in different forms again and again despite receiving the same answer.

"Did you go in the lake after this event?" he asked.

"No," Sam replied.

"Did you wash yourself in the lake?"

"No."

"Did you wash your hair in the lake?"

"I didn't wash anything in the lake."

Two questions later, Gerber tried again.

"Did you wash yourself in the kitchen sink?"

"I washed myself at no time," Sam replied, by now clearly angered.

Then, incredibly, as if the subject had just come up, Gerber said,

"Did you wash yourself in the home or in the lake?"

"No."

Only after the same question was asked and answered five times was Gerber satisfied enough to move on.

Throughout Sam's testimony, which lasted the remainder of that afternoon and continued again Friday morning, a hush hung over the packed gymnasium. Only the occasional shuffle of shoes on the slick floor or the crying of a baby nestled in its mothers' arms broke the chilling silence. The yells and squeals of the children playing outside seemed miles away.

Eventually, Gerber turned to the topic of Susan Hayes, and the housewives sat up in their seats and leaned slightly forward, anticipating a plot twist they'd come to expect in one of the afternoon soap operas they listened to on the radio. Sam acknowledged becoming friends with Susan Hayes when she was a lab technician at Bay View. He also confirmed Gerber's queries about his California trip in March: he did meet Susan there and they did drive to San Diego for the wedding of a friend of Sam's. "I'd like to say at this time," Sam added parenthetically, "that we were good friends and my wife knew about it and suggested that I contact Susan."

The animosity between the coroner and the witness once again surfaced as Gerber asked about the notes Sam left requesting the lost watch be returned to him.

"What did they say?" Gerber asked.

"I can't say for sure," Sam replied.

"Well, you wrote it," Gerber snipped.

Sam sighed and answered, "I've written a lot of things in the past six months."

As Gerber continued railing away at Sam about Susan Hayes, Corrigan, as powerless as any of the housewives in the audience, couldn't suppress his compulsion to object. "Now be fair," he cautioned Gerber in a severe tone. Gerber shot back dismissively, "That's what I'm doing." Corrigan would later tell reporters that the entire proceeding was like a trial in communist China, with the audience serving as the self-appointed jury.

Soon Gerber got to the heart of the line of questioning. He got Sam to acknowledge that he and Susan Hayes had spent four nights in the house of a mutual friend in California. Now Gerber fired his final questions in rapid succession.

"Did you sleep in the same bedroom with Susan Hayes?"

"No," Sam replied flatly.

"At no time?"

"Absolutely not."

"Did you have any sexual relations with Miss Hayes at that time?"

"No."

"Not during any time in California?"

"Not at any time," Sam answered.

"You didn't sleep in the same bedroom?"

"No."

"Four nights in a row?"

"No."

Sam knew all six answers he gave were lies. With Corrigan's encouragement, Sam decided to protect Susan's reputation. And since he figured she had nothing to do with what had happened on July 4, the risk of publicly lying seemed marginal.

Little did he know that just as he was uttering those words, some very different information was being collected in Los Angeles. Detective Robert Schottke and assistant county prosecutor Thomas Parrino had been dispatched to California—accompanied, as it happened, by *Press* reporter James Vail. On Sunday, Schottke led a forceful interrogation of Susan Hayes, during which she varied from the tale she'd told the L.A. district attorney. "Suffice it to say that some of the things she told are not consistent with the testimony by Dr. Sheppard regarding their associations," Parrino would say.

But neither Gerber nor Sam knew this at 1:25 on Friday afternoon as Gerber completed his questioning. After nearly six hours of testimony, the doctor was excused. As he slowly marched out of the auditorium to try to return to as much normalcy as was possible, Sam had no idea he'd just ensnarled himself in a lethal web. The whole point of the inquest was for Gerber to try to catch Sam in a lie. And Sam had cooperated.

Though the star witness had left the stage, there was still some drama that afternoon. Before his testimony, Stephen Sheppard offered a plea to the audience for understanding and proper justice. "This could happen to you, and you could also be completely innocent," he said. "You could also be subjected to hours and hours of interrogation, and you also could be brought into a gymnasium and your family subjected to questioning." His words bounced off the high ceiling and cement walls of the large room, but didn't seem to land.

More tension arose when Gerber questioned Dorothy Sheppard, Stephen's wife. As she recounted a visit with Marilyn, she searched for the proper word to describe Marilyn's mood.

"She was disturbed . . . no, not disturbed . . ." she said, trailing off.

Sensing blood in the water, Gerber pounced. "Disturbed?" he repeated energetically.

"No," Dorothy quickly replied.

Gerber tried again. "Unhappy?"

"No," Dorothy shot back. Then, in an unmistakably sharp tone, she added, "I would appreciate it if you would let me choose my own word, Dr. Gerber."

When she was excused a few minutes later and left the witness table, she glared at Gerber, her eyes sharp and angry. As the crowd watched Dorothy, an otherwise minor character in this drama, step away, a stir worked its way through the room.

Shortly after, the proceedings closed for the weekend, to be continued on Monday. And when the inquest resumed, the fireworks continued as Sam Sheppard looked less and less believable. Nancy Ahern dropped two bombshells. In addition to revealing that Sam hadn't been excited about the news of the new baby, Mrs. Ahern testified that just after Sam and Marilyn returned from California that spring, Marilyn told her that she and Sam had considered seeking a divorce. This was a startling revelation that contradicted Sam's testimony that divorce had never been discussed. Even worse, Marilyn's father then told Gerber that he didn't want to see or speak to Sam "until the air is cleared." To the spellbound audience, Sam's father-in-law had just relayed his opinion that Sam, if not guilty, certainly wasn't innocent.

In between moments of tension, the crowd enjoyed some levity. Gerber made a not-so-subtle slip when questioning a Bay View doctor about Sam's injuries. "Was the examination of Sam Hayes . . ." he began, then paused. "Excuse me, I mean Dr. Sam Sheppard," he continued through the few chuckles that escaped from his audience. During another line of questioning, when audible laughter began trickling out of the crowd, Corrigan jumped up. He stormed over to the stenographer he'd hired and demanded that the record include mention of the laughter.

As he did, Saul Danaceau rose and addressed Corrigan across the room. "You are a spectator," he said, seeming to bite off each word. "You will keep quiet, or you will be removed."

Corrigan spun around to face Danaceau. He'd had enough. One of the most prestigious defense attorneys in Cleveland had been rendered utterly impotent for three days while his client's reputation was battered before him. "No, no," he shouted back, challenging Danaceau. "This is not an inquest room. This is a public meeting hall. This is a gymnasium."

Danaceau ignored him. "Don't you put anything into the record except what the coroner tells you," he warned.

"He is my stenographer," Corrigan countered.

Danaceau ignored him again. "You are only a spectator. You are not to participate in these proceedings."

"This is my stenographer!" Corrigan barked back. "I am taking the record."

"You may take the record as far as the coroner's record is concerned," Danaceau said, "but you are here merely as a spectator."

"It is my record, too, Mr. Danaceau."

"In your private record you can put whatever you want to."

Now it was Corrigan's turn to ignore Danaceau. "I will put in what I want to in the record."

"In your *private* record," Danaceau countered.

Like a father fed up with bickering children at the dinner table, Gerber rose and spoke directly to the stenographer. "You are directed to remove anything at all either now or previously that Mr. Corrigan has asked you or Mr. Petersilge has asked you to put in the record—by either one of them."

Naturally intimidated and stuck in the middle of a very public pissing match, the stenographer ceased his work. "Are you working for me or aren't you?" Corrigan barked, then turned back to Gerber. "Now listen to me a minute . . ." he began.

"There won't be any more discussion," Gerber interrupted.

"I want to ask a question!" Corrigan cried.

"There won't be any more discussion," Gerber repeated flatly.

"You're trying to cut me out," Corrigan snapped. "This is a public room here. You are here in a public building."

Danaceau interjected. "You are here as a spectator, and if you can't keep quiet . . ."

"No—I am not a spectator!" Corrigan shouted. "I am more than a spectator."

"If there is any more difficulty," Gerber proclaimed loudly, his words echoing through the room, "I will ask the officers to put you out."

Corrigan was nearly blind with rage. "No!" he snarled. "You won't put me out!" He swiveled back to the stenographer and continued to give instructions.

Gerber raised a slim, bony finger to Carl Rossbach and growled two words: "Remove him."

Rossbach moved swiftly over to Corrigan and clamped his large hands around the wiry lawyer, who continued to protest. A member of the audience began to clap, another joined in, and soon the entire crowd was applauding and cheering as they watched Corrigan be physically dragged out of the gymnasium. Enraged by what was happening, Corrigan screamed to the people who so visibly approved of his ejection that their own constitutional rights were being infringed by what was happening here. When he and Rossbach reached the corridor, he turned and shouted back into the auditorium, "This is a disgraceful exhibition by American women!" He waved his hand at the crowd jeering him and cried, "These people are all hostile!" As the doors closed in Corrigan's face, the applause rose to a crescendo. By all appearances, the greatest obstacle to justice in the murder of Marilyn Sheppard had just been physically removed.

"These people are supposed to be Americans!" a raging Corrigan shouted to no one in particular in the hallway. "Haven't they heard of the Bill of Rights?" He stormed up and down the hall like a caged tiger. "Someday some of these people or their children may be in a situation where they might want to know the Bill of Rights."

Back inside a few minutes later, satisfied that his work was done, Gerber adjourned the inquest. Seventeen witnesses had testified, but in the final analysis, only one mattered. Whatever other information could be gleaned from the three-day showcase, Gerber had trapped Sam Sheppard in a lie. And, as any American of 1954 knew, anyone who lied was also capable of murder.

As he left the gymnasium, Gerber was swarmed by the adoring crowd. Many women patted him on the back, embraced him, and even planted kisses on his cheeks.

Finally, this horrible story had a hero.

20-LIKE A HOLLYWOOD MOVIE

This was Bob Feller's last chance. And he knew it.

He'd been baseball's greatest, most celebrated pitcher for nearly two decades—maybe its best ever. He'd dominated the game with style and class and made his name familiar in households across the country, making history almost every season. Yet for all the records and statistical domination, all the games he'd won and all the strikeouts he'd collected, there was one thing Bob Feller had never done. It was a void in his career that haunted him, and he was determined to fill it.

He had never won a World Series game.

For as good as he'd been for as long as he'd played, only once had he been part of a pennant-winning team. And while the Indians won the 1948 World Series in six games, Feller had not delivered any of the quartet of victories. Ironically, Feller was the loser in the only games the Indians dropped—first when he lost a 1–0 pitchers' duel to Johnny Sain in the opener, and then when he was battered for seven runs in Game Five, denying the Indians a chance to win the title in front of their home crowd.

To truly be considered the greatest pitcher of all time, Feller knew he needed to showcase his talent on the grand stage of a World Series. He longed to return to the Fall Classic, to get just one more shot at slaying this proverbial dragon. He'd been close enough to taste it the previous four years, only to be denied on the final turn by the Indians' pinstriped nemeses. Now, with Cleveland once again clinging to a narrow lead atop the standings going into August, Feller, in his sixteenth season with the Indians, knew it was now or never. Either this team would finally get over the hump and land Rapid Robert in the World Series once again, or his career would come to a graceful, yet quiet, conclusion sprinkled with the indignity of never having the opportunity to right an old wrong.

He certainly was doing everything in his power to get back to the Series. As the Indians returned from their road trip to begin the final two months of the campaign, Feller stood at 8–1 with a 2.99 ERA, a remarkable turnaround after a wobbly start to the season. After his first three starts of the year, he looked finished. His ERA had ballooned over 12, giving credence to the rumors swirling through town that Al Lopez had actually wanted to release Feller during spring training. Hank Greenberg, fearing a public outcry a general manager on the hot seat could hardly afford, intervened and talked Lopez out of it. In late May, Feller began to turn it around, and Lopez grudgingly made Feller a regular starter. Yet he never completely trusted him, thinking Feller's success was a mirage, that his legendary fastball was what had made him great and without it he couldn't be trusted to win a big game. "It almost seemed that he couldn't wait to take me out if I gave up a couple of hits," Feller wrote in his autobiography. "He'd almost beat the ball back to the mound." Yet even with Lopez's propensity for a quick hook, as 1954 unfolded, Feller thrived.

"One of the more fascinating facts in American League affairs this year," Shirley Povich wrote in the *Washington Post*, "is the resurgence of the Old Man of the Cleveland Indians, Bob Feller, as a winning pitcher. At thirty-five, when most pitchers have had it, Feller is writing a comeback story that has few parallels." Yet for all the satisfaction delivered by his summer resurgence, the only satisfying conclusion to Feller's comeback tale would come in October.

As Feller and the Indians basked in the glow of adoration showered upon them by their fans at the airport on the Sunday night they returned from their triumphant road trip that wrapped up in New York, another group of stars came out at Municipal Stadium.

In a combined concert fittingly called "Star Night," the greatest array of singers ever assembled in Cleveland took a makeshift stage constructed on the Indians' stomping ground. Perry Como, Patti Page, and Nat King Cole highlighted the docket, which drew 14,000 to the ballpark for a four-hour concert on a sweltering summer night. Yet concert organizers were disappointed with the turnout, particularly since nearly 75,000 had attended the concert when it stopped in Chicago a few weeks before. Part of the reason for the modest turnout was because it was inadvertently competing with another civic celebration that night. The real "Star Night" was taking place at Hopkins Airport, where thousands of fans were welcoming the Indians home after their incredible eastern swing. Apparently, Perry Como and Nat King Cole were no match for Al Rosen and Larry Doby.

With a day off Monday, the Indians could bask in the glow of their rousing road trip and look ahead to what promised to be a gracious August schedule. Aside from one home series with the Yankees, the remainder of the month would see the Tribe taking on the American League's second division. Al Lopez felt his club was in such an enviable position that he no longer saw a reason to shuffle his pitching rotation when New York did come calling. The Big Three would pitch when they were scheduled to pitch, period. "We'll take the games as they come and try to win them," he said sincerely, though with great relish. He thought back to the phone call he'd received in the Hotel Kenmore in Boston on that rainy afternoon in April when Red Patterson informed him that Casey Stengel had no plans to adjust his pitching rotation to face the Indians. The roles of the previous five seasons had reversed. It would be the first time the Yankees went into August outside of first place in four years—and the first time the Indians entered the month in first in more than three decades. For the first time in a generation, the Indians were perched in the catbird seat heading into August. "We will regard the Yankees as just another club," Lopez concluded, beaming on the inside.

Cleveland's sorcery over Boston continued as the Indians took two of three from the Red Sox while the Yankees kept pace in Chicago. With the scuffling Senators coming to town for a four-game series and the Yankees heading to Fenway Park for a weekend set with their bitter rival Boston, the Indians saw the final weekend of July as a prime opportunity to cushion their lead.

Ironically, by mid-week the Cleveland Police Department had the same mentality. With the three-ring inquest now complete, Chief Frank Story was as confident as he'd been in weeks. "The case looks more encouraging than at any time since we took it over," he said. Part of the reason for his swagger was the return of Captain David Kerr from his Cuban vacation. His credentials as a top-notch detective were impressive, but the look Kerr brought to the case was even better. With a seasoned, leathery face, short dark hair, and thick eyebrows, Kerr embodied the public's image of a homicide detective—the kind of experienced, savvy gumshoe seen in movies. And Kerr hit the ground running. Before immersing himself in the investigation, he announced his opinion that Sam Sheppard should have been arrested long ago. "If there had been an immediate arrest," he explained, "the case would have been solved in four hours." Then, taking a cue from Louis Seltzer, Kerr stated his distaste for the favoritism that Sam Sheppard had doubtlessly been receiving: "In homicide investigations, I treat doctors and lawyers and everyone else just alike." With trumpets blaring, the cavalry had arrived.

But even more promising than Kerr's arrival were the reports coming from Robert Schottke in Los Angeles. As the inquest wrapped up in the Normandy gymnasium, a continent away, Schottke broke the case wide open.

After hours spent questioning every pertinent character from Sam's March vacation, Schottke and Thomas Parrino confronted Susan Hayes with a trick up their sleeves. Aware that Susan had already denied any extra-marital affiliation with Sam to the L.A. district attorney, Schottke had heard too much from too many people to believe that Sam and Susan hadn't been involved. So he decided to play a hunch. Schottke told Susan Hayes that back in Cleveland, Sam Sheppard had already told them everything about their affair and they knew she'd lied to the district attorney. The best way to get out of this mess, Schottke explained, was to tell them everything.

And Susan, having no idea that Sam had just testified repeatedly and emphatically that he had never had a relationship with her, took the bait. Yes, she explained, not only had she and Sam had an affair when they worked together at Bay View, but they had rekindled it during his trip to California four months before. Though he often showered her with gifts and the two hadn't been all that inconspicuous—some Bay View employees believed that Sam and Susan had used unoccupied examination rooms for their sexual escapades—she had never expected Sam to leave Marilyn for her.

With that, the investigation had taken its final, fateful turn. Susan Hayes would be brought to Cleveland for further questioning, but before her arrival, her confession was relayed by James Vail, the only reporter to accompany Schottke and Parrino out west, back to the *Press*. "I've told the truth," Susan told him, admitting she regretted lying to the district attorney but only did so because she figured her relationship with Sam had nothing to do with what happened on July 4. And ultimately, she didn't want to get involved. "I never realized how good it is to get something like that off your chest," she added.

This news was music to Louis Seltzer's ears. His headline in Tuesday's edition skipped over Susan Hayes's game-changing story and cut directly to the quick: "Doctor's Indictment Near in Murder of His Wife." The subsequent article detailed Susan Hayes's new tale and informed readers that she was already in the air on her way across the country.

During a brief layover in Chicago, she was swarmed by eager reporters barking questions. "I am coming back to tell all I know," she said succinctly as more questions were shouted. One reporter asked her about the four days she stayed in the same house with Sam, and for the first time, Susan pulled away from the attention. "Now, that's asking too much," she said, and would answer no more questions. Shortly afterward, she boarded her flight to Cleveland. For anyone wishing to meet her at the airport, the *Press* included her flight number and arrival time of 6:50 p.m. The *Plain Dealer*, already scooped by the *Press* and trying to keep up, took credit for having found Susan Hayes in California and bringing her into the investigation. "I can't see why the police think I'm so important in this case," she said at one point. "But I will do what they want."

Meanwhile, Schottke and Parrino tried to deflect any potential interest from their about-to-be-famous passenger. She was registered on American Airlines Flight 40 to Chicago under the name "Susan Hamilton" and Schottke remained by her side through the entire trip. As she boarded the plane under an obvious umbrella of protection, she caught the interest of other passengers, who wondered who she was. Some even asked their flight attendants, who approached Schottke and inquired which movie star they were accompanying.

Susan Hayes appreciated the attention she was receiving. "If this wasn't such a serious matter," she said with a girlish smile, "it would be more like a Hollywood movie than anything happening in real life."

She arrived in Cleveland on Tuesday evening, and like the Indians two weeks earlier, she was met by a large crowd as she came down the stairs from the airplane to the tarmac. Before the masses could get a good look, a police car slid up to the ramp. She stepped in and was whisked away to the Cleveland central police station downtown, where she was questioned for three hours. Outside the station, a crowd began to gather, hoping to get a peek at the femme fatale of the Sheppard case.

Meanwhile, as Susan Hayes was questioned long into the night, the Bay Village police responded to yet another call of a suspected burglar in a home. This one turned out to be nothing more than a defective light bulb that cast peculiar shadows through the window, yet it was the continuation of a disturbing trend stemming from the Sheppard circus. For the previous two weeks, the department had received an average of six calls a night reporting suspected prowlers. The citizens of Bay Village were jittery and terrified that Marilyn Sheppard's killer may attack again.

Assuming, of course, Sam Sheppard actually didn't do it.

21 - BRING HIM IN

D espite the dramatic change in the tone of the investigation over the previous week, Louis Seltzer still wasn't happy.

True, the Cleveland police had taken over the investigation and Samuel Gerber had conducted a no-holds-barred inquest—both at his behest. Better still, the *Press*'s circulation soared. As the inquest unfolded, copies flew off of newsstands, further cementing its reputation as the most popular paper in the state.

Yet for Louis Seltzer, there was still one large loose end left untied. In his mind, a guilty man was still free. On Tuesday afternoon, in the first edition printed since the conclusion of the inquest, like a kidnapper discussing ransom, Seltzer made his latest demand. The third round of his editorial artillery was titled: "Why Don't Police Quiz No. 1 Suspect?" The title alone suggested Seltzer was unfamiliar with the details of the investigation, principally that Sam Sheppard had now indeed been "quizzed" in one fashion or another for a total of thirty-seven hours.

"You can bet your last dollar the Sheppard murder would be cleaned up long ago if it had involved 'average people,'" the editorial began. "They'd have hauled in all the suspects to police headquarters. They'd have grilled them in the accepted, straight-out way of doing police business. They wouldn't have waited so much as one hour to bring the chief suspect in. Much less days. Much less weeks.

"Why all this fancy, high-level bowing and scraping, and super-cautious monkey business? Sure, it happened in suburban Bay Village rather than in an 'ordinary' neighborhood. So what? What difference should that make?

"When they called the Cleveland police in, everybody thought: 'This is it. Now they'll get someplace. Now we'd have vigorous, experienced, expert, big-time action. They'd get it solved in a hurry. They'd have Sam Sheppard brought in, grill him at police headquarters, like the chief suspect in any case.'

"But they didn't. And they haven't.

"In fairness, they've made some progress. But they haven't called in Sam Sheppard. Now proved under oath to be a liar and still free to go about his business, shielded by his family, protected by a smart lawyer who has made monkeys of the police and authorities, carrying a gun part of the time, left free to do whatever he pleases, Sam Sheppard still hasn't been taken to headquarters.

"What's wrong in this whole mess that is making this community a national laughing stock? Who's holding back—and why? What's the basic difference between murder in an 'ordinary' neighborhood and one in a Lake Road house in suburban Bay Village? Who is afraid of whom?

"It's just about time that somebody began producing the answers—and producing Sam Sheppard at police headquarters!"

Seltzer had now awakened the inner pride of each citizen of Cleveland. No one should be permitted to make their great city into a laughing stock, certainly not a privileged doctor—an osteopath no less—in uppity Bay Village. The words inflamed the passion of the countless "average people" who read the *Press* and trusted Louis Seltzer to be their guardian as they went about their everyday lives. Now the watchdog was snarling, further fueled by an editorial cartoon that ran the following day. It depicted a set of hands labeled as "officials" and "police" restrained by a pair of handcuffs and straining to reach a figure hidden behind a blanket—though the top of his head peeked out and just happened to match Sam Sheppard's receding widow's peak—held by a collection of well-dressed men labeled as "lawyers" and "friends." The caption of the cartoon read "Handcuffs on the Wrong People?"

Seltzer's questions echoed through Greater Cleveland, and as always, generated action.

On Wednesday afternoon, while Susan Hayes spent the day secluded in a downtown hotel, the key figures of the investigation—Spencer Houk and John Eaton from Bay Village, David Kerr from Cleveland homicide, and Thomas Parrino from the county prosecutor's office—met with Chief Frank Story in his office for a tense three-hour conference. Yet once again, the result was simply that the group found out they were nowhere. "We don't have the evidence now to make an arrest," a frustrated Story announced. "If I thought we had the evidence, he would be in the 'can' now." Yet Story added that even if they had Sam in custody, they wouldn't get any answers. "I don't think you will shake that guy down in twenty-four minutes or in twenty-four hours," he said.

Then Story made a surprisingly candid comment that would echo through the corridors of history. "Our feeling is that Sam Sheppard killed his wife, even though we can't prove it," he said. "If we had a single shred of solid evidence against him, I'd send the janitor out to make the arrest."

Such a comment from a police chief was essentially like adding the words "The End" at the conclusion of a paragraph. That was, putting it in baseball terms, the whole ballgame.

But not when the story was being written by Louis Seltzer, who had one final, devastating round to fire from his editorial artillery.

The nitty-gritty details of the investigation were insignificant.

". . . we can't prove it."

Nearly two centuries establishing the greatest legal system in world history were unimportant.

"We don't have the evidence. . . "

The reputation of Cleveland was at stake. The pride Clevelanders took in living in the Best Location in the Nation hung in the balance. Citizens in one of the greatest cities in the world couldn't live in fear that it couldn't effectively govern itself, couldn't scrub out an obvious stain. "I was convinced," Seltzer wrote in his autobiography, "that a conspiracy existed to defeat the ends of justice. And that it would affect adversely the whole law-enforcement machinery of the county if it were permitted to succeed. It would establish a precedent that would destroy even-handed administration of justice."

Seltzer began his fourth front-page editorial in two weeks just as he'd started the previous one—as a question. The original headline, which was published in the early editions, read "Why Isn't Sam Sheppard in Jail?" But at some point that Friday afternoon, Louis Seltzer decided he was finished making polite inquiries. He was no longer submitting requests. He was making a very specific demand.

The change was made soon enough that most readers never saw the original headline. The one that appeared on most of the thousands of copies that were sold that afternoon was the one that would be remembered: *Quit Stalling—Bring Him In.* Beneath these words was a grainy photograph of Dr. Sam in his insectile sunglasses and animal-like collar.

The 511 words that followed accomplished precisely what Louis Seltzer intended. Of course, as he sat in the newsroom, proudly examining the edition like a father leafing through a photo album on his son's graduation day, he had no idea that his words would also alter the course of legal history.

"Maybe somebody in this town can remember a parallel for it," it began. "The *Press* can't. And not even the oldest police veterans can, either.

"Everybody's agreed that Sam Sheppard is the most unusual murder suspect ever seen around these parts. Except for some superficial questioning during coroner Sam Gerber's inquest, he has been scot-free of any official grilling into the circumstances of his wife's murder.

"From the morning of July 4, when he reported his wife's killing, to this moment, twenty-six days later, Sam Sheppard has not set foot in a police station. He has been surrounded by an iron curtain of protection that makes Malenkov's Russian concealment amateurish. His family, his Bay Village friends—which include its officials—his lawyers, his hospital staff, have combined to make law enforcement in this county look silly.

"The longer they can string this whole affair out, the surer it is that the public's attention sooner or later will be diverted to something else, and then the heat will be off, the public interest gone, and the goose will hang high.

"This man is a suspect in his wife's murder. Nobody yet has found a solitary trace of the presence of anybody else in his Lake Road house the night or morning his wife was brutally beaten to death in her bedroom. And yet no murder suspect in the history of this county has been treated so tenderly, with such infinite solicitude for his emotions, with such fear of upsetting the young man.

"Gentlemen of Bay Village, Cuyahoga County, and Cleveland, charged jointly with law enforcement—"

The type now switched to all capital letters, as if Seltzer were yelling at the entire city.

"THIS IS MURDER. THIS IS NO PARLOR GAME. THIS IS NO TIME TO PERMIT ANYBODY-NO MATTER WHO HE IS-TO OUTWIT, STALL, FAKE, OR IMPROVISE DEVICES TO KEEP AWAY FROM THE POLICE OR FROM THE QUESTIONING ANYBODY IN HIS RIGHT MIND KNOWS A MURDER SUSPECT SHOULD BE SUBJECTED TO AT A POLICE STATION.

"The officials throw up their hands in horror at the thought of bringing Sam Sheppard to a police station for grilling. Why? Why is he any different than anybody else in any other murder case? Why should the police officials be afraid of Bill Corrigan or anybody else, for that matter, when they are at their sworn business of solving a murder?

"Certainly Corrigan will act to protect Sam Sheppard's rights. He should."

Again, Seltzer pressed the caps lock key on his typewriter and raised his voice.

"BUT THE PEOPLE OF CUYAHOGA COUNTY EXPECT YOU, THE LAW ENFORCEMENT OFFICIALS, TO PROTECT THE PEOPLE'S RIGHTS.

"A murder has been committed. You know who the chief suspect is.

"You have the obligation to question him—question him thoroughly and searchingly—from beginning to end, and not at his hospital, not at his home, not in some secluded spot out in the country. But at police headquarters—just as you do every other person suspected in a murder case.

"What the people of Cuyahoga County cannot understand, and the *Press* cannot understand, is why you are showing Sam Sheppard so much more consideration as a murder suspect than any other person who has ever been suspected in a murder case.

"Why?"

Seltzer knew he was sticking his neck out, and he anticipated the *Press* would receive some criticism. Yet he never wavered in his commitment to publish such a dramatically worded article. When he looked back upon this column years later, Seltzer admitted he "would do the same thing over again under the same circumstances."

By sticking his neck out, Louis Seltzer was challenging—perhaps even commanding—others to do the same. And as they'd done throughout the past four weeks, the cast of characters in this drawn-out drama followed suit.

Now that the big boys from Cleveland were in charge, it would be counterproductive to offer blanket criticism of the investigation. It had been more than a week since the Cleveland police had ridden to the rescue and, to Louis Seltzer at least, no tangible results had been seen. So Anthony Celebrezze tried a different approach.

After an impromptu meeting with Story and Kerr, the mayor came out with both barrels blazing. "We're getting impatient about all the dilly-dallying in this case," he said in a comment that should have been construed as a criticism of his own police force, which had enjoyed carte blanche over the entire investigation for more than a week. But Celebrezze went on to amplify his statement and take the Cleveland police off the hook.

The reason his police department hadn't made any headway in its investigation, he explained, was that Bay Village authorities were standing in the way, having drawn "a protective cloth" around Sam Sheppard. "We feel that we have not received the fullest cooperation from Eaton and Houk," Celebrezze said succinctly. "We have furnished them all our information. They seem to be withholding some of theirs." Further, Celebrezze announced that if Bay Village refused the "advice" of the Cleveland homicide squad and unless Houk "shows more aggressiveness," then Celebrezze would rescind his police force's agreement to conduct the investigation and it would be dumped back in Bay Village's lap.

In a month of outrageous declarations, Celebrezze's took the prize. As publicly proclaimed at its last city council meeting, Bay Village had cooperated fully during the entire episode. From day one, Spencer Houk and John Eaton recognized that their modest, inexperienced police force couldn't properly handle an incident of this magnitude and requested assistance. Along the way, there had been miscommunication and ego-driven horn-clashing. But for Celebrezze to blame Bay Village for the Cleveland police's inability to find any evidence that would lead to the arrest of a suspect was both stunning and incredibly unfair, particularly since few readers of the *Press* were able to understand the context of the situation. They had been told for weeks that everybody in Bay Village—from the mayor and his neighbors to the staff of Bay View Hospital and its fledging police department—had been hiding Sam Sheppard behind a curtain and thwarting Samuel Gerber's and

Louis Seltzer's attempts to shine the light of justice into their well-to-do lakeside hamlet.

Louis Seltzer wanted action, and Celebrezze, who never would have been elected without Seltzer's support eight months before, took it. Now that the mayor of Cleveland had made demands, everyone expected them to be met.

Yet there was a twist.

While the Cleveland police were calling the shots of the investigation, they did not have the legal authority to make any arrests. That power still rested with the city of Bay Village—specifically, with its mayor.

That Friday afternoon, the eyes of northeast Ohio settled on Sam Sheppard's neighbor, the man who had been the first to learn about Marilyn Sheppard's death and the first to arrive at the scene of the murder at dawn on Independence Day.

Spencer Houk had an impossible choice to make: authorize the arrest of his good friend based on nothing but circumstantial evidence and speculation or become the next target of a devastating artillery barrage launched by the holy trinity of Cleveland's political power: Celebrezze, Gerber, and Seltzer.

Houk spent the afternoon agonizing over the decision he had to make. He stayed in his house—three down from the still-vacant Sheppard home—for the entire day. In the end, he realized he had no choice. Considering the vehemence with which Cleveland's power elite had ambushed him, Houk knew that even if he tried to bring reason to bear, one way or another, Sam Sheppard was going to jail. And if he tried to swim upstream against the tidal wave coming his way, he would be utterly destroyed in the process. So he did the only thing he could do.

Citing his personal connection to the case, Spencer Houk recused himself as mayor of Bay Village and yielded all his decision-making power on this matter to city council president Gershom M.M. Barber. As dinner tables were cleared around Cleveland that Friday evening, Barber signed the warrant for Sam Sheppard's arrest.

Meanwhile, Clevelanders enjoyed a beautiful summer Friday night. At 8:30, just as the sun began to set and long shadows were cast across backyards and street corners, radios were flipped on to WERE as the Indians took the field to face the Washington Senators. There was already good news with the word that the Yankees were in the process of being stomped 10–0 in Baltimore, giving the Indians a chance to extend their lead to two and a half games. But they started slowly when Art Houtteman gave up three runs in the first inning. His offense came to his rescue, plating five runs in the bottom of the inning, but Houtteman struggled again in the third, surrendering a leadoff single and then delivering a wild pitch. The tying run came to the plate in the form of Washington right fielder Tom Umphlett, who delivered by crushing a Houtteman pitch toward left center. From just the crisp crack of the bat, Umphlett knew he had at least a double and an RBI, but as the ball continued to rise on its journey through the outfield, everyone in the ballpark concluded that he'd just tied the game.

Perhaps the only person who didn't believe this was Larry Doby. As soon as the ball left Umphlett's bat, Doby read the trajectory of its flight path and launched himself like a rocket from his starting position in shallow center toward the five-foot fence in left-center field. He thought he could catch it.

He glided across the grass, focused entirely on the baseball. The members of the Senators bullpen, which was stationed beneath an awning just behind the fence, rose to their feet as they saw the ball coming directly toward them. Then, in a flash, Larry Doby appeared and launched himself into the air. Instinctively, he planted his left foot into the chain-link fence and propelled himself even higher, guiding himself upward by clasping his right hand around the top of the fence.

A groundskeeper who had been standing just behind the fence watched in awe. He literally could not believe what he was seeing: Doby's shoes were two feet above the five-foot fence, and his head was two feet behind it. With his left arm stretched out to its fullest length, he opened his glove just wide enough to allow the baseball to slap into its webbing.

As it did, Doby bounced atop the canopy covering the bullpen (which, witnesses later revealed, Doby's right hand had ripped through on contact) and, like a rubber ball thrown against a front stoop, caromed back onto the field and crashed onto the grass at the base of the fence. He lay flat on his stomach, completely motionless. As Al Smith neared his fallen teammate on his long run from left field, he was sure Doby had broken his back.

Then Doby raised his left arm, hoisting his glove with the ball nestled inside it. Umpire John Flaherty raised his right hand emphatically and folded it into a fist. Tom Umphlett was out.

It was the greatest catch anyone had ever seen—Al Lopez and Washington manager Bucky Harris, who'd both witnessed thousands of games, agreed that they'd never seen better. Hall of Fame pitcher Dizzy Dean, in town to broadcast Saturday's game on national television, knew that they'd witnessed something amazing. "I've seen them all," he said. "Moore, DiMaggio, and this here fellow named Mays, but I never seen a catch as good as this one." After the game, when the reporters and most of their teammates had cleared out, Houtteman would approach Doby. "I wanted to talk to you alone," he said quietly. "I wanted to thank you for that catch. As long as I live I'll never forget the greatness of that play."

Neither would any in the modest crowd of 17,000 who witnessed it. As the fans slowly began to understand what they'd just seen, an alert Smith dug the ball out of Doby's raised glove and fired it back to the infield to prevent the runner from tagging up. As the disbelieving crowd began to applaud, Doby rolled onto his back with his legs splayed out. For all intents and purposes, it looked as if a corpse was laying in left-center field.

After making one of the greatest catches in Indians history, Larry Doby remained motionless in the outfield grass for several tense moments.

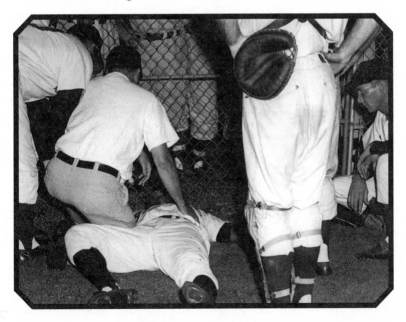

The applause softened into silence as an entourage of Indians motored to Doby's side. Wincing at the sharp pain in his shoulder, Doby sat up and was helped to his feet. He rotated his arm in a circular motion to loosen it up and walked around to get his bearings. As he started back to the dugout, the cheers began again, tumbling into a standing ovation as he crossed the outfield. As he neared the infield, he met Lopez, who asked Doby how he felt. The outfielder admitted he wasn't too bad and that the pain was beginning to subside. Lopez nodded and left it up to Doby. With the roar of the crowd continuing to grow, Doby slapped his cap back atop his head, slid his glove back onto his hand, and turned to run back to center field. He would stay in the game. The applause began again. The fans may not have particularly liked Larry Doby, but they recognized an astonishing play when they saw one. Their cheers swelled to a standing ovation after Houtteman retired the next batter and Doby jogged back to the dugout. In this rare moment, Larry Doby was both appreciated and adored—his perceived moodiness and sullen personality rinsed away by his remarkable talent.

As the triumphant Doby rejoined his teammates on the bench, thirteen miles away, an ordinary blue Ford sedan coasted through the streets of Bay Village. Inside sat three young men wearing civilian clothes, each with a solemn look on his face. The Ford, passing a line of other cars parked like jackstraws along the road, turned slowly into the narrow driveway of a spacious white colonial home on a bluff overlooking Lake Erie and puttered toward the front door. The three men got out slowly and marched up the steps of the spacious front porch. In the lead was Fred Drenkhan, now assigned with one of the most difficult tasks of his career.

He reached the front door and rang the bell. The door opened a crack and the wary face of a man who had encountered more than his share of unwelcome visitors peeked out. The weary eyes of Richard Sheppard Sr. scanned the three men. In that instant, he knew what they were here for.

"Is Sam here?" Drenkhan asked, polite yet determined.

"Yes," the elder Sheppard replied, his voice soft and thick.

"We'd like to see him," Drenkhan said.

Sam's father nodded and, as if in defeat, slowly pulled the door open. "Come on in," he said in a tone that did not at all match his hospitable words.

It had already been a disastrous evening for Sam. Less than an hour before, he had been at his brother Stephen's house, which was surrounded by four cars outside, each containing reporters. He had planned to enjoy a relaxing boat ride with his brother and sister-in-law Betty that evening, but they were wary to go anywhere lest they be harassed by the reporters following him. Earlier, Stephen had even gone out to ask the reporters to leave. "You're wasting your time," he told them. "There won't be any arrest tonight." The plea did no good. So Stephen returned inside and began crafting a plan.

The reporters were sparked into action when the garage door opened and Stephen's station wagon swiftly backed out and motored down the driveway. Visible inside were Stephen, Betty, and Sam. As the bystanders roared their own car engines, the station wagon's wheels squealed across the pavement, and it sped off into the night. The four cars roared after it.

The station wagon tore east through the dark avenues of Bay Village, veering wildly onto side streets and making sudden u-turns in an attempt to lose its pursuers. It would slow as it neared a traffic light and then speed up to clear the intersection just before the light turned red. But the reporters, sensing the biggest story of their careers about to break wide open, stayed close. After a few more wayward turns, the station wagon shook three of the cars at a railroad underpass on West Lake Road. But one, which contained a determined *Plain Dealer* reporter, continued the pursuit.

Finally, the station wagon coasted into the parking lot at the Cleveland Yacht Club, where the Rocky River spilled into Lake Erie. The three Sheppards quickly jumped out and headed for Stephen's boat for the nighttime ride and picnic they'd planned. But before they could get on board, the final reporter squealed his car to a stop and began snapping pictures of Sam.

As they reached the boat and climbed aboard, Sam shook his head in disgust. He'd had enough. He couldn't possibly enjoy a relaxing boat ride under these conditions, even if it served as a temporary respite from the media stakeout. And he knew that they would have to once again run the blockade to get home.

Defeated, Sam returned to the station wagon with Betty. Stephen remained on the boat and waited for Betty to return after she dropped Sam off. The final reporter got back in his car to follow as the station wagon pulled out again, this time with Betty at the wheel and Sam ducked down beneath the dashboard. There was no high-speed chase back to Bay Village. Betty simply maneuvered the station wagon to her in-laws house, knowing there was no sense in trying to shake their irritating follower. A few minutes later, she dropped Sam off at his parents' house and returned to the Yacht Club. Within minutes, news of Sam's new location spread through the grapevine, and reporters

Sam ducks down in his sister-in-law Betty's car
as he retreats from reporters who had pursued him
on a high-speed chase through Bay Village.
He would be arrested later that night.

began emerging out of the darkness like the crickets that sang in the trees on this summer night, silently stalking their target.

Most had stepped out of their cars and were approaching the house as Drenkhan and the two other officers entered the front door. There Drenkhan saw his friend and colleague, a man who'd he'd come to respect highly over the years they'd worked side by side at the sites of accidents. The reason for this visit felt absurd to Drenkhan, particularly since the man he'd come to see had helped Drenkhan bring reason and order to disastrous situations.

"Sam," he said solemnly, the words seeming to come from outside of him, "I have a warrant for your arrest."

As if trying to convince himself that he truly did, Drenkhan held it out. And Sam, who, like his father, wasn't surprised by this visit, reached up and took it from him. Wearing summer pants and a white t-shirt—almost the identical outfit he'd been wearing the night of his wife's murder—he stared down at the warrant, his expression a mixture of amazement and inner pain. He saw that the signature on the warrant was that of Gershom M.M. Barber, identified in the document as Bay Village's acting mayor. Sam knew that after a day of agonizing inner turmoil, Spencer Houk had finally stepped out of the way of the oncoming freight train.

Drenkhan apologetically pulled out a pair of handcuffs and reached for Sam's right hand.

"Do you have to use handcuffs?" Sam's mother, Ethel, asked in a voice that suggested she thought she was dreaming.

"Yes, ma'am," Drenkhan replied in the same flat tone as he attached the other cuff to his own left wrist. Sam shrugged, as if acknowledging that getting upset about wearing handcuffs would make no difference.

Sudden flashes of light seared through the windows as a murmer grew outside. Richard Sr. went to the window and saw a swarm of reporters and photographers covering his front lawn. Some of the more ambitious in the crowd had marched directly up to the house, traipsing through the landscaping and trampling the flowerbeds to peer through the windows at what was happening inside. In addition to the reporters assigned to follow Sam's every move, a handful of others had been tipped that the arrest was in motion. Yet while essentially every reporter and photographer in Cleveland knew it was coming, attorney William Corrigan had not been notified.

"There are reporters outside," Drenkhan said unnecessarily. "Do you mind having your pictures taken?"

"Yes!" Richard Sr. snapped. "I want them off my property!"

He stormed out his front door. Flashbulbs popped as he proclaimed from his front porch, "I want you men off this property! You are trespassers! Do I have to put you off myself?" He stormed back inside and slammed the door. None of the reporters or photographers moved.

Drenkhan suggested they try waiting out the crowd. After a few minutes, he stepped outside and told the reporters they might as well leave because Sam wasn't coming out until they were gone. But Drenkhan was bluffing with a lousy hand and they knew it. These men had been following this drama for the past twenty-six days, and they weren't about to miss its climax. Sooner or later, Sam would have to come out, and they would be there when he did.

Finally, Drenkhan blinked. One of his colleagues came out to strike a deal with the reporters—they would clear a path for them to leave the house in a civil manner and in return, the police would drive deliberately slowly to City Hall to allow all the reporters and photographers to get there in time to witness the proceedings.

At 10:15, the door opened. Drenkhan and Sam Sheppard, now wearing a leather jacket and a sturdy pair of eyeglasses, stepped out, and the flash bulbs lit up the steamy July night. With neighbors hearing the commotion and word spreading through Cleveland, the crowd had grown dramatically. The starburst of flashbulbs was accompanied by shouts of "Murderer!" from the bystanders, followed by barks of encouragement: "Go get him!"

Seeing the mammoth crowd for the first time, Sam shook his head slightly and muttered, "Apparently the *Press* got its way."

He, Drenkhan, and the other officers pushed through the crowd to the blue Ford in the driveway and got in. As soon as the door slammed, photographers climbed over one another to snap more pictures of Sam in custody while reporters dashed to their cars to follow. The caravan's

Still wearing his neck brace, Sam looks on in disbelief
as he's arraigned at Bay Village City Hall.

first stop would be Bay Village City Hall, where Sam would be arraigned. During the five-minute drive, Drenkhan made a point not to discuss the situation. The quartet traveled in silence. Only once did Sam speak, and then almost to himself. "I can't believe this can happen," he said. "No matter what happens, I can't confess to something I'm not guilty of." The comment went unanswered.

They arrived at City Hall just ahead of the pack of reporters and swiftly maneuvered into a small conference room. Sam sat at one end of the table, facing M.M. Barber, the man who had authorized his arrest. Before the official proceedings could begin, there was a patterned knock on the door—one thump, a pause, and then two more thumps. It was the "secret" knock designated only for those with clearance to attend the arraignment. The door was opened and Spencer Houk stepped into the room. Though he was wearing a stylish suit, Houk looked awful—his eyes buried in dark circles, his face pale and haggard, his posture slumped and defeated. Under these circumstances, he couldn't make eye contact with his old friend.

"Have you read the charge?" Barber asked.

"No," Sam replied despondently.

"I will now read it," Barber replied, and began to recite. "I, Gershom M.M. Barber, acting mayor, on information supplied by police chief John Eaton, charge that you, on or about July 4, did purposefully and of deliberate and premeditated malice kill one Marilyn Sheppard. How do you plead?"

Sam shook his head slowly and his reply was nothing more than a whisper: "Not guilty."

The preliminary hearing was set for August 17, and for all the subterfuge and secret knocks, the arraignment was complete in just over a minute. The next course of action would be to transfer Sam to the county jail downtown.

Sam looked around at the room full of familiar faces. "May I wait until my counsel arrives?" he asked in a dull voice.

The gentlemen across the table looked at each other. No one seemed to have a definitive answer.

"When was he notified?" asked Bay Village solicitor Richard Weygandt.

"At the time I was . . ." Sam raised his right hand weakly and made a dusting gesture.

Weygandt shrugged and looked around the room again. "I see no harm in it," he said.

But Barber, who as acting mayor was technically in charge of the situation, weighed in. "I'm not depriving him of any rights," he began, "but he can see him in jail. I want to clear this room."

So in the spirit of good logistics, Sam was hustled back into the blue Ford and made the drive through the darkness into downtown Cleveland. As on the drive to City Hall, Drenkhan didn't discuss anything to do with the matter at hand. Over the course of their twenty-minute journey, they chatted about a number of bland topics, as if they were on their way to an accident scene together just as they'd done many times before.

Around the time Sam was being escorted into the county jail, William Corrigan arrived at Bay Village City Hall. He was stunned to discover the lights out and the doors locked. Not only had they not notified him of Sam's impending arrest, they'd held the arraignment without him and then whisked his client to prison. By the time Corrigan arrived at the county jail, it was 12:45 Saturday morning, and Corrigan was politely informed that lawyers weren't allowed to visit with prisoners after seven p.m. He would have to return the following morning to confer with his client, nearly twelve hours after his arrest.

Needless to say, Cleveland's power brokers were pleased with the happenings of this Friday night. "It's about time," an appeased Frank Story said. "This was long overdue. This should have been done right after the murder was discovered."

Mayor Celebrezze was equally satisfied. "I am happy to see that the Bay Village officials finally have cooperated with the Cleveland Police Department," he proclaimed, getting in one final dig at his suburban brothers. "I feel the investigation is moving along now as it should have some time ago." Then, incredibly and inexplicably, he added, "I have no opinion as to the guilt or innocence of Dr. Samuel Sheppard."

As Corrigan tried to argue his way in to see his client, Sam was given a cursory medical exam, slipped into a jailhouse jumpsuit, and taken to a solitary confinement cell on the fourth floor. "I didn't think it could happen in this country," Sam stated emotionlessly to the gaggle of reporters as he was led past them. He was guided down a long corridor into a cellblock already filled with a probation violator, a car thief, and a panderer. One of Cleveland's most promising young doctors was led into a small box of concrete that couldn't hold a piece of furniture from the Sheppard living room. The door rattled shut, and Sam was alone, with nothing but a squeaky cot beside a dingy wall crisscrossed by the segmented shadows of the bars. In a corner of the room was a filthy metal pail that was to be used as a toilet.

Sam closed his eyes and tried once more to wake himself from the worst nightmare of his life. "Could this be Cleveland, Ohio," he thought, "or is this a prolongation of the hideous dream that started on July 4?"

But as Sam endured his first night in prison, he gradually began to realize that this was no dream. This was indeed Cleveland, Ohio.

The Best Location in the Nation.

22-THE GUNS OF AUGUST

Adolph Tomsick could tell this was trouble.

As he walked up East Fifty-Seventh Street toward his modest house on Cleveland's East Side, the police detective noticed his neighbor, Homer Wentworth, sauntering up the sidewalk toward him. The unnatural lolling in his slow, methodical gait told Tomsick that Wentworth had likely been drinking, which wasn't all that unusual for a Tuesday afternoon. What did capture Tomsick's attention was the blood splattered all over Wentworth's shoes.

Wentworth, a painter by trade, spotted Tomsick and approached him. In many ways, he looked no different than usual, with his narrow, haggard face topped by a mess of fading white hair that made him look much older than his fifty-five years. But his eyes, caught in nets of wrinkles, were wide and crazed, as if they couldn't quite believe what they'd just seen.

"I'm in trouble, Adolph," he said to Tomsick in a raspy, wheezy voice.

Tomsick glanced at Wentworth's shoes again. "I'll say you're in trouble," he replied with the calm only an experienced police detective could muster. But before he could inquire further, Wentworth stated the situation as if he were describing the weather.

"Elsie is dead."

"Elsie" was Elsie Rhodes, who lived with Wentworth down the street from Tomsick. Not exactly a sweeping romance, they had been living together for some time in what was quaintly referred to as a common-law marriage. They were to be legally married the following Saturday.

Tomsick gently took Wentworth's elbow and turned him to his house to try to figure out what had happened. Before they got there, Wentworth erupted with sudden, bizarre enthusiasm. He grabbed the t-shirt he was wearing and pulled it off his sunken chest. "Look!" he cried. "My t-shirt is clean! There's no blood on it!"

As detached as Homer Wentworth was from reality in that moment, he'd made two things clear: that he'd killed his bride-to-be and that he had closely followed the Sheppard murder case.

Sure enough, when they arrived at the house, Elsie's body was stretched across the living room floor, the right side of her face caved in and her ear almost completely torn off. Beside her lay a bloody claw hammer. As best they could piece it together later, Wentworth and Elsie had been sharing a bottle of wine when they got into an argument. Believing Elsie was seeing other men, Wentworth began beating her and kicked her all over her body before grabbing the claw hammer. By that evening, Homer Wentworth had signed a full confession.

While Sheppard mania reached a new level, Wentworth became a hot topic too, joining the upper echelon of conversation starters: Sam Sheppard, the Indians, and the miserably high temperatures.

The heat wave, which had started gradually two weeks before, had now become almost unbearable as temperatures topped 95 by the middle of July's final week. But making the heat even more oppressive was the continuation of a record drought. As weeks passed since the last substantial rainfall in early June, most of the suburbs enacted sprinkling bans to preserve their water supplies. It had become the longest drought in a quarter-century and the driest July in Cleveland history as the number of consecutive days without rain topped fifty.

Helping ease these sweltering afternoons, the Indians also refused to cool off. Bob Lemon and Early Wynn pitched back-to-back complete-game victories over the Red Sox to start a fourteen-game home stand. Then on the weekend of Sam Sheppard's arrest, Cleveland put on a clinic in a four-game sweep of the Senators, highlighted by Larry Doby's mesmerizing catch Friday night, Lemon's three-hit shutout on Saturday, and a pair of home runs by Vic Wertz in Sunday's doubleheader. Wynn also flirted with history in the final game of the series, striking out five consecutive Washington batters and pulling within one strike of tying the American League record of six. Despite winning twelve of their last fourteen, the Indians still only led New York by two and a half games. And now those damned Yankees would come sauntering back into town, with Casey Stengel pushing every motivational button he could think of.

"If the Yankees don't win the pennant," he told reporters as his club packed up for the trip to Cleveland, "they ought to fire me."

It was a peculiar comment. It carried little weight, since even the highbrow Yankee organization could hardly justify firing its manager after falling short following a run of five straight championships. But Stengel used it to deliver two messages: first, that his players weren't to blame for the team's shortfalls, and second, that the New York Yankees were simply supposed to win the pennant every year. If they didn't, no matter why, there should be consequences.

But Stengel didn't think his job security would come into question simply because he still genuinely believed his club would come out on top. During a trip to Chicago the previous week, Stengel had run into Mickey McBride, a nationally known sportsman who, ironically, would be remembered best for founding the Cleveland Browns.

"How does it look, Casey?" McBride asked jovially.

"We'll win it," Stengel replied without needing clarification on what McBride was talking about.

McBride's eyebrows arched. "How are you going to beat those Indians?" he asked.

"We'll win it," Stengel repeated, "because I've got the money players."

As much as those words struck a nerve with Indians fans—and Hank Greenberg, for that matter—they knew the only way they could retaliate after the last three years was if their club gave them some ammunition.

More than 60,000 fans, the largest home crowd of the season, piled into Municipal Stadium to see Don Mossi match up with Whitey Ford in the opener. While the crowd was impressive, it still seemed somehow disappointing. Even Stengel, watching from the dugout as the fans trickled into the ballpark that evening, noticed the difference. "They don't catch fire here like they used to," he commented. "Doesn't look like it did four, five years ago. Used to pack 'em in here then."

Still, the Yankees' arrival was the talk of the town. In the county jail not far away, as Homer Wentworth was being booked for murder four floors below, Sam Sheppard cut short a letter to his mother to listen to the game on a small radio brought to him by his brother Stephen. Sam tuned in to hear the Tribe creep to a 1–0 lead on a Larry Doby homer in the first, but the evening began to turn sour along with Mossi's stomach. The Sphinx was forced to leave the game after one inning, and Art Houtteman gave up a two-run single to Yogi Berra in the third that gave the Yankees the lead and all the runs Ford would need. The Chairman of the Board, who told reporters afterward he felt much stronger since giving up cigarettes a few weeks before, went the distance, surrendering four hits in a 2–1 win that pulled New York back within a game and a half of the Indians.

Things looked grim again for the home team the following day. This time with 58,000 fans enduring an overcast, muggy evening, Yogi Berra again delivered an early RBI single that sparked the Yankees to a 2–0 lead on Bob Lemon. New York hurler Allie Reynolds, 10–2 on the year, set the Indians down in order in the first two frames, but in the third Bobby Avila lofted a two-out, three-run home run that just cleared the fence to put the Indians ahead. Vic Wertz, beginning to settle in at first base, made nifty stops on back-to-back plays to thwart a rally in the top of the fourth, and then added a homer of his own to lead off the bottom of the frame. With Lemon cruising, the Tribe coasted to a 5–2 triumph—Lemon's fourteenth of the season and third over New York.

The rubber match on Thursday afternoon appeared destined to be a pitchers' duel as Early Wynn and Bob Grim matched one another with scoreless frames into the fourth. But Mickey Mantle broke the stalemate with the first of two home runs, and Johnny Sain held off the Indians to preserve New York's 5–2 decision. The Yankees' trip to Cleveland had shaved a game off the Indians' meager lead, but more impressively, had drawn more than 150,000 fans to the ballpark for the three-game series—the largest mid-week gate in Cleveland history.

Now having won six of nine games in Cleveland in 1954, the Yankees would come back just once more—for the much-anticipated September doubleheader that, with each passing week, looked more and more titanic.

As New York rode the rails around Lake Erie to Detroit for a three-game weekend series, the Indians stayed home to host Philadelphia, hoping to pad their lead ever so slightly. While the Indians dismantled the Athletics in a quartet of rousing victories, the Yankees struggled with the Tigers, losing on Saturday, then dropping the finale in ten innings the following afternoon. When the Yankee score was hung on the center-field scoreboard in the final moments of the Tribe's second win on that blustery, dreary Sunday, the crowd erupted into cheers. Cleveland's lead swelled to four games, its largest in a month.

Buoyed by the promising weekend, thousands of Clevelanders tuned in to WXEL to watch the Indians play in Detroit the following evening. As Ney, Ohio, native Ned Garver continually sawed off the Indians' bats, the Tigers took a 1–0 lead into the seventh. After Garver led off the Detroit half of the frame with a single, at precisely eleven o'clock, the television broadcast back in Cleveland came to an abrupt end. In the following minutes, WXEL's switchboard lit up like a Christmas tree, with hundreds of calls pouring in from as far as Youngstown and Akron to find out what happened. Operators explained that the interruption, as abrupt as it seemed, had been scheduled all along. The coaxial cable being used to send the signal from Detroit to Cleveland, owned by the American Telephone & Telegraph company, was needed for a previous commitment to a program linking several local stations in Michigan. The plug was pulled on the Indians-Tigers game, and the cables were redirected.

As it turned out, the irate fans were saved from watching the Tigers plate three more runs in the eighth and coast to a 4–0 triumph. The lead was back down to three games as the Yankees snapped their two-game skid by beating the Athletics. The Indians didn't know it yet, but that victory would kick-start their nightmare scenario: the Yankees, prone to explosions of baseball perfection, were about to get unnaturally hot just as the plot of the pennant race thickened. Starting with their tide-turning victory in Philadelphia, the Yankees wouldn't lose a game for the next nine days.

But neither would the Indians.

23 - A GHOUL'S PARADISE

Amidst the triumphant afterglow that cast across town on the Sunday morning following Sam Sheppard's arrest, the city of Cleveland was scolded by an angry voice from the pulpit.

In mid-July, Alfred Kreke, the pastor at Bay Village Methodist Church who had presided over Marilyn Sheppard's funeral, had been so dispirited by the day-to-day drama of the Sheppard case that he took his family out of town for a week's respite. Just as the inquest reached its ugly conclusion, the Krekes returned to Bay Village refreshed in both body and soul, not having read a Cleveland paper or listened to a local radio station for seven days.

What they witnessed over the next seven days was so troubling to Pastor Kreke that he set aside ten minutes of his sermon that Sunday to discuss the dark cloud of hatred and fear that had settled over their previously peaceful, friendly community. He segued away from his sermon with a general statement: "We are fickle to God and our American heritage of human rights when, without just cause and before a fair trial, we condemn any person."

Kreke told of his family's vacation and the relief they found in escaping the cauldron of accusation that Bay Village had become. "We returned," he told his congregation as they fanned themselves in the morning heat, "to find our community the center of an open inquest with a miniature McCarthy at the head of what seemed from all appearances to be a carefully planned persecution of not only one individual, but the defamation of an honored family name, a deliberate attempt by publicity seekers and little professional men to undermine in the eyes of the public the qualifications and efficiency of our hospital staff and personnel."

The well-dressed churchgoers sat frozen in silence, riveted by the most interesting sermon most of them had ever heard.

"I was mortified at the subtle innuendoes and implications suggested in the questioning," he continued, "which was not conducted as an inquest, but as a trial with a prosecutor suggesting most of the questions. There were all the earmarks not of an inquest, but of a medieval inquisition. The morbid, sadistic attitude of the audience," many of whom, Kreke knew, were also in *this* audience, "reminded one of the blood-letting arenas of Nero days."

Some of those women in the church sunk a little lower in their pews. In the cold light of Sunday morning, their behavior at that inquest seemed inappropriate, even childish. But at the time, it made perfect sense. Before they could ask themselves exactly why, the pastor shifted to another topic.

"The publicity seekers, with an eye for personal gain and for profit, seem to be seeking each day a new angle, a new picture to add in a feeble way some semblance of newness to the old story which has been hashed and re-hashed for almost a month."

He did not mention Louis Seltzer by name. And as he spoke these words, a line of cars—which had begun to form at seven that morning—slowly crawled past the Sheppard house on Lake Road, packed bumper-to-bumper. The line would remain continuous until well past sunset.

After a deep breath and one final disappointing gaze cast out at his congregation, Kreke concluded with a sentiment never before introduced within this beacon of spiritual guidance and worship. "When one says that it is pretty difficult to believe in people anymore," he said, "I think I understand."

The words echoed through the chamber like a whisper in a dark tunnel, and the pastor gave them a moment to sink into each and every one of the people sitting before him.

Message delivered, he continued with the service.

That evening, Kreke received dozens of angry and threatening phone calls.

Since this Sunday marked the beginning of a new month, some hoped that perhaps the ugliness that had covered Cleveland like a plague would be forgotten. J.F. Saunders wrote a telling column in the *Plain Dealer* capturing this spirit, titled "Evil the Days of July."

"No July within our memory has produced such a sultry climate of community evil as the month now preparing to blow the whistle on the simmering kettle of its conclusion," he began. "Even Public Square, by night, is crisscrossed with strange and sinister shadows because widening work being done there has darkened many of the lights."

He said this fateful July had been defined by "an aura of wickedness that seemed to engulf the town like an ooze that follows a receding flood, encroaching upon more and more space and suffocating the puny Sunday struggles of men of wisdom to extricate us from the swirl of sin and abnormal living." When Clevelanders heard of Marilyn Sheppard's killing, they "learned how savage violence had invaded a quiet suburb under cover of night, the erosion of crime biting deep into an unfamiliar area, where a greedy lake chews away steadily at the helpless land."

As if a young wife and mother being annihilated in her own bed in a safe neighborhood weren't enough, Saunders was equally appalled by the aftermath. "Around every green blade of fact," he wrote, "there sprung up acres of the cockle and gossip, much of it malicious, some of it benign, none of it worth stooping to inspect unless to pluck it angrily from the broad lawn of reason. In barroom and living room, on golf course and in supermarket, choice bits of rumor and fantasy were passed along hastily like the hot dish at a long picnic table. Telephone lines sagged with the very weight of supposition and theory being transmitted over them without interruption. Truth languished, discarded for the summer like a sable scarf."

Saunders concluded that the city entered August grateful to depart July, which was "a month that can only be regarded as an evil interlude, not only for the actors in the tragic dramas, but for many of the audience whispering unsupported tattle behind their programs."

Kreke's sermon and the Saunders column proved that reason, as sound and strong as ever, did have a voice. What it did not have, however, was an audience. Cleveland was utterly enraptured with the continuing storylines of the investigation, embracing its colorful cast of characters and wondering what would happen next. It was discussed over breakfast and cocktails, on buses, in grocery stores, and on street corners. In the cool basements in which children had spent the first half of the summer playing games, they now played a new one—reenacting the murder and investigation. After careful negotiation and debate, someone would be selected to be Marilyn, someone would be Sam (who would then don a towel or rolled-up piece of cardboard to symbolize the neck brace), and others would be the police, the coroner, and the sinister defense lawyer. Many versions of the game even tacked on a natural ending: the "Sam" character tied with rope to a kitchen chair and "electrocuted."

In this environment, Sam Sheppard's first full day in custody raised no alarm bells. After a simple breakfast of coffee and cereal and a brief meeting with William Corrigan, who was finally permitted to speak briefly to his client, the police began their questioning. Patrick Gareau and Robert Schottke, essentially picking up where they left off at Bay View on July 4, conducted a tag-team inquisition that lasted the next twelve hours. To call the interrogative statements the detectives made "questions" would be sugarcoating them.

Since by now they were well past "Did you kill your wife?" they skipped ahead to "Why did you kill your wife?" They showed him pictures of Marilyn's bludgeoned body. They called him names. They said they knew Chip wasn't his son and neither had been the baby Marilyn was carrying.

"Now look here, you dirty, no good son of a bitch," Sam remembered one of them snarling. "You killed your wife in cold blood. We know it. You know it. The whole town knows it." The detective paused and chuckled. "For Chrissake, it's been in all the papers!"

Sam sat in silence, as if waiting for a storm to pass before going outside.

"Wake up, you horse's ass!" the detective screamed. "We're going to burn you if you don't confess!"

As the nightmarish day went on, Sam understood that what they really wanted was to strike a deal. If he would just admit that he killed

Marilyn, his charge would be lessened. "They have admittedly gone on percentage, and I am therefore guilty in their eyes until I can prove myself innocent," he wrote in a letter to his mother. "This is hard to believe in the U.S.A."

It also became apparent over the course of that weekend that detectives were working on a very tight deadline. Rumors swirled both inside and outside official circles that Sam was a dope fiend, and that's why he was arrested in the dead of night on a Friday. Without a fix for two full days, they deduced, he would be much more willing to confess. Once the pulse of the legal establishment began pumping again Monday morning, their window of opportunity would close, so they wanted to obtain a confession before the weekend was over.

Detectives entered the interrogation room in waves, relieving their comrades and starting a whole new style and line of questioning. "It was like brainwashing behind the iron curtain," Sam said. "Physical beating would have been a pleasure to me by comparison." Yet Sam, showing no signs of physical withdrawal from any substance, never changed his story. David Kerr snorted that this was simply because Sam had been "well-coached" by his attorneys.

Around 4:30 p.m. on Saturday, Sam was permitted to take a short break for a shower and dinner. Stephen and Betty Sheppard arrived that afternoon to see him but were denied. Instead, they dropped off some clean clothes, his shaving gear, and a portable radio for him to listen to classical music and Indians games in his cell.

At 7:25, just as detectives prepared for the day's final push of heated questioning, outside the thick cement walls of the jail, the temperature plummeted as a cold front swept east. The sun, which had baked Cleveland throughout the day, was buried behind an arsenal of thick gray clouds and a premature darkness settled over the city. The cool relief of the evening brought something else, as well. Large drops of rain began falling, leaving circular spots the size of quarters on the sun-singed streets and sidewalks. But unlike a number of times over the previous two months when these few drops would be all that the bloated clouds would release, this time heavy rain pelted the city, rinsing away the sticky residue of the fifty-seven-day drought. As it did, deep belches of thunder rumbled over the landscape and jagged strokes of lightning lit up the sky. Heavy swirls of wind scattered garbage into alleys and pulled browning leaves off parched trees. The storm knocked out power all over town that night, but residents were so happy for the moisture that the minor inconvenience was worth it.

As the tempest raged outside, within the county jail, detectives continued their mission. With their questions punctuated by sharp claps of thunder and underlined by the constant hiss of rain beating against the building, they spent the rest of this stormy Saturday night trying to pull a confession out of Sam Sheppard. Finally, at twenty minutes before midnight, after almost twelve straight hours of interrogation, detectives sensed a change in Sam's attitude. He now seemed nervous, his Adam's apple bouncing as he constantly swallowed the collecting saliva in his mouth. But before they could play it out, the deputy sheriff interrupted to call off the session, saying the prisoner had been questioned enough for one day. "After all," explained David Kerr, "we don't want to give the man the third degree. We don't want our questioning construed as anything like a third degree."

Corrigan struck back the only way he could on Sunday. He arrived just after eight a.m. and began a marathon conference with his client. It had endured for more than two hours when they were joined by Arthur Petersilge at 10:30, and the meeting continued to stretch out like caramel until early afternoon. Corrigan's "filibustering" infuriated the police, who noted that Corrigan spent a long portion of the meeting reading the Sunday *Plain Dealer* aloud to Sam. Corrigan had once again lit the pilot light of their disdain for the suspect and his fancy lawyers. "I've never heard of another case in which a defendant's attorneys have used up so much time interfering with his interrogation in county jail," Frank Story declared to reporters. Then in the same breath, he added, "On the other hand, there's never been a case where the Cleveland police have spent so much time talking to a prisoner in county jail."

Kerr sniveled that Corrigan seemed to be running the jail. Yet after Corrigan returned from lunch, he was refused access to Sam. As he was turned away, a reporter in the corridor asked accusatorily, "What is the purpose of all your visits?" Corrigan glared at him. "Have you ever been arrested and charged with first-degree murder?" he snapped. "What do you think a lawyer is for? We're here to protect him."

When the questioning finally continued, Sam refused to talk. "On advice of counsel," he would repeat emotionlessly, "I will not talk about anything to do with the murder."

It sent Kerr over the edge. They finally had Sam and still were running into roadblocks. "It is far from an ideal situation where you can interrogate anyone in a proper manner," he barked to reporters. "We have absolutely, positively no control over the prisoner." That is, of course, aside from having him in full police custody with the ability to question him for twelve hours at a time.

Meanwhile, Corrigan was telling his own story to the *Press*, offering "spin" decades before the term would be coined. "This man is innocent," he stated simply. "They arrest the man on a charge of first-degree murder and then they try to get the evidence to make the charge." The Sheppards tried to maintain the façade of everyday business. Sam's father visited him, bringing a set of x-rays taken of one of Sam's patients for him to examine. But the circumstances were too surreal to mirror reality. When Marilyn's aunt came to visit Sam, she was astounded by the phalanx of photographers taking pictures of her and all other visitors. "This certainly is a ghoul's paradise, isn't it?" she muttered bitterly.

While Corrigan and the family tried to turn the tide of public opinion, Sam did little to endear himself or his plea of innocence to the masses. When not being questioned, he would sit on the cot in his dingy cell, smoking his pipe and listening to his radio. He would leave his neck brace off until being led to meet someone—or anywhere near photographers and reporters. This habit, combined with the results of a police-sanctioned examination of the prisoner that deemed him healthy with "no serious disability," sank Sam even lower in the public estimation. A *Plain Dealer* editorial cartoon depicted the Egyptian Sphinx wearing an orthopedic collar. The caption read: "'I Will Do Everything in My Power to Help Solve This Terrible Murder.' – Dr. Sam Sheppard."

After two days of questioning, Sam simply stopped acknowledging his interrogators. He would leaf through hot rod magazines while detectives railed at him, ignoring their queries and threats. When the now-infamous Pastor Alfred Kreke visited him on Monday (delivering a Bible that Sam would also use to pass the time during questioning), Sam told him the reason he was ignoring the police was that they kept asking the same questions he'd answered over and over. Frank Story eventually had enough, calling off all questioning sessions because of the suspect's uncooperative attitude, as well as ceasing constant reports to the media. "There has been all kinds of yakety-yak going on and it has helped the other side," he said. He also scoffed at suggestions that Sam had been treated badly, explaining that police had been "bending over backward" to treat the suspect gently.

On Monday, Sam went before the court of common pleas for a hearing on a writ of habeas corpus to free him, based on Corrigan's argument that the warrant for Sam's arrest was invalid because it wasn't signed by Spencer Houk, the actual mayor of Bay Village. Less newsworthy to reporters than the results of the hearing was the judge's decision to only allow the principals into the courtroom—no spectators or reporters. He didn't want a mob scene in his courtroom, he explained. Yet when the hearing began just before 10:30 on Monday morning, there were more than 100 spectators on hand, creating a courtroom so cluttered that Arthur Petersilge had a difficult time fighting through the crowd to join Corrigan and Sam at the defense table. Yet no one made any attempt to ask the overflow audience to leave. The writ was denied, and on the way back to the county jail, Sam was taken to central police station for the obligatory mug shots and fingerprints.

While the news coming out of the county jail slowed to a trickle that week, reporters found leads elsewhere. Most notable were the results of a police simulation of Sam's version of the story held at the Sheppard house. David Kerr lay on the daybed at the foot of the stairs, and when given the signal representing Marilyn's scream for help, pounced up and raced up to the bedroom. It took Kerr only six seconds to mount the fourteen stairs. Police estimated it would have taken a minimum of forty seconds for the killer to deliver the twenty-seven blows. By that estimation, it left thirty-four seconds unaccounted for. Corrigan rolled his eyes when he heard of the little pageant. "Gerber should have knocked Kerr out with a club when he got to the top of the stairs," he snarled, "and then observed what a dazed man would do under the circumstances." But his objections were drowned out by the heavy ink of the three Cleveland papers. Readers wondered: could Marilyn have been screaming for her life for several seconds before Sam awoke? Or did the killer begin beating Marilyn, stop to clobber Sam, then return to deliver an additional twenty-some blows upon Marilyn? Either way, Sam's story was sinking like a rock.

Simultaneously, Corrigan and the Sheppard family began shopping around alternative suspects. Corrigan constantly implored the police to further examine Les Hoversten, the houseguest who mysteriously left town a few hours before the killing, suggesting Hoversten had already left the country. But when police did call Hoversten in for further questioning, he was at a medical conference in California and came willingly. After a brief session, he was released and once again dismissed as a suspect.

With Hoversten out of the mix, the Sheppards turned their attention closer to home. Stephen Sheppard informed police that Spencer Houk had told Marilyn of his love for her, and because Marilyn didn't feel the same, Houk had become jealous of Sam. Following up on the lead, detectives picked up a stunned Houk at his home and took him to the private office of chief of detectives James McArthur for further questioning. When they explained why, Houk's face narrowed. "The damndest lie I ever heard!" he shouted, the words bouncing off the walls of the tiny office. Detectives spoke with Houk for the next four hours, assessing his answers to carefully worded questions.

Then, in a scene reminiscent of a low-budget cops-and-robbers film, Stephen Sheppard was brought in to verify the wording of his

Mayor Spencer Houk (left) and Police Chief John Eaton
found themselves and their quaint town of Bay Village
at the center of a firestorm of controversy in the weeks
following Marilyn Sheppard's murder.

concerns—essentially confronting Houk with his accusation face-to-face. As McArthur read Stephen's statement, Stephen's eyes darted uncomfortably around the room, refusing to settle on the mayor of Bay Village, and Houk once again became visibly angry.

"Lies!" he shouted at one point during the reading. "Damn lies!" When McArthur finished, all eyes settled on Stephen. He paused a moment, his eyes again dancing across the office. He then didn't merely offer a simple affirmative statement but actually complimented McArthur on the accuracy with which his statement had been recorded. McArthur, amazed at the nerve of this jittery little man, felt his lips curl into a small smile as his eyes turned to Houk for the outburst everyone in the room anticipated.

Houk leapt to his feet and started toward Stephen. "The biggest lie I ever heard!" he screamed as he charged at his neighbor's brother. "You're a liar!" The officers in the room grabbed him and held him back. Regaining control, the detectives told Stephen that Houk was still not a suspect. Stephen pursed his lips and replied, "I am very, very glad to hear that."

Moments later, Stephen left the room, entered the hallway, and pressed the button for the elevator. As he lifted his finger off the button, Houk entered the corridor smoking a cigarette. Still wearing the simple white t-shirt and baggy blue trousers he'd worn when police picked him up that morning, he sauntered to the elevator and stood beside Stephen Sheppard, who wore a slick blue suit and hat. They didn't say a word to each other, absorbed in the silence of the hallway. Just before the elevator arrived, Stephen stepped away to a nearby water fountain. As he sipped the water, the elevator doors opened. Glancing away from Stephen, Houk stepped on and turned to face the doors.

Timing the process perfectly, Stephen lifted his head from the fountain and walked back to the elevator to wait for the next car.

As he did, the door between the Sheppards and the Houks slid closed.

24 - DESTINY

On an otherwise ordinary Thursday afternoon, August 16, 1954, the entire culture of American sport went through a dramatic change—though nobody knew it at the time.

All over Cleveland—and across the country—beefy newsstand operators and whistling drug store clerks made room on their magazine displays for a new title. Though the inaugural issue looked nice—its cover emblazoned with a color photograph of Braves third baseman Eddie Matthews taking a cut at home plate during a night game at Milwaukee's sparkling new County Stadium—no one could have predicted the influence this new publication would have on its subject. On the way home from work that evening, men all over Cleveland picked up the eye-catching magazine for twenty-five cents. As they leafed through the 144 pages, readers quickly realized this was not *Sporting News*. Whereas the unofficial publication of baseball was saturated with spider-web strands of black ink comprising statistics and box scores, opening this new magazine was like watching Dorothy enter Munchkinland in *The Wizard of Oz*.

The first issue was sent out to more than 350,000 readers who'd paid $7.50 apiece for a year's subscription. Of those first subscribers, more than two-thirds had signed up even before the magazine had announced its official name the month before. And that name was nothing special. In fact, at least two other publications had tried the same title years earlier but quickly folded. Yet this version, founded by *Time* magazine creator Henry Luce, was something else altogether. He called it *Sports Illustrated*.

It was overflowing with color photographs, mixed among full-page ads for fur hats, slide projectors, cigarette lighters, bowling balls, vermouth, and scotch. Its first foray into covering the national pastime was a long article about the growing popularity of bubble-gum cards among young fans. Included were three pages of full-color simulated cards of the game's biggest stars. Cleveland fans were pleased to see Al Rosen's All-American grin on one and Larry Doby's intense scowl on another. The Best Location in the Nation received another nod inside when a piece by *Plain Dealer* sports editor Gordon Cobbledick was spotlighted as the "Column of the Week."

The highlight of the first issue was an article titled "The Golden Age Is Now," which offered the opinion that in terms of attendance, excitement, and broken records, the current era was the greatest in the history of sports. Running alongside the article was a photograph of Municipal Stadium from the 1948 World Series, when the Fall Classic's all-time single-game attendance record was set. Yet more than just about baseball or football, the new venture spotlighted other, more upscale sports such as polo, yachting, fishing, and hunting.

So impressed with the inaugural issue, Samuel Goldwyn wrote a letter of congratulations to the editorial staff, as did Marshall Field Jr. and publishing magnate M. Lincoln Schuster. In the ten days after its premiere issue hit the stands, the magazine would pick up 25,000 new subscribers. It would take almost a decade for this enterprise to begin to turn a profit (coinciding with its initial and controversial "swimsuit" issue in 1964) but by the end of the century, more than twenty million people would read *Sports Illustrated* each week—including nearly one out of every five men in America. To have your photograph placed on its cover was akin to being knighted, and in years to come, the magnitude of the aftermath led many to believe bad luck would follow whoever was deemed worthy of the cover shot.

Over the next seven months, two Indians would carry that honor, including the first pitcher ever to grace the cover of *Sports Illustrated*. Ironically, it would not be any of the Big Three, nor would it be eventual Hall of Famers Bob Feller or Hal Newhouser. The following spring, cherub-faced Herb Score would be pictured in a crisp Indians uniform beginning his windup, his head centered perfectly in the "o" of "Sports." Inside was a feature article noting that Score's arrival marked a changing of the guard for American League pitchers—and the beginning of a dismal new chapter for its hitters. In the summer of '54, the batters of the American Association could have warned them what was coming.

At tiny Victory Field in Indianapolis on August 19, minor-league catcher Joe Ginsberg stepped into the dugout moments before his game was to begin, peeled his mitt off his hand and tried to shake the soreness out of it. "He's got it tonight," he muttered, glancing down at his palm, already pink and tender from warming up Herb Score. In the sixth inning of that game, Score would strike out his 265th batter of the season, breaking an American Association record that had stood for forty-eight years and had been thought to be unbreakable—one that had been set in more than 150 additional innings pitched than it took Score, who received a well-deserved standing ovation. He struck out twelve that night, but managed to keep the ball with which he broke the record. "Well," Score said afterward, "I've got something to show my grandchildren." Reporters smiled at his sheepish appreciation—as if he wouldn't have countless other baseballs from countless other broken records to show off.

Long since forgotten, one of Score's teammates had the opposite experience on the mound a week earlier. Whereas Score was dominant, eyeing a future spread out before him on a golden track, fellow pitcher Bob Kelly couldn't last three innings, unable to shake the notion that his life was falling apart around him.

Just before a game in Columbus, Kelly had been stunned to read his wife's name in the local newspaper. As the well of information pertaining to the Sheppard murder case began to dry up, reporters couldn't help themselves from printing rumors about other women Sam may have had affairs with—usually referring to these women only by their first names and hair color. One of these rumors was traced to Sandra Kelly, Bob's angel-faced, blonde-haired wife, who had been friends with the Sheppards for years, at one time engaged to a cousin of Marilyn's. Sandra had even briefly lived with Sam and Marilyn in California before meeting Bob, and this detail ignited the bonfire of gossip concerning her relationship with Sam. As far as Bob knew as he took the mound that night, his Sandra was about to become the case's next Susan Hayes.

Not surprisingly, the distracted pitcher was shelled to the tune of three walks, four hits, and five runs in just over two innings, and Indianapolis lost. Though Sandra was quickly cleared of any suspicion of having an affair with Sam Sheppard, the case had now crossed yet another medium, affecting the outcome of a professional baseball game.

Meanwhile, several of the Indians' minor-league players had been rocked on their heels when Cleveland's Class B team, the Peaches of Spartanburg, South Carolina, (coincidentally Al Rosen's birthplace) suddenly pulled out of the Tri-State League with a month left in the season. The team president explained he was simply making good on a promise he'd made to Spartanburg fans before the season. When the Knoxville Smokies took the field for a game against the Peaches with a black player in the lineup, the Peaches were forced to go against their pledge to their fans that they wouldn't play in a game against any "negroes." Their decision pushed the Tri-State League to the verge of collapse, and Spartanburg players were quickly shuffled onto other Indians farm teams.

With turbulent undercurrents flowing through its minor-league system, topside it was nothing but smooth sailing for the parent club. The Indians avenged their shutout loss in Detroit with back-to-back dominant pitching performances by Garcia and Lemon and then returned home to bully the Orioles in a four-game sweep. The highlight of the home stand was a thrilling extra-inning marathon in which the Tribe endured an eighty-minute rain delay and a three-run Baltimore lead to tie the game in the eighth inning on a three-run home run by Bobby Avila. The Indians then ended the marathon and won it in the eleventh on a two-out RBI single by backup catcher Hal Naragon. Appropriately, the winning hit came off Bob Chakales, whom the Indians had traded for Vic Wertz two months earlier. Whether they liked it or not, these Indians had become a team of destiny, and Hank Greenberg had become King Midas.

This win marked Cleveland's forty-first come-from-behind victory of the season, its fifteenth triumph in its last at-bat, and improved the

Tribe's record in extra-inning games to 11–3 and in one-run games to 23–9. "Cleveland fans have learned to stick around no matter how far their club may be trailing going into the final innings," Hal Lebovitz wrote. "When the team is on the road, they don't dare turn off their TV sets or radios and go to bed early. The stick-to-the-finishers have found this edition of the Indians never quits, and, in fact, has made a delightful habit of staging last-ditch rallies." They did it again to open the next series. With Bud Abbott and Lou Costello watching from box seats near the Cleveland dugout, the Indians scored two in the bottom of the ninth to beat the Tigers. Two days later, they rattled Ned Garver, who'd shut them out the previous week, in another one-run triumph— the Indians' ninth straight. While impressive in its own right, the streak served as a psychological body blow to the Yankees, who'd won ten straight over the same period and only managed to pick up a half game. No matter what the Yankees did, the Indians were better. It was a beat that matched the tempo of this strange, steamy summer.

Home to an untouchable baseball team and a riveting murder mystery, Cleveland had become the very nucleus of America.

25 - WHAT EVIDENCE IS THERE?

Common Pleas Court Judge William K. Thomas couldn't believe what he was seeing.

As he heard arguments in Sam Sheppard's motion for bail, he kept mulling the same question over in his mind. Finally, once William Corrigan and the prosecutors had finished their sparring, Thomas put his astonishment into words.

"What evidence is there in front of me here?" he asked. "Nothing, except the application of the defense for bail and a statement by the prosecution in opposition."

Corrigan and Sam felt their chests ignite with relief and verification. Finally, here was a voice of authority standing up to the nonsense that had plagued them for the past six weeks.

"This court cannot go beyond this courtroom," Thomas went on. "We cannot deal in surmise. I must find that there is nothing before me here to sustain a finding that proof is evident or presumption great." The prosecutors—John Mahon, Saul Danaceau, and Thomas Parrino—stewed in silence as Thomas completed his finding, noting that a defendant is entitled to bail except in capital cases where "the proof is evident or the presumption of guilt great." This was, after all, Thomas declared, "an American court, operating under our Constitution and Bill of Rights."

"I do not pass on the question of innocence or guilt, but merely upon what evidence has been presented here," he said. He then added four powerful words: "I find no evidence."

Sam Sheppard's bail was set at $50,000, requiring his family to pay $2,500. David Kerr snorted when he heard the figure. "I guess law and order are for poor people," he said. Wearing the same gray suit he'd worn to Marilyn's funeral, Sam felt a surge of emotion crack through his outer shell and a modest smile momentarily brightened his face. Corrigan himself couldn't believe it. Over the course of his long career, he'd never successfully received a ruling in favor of bail for a defendant charged with first-degree murder. Both he and the prosecutors conjectured it was the first time it had occurred in Cuyahoga County in at least thirty-five years.

Yet as Sam shuffled through the obligatory paperwork and formalities of posting bond, thirty feet away, the wheels of justice were spinning once again. The Grand Jury was in the midst of a two-day session of testimony, which included statements from Samuel Gerber, Spencer Houk, and of course, Susan Hayes. Sam could feel his sudden freedom after two weeks in prison becoming like a cool breeze on a hot summer afternoon: refreshing but maddeningly brief. After picking up his personal effects from his cell, he, Corrigan, and his brother Richard headed toward the prison exit.

Before they reached the door, chief jailer Mike Ucello called out to them. "Where's your radio?" he said. "Do you have it with you?"

Sam glanced over his shoulder and shook his head. "You keep it for me," he said somberly. "I'll be back."

With his neck brace packed in a bag carried by Corrigan, Sam followed Richard through the rush of reporters and photographers and got in his brother's green Ford convertible. They sped off toward Bay Village, driving directly into a horizon blanketed by black storm clouds steaming eastward. Just as they reached their father's house on Lake Road, one of the most ferocious thunderstorms of the summer erupted onto northeast Ohio, pouring heavy rain and dangerously strong winds gusting up to 55 miles per hour. Seven people were injured over the course of the storm, and a man was killed on the East Side when he tried to move a fallen power line.

Once the storm had rumbled away, leaving death and widespread damage in its wake, Dr. Sam went back to work. He returned to Bay View Hospital for a late-afternoon tour of patients. As he did, his brother Stephen received a call from police captain David Kerr, who invited him to his dimly lit office.

As Stephen settled into a chair, across the desk Kerr tilted back in his own chair and surveyed the stiff young doctor whose brother was now a free man, much to the dismay of the chief of homicide.

"You know you people are going about this in the wrong way, don't you?" Kerr asked casually.

Stephen's eyebrows narrowed, not following.

"Your brother is guilty as hell and you know it," Kerr continued.

Stephen, no longer surprised by such comments, shook his head, and carefully constructed his reply. "I know just the opposite," he said. "And so do you, Captain Kerr."

Kerr snorted and shook his head. "Well," he started, almost good-naturedly, "I'm going to tell you something." The legs of his chair dropped onto the floor and Kerr leaned forward across the paper-littered desk. "I'm going to tell you something," he repeated, "and if you ever tell anyone I said this, I will call you a liar."

He paused, allowing Stephen the chance to absorb this prologue.

"Now then," Kerr began again, "you go see your brother and tell him to confess."

This comment did catch Stephen off guard, and his expression mirrored his surprise. Kerr noticed, and it seemed to energize his argument. "God damn it, he can plead insanity or whatever he wants," Kerr said. "He will do six months in a hospital and come out cured. He can return to the practice of medicine and there will be no further difficulty."

Stephen's expression melted back into the poker face he shared with his brothers and father. Kerr must have thought he was foolish to float such a concept as pleading insanity and spending only six months in prison. No district attorney would agree to such terms, and both Stephen Sheppard and David Kerr knew it. But Stephen could see Kerr's real offer: the authorities were willing to deal. They didn't care about how much time Sam spent in jail, or for that matter, if he even went to jail.

All they wanted was a confession.

Come what may to Sam Sheppard afterward, they had to be proven right: the police, the mayor, Samuel Gerber, Louis Seltzer. They had all come too far to risk letting a jury allow Sam Sheppard to slip through their fingers.

"And if he refuses to confess to a crime he didn't commit?" Stephen asked.

Kerr's response was quick and forceful. "Don't give me that crap, Doc," he said. "But if he is silly enough to refuse, you can tell him for me that we'll burn him." Then, leveling his gaze into Stephen's, he added dismissively, "That's all."

Back at the courthouse, testimony continued. The following morning, Gerber testified for an hour and forty-five minutes, displaying the blood-drenched pajamas Marilyn died in and the brown trousers Sam was wearing the night of the murder. When asked how he came to the conclusion that the murder had not been committed by an intruder, Gerber's answer was surprisingly brief. "From my experience," he said. "That's all."

Fidgeting like a nervous schoolgirl, Susan Hayes told the Grand Jury how she and Sam had lived "as man and wife" for a week in Los Angeles that spring and that Sam had told her he didn't love Marilyn but couldn't divorce her because of how his family would react. Elsewhere in the building, when he arrived in his chambers that morning, Judge Thomas, who'd freed Sam hours before, received an anonymous postcard: "Get off the bench, you don't belong there," it read. "Get a job sweeping streets."

Chief of Detectives James McArthur complained to reporters camped out in the corridors that many prisoners in the county jail were now refusing to answer police questions, thinking that if Sam Sheppard could get bail, then so could they. As far as he was concerned, McArthur had heard enough about defendants' rights. "And who is protecting the constitutional rights of Marilyn Sheppard?" he asked rhetorically.

In this climate, it certainly came as no surprise that afternoon when the Grand Jury indicted Sam Sheppard on the charge of first-degree murder. Now celebrities, the fifteen members of the Grand Jury would have a group picture taken and printed on the front page of that day's *Press*, along with their names and home addresses. When warned not to discuss the case outside of the courtroom, not even with his own spouse, jury foreman Bert Winston shrugged. "My wife told me she already knew all about the case," he said, "so there was no need to discuss it."

Just past five p.m., less than thirty hours after Sam was released from jail, three sheriff's deputies were dispatched to Bay Village to re-arrest him. It was an eerily familiar scene. At quarter of six, a blue Ford sedan eased into the driveway of Dr. Richard Sheppard Sr. As it did, a swarm of men carrying notepads and cameras rushed up the front lawn toward the porch, retracing the footsteps they'd made in the grass eighteen days before. Carl Rossbach led the group, marching up to the front door and ringing the bell. The elder Richard opened it.

"Good evening," Rossbach said simply, just as Fred Drenkhan had. "We'd like to see Sam."

And just as he'd done before, Sam's father was surprisingly respectful. "Step in, gentlemen," he replied. "He's just starting to eat."

Sure enough, as Rossbach and his subordinates entered the house, passing Sam's father and mother, they saw Sam hunched over a plate at the dining room table. He glanced up to look at them, but there was no surprise in his eyes.

"The Grand Jury returned a true bill of first-degree murder against you, Sam," Rossbach explained. "We've come to pick you up."

Ethel Sheppard's eyes welled with tears, but her son showed no emotion. He sighed with the resignation of a man who finally was faced with tending to a chore he'd been putting off. "Can I pack a few things?" he asked dejectedly. "Sure," Rossbach agreed. "And you can finish your dinner, too."

As Sam slowly ate the last meal he would enjoy as a free citizen for the next decade, his mother rushed around the house, packing clothes into a paper bag along with peaches, bananas, and grapes into another. Sam polished off his cherry pie dessert and stood up. He saw his mother stuffing underwear and handkerchiefs into the paper bag, and he asked her to stop. "I've got enough of that stuff in jail," he said.

Seeing her lips quiver, Sam embraced his mother, holding her tight as if to shield her from this horror. After a long moment, she released him and kissed him good-bye. His father, maintaining as much decorum as the situation allowed, reached out and took Sam's hand. "Take care of yourself, son," he said. Sam nodded casually, as if the statement didn't carry any more meaning than all the other times in his life he'd heard it.

Sam turned to face Rossbach. His lips curled into a small, sheepish grin as he held out his left hand to the deputy—looking not unlike all the young boys around Cleveland who had spent their afternoons in basements rehearsing and acting out this scene. Without another word, Rossbach snapped a moon-shaped cuff over Sam's wrist and then circled the other cuff around his own. Sam picked up the leather jacket he'd worn out of this house eighteen nights before and gracefully placed it over the handcuffs.

They stepped out of the house together into a supernova of flashbulbs and slid into the back seat of the blue Ford sedan, which, coincidentally, had carried Susan Hayes to the courthouse to deliver her testimony earlier that day. In addition to the enraptured reporters, dozens of patients watched silently from the balcony of nearby Bay View Hospital. Sam's parents gazed out their front window as their son was once again taken away from them, not knowing they would never again see him as a free man. For in five months, both Richard and Ethel Sheppard would be dead.

The Ford backed slowly out of the driveway and began its journey to the county jail. His brief allowance of freedom—which cost his family roughly $100 per hour—now over, Sam didn't say a word. When he arrived, he changed into the denim pants and t-shirt that had become all too familiar over the past few weeks. "Your old cell is waiting," Mike Ucello told him. "We've got the radio you left waiting, too." Sam nodded sadly as he was led back to his new home and settled in for the night. As he did, his radio delivered the play-by-play story of the Indians extending their winning streak to nine and keeping the Yankees two and a half games back with a dramatic ninth-inning rally to defeat Detroit.

The contrast between his situation and his beloved baseball team was painful. Sam Sheppard would enjoy no more ninth-inning rallies. This time, there would be no reprieve—no more rounds at the hospital, no more convertible rides with his brother, no more homemade cherry pie. Though just yesterday a judge had decreed there was no evidence against him, Sam Sheppard was now in jail for good. And there he would stay for the next ten years.

That night, Cleveland slept sounder than it had in weeks.

26 - NOT THE FOLDING-UP TYPE

Red Skelton was sure he'd broken his neck.

The gag was going to be the highlight of CBS's *The Red Skelton Show* on Sam Sheppard's first night back in jail. The popular comic was going to ram his head through a fake jail door with a block of cement tied to his head. In the final rehearsal, Skelton wanted to make sure it looked right. With the cement block attached, he put his head down and charged toward the door. But the door didn't break. Skelton bounced backward and tumbled to the floor, unconscious. He was rushed out of CBS Television City and to a doctor, slipping in and out of awareness of the pain orbiting his head and neck. He hadn't actually broken his neck, merely sprained it badly, and he'd suffered a concussion. He'd be up and around in a few days, but in the meantime, his producers were scrambling. They had a show to broadcast on national television in a matter of hours and nobody to host it.

In desperation, they turned to one of Skelton's writers to keep his seat warm for the night. Just twenty-nine years old, he was a little-known nightclub comic who had picked up minimal on-air comedy experience while working for a local station in Omaha, Nebraska. He was in way over his head on a national broadcast. He was rushed into the studio thirty minutes before air time, quickly familiarized himself with the script, and before he could get rattled, Johnny Carson's smiling face and quick wit was beamed into homes across the country. With a flavor of self-deprecation, he introduced himself as "the poor man's Red Skelton."

After somehow maneuvering through the show that August night, Carson faded back into oblivion. Eight years later, he took over as host of NBC's *The Tonight Show* and during the next three decades, he would become a household name, turning a simple talk show into a television icon. Along the way, during many of his thousands of opening monologues, Carson would get big laughs for his jokes about the sad state of Cleveland, Ohio.

But on the night of Johnny Carson's national debut, Cleveland's status was nothing to joke about. Neither was its baseball team.

After wrapping up a 7–1 home stand, as August entered its final ten days, the Indians would take their act on the road for a trip that likely would determine whether or not they won the pennant. Cleveland would play nineteen straight games on the road, visiting every American League park but Briggs Stadium in Detroit, not to return to Cleveland until Labor Day. Over that same stretch, the Yankees would play eleven of fourteen games at home—including a three-game set with the Tribe.

The trip started badly with news that Al Rosen had re-injured his finger tagging a Detroit runner in the final game before the Tribe left town. This latest setback would again stifle his productivity. Rosen was now batting under .300, had gone nearly two weeks without hitting a home run, and went twelve straight games without an RBI during an abysmal 0-for-21 streak.

Yet the Indians kept winning. Inexplicably, every time it appeared the team was destined to stumble, it soared. When one player got hurt, another rose to the occasion. When the offense sputtered, the pitching was sublime. On the rare occasion when one of the Big Three didn't have it, the Cleveland batters would scratch out a few extra runs. "Somehow we win games," a *Press* editorial explained. "Somehow we stay in front. And somehow—because of all this—we suggest to the East Coast calumniators that the 1954 brand of young men wearing the Cleveland uniform are not the folding-up type. It may be that in 1954 we will find somebody else folding up—and we'll give you at least one guess who we might have in mind."

"Ho-hum," yawned the *Plain Dealer* after a doubleheader victory over Baltimore that capped a four-game weekend sweep, "just another double victory and another series sweep for the Indians yesterday. Nothing to it." For as well as things had gone, and for as confident as the Indians and their fans had become, a tacit sense of trepidation ensorcelled the club as it began its journey. Would this be the biggest collapse of them all?

Things started well in Baltimore. After a 7–2 trouncing of the Orioles in the opener, combined with a Yankee loss in Fenway Park, the Tribe used a triple play as the catalyst to wipe out an early deficit and rally for another victory on Saturday afternoon. After the game, the Indians gathered in the clubhouse for a belated birthday party for Al Lopez, who turned forty-six the day before. As they stuffed themselves with chicken cacciatore, spaghetti, and birthday cake, they listened on the radio to the conclusion of a thriller in Boston. Twice the Red Sox had rallied with last-minute runs to prevent defeat and extend the game, but they came to bat in the bottom of the twelfth once again trailing by one. Facing Whitey Ford, Boston loaded the bases with one out as the Indians listened intently in Baltimore. Then, at the top of the hour, the game broadcast abruptly ended as the station switched to its regularly scheduled program. The players went berserk, some racing through the clubhouse trying to find out what was happening in Boston, others venting their frustration by pounding on the radio that had betrayed them. Before their frenzy became too violent, the news crackled through the speakers: Don Lenhardt had singled with two out to bring home the tying and winning runs. Incredibly, the trend continued the following day as Boston thwarted New York 8–2 while the Indians mopped the floor with the Orioles. Thanks to the pluck of the Red Sox, the Indians were now five and a half up, their largest lead of the season. The following day, Red Sox manager Lou Boudreau was added to the Indians' team Hall of Fame for his achievements as the Tribe's star shortstop and manager throughout the 1940s. Though Cleveland officials shrugged it off as coincidence, the timing of the announcement—just hours after Boudreau's current team had provided such a dramatic boost to his old one—seemed conspicuous.

Following the idyllic start to the Tribe's barnstorming journey, it was only natural that the road would get bumpier. The Indians steamed into Philadelphia and lost to the miserable Athletics. They seemed destined for a second straight defeat the following day when the A's took a 3–1 advantage into the eighth. With the Yankees notching back-to-back wins over Baltimore, the Indians knew they couldn't afford to allow their cushion to be further punctured. A clutch RBI double by Vic Wertz tied the game in the eighth and then pinch-hitter Hal Naragon rapped a two-out triple in the tenth to deliver one of his twelve RBIs for the season and yet another Cleveland victory. Once again, an unlikely hero had saved the day. "I've never seen the likes of it," Lopez admitted. "There isn't a man who hasn't helped us win a game somewhere along the line."

After winning two of three in Washington, the Indians arrived in Boston with their lead trimmed to three and a half games. The Yankees' hopes that the Red Sox would show the same spoiler determination they'd displayed the previous weekend dissolved when the Tribe swept a doubleheader on a cloudy, chilly Sunday afternoon before the largest Fenway crowd in twelve years. In the first game, Bob Lemon secured his twentieth victory of the season—the sixth time in his career he'd reached that plateau. Then on Monday afternoon the Indians scored five runs in the seventh to wipe out a four-run Boston lead and complete not only a series sweep, but a complete season sweep of the Red Sox in Boston. With eleven Cleveland victories in eleven attempts, for the first time a visiting team had won every game it played in Fenway Park over the course of a season.

With their lead back to four and a half games, the Indians headed to Yankee Stadium for the last time in 1954. The stakes were clear: by sweeping the three-game set or even taking two of three, the Indians could all but put the nail in the Yankee coffin. Conversely, a New York sweep would tip the scales in the other direction, giving the defending champs momentum heading into the season's final month. The Gotham writers laid in wait for the Tribe, anticipating that this was the week that would signal the beginning of this year's annual collapse.

Yet when the Indians' train arrived in New York that night, they showed no signs of melting under pressure. As they marched through Grand Central Station, the players joked and clowned around, catching the attention of all the Yankee rooters on their way home from work. Outside, the remnants of an immense hurricane that had belted the East Coast pelted rain into the streets and sidewalks of the Big Apple. The showers would continue throughout the night and into Tuesday morning, putting the first game of the series in doubt. By mid-day, the stiff winds that had accompanied the rain remained, but the front itself hovered into the Atlantic, and that night, the Indians and Yankees took the field before 58,859 paying customers.

A slight logistical problem greeted the Indians on Wednesday, as they discovered that the Yankees' visiting batboy hadn't shown up at the ballpark. Jim Hegan solved the problem. His twelve-year-old son, Mike, had accompanied his dad on the trip, and now he was drafted into service as the team's batboy. It wouldn't be the youngster's last time in the Indians dugout. Mike, already a dazzling Little League player, would follow his father's footsteps into the big leagues, making his major-league debut in this hallowed ballpark ten years later as a promising Yankee infielder. In his twelve-year career, Mike Hegan would collect more than 500 hits and play in four World Series and then return to Cleveland to become an Indians broadcaster. But on this September day in 1954, he was a starry-eyed kid sitting in a dugout at Yankee Stadium.

Across the field, as he sat in his own dugout prior to the game, Casey Stengel looked tired and haggard and spoke like Captain Ahab in the middle of his impossible quest for Moby-Dick. "Lopez never loses a game, and I can't do nothing about that," he sighed. "But I know what I got to do. I got to win every game from here in. I can't wait around for somebody else to beat him."

Eighteen-game winner Early Wynn was matched with seventeen-game winner Bob Grim in what promised to be a pitching duel. There was no score through three innings, though Grim had been shaky. Wynn, meanwhile, was dominant, retiring the first eleven Yankee batters and not allowing a hit until the seventh. When Cleveland surged ahead 2–0 in the fourth, a group of fans paraded around Yankee Stadium holding up a banner reading "Down With the Yankees—Bye-Bye Casey." The Tribe then put the game away in the eighth on an RBI single by Rosen and a two-run home run by previously slumping Dave Philley, one of several newcomers to the team who shined in 1954. "It's that magic Indians uniform," Lopez said, a sideways acknowledgment of the baseball axiom that just by putting on a Yankee uniform a player becomes much better than he actually is. The final was 6–1, Cleveland, and the Indians' lead was back to the high-water mark of five and a half games on the strength of their twenty-sixth victory of the month—tying an American League record. Afterward, reporters tried to get Lopez to say that this victory had given the Indians the pennant. He refused. "He'd better not say it!" a grumpy Stengel barked when he heard.

The following afternoon, the first of September, Ed Lopat and Mike Garcia squared off, and the Indians crept to an early lead when Jim Hegan tripled to start the third and scored on a sacrifice fly by Garcia. New York went ahead in the fourth when former Indian Eddie Robinson slashed a two-run double. Then Yogi Berra made it 4–1 with a two-run homer in the sixth. With his next pitch, Garcia threw high and tight to Irv Noren, sending him flailing out of the batter's box and bringing the Yankees to their feet in the dugout, shouting at The Bear. Though Garcia was simply demonstrating he wasn't about to give up, the damage had already been done. The Yankees coasted to a much-needed victory.

On Thursday, a Hollywood movie crew was on hand at Yankee Stadium to film background scenes for the upcoming Marilyn Monroe film *The Seven-Year Itch*. Two weeks later, in front of a thousand spectators on Lexington Avenue and Fifty-Second Street, the same crew would capture the movie's trademark scene, when Monroe unsuccessfully tries to keep her dress from flying up to her waist as she stands on a subway grating. It's rumored that this scene was the last straw, shattering Monroe's troubled marriage to former Yankee superstar Joe DiMaggio, who was outraged by it. A month later, 274 days after they were married, Monroe filed for divorce.

Fittingly, the game that marked the beginning of production for an iconic movie and the memorable breakup that followed in its wake would mirror the theatrical element. Win or lose, the game would represent a pivotal moment of New York's season. A win would pull the Yankees back to within three and a half games with three weeks to play, while a loss would put them five back in the loss column—a tough row to hoe against a hot team that very well could go the remainder of the season without losing five more games. While Stengel's squad entered focused on survival, the Indians hoped to deliver a knockout punch.

Baseball's two best teams would send their best pitchers to the mound, both carrying ERAs under 3.00: Bob Lemon against Whitey Ford. While Ford cruised through the first three innings, Lemon wiggled out of jams in the second and fourth. With two out in the top of the fifth, Sam Dente, still filling in at shortstop while George Strickland's shattered jaw healed, blasted his first and only home run of 1954 to give Cleveland a 1–0 lead. To jubilant fans back in Cleveland, it seemed like an appropriate way to turn the lights out on the hated Yankees: an unsung substitute driving in the stake. But before rumors of New York's demise could begin, Mickey Mantle led off the sixth with a game-tying home run. Then Hank Greenberg and the Indians finally paid a price for the Vic Wertz experiment. After thriving at his new position of first base all summer, Wertz committed two errors in the inning that led to a pair of unearned runs and a 3–1 Yankee lead.

With Rudy Regalado on first and one out in the eighth, Hank Majeski pinch-hit for Bob Lemon and lofted a long drive to left field that had enough juice to reach the seats and tie the game. But Irv Noren made a stretching catch against the fence to rob Majeski of a dramatic home run and maintain the Yankee lead. Noren's theft proved even more painful when Larry Doby blasted a one-out home run in the ninth to pull Cleveland within a single run. Rosen walked, and Wertz came to the plate with a shot at redemption, representing the go-ahead run. Instead, he popped out, and Dave Philley grounded out to end the game. Once again, the Yankees had persevered. "This was the big one that got away," Gordon Cobbledick lamented. "It was the one that would have killed the Yankees, and because they won it, they're still very much alive."

As the Indians' DC-3 soared over the city on its way to Chicago, a despondent Vic Wertz looked out the window. Far below, he could see Yankee Stadium, where just a few hours before he had committed the two biggest mistakes of his career. Finally, his inner turmoil boiled to the surface. Wertz turned, placed his knee in the cushion of his seat, and leaned on the backrest to face Bob Lemon sitting just behind him.

"Dammit, Lem," Wertz said in a raspy voice, "you know how sorry I am that those things happened out there today." Lemon's eyes met Wertz's, and he could see the emotional weight his teammate had been carrying. Lemon, who'd been the victim of countless instances of good and bad breaks in his career, shook his head and offered a small smile. This bald kid was something else. "Forget it, Vic," he said. "Nobody told you when you came to this ballclub you were going to play first base. You're an outfielder playing first base and you've done a fine job."

Now it was Wertz's turn to smile. "I'll make it up to you," he promised. "Bet on that, I'll make it up." Once again, he felt a part of the team, and the mood on the plane instantly lightened. His face still curled into a satisfied grin, Wertz glanced back out the window. This time, he noticed not only Yankee Stadium, but his eyes flowed east across the Harlem River to the dark, oblong shadow of the Polo Grounds. In that moment, Wertz couldn't have known that in less than four weeks, it would be there he would deliver his promise to Bob Lemon.

With lightning bursting through black clouds in the distance, the plane soared west. Now the Indians would return to Comiskey Park, the site of their most horrifying display of the season. On their last trip to Chicago two months before, the Indians had lost four straight, scoring just five runs. Now, with the Yankees re-energized, the White Sox had a golden opportunity to play spoiler. On the Friday night that opened Labor Day weekend, the Indians took a 3–2 lead into the bottom of the seventh but ran into trouble when the White Sox loaded the bases with one out. With the Comiskey crowd riled, and the Yankees stomping the Senators in D.C., Al Lopez knew he couldn't let this one get away. He called on Mike Garcia, who'd pitched six innings in Yankee Stadium two days earlier, to rescue his club from disaster.

But before Garcia could throw a pitch, the clouds opened and thick drops of rain pummeled the humid Chicago landscape. Umpires suspended play, and Lopez and his players sat and paced in their dugout like expectant fathers in a hospital waiting room, with nothing but worrisome thoughts whirling through their minds: What if Garcia didn't have it tonight? What if this turned into a big inning that led to defeat, pulling the Yankees to within three games? What if defeat here set the tone for another disastrous weekend in the Windy City and the

Indians returned to Cleveland Sunday night clinging desperately to a half-game lead? What if, as soon as the rain passed, their most colossal September swoon would begin?

After thirteen agonizing minutes, the front swayed over Lake Michigan and the game resumed. And those jittery thoughts faded into the Chicago night as smoothly and silently as the rain showers. Garcia got catcher Matt Batts to pop out, then enticed Johnny Groth to ground to second to quell the White Sox threat. The Bear did indeed have it tonight, and he cruised through the eighth and ninth, permitting only an infield single, to collect what would retroactively be ruled his sixth save of the season. The Tribe had dodged yet another bullet.

Things didn't go as well on Saturday night when a 3–1 Cleveland lead vanished in the wake of two sixth-inning errors that opened the floodgates for five unearned runs and an easy Chicago victory. Luckily, the Yankees had stumbled in Washington, minimizing the damage. The Tribe bounced back Sunday afternoon, sprinting to a 5–1 lead in the fourth and coasting to an 8–2 triumph. Meanwhile, in the nation's capital, Eddie Yost delivered a two-out RBI single in the bottom of the ninth to give the Senators another stunning victory over New York.

As dusk fell across the Midwest that balmy evening, the Indians flew east to Baltimore for the final stop on their nineteen-game gauntlet before returning home on Labor Day. Back in Cleveland, the start of the holiday weekend was celebrated much like the previous one, with a repetition of the Independence Day cookouts and outdoor activities amidst record temperatures that soared into the mid-90s. Attending these backyard barbeques were the uneasy memories of the story that greeted Cleveland the last time the city paused for a summer celebration: a pretty young housewife murdered in her own bed in upscale Bay Village.

Over the past two months, the Sheppard case had turned the city upside down and inside out, shattering the veil of safety people felt protected them in their own backyards and the trust they'd invested in upstanding neighbors like Sam Sheppard. Marilyn Sheppard's murder rattled not only Bay Village but Cleveland itself, and for many on this Labor Day weekend, their hometown seemed a dramatically different place.

For all that had changed between these two summer holidays, one constant remained. On the morning of Independence Day—the morning of Marilyn Sheppard's murder—the Indians held a four and a half game lead. Now, with Dr. Sam locked away, Cleveland newspapers enjoying a surge in readership, the national media descending on northeast Ohio, and sleepy Bay Village torn apart by publicity-seekers, ghoulish tourists, and the dramatically differing opinions of its own citizens, the Indians' lead remained four and a half games.

Amidst this mixture of anxiety and constancy, the final act in this fateful summer of shadows was about to begin.

A·U·T·U·M·N
Interlude

Game 4

CASEY STENGEL SAT ALONE among the sparsely filled box seats at Municipal Stadium, staring at the field with a leathery hand resting on his cheek, looking like a man who'd just had his car stolen while he sat in it. He studied the field as if trying to convince himself of the reality of his surroundings. Beyond all expectations, Casey Stengel was watching another American League team in the World Series.

Though the seemingly impossible—his Yankees being bested in a pennant race—had happened, Stengel's mid-summer suggestion that he should be fired as New York manager did not come to pass. He signed a new two-year contract three days after the Yankees were officially eliminated and immediately began reflecting on what had happened in 1954 and how he could prevent it from happening again in 1955.

"Now, you might think that I am worrying about myself," Stengel explained to a reporter, "which would be as far from the truth as we are from the Indians." Bouncing off topic as he often did, Stengel began talking about what had happened to his Yankees in September. "We tumbled from four and a half to eight and a half faster than the stock market in 1929," he explained, then added with a wink, "which didn't do

me no good, either." The turning
point in the pennant race, Stengel
felt, was the three-game losing
streak at Fenway Park in late
August.

The reporter asked what
had put Cleveland over the top.
"Yeah, the pitching," Stengel
finished for him. "It beat us."
Before another question could be
asked, Stengel pulled back from
the specifics to ruminate on the
overall. "So down we go after five
straight world's championships,"
he sighed, "and up comes
Cleveland. And that is life."

In the time it took the
reporter to scribble down this
thought, Stengel turned to the
future. "I feel good because we
can, and will, do a lot better in
1955," he said, "and the Indians
cannot—and will not—improve
on their 1954 showing. I think
they have a one-shot. Their club
reached its peak this season and
will slip next year."

Yet as Stengel looked
out at the Municipal Stadium
infield being prepared by the

groundskeepers for the fourth
game of the World Series, he
knew, just as everyone did, that
the Indians had already begun
slipping.

Somehow down three
games to none, the Indians were
now less interested in winning
the Series than they were simply
in salvaging some of their pride.
And in that desperate spirit, Al
Lopez made a trio of changes to
his lineup. First, though he was
no healthier than he'd been the
day before, Al Rosen was inserted
back at the cleanup spot. George
Strickland, who'd gone hitless in
nine at-bats in the Series thus far,
was benched in place of backup
Sam Dente. And most notably,
Lopez felt forced to make a move
that would haunt him through
the coming decades. Rather
than giving the ball to Bob Feller
for Game Four, with the season
hanging in the balance, Lopez
opted to start his ace. Three days
after throwing 142 pitches in the
Polo Grounds, Bob Lemon would
take the mound again in the hope

of earning a stay of execution for the battered Tribe. "In a spot like this," Lopez explained at the time, "you have to go with your best." Four decades later, Lopez would give an even more succinct reply on why he didn't go with Feller with the entire season hanging in the balance: "He wasn't that good of a pitcher anymore."

At first, the choice appeared sound. Beneath a warm October sun and crystal blue sky, Lemon cruised through the first inning, and for the first time in the Series, neither team plated a run in the initial frame. But trouble began in the second when Lemon walked Hank Thompson, then surrendered a double to Monte Irvin. With runners on second and third, Davey Williams hit a screaming liner directly to Vic Wertz at first, who snagged it for the first out. Then Wertz, following the desperate mood of the club and trying to extinguish the scoring threat, saw Irvin had drifted off second and knew he would have to scramble to get

back. Envisioning a momentum-killing double play, Wertz fired the ball to second. Dente read the situation and started to the bag to receive the throw but didn't react quickly enough. Wertz's bullet sprayed over the bag and into left center field. Thompson waltzed home with the first run and Irvin took third. The giant crowd, totaling better than 78,000, groaned.

Things got even worse seconds later when Wes Westrum lifted a routine fly ball to right field. Wally Westlake approached the ball and prepared to fire it quickly to home plate in case Irvin had any thoughts of trying to score after the catch. But in the process, the ball jostled out of his glove and bounced to the grass, Cleveland's second error in less than a minute. Irvin scored and Westrum was awarded first base. The beleaguered fans again grunted in disbelief. Their beloved baseball team, which had played symphonic baseball all summer, now looked like the Keystone Cops.

Lemon got out of the inning, but immediately dug another hole in the third by allowing back-to-back singles, followed by an RBI double from Willie Mays to make it 3–0. Though Lemon dug deep and struck out Irvin on a full count with the bases loaded (Leo Durocher had considered sending up Dusty Rhodes as a pinch-hitter but opted against it), then got a ground out to end the rally, it had become clear that the Indians' ace just didn't have it today. After the Giants loaded the bases again with nobody out in the fifth, Lemon was replaced by Hal Newhouser.

But even the revitalizing magic that had fueled Newhouser all summer was now gone. He promptly walked in one run then gave up a single to Irvin to score two more. When the mess was finally swept away by Ray Narleski, the Giants had plated four runs, making the score a surreal 7–0. And since to this point the Indians had collected only one hit themselves, much

of the crowd began filing toward the exits, looking to salvage something of this beautiful Saturday afternoon. Or perhaps more appropriately, to permit this magnificent baseball team to salvage what little dignity it had left and die alone. As the subdued line of fans slowly streamed out of the ballpark, it re-entered a city that was somehow different. "Even the buildings looked shocked," Ed McAuley wrote in the *Cleveland News*. As it often does, shock and disappointment evolved into violence. Police were called to break up a fight between two men on East Ninth Street that had begun as an argument over whether Feller should have started instead of Lemon.

The few thousand who did remain until the bitter end did so primarily because they'd been paralyzed by disbelief. As a result, the *Plain Dealer* wrote, they became "witnesses to the embalming." As if trying to make it interesting, the Giants committed two uncharacteristic errors in the fifth, then Don Liddle served up a home run to pinch-hitter Hank Majeski to make it 7–3. Cleveland scratched together another run in the seventh and Don Mossi and Mike Garcia tamed the Giants' bats, but by now the result was a foregone conclusion. The Tribe had one final chance to come alive in the eighth, but with runners on the corners and only one out, Vic Wertz and Wally Westlake, each representing the tying run, struck out. It brought Cleveland's Series tally with runners in scoring position to a horrific four-for-forty—a batting average of .100, only slightly worse than the team's .190 overall batting average. After a season of breaking records and rewriting history, the Indians managed to do it one final time: they left thirty-seven men on base, more than any other team in a four-game World Series.

The thirty-seventh and final stranded runner was Sam Dente, who stood alone on first base with two down in the bottom of the ninth as Dale Mitchell pinch-hit for Dave Pope. The crowd, by now beaten into a coma of indifference, sprang to life with an unrealistic enthusiasm as it cheered for longtime fan-favorite Mitchell, who'd been one of the heroes of the 1948 World Series six years before. But now he reflected the sudden, inexplicable impotence of the greatest team in American League history. He weakly popped a Johnny Antonelli pitch along the third-base line. Hank Thompson caught it, and just like that, at 3:55 p.m. on Saturday, October 2, the New York Giants were world champions.

As the players piled out of the dugout and celebrated between third and home, the natural question telegraphed its way through the baseball world.

How?

How on earth could a team this good, this historically significant, be emasculated on such a grand stage? How could a team that had bested the Yankees be exterminated by New York's other, afterthought ballclub? "Maybe we simply caught them at the right time," Giants captain Alvin Dark conjectured. In the afterglow of his greatest triumph as manager, even more significant than coming back from the netherworlds of the standings to win the 1951 pennant, Leo Durocher had to admit that the Series was a bit of an aberration. "Everything we did seemed to be right," he said. "Everything they did seemed to go against them." Al Lopez was even more on the nose with his assessment: "We're not that bad and they're not that good."

And it was Lopez who bore the brunt of the shocking disappointment. Al Lopez, who thought he'd finally made it over the frustrating hump that had constricted him the previous three seasons, sat in his office, his eyes glassy and unfocused, with his feet up on his desk. Though he never drank, on this afternoon, he sipped on a beer. As they carefully approached him, the Cleveland

reporters who'd witnessed his disappointments over the past three years had never seen him quite like this. They gathered around him like timid children, none of them really wanting to begin the process of making him relive this miserable experience. They stood in silence for a long moment, not sure how to proceed.

Finally, one writer, his eyes darting to the floor, mumbled, "You know how we feel, Al. What can we say at a time like this?" The comment eroded Lopez's final layer of control. His eyes filled with tears, and he lifted a shaky little finger to flick away the droplets like dust. "Thanks, fellas," he choked. Then, as best they could, they began the questions.

"They faced our best and still beat us," Lopez explained somberly. "That's all there is to it." When late-arriving photographers asked him to put his hands to his head and appear dejected, Lopez snorted, "What's the matter with the way I am? I don't see how I can look any worse than I feel." Neither could his players. By all appearances, they didn't look or act as if they'd just been swept in the World Series. "There wasn't any moaning or despair in our locker room," Bob Feller would say. "It all happened too fast for any of that. It was painless at the time . . . . The pain set in later."

Yet Feller's own disappointment was both immediate and lasting. Having seen his last chance to capture a victory in a World Series slip through his fingers, the pitching legend was crushed. Not only had his teammates let him down, but he never got a chance to aid the cause, not pitching a single inning of the four games. He never publicly expressed any bitterness about Lopez's decision, nor did he ever ask him about it. But the experience would weigh on Feller through the coming decades.

Early Wynn, who'd agreed to serve as a guest columnist for the *Cleveland News* for the Series,

shook his head as he looked at Gordon Cobbledick. "This is a tougher racket than I thought," Wynn sighed. "What can you write about a thing like this?" The players tried to console each other, but admitted that it would be a long winter, particularly for those who lived in Cleveland.

Then somebody mentioned the Browns. A cloud of relief passed through the clubhouse. The Browns would ease the Indians' suffering, just as they'd done the previous three years after the Tribe's heart-wrenching second-place finishes. In each of those autumns, the Browns had started fast out of the gate and reached the NFL Championship Game, only to lose three successive times to what they felt were inferior teams. The '54 Browns had begun the season six days earlier by getting dominated by a mediocre Philadelphia squad, an indication that their days as an elite National Football League team were over. Thanks to the Indians, the Browns got a reprieve by not having to face the defending world champion Detroit Lions the next day (after all the fuss about scheduling and debates about whether or not the stadium could host two big events in one day, the ballpark would now sit empty on Sunday afternoon), but it would only be a temporary reprieve. Over the next few weeks, many Indians players agreed, Cleveland fans and sportswriters would shift from asking "What happened to the Indians?" to "What happened to the Browns?"

Yet even in the coming winter months, Hank Greenberg would still be asking how this sweep had happened. As he slowly walked through the dim clubhouse, he looked haggard. Dark circles were brushed under his eyes and the wrinkles on his face somehow looked deeper and longer than they had a week earlier. He approached each player and shook his hand, thanking him for all he'd done to contribute to

what—until Wednesday—had been a rhapsodic season. Then he approached Vic Wertz, who more than anyone had symbolized the uniqueness of 1954 and represented the indefinable ingredient of a championship.

"Vic," Greenberg said heartily, "you were wonderful." Wertz took Greenberg's hand and shook it, offering a small smile in return. "You've helped the ballclub tremendously." The general manager then looked into the eyes of the man he'd traded for four months before and with a bit more sincerity than he'd offered the other players, said, "Thanks a lot."

Wertz nodded and replied, "I want to thank you, too. If it hadn't been for you, I never would have had the chance." Their handshake seemed to last longer than the others, as if each man knew what it represented and what it would mean to let go. But eventually, they did.

Greenberg, the clock now having struck midnight on his

fairy tale, melted back into the mass of humanity crowding the clubhouse, and Wertz prepared to appease the gaggle of reporters heading toward him. The only Indian batter to even approach competence in the World Series, Wertz tried to maintain the confidence and optimism he exuded the day before. He answered the questions patiently and softly, then, as if talking to himself, added a final thought. "We're gonna come back next year and win 112 games," he said, his voice cracking with emotion. "Then we'll beat those guys."

But they'd had four chances at them with the best team the American League had ever seen. And they'd failed each time.

Saturday's loss turned out to be the most painful of all, even for those who had no interest in baseball or the Indians. By eliminating the prospect of a fifth game the following day, the Indians had stripped more than a million dollars out of the coffers of their city as out-of-town guests

left their hotels and started home a day earlier than planned. The biggest crowd of the weekend had been expected for Sunday, one that was to mirror the colossal gathering that had descended upon downtown Cleveland for the Yankee Doubleheader three weeks before.

The city had been set to take in another $6,000 for rental of the stadium, $6,700 from the concession receipts, and a delicious $14,000 in sales tax from the tickets. But that was nothing compared to the $526,000 the team would lose in ticket sales. Instead of raking in the profits of another record day, money began gushing out of the Indians front office, which announced it would give refunds to all fans who had purchased tickets for Game Five (prompting several quick-thinking youngsters to purchase unused Game Five tickets from fans headed out of town). Stadium concessioners, who'd spent much of the week concerned they wouldn't have enough supplies to satisfy the weekend crowds, were suddenly stuck with truckloads of food. They were lucky enough to be permitted to return the hot dogs but had to suffer losses on the buns, popcorn, and peanuts. Better than 50,000 programs remained in boxes, unsold. In addition to the lost profits as a part-owner, Bob Hope, who had hurriedly wrapped up production on his latest movie and bought tickets and transportation for countless friends and acquaintances, had invested even more in the weekend. "I spent plane fare and everything to see this," he complained afterward. "I could have gotten a bad stomach by just staying in Los Angeles." Just as Hope could look to more promising days in 1955, local hotels and restaurants could be reassured they would make up for some of the lost revenue with a second wave of visitors set to arrive in two weeks for the start of the Sheppard trial.

But on the night following Game Four, downtown Cleveland's restaurants and bars stood abandoned and quiet. For the first time in recent memory, Cleveland was anything but a Saturday-night town. Signs in bar windows announcing that they would be open for patrons to watch the game on Sunday were removed and torn to pieces. The highly publicized Alpine Village victory celebration scheduled for Sunday night was cancelled. As the evening crickets began their symphony, it no longer felt like summer. Because of the long drought that had roasted lawns through July and August, the leaves of the parched trees had begun their colorful metamorphosis early and were already beginning to fall. They crackled across sidewalks and swirled through backyards, and the tangy smell of burning leaves lilted through neighborhoods at twilight. On this Saturday evening, fall arrived. Which meant, of course, that winter was coming.

As Cleveland brooded, the Giants jetted back to New York

(with a banner painted on the outside of the fuselage reading "World Champions 1954"), where they were greeted by 2,500 adoring fans at LaGuardia Airport. They then were whisked to a festive victory celebration at the Biltmore Hotel, in the same ballroom where four nights before the Mutual Network had broadcast a World Series preview show that had essentially crowned the Indians world champs. In the days to come, accusations and explanations for what had happened were exchanged like baseball cards. Chicago GM Frank Lane, who had come to the Indians' defense all summer and stood up for them when they were labeled as chokers, was now whistling a different tune. "The other clubs in our league ought to sue the Indians for libel," he said. St. Louis sportswriter J. Roy Stockton called Cleveland "the most overrated club that ever went into a World's Series." *Sporting News* surmised that the Indians had "embraced their entire league

in the humiliation which befell them." In the *Washington Post* Shirley Povich icily declared "The Indians demonstrated by their futility in the Series that they are never to be confused with the fine Yankee teams which used to knock off the National Leaguers in October." While the Indians' play in the Series was certainly worthy of criticism, one can only wonder why these insightful scribblers hadn't noticed the team's flaws in time to keep them from predicting that Cleveland would cruise to a Series victory.

Even George Weiss, general manager of the disposed-of Yankees, could afford to be smug. "I thought we would have a long, tough struggle to get back up there," he said. "Now, maybe not. I can't see how the Indians are going to recover from this." Casey Stengel and Yogi Berra also got into the act, publicly criticizing the Indians for their embarrassing play. When word got back to Cleveland, the Indians were not amused. Sam Dente, however, simply shrugged it off, saying, "The Yankees had their chance."

Of course, so had the Indians.

Al Rosen, his body aching and creaking from a season of constant injury, phoned his home in Shaker Heights, where his in-laws were watching his young son. He asked if they could stay an extra day—he planned on remaining in the city that night. Rosen borrowed a couple of sleeping pills from the trainer, checked into the Statler Hotel at Euclid and Twelfth Avenue, eased his weary muscles into bed, and slept for the next eighteen hours.

"We finally beat the Yankees," he would say years later. "And in what should have been a glorious year, we wound up absolutely in the depths of despair."

And as Rosen slept on that drizzly Sunday morning in downtown Cleveland, where a scheduled World Series game wasn't played that afternoon, no one could know just how deep or how broad that despair would extend.

PART FOUR

TWILIGHT OF THE GODS

AMERICAN LEAGUE STANDINGS
ON THE MORNING OF LABOR DAY
MONDAY, SEPTEMBER 6, 1954

	W	L	PCT	GB
CLEVELAND	97	39	.713	—
NEW YORK	92	43	.681	4½
CHICAGO	87	50	.635	10½
BOSTON	60	74	.448	36
DETROIT	59	76	.437	37½
WASHINGTON	57	77	.425	39
PHILADELPHIA	45	90	.333	51½
BALTIMORE	44	92	.324	53

27 - WHAMMY BE DAMNED

E ach time the twinkling lights of an aircraft began to glide toward them through the steamy darkness, the crowd murmured, wondering if this was it—if the massive celebration that would last throughout the winter could finally begin.

Many of the 10,000 fans at Hopkins Airport that Labor Day evening had been waiting more than three hours to participate in the welcome back rally planned by a city council subcommittee. Even as the wheels of the Indians' plane left the ground in Baltimore, where the Tribe had split a holiday doubleheader with the Orioles to conclude their epic nineteen-game road trip, the parking lots at Hopkins were full. Late-arriving fans resorted to pulling their cars over along Hummel Road and hiking into the airport on foot. Thirty policemen and a battalion of civil defense officers helped direct the snarled arteries of traffic.

They began jamming the observation deck just after sunset on what had been an unbearable Labor Day, the hottest in Cleveland history, with the temperature reaching a record-breaking ninety-eight degrees by mid-afternoon. Even as midnight approached, with the scorching sun departed and an inky blackness having settled over the city, thermometers still registered in the mid-eighties. While those on the outdoor observation deck were sticky, others jammed inside the

348

airport's recently constructed concourse and administration building felt as if they were evaporating in the still, stifling air. Yet even the record heat couldn't stifle the enthusiasm permeating the airport. The fans cheered the baton twirlers and bounced to the peppy tunes played by a twenty-piece band and clapped as council members Mary Sotak and Joseph Horwitz danced an impromptu polka on the tarmac to amuse the masses. Nearby, the players' wives stood together, wreathed in smiles, with beautiful corsages pinned to their dresses.

Just before eleven p.m., the anticipation throbbed as the Capital Airlines plane pulled up to gate five. WERE interrupted its usual programming to broadcast the arrival to its listeners. The steady hum of the crowd, which to those listening on the radio sounded like water running into a bathtub, swelled to a roar as the stairway was wheeled into place and the passengers filed out, wearing the tired smiles that accompanied sleeping in foreign beds every night for three weeks. The scene was unlike any the players had ever witnessed. Across the observation deck, wildly cheering fans held up distributed signs reading "Indians Welcome Home." They'd also been given car stickers showing Chief Wahoo standing inside the Municipal Stadium bowl holding a tomahawk in one hand and the '54 pennant in the other. "Let's Help Bring Home a Winner," the message below read.

And winners the Indians were, having taken thirteen of the games on the trip, actually increasing their lead over the Yankees by two games along the way. Even dropping a heartbreaker in the nightcap in Baltimore that day proved painless. Though the Indians rallied to score two runs with two out in the ninth to tie the contest and force extra innings, the Orioles pulled it out in the tenth, opening the door for New York to creep closer. Yet after taking a 7–0 lead into the sixth inning of the second game of their doubleheader against Boston, the Yankees imploded, allowing eight runs in the next three innings to fall to the Red Sox once again. When Tribe fans heard the final from Yankee Stadium, many thought back to the talk emanating from New York all summer about how the Indians were bound to collapse when the going got tough. "Who's choking now?" became the evening's unspoken mantra.

Thus the Cleveland lead remained four and a half games with just sixteen to play, and Cleveland's magic number for mathematically eliminating the mighty Yankees stood at thirteen. "The old you-know-what is practically floating in the breeze atop the flag pole at the stadium," the *Plain Dealer* offered with a wink, alongside an editorial brazenly titled "Welcome Home, Champs!" Their Indians were back home, "looking and acting like champions," it stated. "You've been a credit to yourselves, to your city, and to baseball. Tie it up now, as quickly as possible. No sense in prolonging the agony for Mr. Casey Stengel. He may not admit it, but he's had it! You gave it to him—but good!

"When you put yesterday's results into the hopper you can come up with only one conclusion—whammy be damned—the Indians are headed for the pennant, and they won't be stopped."

In contrast to Stengel's agony, as Al Lopez stepped off the plane, he was handed a bursting bouquet of red carnations and was kissed on the cheek by Councilwoman Sotak. Mayor Celebrezze stood beaming nearby, offering Lopez a handshake as Jimmy Dudley began introducing each player over a hastily assembled public-address system. After basking in the glow of civic appreciation, the players boarded a bus that followed an escort of ten motorcycles and several police cars back to their parking lot.

Yet for all the festivity and festoonery, organizers emphasized this was not a victory celebration. There would be plenty of time for that later. Right now, there was still work to be done and—though none at the airport pep rally that night would say it out loud—still time for the wheels to come off the wagon. Just six years before, when the Indians last won the pennant, they stood in third place on Labor Day, four and a half games behind front-running Boston, and wound up finishing the season tied with the Red Sox for first. But few Clevelanders dwelled on such details on this holiday. Somber thoughts and cruel twists of fate were for others—like Sam Sheppard.

As Clevelanders celebrated the final weekend of summer at the zoo or at one of the sixteen city pools that would close for the season on Tuesday, Dr. Sam spent Labor Day on a rusty cot in his tiny jail cell, glistening with sweat while listening to the Indians on his radio before enjoying a dinner of frankfurters, potatoes, beets, and coffee. As the mayor who had condemned him hobnobbed at the airport, where members of the city council who had watched as he was publicly crucified danced a polka, Sam's thoughts joined theirs in planning for the forthcoming October. Yet his were focused on the trial, scheduled to begin two weeks after the World Series.

Cleveland businessmen, meanwhile, were also getting nervous. If the Indians could indeed seal the deal, account managers and salesmen would be barraged with requests from customers and clients for World Series tickets and hotel rooms for the first weekend in October. And in some cases, their livelihood would be affected by their ability to deliver seats to the Series. Very quietly, the Indians front office began soliciting many of these same businesses to purchase ads for a potential World Series program.

But before the World Series could come to Cleveland, the hated Yankees would come to make one final attempt to prevent it. And as the short workweek began, all of northeast Ohio prepared for the following Sunday, when baseball's two best teams would play two games at Municipal Stadium. Sportswriters flooded into Cleveland for the doubleheader that had become the primary topic of sports discussion in every coffee shop and bar across the nation. So many reporters and photographers were now following the Indians that the players laid down a new rule: no outsiders were permitted in the clubhouse within one hour prior to the start of each game and for fifteen minutes after the conclusion. Even veteran Bob Feller, who had received more than his share of media attention and been through pennant races before, was amazed at the interest. "It was getting so we couldn't tie our shoelaces without a stranger staring at us," he said.

Prior to the next game, the Cleveland Chamber of Commerce presented each player with a leather billfold with his name stamped on it in gold letters, subtly hinting that they would need these billfolds to hold all the World Series bonuses. Yet neither the presentations nor life under the microscope affected the team on the field. After a welcomed off day, Early Wynn picked up his twentieth and the team's ninety-ninth win of the season, followed by the 100th in a comeback victory in extra innings over the Athletics the following afternoon. They became the first American League team to reach the centennial mark in eight years and just the nineteenth in league history. For all their dominance, the Yankees hadn't won a hundred games in a season in twelve years.

Better still, unknown Baltimore pitcher Joe Coleman held the Yankees to one hit that afternoon in a 1–0 Oriole triumph that extended the Indians' lead to five and a half games. With the bright lights of

September now upon them, the Yankees had suffered their fourth loss in seven games.

On Friday night, Cleveland honored Lou Boudreau for his recent induction into the Indians Hall of Fame (and, unspoken, for his Boston club's success against the Yankees) by presenting him with a gold clock prior to its game with the Red Sox. Even with Al Rosen out with a leg injury suffered the previous afternoon and Larry Doby forced to leave the game with a charley horse, the Indians cruised to a 4–2 triumph, followed by a dominating performance on Saturday afternoon as "Hard Luck" Houtteman pitched a complete-game shutout for his fifteenth victory of the year—the number he predicted would foretell an Indians pennant. In Chicago, the Yankees blew a two-run, ninth-inning lead and lost to the White Sox in ten. "Oh, Casey!" Frank Lane shouted from his box in the second deck at Comiskey Park following the game. "Now let's see how good you are!" The Indians' lead had now swelled to six and a half games with twelve remaining.

It would take a miracle for the Yankees to catch the Indians now, yet miracles seemed to be woven into their pinstripes. If their greatest triumph—and Cleveland's ultimate collapse—was forthcoming, it would begin the following afternoon, when the two best baseball teams on the planet would play the doubleheader for which both had been waiting for six months.

On Sunday, September 12, 1954, Municipal Stadium would be the site of a shootout between these longtime rivals, with the American League pennant blowing in the September breeze between them.

28 - THE YANKEE DOUBLEHEADER, ACT ONE

The sun rose in Cleveland that Sunday at 7:04 a.m. Usually this mundane occurrence went unnoticed, but on this day, the bright, cloudless dawn foreshadowed history. Sunshine gradually crept across the landscape, stretching long shadows across front lawns and living room carpets, and in those shafts of light, the Indians front office saw the pot of gold at the end of the rainbow.

After a week of conjecture and prognostication, the morning light warmed the chill off a crisp Saturday night and informed Greater Cleveland that yes, the weather would indeed cooperate. Team officials knew the crowd for the doubleheader would top 70,000 no matter what the conditions, but if September 12 turned out to be one of those shimmering days that straddled between summer and fall, even more fans would be drawn to Municipal Stadium. And sure enough, at nine a.m., with the temperature creeping into the sixties, fans wearing light topcoats and hats began descending on the mammoth ballpark to snatch up the 20,000 bleacher and standing-room seats that remained at sixty cents and $1.25 apiece, respectively. By the time the gates opened at 10:30, the remaining stockpile of tickets had been picked clean. Indians publicist Nate Wallack admitted he'd never seen such demand for tickets for a single date. Even Tris Speaker, the Hall of Fame center fielder who had managed the Indians to the 1920 world title and remained a franchise emissary, was affected by the demand. Though he'd spent much of the summer in the hospital recovering from heart ailments, he'd still been barraged with requests for tickets for the event that simply came to be referred to as "the Yankee Doubleheader."

The city, too, was prepared for the onslaught. Every downtown hotel was filled to capacity and parking lots were already jammed. The traffic commissioner assigned 115 officers to help direct cars and control busy intersections, and, starting in the seventh inning of the second game, East Ninth Street would revert to one-way traffic going south between Lakeside and Carnegie and would remain so until all the stadium lots were empty. The Cleveland Transit System provided "Baseball Specials," trains running downtown from the suburbs every few minutes. Nineteen specially designated trains consisting of more than 300 cars would bring fans from all around Ohio, Pennsylvania, and New York, some from as far as Niagara Falls. For those driving to the game, parking would come at a premium. Parking was prohibited along all main roads downtown, and police were quick to enforce, issuing hundreds of tickets and authorizing the towing of dozens of cars. Many drivers who found empty spots in private lots discovered a new problem. Since many of the smaller lots weren't operated full-time, their owners weren't required to register with the city and obtain a license. As a result, they weren't held to the city's price guidelines and could charge whatever they wanted. Many motorists were outraged when they discovered they'd have to pay upward of $1.50 to park their cars.

Inside the ballpark, concessioners were ready. Employees of the team's vending company had worked until one a.m. preparing the thirty-five refreshment booths with necessary supplies. Before the day was over, they would sell more than five tons of hot dogs and roughly 100,000 bottles of beer. And with the afternoon slated to be cool on the lake, the stands were primed with steaming coffee and hot chocolate.

And for many fans, the doubleheader became a daylong experience. By 11:30, one hour after the gates opened and two hours before game time, the standing-room area behind the outfield fence was completely filled with more than 10,000 fans. Latecomers were forced to look elsewhere for real estate, and many resorted to sitting on concourse guardrails and hunching down on sloping ramps. Even those fans lucky enough to find prime standing room were lucky if they could see half the field. The tight quarters—and record sales of beer—ultimately led to several fistfights breaking out. Before a single player took the field, tension pulsed through Municipal Stadium.

Even those who didn't have tickets woke up with a mixture of excitement and unease. The *Plain Dealer* addressed the pulse of the city that morning with an editorial aptly titled "Relax."

"Tense this morning?

"Feel a bit more on edge than usual, especially for a Sunday?

"Has breakfast tasted a little less palatable than usual, the voices of those around you a bit more grating? Has the neighbor's dog been barking louder than you've heard him?"

Readers nodded their heads in silent agreement. Some even wondered if the barking dog might have been a gentle nod to the Sheppard's dog Kokie and his well-documented silence the morning of July 4.

"Relax," the article continued, "at least until 1:30 this afternoon. It's just that you're on the edge on D-H Day, a common affliction.

"For the old nerves are just achieving a fine stage of balance and responsiveness in anticipation of this afternoon's doubleheader between the Indians and the Yankees.

"Good luck and may the better team win at least one. Indian rooters think they know without a doubt which team that is."

Yet for all their confidence in their ballclub, Indians fans couldn't forget that this scenario was eerily reminiscent of past disappointments. Two years before, better than 73,000 packed into Municipal Stadium on the second Sunday in September expecting to cheer the Indians to a victory over New York that would pull them within a half-game of the Yankees. Instead, Casey's crew blitzed the Tribe 7–1 behind Eddie Lopat and cruised to the pennant. The year before that, the Indians traveled to New York in mid-September for a Sunday afternoon showdown with a one-game lead. With 68,000 packed into Yankee Stadium, the home team won, 5–1, to pull into a tie, then won the next day as well, again behind Lopat, and took over first for good. The lead may have been greater on this September Sunday, but the Indians were battling history, not just the Yankees.

With thermometers holding steady at sixty-five degrees at noon, fans continued to flood downtown, strolling through the busy streets and stopping in restaurants and hotels, "giving the city the air of a Midwest college town on a Saturday afternoon." Those without tickets were now turned away—all seats had been sold and all standing-room corrals had been filled. Most fans remained outside the stadium, basking in the glow that emanated from within. Some grumbled about Hank Greenberg's stubborn refusal to televise the games. He'd been offered $60,000 for a national telecast but turned it down. Then when Mayor Celebrezze phoned to ask him to televise the games locally, Greenberg once again offered his regrets. He explained that the "complications involved would be insurmountable" but more importantly, the team had promised the fans the previous winter that no home games would be televised, and Greenberg felt he owed it to the fans to keep his word.

Thus, most fans flipped on radios to hear the play-by-play. Yet even Jimmy Dudley's descriptions couldn't capture the majesty of the scene as game time approached. It was a baseball sonnet: beneath a shimmering blue sky, a gentle breeze, and the narrow condensed heat of the autumn sun, the largest ballpark in the nation was filled to capacity and the sport's two finest teams gathered to showcase the game for the world.

When the final tally was conducted, stadium officials couldn't believe their eyes. For all their optimism, they never expected this. At 1:30 p.m., as Bob Lemon prepared to throw the first pitch to Gil McDougald, 86,563 fans watched and waited—the largest crowd ever to attend a game in the history of baseball. The one-day total represented more than 10 percent of the 823,000 fans who had attended the twenty-two Indians-Yankees games of 1954, a number that topped the overall season attendance of six major-league teams. In the final, breathless moments before Lemon's first pitch, Hank Greenberg leaned forward in his seat in his private box and studied the gargantuan gathering with a dark intensity. Whatever happened next, it would be remembered in this town forever.

With the anticipation unbearable, Lemon settled in and got McDougald to pop out to second to start the game. Joe Collins followed by lacing a single to left, but Lemon set the tone for the day when he fanned Mickey Mantle for the second out. Still, Lemon faced trouble when Yogi Berra rifled a single to center that moved Collins to third. Irv Noren stepped to the plate and launched a rocket down the first-base line, but Vic Wertz speared it to save a run and end the inning.

Ford cruised through the bottom of the inning before Lemon once again found himself struggling in the second. He issued a one-out walk to Andy Carey, who reached second when Bobby Avila misplayed a potential double-play grounder from Willy Miranda to put two Yankees on with only one out. Casey Stengel played it safe, sending Ford to bunt the runners into scoring position, and with two down, it was up to McDougald to bring them home. Lemon got him to pop to second again and once more escaped unscathed. Ford then set down the Indians in order in the second. The mammoth throng didn't like the flavor of the first two frames, with a shaky Lemon and a dominant Whitey Ford foreshadowing a Yankee victory. But in the third, the roles reversed.

This time, it was Lemon who got on a roll, retiring the side in order, while Ford surrendered an infield single to George Strickland, then committed the cardinal sin of walking his counterpart Lemon to push Strickland into scoring position with one out. Ford rebounded to retire Al Smith and Avila on fly balls to get out of the inning, but his shiny pinstriped armor had been dented. And he would encounter more trouble in the fourth. An Al Rosen single followed a leadoff walk by Larry Doby, and the Indians had runners on the corners with nobody out. The stadium crowd—which would have comprised one of the largest cities in Ohio—crackled with excitement. After Wertz struck out, the anticipation grew when Ford walked Strickland to the load the bases. On the brink of watching their team take the lead, the fans moaned as Strickland bounced a routine ground ball to McDougald at second, who flipped to Miranda covering the bag, who then fired across to Collins at first for an inning-ending double play. Both pitchers had now survived threats and the stage was set for an epic pitchers' duel.

After getting Miranda and Ford to pop out to start the fifth, Lemon looked dominant, having retired ten straight batters. After McDougald singled, Lemon got Collins to bounce the ball back to him to end the inning. While Lemon had put his early turbulence behind him, Ford still couldn't shake his. Jim Hegan singled to center to start the Cleveland fifth, then advanced to second on Lemon's bunt. It appeared as if Ford would escape again when Smith popped out, but the league's batting leader wouldn't allow the rally to perish. Bobby Avila looped a single to center to bring Hegan around as 86,000 fans roared in jubilation. The cheering continued when Doby followed with a single and Rosen walked. Once again the bases were loaded. But with the Indians poised to open the floodgates, Ford dug deep to whiff Wertz and snuff out the threat. The crowd groaned in disappointment but remained energized. The way Lemon was pitching, a 1–0 lead just might hold up.

But in the sixth, they were reminded that these were, after all, the mighty Yankees. Mantle led off with a double, moved to third on a single by Berra, and came home on a sacrifice fly by Noren. In less than five minutes, Cleveland's tenuous lead had vanished, and now it appeared Lemon might be running out of gas. He caught a break when Berra—who hadn't stolen a base all year—was caught trying to swipe second. He then retired Enos Slaughter. Reversing roles once again, Ford picked up where Lemon had left off an inning earlier, quickly putting down the Indians in order and sending the 1–1 game into the seventh. The largest crowd in the game's history was getting every penny's worth.

Andy Carey singled to lead off, but Miranda grounded into a fielder's choice. With Ford due up, Stengel sent out former Indian Eddie Robinson to pinch-hit, a move that surprised many in the crowd considering how strong Ford had looked the previous inning. Yet in the process, Ford had injured his shoulder and couldn't continue. Robinson flied out to right, then McDougald did the same. As fans rose to their feet during the tension-filled seventh-inning stretch, they wondered if the Indians had just caught the break they'd needed for the past five years.

Stengel handed the ball to aging star hurler Allie Reynolds, who'd been strong over the past two seasons but nowhere near as dominant as he'd been in 1952, when he won twenty games with a league-best 2.06 ERA. Along the way, he'd become one of the game's biggest Indian killers. Ironically, Reynolds began his career with Cleveland under the clouds of World War II before being traded for second baseman Joe Gordon after the 1946 season. Gordon would enjoy three spectacular years with the Tribe, helping deliver the '48 title, but the Yankees still got the better end of the deal. Reynolds would win 131 games over the next eight seasons—including a no-hitter against the Indians—plus seven more World Series victories, along with five All-Star Game appearances. Now, at the age of thirty-seven, and with less than a week remaining in his baseball career, Reynolds would try one final time to do what he'd done nineteen times since leaving Cleveland: beat the Indians.

Both the Tribe and its fans saw the script unfolding before their eyes. If one player had personified the Yankees' success against the Indians over the previous three seasons, it was Reynolds. To lose this game now, to lose once more to Allie Reynolds, would again underline Cleveland as a team that choked up when the pennant race got hot. It would prove that no matter how many star pitchers the Indians had, the Yankees' pitchers would have their number. And in a broader sense, it would once again prove that no matter how good the Indians were, the Yankees would always be better.

The Indians could not lose to Allie Reynolds—not today, not ever again.

Lemon opened the bottom of the seventh by flying out to center and then Smith pushed a bunt past Reynolds for a hit and Avila walked. With the mammoth crowd beginning to sizzle in anticipation of a big inning, Reynolds got Doby to ground out, sending the runners to second and third, but recording the second out of the inning. As had been the case countless times over the previous two seasons, it would be up to Al Rosen.

The battered slugger limped into the batter's box, an aching shell of the triumphant gladiator who stepped to the plate for his first at-bat in the home opener back in April. The magic of 1953 had evaporated amid the myriad injuries he'd endured over the course of the summer, but he still managed to show an occasional gleam of the hitter he was— breaking up Bob Turley's no-hitter in Baltimore, crushing two home runs without using his index finger in the All-Star Game. Now, with this season of stardust at its apex, Al Rosen wanted nothing more than to come through one last time.

With his ice-blue eyes frozen on Reynolds, Rosen blasted a slider into right center. It landed perfectly between Enos Slaughter and Mickey Mantle and caromed to the fence as the fans erupted. Smith scored. Avila scored. And as the ball floated back to the infield, Rosen hobbled into second to complete the biggest hit of his career and put the Indians on the cusp of the pennant. He stood at second, wincing from the strain on his leg, absorbing the cheers of the crowd as if standing beneath a waterfall. Once again, Al Rosen was the hero, knocking in his ninety-ninth and 100th RBIs of a difficult season. This time, the entire team shared his glory.

With the game's first full-time Hispanic manager guiding a lineup that featured a Jewish slugger (Al Rosen,
left), two African-American outfielders (including
Al Smith, center), and a second baseman from Mexico
(Bobby Avila, right), the 1954 Cleveland Indians could
be considered baseball's first truly modern team.

Reynolds loaded the bases but slipped away with no further damage, and Lemon was handed a 3–1 lead along with the baseball in the eighth. He retired the first two batters—Mantle on a strikeout—then after walking Berra, whiffed Irv Noren for his fifth strikeout of the game to end the inning.

Already tasting victory, the fans were treated to the proverbial cherry atop the sundae in the bottom of the frame when Al Smith reached on an error with two out and scored on Bobby Avila's sharp single to right to make it 4–1. On their feet in the ninth, the fans didn't have to wait long to celebrate. Bob Lemon cruised through his easiest inning: retiring Slaughter on a weak grounder to the mound, then Andy Carey and Hank Bauer on lazy flies to left. As Bauer's fly slapped into Al Smith's glove, the ovation escalated into a roar that vibrated the entire park.

Lemon was swarmed by his teammates as he departed the field, shaking hands and savoring his twenty-second victory of the season, his fourth over New York. And it was a beauty: nine innings, six hits, one run. "I'll take that game even over my no-hitter," he would say later. "I never saw a game I wanted more or one that meant more."

The lead was now seven and a half games. And there was still one more game to play on this magical Sunday afternoon on the lake.

29 - THE YANKEE DOUBLEHEADER, ACT TWO

s the Indians and Yankees prepared for the second act of their matinee performance, in Brooklyn, NBC technicians were scrambling. At seven o'clock, the network would inaugurate its new studio with a live broadcast of its first ninety-minute color "Spectacular." That night's presentation was a musical titled *Satins and Spurs*, which the network was certain would "explode television entertainment to a new high," as NBC's president declared that week. The production was immense, costing nearly $300,000, yet its impact was limited. For the 7,000 American households with color television sets, viewers were treated to what was indeed a bouquet for the senses. But for the viewers of the thirty-one million black-and-white television sets, *Satins and Spurs* was nothing special. In fact, many switched to CBS to catch the premiere of a new show featuring the adventures of a female collie and her efforts to protect her farm family. Starting that evening, *Lassie* would be a CBS fixture on Sunday evenings for the next seventeen years and endure as a cultural icon.

But before any of the Indians fans at Municipal Stadium could mull over their evening entertainment options, they would enjoy more baseball. Their club already had secured at least a split and avoided an embarrassing sweep that could cause a disastrous final two weeks. And yet Clevelanders wistfully looked skyward like children on Christmas Eve. "But what if they should win the second game, too?" a playful *Plain Dealer* editorial conjectured. "That's almost too much to expect."

Considering the context, it would be nearly impossible. As the Veterans of Foreign Wars Junior Military Band entertained the fans between games, a Yankee victory seemed as inevitable as the sunset at the end of this long, golden afternoon. The Yankees hadn't lost both ends of a doubleheader all season. Now, with their pride battered and the Indians satisfied that their mission for the day had been accomplished, it was only natural to expect a New York romp in the nightcap. Plus, with the day's heavy lifting done, both Al Rosen and Larry Doby would sit out the second game to nurse their injuries. Hank Majeski was inserted at third, and Wally Westlake took center field. Accordingly, the festival atmosphere of the first game dulled somewhat, and the colossal gathering took on a relaxed, more business-like demeanor. The mood remained subdued when Early Wynn struggled in the first. He struck out Hank Bauer to open the game and Mickey Mantle a batter later, but in between Andy Carey rifled a double to left. With two out, Yogi Berra cracked a knuckleball into the upper deck in right field to give New York a 2–0 lead.

His pitching staff exhausted, Casey Stengel handed the ball to Tommy Byrne, purchased from the Pacific Coast League Seattle Rainiers nine days before. Byrne was no stranger to Stengel and the Yankees, having won thirty-eight games for New York between 1948 and 1950. And like seemingly every Yankee pitcher of this era, his résumé included memorable victories over Cleveland, in his case three clutch late-season triumphs, including two Sunday shutouts before huge crowds at Municipal Stadium. Though he hadn't won a major-league game in nearly sixteen months, Tommy Byrne seemed to personify Yankee dominance over the Indians.

Sure enough, after walking Al Smith to start the Cleveland half of the first, Byrne looked as dominant as he had half a decade before, retiring the next eight Indians and cruising into the third in command. When Smith and Bobby Avila rifled back-to-back singles with two out, Byrne settled and enticed Westlake to pop out to retire the side. He then put down the Tribe in order in the fourth. Yet while Byrne was reigniting his career and pushing the Yankees to a victory that would stop the bleeding and extend the pennant chase, Early Wynn had shaken off his early struggles and was just as dominant. He didn't allow a hit over the next four innings, striking out five along the way. But for as strong as he'd been on the mound, it seemed only fitting on this unpredictable Sunday that Wynn would turn the game around at the plate.

Byrne had mowed down the first two Cleveland batters in the fifth, and needed only to retire Wynn, a .183 hitter for the season, to end the inning. But Wynn slapped a single up the middle to bring up Smith, who'd reached base in both of his previous at-bats. He chopped another bouncing ball through the infield into left to send Wynn to second and bring the red-hot Avila to the plate. The league's leading hitter collected his fourth hit of the day with a line drive to left that brought Wynn around to score just beneath a throw to the plate to make it 2–1 and energize the throng once again. The enthusiasm dulled, however, as the fans realized Larry Doby wasn't coming up in his usual third spot in the lineup. Instead, into the batter's box stepped his replacement—journeyman Wally Westlake, the colorful castoff who'd pinballed from team to team in the National League before being purchased by the Indians two years before. Just over a year removed from his nerve-racking march to Hank

Greenberg's office, where he believed he was going to be informed his career was over, Westlake felt the gaze of the baseball world upon him. Focusing on the technique Greenberg and Al Lopez had illustrated when they showed him the film of his batting stance, Westlake cocked his bat and waited for whatever Tommy Byrne, who he'd never faced before, threw to him.

The ball exploded off Westlake's bat and soared into left field. He knew right away from the trajectory Irv Noren was taking that the ball would drop, but as Westlake sped toward first, running harder than he'd ever run in his life, he was sure he could stretch it into a double. As he rounded the bag, he saw the ball bounce off the grass in left field, which looked miles away. Somewhere he heard first base coach Red Kress shout, "You can't make it!" It didn't matter to Westlake. A year ago, his baseball career was all but over. Now he'd delivered the biggest hit of his life and the biggest hit of the season for the greatest baseball team he'd ever seen. Come hell or high water, he was going to second base.

As Westlake's legs pumped furiously on the dirt between first and second, he didn't see Smith cross home plate with the tying run or Avila with the run that put the Indians ahead. The only thing he saw was the white oasis of second base, drawing closer with each stride. Irv Noren collected the ball and rifled it toward second base. Westlake bounced upward and began his slide just as Gil McDougald crouched to receive Noren's throw. A thick cloud of dirt exploded upward as Westlake's legs floated into the base. When the plume cleared, Waldon Thomas Westlake's right foot rested on the bag and McDougald stared down with a grimace as second base umpire Red Flaherty emphatically stretched his arms outward.

Only now did Westlake hear the crowd: the collective roar of 86,000 fans celebrating not just Westlake's hit and the lead he'd given his team, but this entire magnificent summer. The cheers echoed through downtown and over the airwaves, crackling through the small radio in the corner of Sam Sheppard's cell. It's likely that a small smile worked its way across his troubled face, the first smile he'd enjoyed in weeks.

It would have mirrored the smile on Wally Westlake's face as he stood at second base. His cherub cheeks couldn't help but stretch into a modest grin as he brushed the dirt off his uniform. He looked over to Kress, who was clapping and smiling, grateful Westlake hadn't heeded his advice. And as Westlake's eyes brushed over the white square at Kress's feet, he came to a sudden realization: he hadn't touched first base.

It was perhaps the only thing that could have ruined this moment. Westlake had come through dramatically, delivering one of the most memorable hits in Indians history, but if any of the Yankees had noticed what he'd just realized, he was about to be humiliated before the largest crowd to attend a baseball game. As McDougald tossed the ball back to Byrne, Westlake closed his eyes and quickly prayed for Byrne to throw another pitch, for him not to lob the ball over to Eddie Robinson at first and then turn to first base umpire Jim Honochick for the ruling. Even if his being called out for failing to touch the bag wouldn't have wiped out the two runs scored, Westlake couldn't imagine having to jog back to the dugout in the middle of this colossal crowd like a disgraced bullfighter. *Please*, he whispered inwardly to fellow journeyman Tommy Byrne. *Please just throw another pitch.*

After an interminable stretch of a few seconds, Byrne did. Westlake sighed in relief, finally allowing himself to soak in the weight of his accomplishment. He'd put the Indians ahead of the Yankees, wiping out a lead that a few minutes earlier seemed insurmountable. Now, with the way Wynn was pitching, the Indians had a very good shot at sweeping the doubleheader from the damned Yankees and putting the final nail in the coffin no one had been able to close for six long years.

Hank Majeski popped out to end the inning, but the cheers and shouts of the crowd began again as the sides changed. After this fantastic fifth inning, their team was ahead, and the subdued nature of the early going vanished. The crowd smelled blood in the water, and now it was up to Early Wynn to close it out.

As Wally Westlake jogged to center field to start the sixth, he heard a deep, authoritative voice bark at him from the right. "Hey, pal!" it said. Westlake turned his head and saw umpire Honochick looming at first base in his black suit and cap. "Next time you come by," he continued, motioning down to the bag, "you'd better touch that thing." Westlake smiled and nodded. Like everything else in Cleveland in the summer of 1954, it had all worked out.

The newfound lead was suddenly in peril when Hank Bauer laid down a perfect bunt single to open the inning and then advanced to second on a sacrifice bunt. With Mantle and Berra due up, the Yankees were poised to knot the contest once again. But Wynn was having none of it. He promptly struck out Mantle and got Berra to lift a lazy fly to Westlake in center, and the lead was safe once again. And Bauer, who'd collected New York's first hit since the first inning, would be the last baserunner Wynn allowed.

After the Yankees were retired in order in the seventh, the crowd's singing of "Take Me Out to the Ballgame" was remarkably enthusiastic, even more than in the first game. "They were convinced," the *Plain Dealer* explained, "beyond any more doubting, that Cleveland was to become the capital of the baseball world." This confidence grew in the eighth. With the sun settling into the lake at the end of a long, copper track, the stadium lights tripped on behind the plate as Wynn once more put down New York in order. But he would have to face the meat of the lineup in the ninth with Mantle and Berra due up. Down to his last gasp of the season, Stengel sent in Enos Slaughter to pinch-hit to open the final frame. Five months before, New York's stunning trade for the future Hall of Fame outfielder seemed to signal that the Yankees would once again be unstoppable, that just wearing the pinstripes would invigorate a capable veteran at the end of his career, and Slaughter would provide enough power and run creation to hold off the Indians and any other teams that believed they could stand up to the mighty Yankees. Instead, for the first time in memory, a key Yankee addition had provided little of what had been expected. Now Stengel hoped there was enough magic left in Enos Slaughter's bat to extend the Yankees' season.

But this time, the thirty-eight-year-old legend was no match for Early Wynn. Working even quicker than usual, Wynn got ahead in the count, then froze Slaughter with a two-strike knuckleball that sent him back to the dugout shaking his head. Yet Slaughter had been just the warm-up. Up to the plate stepped the blonde-haired, twenty-two-year-old slugger who was on the cusp of creating a legend that would buoy the game of baseball for the next century.

Mickey Mantle had endured a tough day, collecting just one hit in six trips to the plate, while striking out five times. Already with twenty-seven home runs and 100 RBIs on the season, Mantle was capable of changing the complexion of a game with one swing, as he would do countless times over the course of his storied career. But not this time. Wynn quickly got ahead and then blew a fastball past Mantle, whose mighty swing touched nothing but the cool air around home plate. As Mantle strode back to the dugout, defeated, the fans' delirium reached a fever pitch. It quieted somewhat as the next batter stepped to the plate. To complete this magnificent achievement and sweep away the Yankees once and for all, Early Wynn would have to retire the most important player on the Yankee roster, the man who'd sent one of his knuckleballs soaring into the stratosphere in the first inning: Yogi Berra.

Though Berra, not yet thirty, had been the anchor of six world champion teams, been selected to seven All-Star Games, and already collected the first of three American League MVP awards, he was no match for Early Wynn in this moment. As he'd done with Slaughter and Mantle, Wynn outsmarted Berra for the first two strikes, then overpowered him for the third, sending a fastball spiraling through the strike zone as the Yankee catcher flailed his bat helplessly outward.

With Wynn's twelfth and most dramatic strikeout of the day, almost precisely twelve hours after the sun had risen on this sparkling September Sunday, the Indians' improbable sweep was complete.

As the fans cheered, players rushed from the Cleveland dugout, shouting and hollering at the top of their lungs. Some embraced Wynn, while others turned toward the Yankee dugout and defiantly shouted, "Choke-ups!" Sportswriters couldn't recall the last time any team had openly taunted the New York Yankees. Other players gaping at the Yankee dugout weren't taunting their opponent as some thought, but rather had been distracted by a violent fistfight that had broken out in the stands just above the Yankee dugout.

The Indians' victory cries echoed down the clubhouse tunnel, along with applause and the happy peppering of bats against the floor and walls. "So we're the choke-up champs!" Hal Newhouser screamed when he reached the clubhouse, enticing another satisfying roar. As local and out-of-town photographers descended and snapped pictures of the victors, the players howled "choke-up" into the lens instead of the traditional "cheese." Meanwhile, across the ballpark, photographers and reporters hoping to capture the mood of the New York locker room were stunned to find that Stengel had barred all visitors. "Don't let anybody in," he snarled to a Cleveland policeman. "I don't want nobody in here." With no distractions or questions to answer, the Yankees were left with nothing but their thoughts as they quickly showered and dressed in silence, as if preparing for a funeral. The *Plain Dealer* echoed the sentiment in its front-page story Monday morning: "No gambler, actor, or politician ever had a funeral like the one that 86,563 persons saw in the stadium yesterday." Roger Kahn would go one better describing the afternoon in *Sports Illustrated*, calling it "The Twilight of the Gods."

Stengel got back into the brown suit he'd worn to the park that morning and quietly slipped out of the clubhouse into the evening, where the cheers and chants of the victorious crowd echoed through downtown as it headed off to fill the restaurants and bars for impromptu celebrations. A reporter saw Stengel and offered him a ride to the Yankee hotel. "Nope," Stengel said without returning eye contact. "I'll walk." With that, baseball's Old Perfessor melted into the streaming crowd and vanished. It was the perfect symbol for the sentiment expressed by the headline of the next day's *New York Telegram & Sun*: "The Mighty Casey Has Struck Out."

Meanwhile, inside the Cleveland dressing room, the grandest party the city had seen since the '48 World Series was under way—"the frosting on such an ideal autumn cake," as a *Press* editorial described it. Bobby Avila, who had saved the best performance of his storybook season for its climax, shook his head and offered his toothy smile. "What a day, what a day," he repeated quietly. In the two games, Avila had provided an almost perfect contrast to Mickey Mantle. Whereas Mantle collected a half-dozen strikeouts, Avila rapped five hits, raising his season average to .340, while knocking in a run in each contest. "Maybe I've had better hitting days," he admitted, "but never one that meant as much as this." Appropriately, in the week to come, as his teammates were bombarded with accolades and public appearance offers, Avila would receive the most unique of all. He was notified he'd been named the honorary mayor of the tiny seaside community of Avila, California.

"We wanted to beat the Yanks ourselves," said Al Lopez. "This was the way we wanted to win the pennant. . . . To win it without beating the Yanks would have left something to be desired. Now nobody can knock us. It's the most wonderful day I ever had in thirty years of baseball." Even Lopez, who'd nearly walked away from the game in frustration after seeing opportunities to win the pennant evaporate the past three seasons, couldn't help but smile when asked of his team's chances at clinching the flag—a topic he'd avoided for weeks. "Yeah," he sighed, "I guess I'll have to admit now that things are looking pretty good."

Still, per Lopez's order, there was no champagne uncorked in the clubhouse. There would be time enough for that when mathematics complied with reality, probably later in the week. The players would gather at Cavoli's Restaurant for a quiet team party that evening, but as it happened, no alcohol was needed to entice emotion. Through the cascade of handshakes and embraces, the day's two primary stars found each other. Bob Lemon reached out with a beefy left hand and pounded Early Wynn on the shoulder. "Meat," Lemon said, "you were great." Wynn smiled, placing his arm around Lemon's shoulder. "Meat," he replied, "you were wonderful."

Like many players, Hank Majeski sat on a stool in front of his locker appearing happily stunned. He watched his celebrating teammates with tears in his eyes. He'd never won a pennant in his thirteen-year career and had been primarily on the bench the previous two Septembers as Cleveland's World Series hopes disintegrated. "I've been around a long time," he said, "and I've been waiting a long time to see those Yankees beaten. Now we've done it. We really broke their backs."

He'd given the reporters the quote they needed, but he went on, knowing that words couldn't effectively capture the spirit of the moment. "Look around," he said. "Look at all these guys. Not one who didn't do a great job when we needed him." He pointed at Sam Dente, beaming in a corner. "Strickland gets hurt and Sam takes over." He then motioned to young Rudy Regalado, who looked like a kid coming down the stairs Christmas morning. "Rudy helped at third at the start of the year," he said, and then swept his arm across the room to The Sphinx and his sidekick, "and those kids in the bullpen—Mossi and Narleski—we'd have been dead without them." Majeski shook his head again and his face swelled into the smile of a proud father. "No, I don't think I ever had a day like this one. This is a real team. Greatest team spirit I ever saw."

No one was happier than Wally Westlake, who played in barely half of the season's games but had delivered the climactic hit to defeat the team's longtime nemesis. "Old Hankus Pankus," a *Telegram & Sun* column stated, referring to Hank Greenberg, "may have found himself a pennant in the five-and-ten-cent store of baseball."

"It wasn't just making such a sure thing of the pennant—that played a big part," a *Plain Dealer* editorial declared, "but beating their worst tormentors, and in front of the biggest crowd ever, that climaxed everything.

"After yesterday," the article concluded, "the World's Series will be an anticlimax."

30 - WE'RE IN

As the Indians spent that Sunday night celebrating their monumental achievement, Herb Score was rushed to the hospital.

The club's almost mythical minor-league prospect had just completed the most incredible individual season in American Association history just two days before, striking out sixteen St. Paul batters, and his Indianapolis club was looking forward to participating in the league playoffs the following week. But now Score, the league MVP, felt miserable as the bad luck that had plagued his childhood once again visited him like a dark angel. He started showing symptoms of illness on Saturday night and was flown back to Indianapolis. When his condition worsened on Sunday, he was admitted to the hospital, and that night was diagnosed with pneumonia. His availability for the minor-league playoffs was questionable, and more disappointing for Cleveland fans, any possibility of Score getting a call-up to the Indians and making his highly anticipated first start in the final two weeks of the season was eliminated. In the aftermath of the Yankee Doubleheader, even Casey Stengel noted the shadow of Herb Score looming over the Yankees' future chances. "This Cleveland team has the best pitching in the league," Stengel said, "and it's going to be better next year when they bring up that Herb Score from Indianapolis."

Still, with talk settling on the World Series, fans eager to see the "Howitzer" could wait until 1955. Score was so good that even an attack of pneumonia couldn't keep him from reaching his almost limitless potential. Quite frankly, they concluded, nothing could.

As Score recovered and his future teammates enjoyed a day off the following Monday, the Indians ticket office began the hectic work of preparation for the World Series. Tickets were being printed and the process for ordering them—a lottery system that could be entered strictly through an application sent by mail—was arranged. Those lucky enough to be selected (the odds were conservatively set at one in eight) would pay almost double regular-season prices: two dollars for a bleacher seat, seven dollars for reserved, and a lofty ten dollars for box seats for each game. And, in a surprising variation to the 1948 method, the seats could only be bought in packages. If selected, you were obligated to buy tickets for all three home games. To some fans, this seemed like an obvious ploy by the team to ensure higher ticket sales, particularly since the Indians' dominance might result in a quick Series and eliminate the possibility of a third home game.

On the first day of the ordering process, the stadium, which generally received a half-bag of mail each day, was flooded with more than fifty bags overflowing with orders for tickets. Post office workers complained of the long lines of people awaiting service, and bank tellers were overwhelmed with requests for money orders or certified checks to be sent along with the requests. In all, more than 900,000 requests encompassing six million dollars came into Municipal Stadium—the largest demand for tickets for any sporting event in history. With the irons on the fire, stadium officials also cleared the decks. Since the three home World Series games were set for the first weekend of October, the Browns' highly anticipated showdown with the two-time defending NFL champion Detroit Lions that Sunday was moved to mid-December to free the stadium for Game Five.

For all of this planning and preparation, the Indians still had yet to clinch anything. It was, however, just a matter of time. Even if the Yankees won all eleven of their remaining games, the only way they could catch up would be if Cleveland lost eight of its remaining ten. The magic number had been whittled to three: a combination of three Indian wins or Yankee defeats would end what still was technically

The Indians front office was flooded with nearly a million ticket requests for the World Series— at the time the largest demand for tickets for any sporting event in history.

a pennant race. Yet as they returned to the clubhouse on Tuesday for a game with the Senators, the players noticed a small note tacked to a bulletin board. It was from Mike Wilson, the team's president, and consisted of just five words:

"Congratulations. Now let's win 111."

The number 111 was to American League teams what visiting the moon was to the world's scientists. For as powerful as the Yankee teams had been for many years, none had matched the utter domination of what was considered the greatest baseball team ever assembled, the Yankees of 1927. It was the year Babe Ruth hit sixty home runs and drove in 164 RBI, while Lou Gehrig hit .373 and belted forty-seven homers to go with an astonishing 175 RBI. The New York lineup that summer consisted of two additional future Hall of Famers in Tony Lazzeri and Earle Combs and boasted a pitching staff with two more destined for Cooperstown, Waite Hoyt and Herb Pennock. The Yankees' offense led the league in hits, runs, and batting average, while its pitching staff was tops in team ERA and shutouts. The '27 Yankees steamrolled to 110 victories and won the pennant by eighteen and a half games. Since then no team had come close to topping that number of victories.

The 1954 Indians had a chance. Having collected 104 wins with ten games remaining, they needed seven triumphs to etch their names in the history books.

The mission began Tuesday night. The Indians scored all the runs they needed in the first inning and coasted to a 4–2 win over Washington. After two off days, they left for a weekend series in Detroit—where the Yankees had just won a pair to postpone the pennant-clinching— promising to return home Sunday night with the pennant in hand.

On Friday night, as thousands back in Cleveland attended

the season's first high school football games, Bobby Avila blasted a grand slam in the seventh to break a 2–2 tie and deliver Bob Lemon's twenty-third victory of the season. Though the Yankees also won in Philadelphia, Friday's triumph secured at least a Cleveland tie for the pennant. With another win or New York defeat the following afternoon, the flag would fly at Municipal Stadium.

The day was overcast, with intermittent rain showers. Matching the weather, neither team could find a rhythm, and the game seemed to toil onward in spurts. The Tigers crept to a 1–0 lead in the third, and the score held through a long rain delay. Finally, in the seventh, the Indians got on the scoreboard. Dale Mitchell, one of the key components of the 1948 pennant drive now at the end of his career, was called on to pinch-hit for George Strickland with one on and one out. Rain pelted the infield, but the umpires urged the game forward, knowing with just a week left in the season, rescheduling the contest would be nearly impossible. On the second pitch from Detroit hurler Steve Gromek, who'd been Mitchell's teammate six years before, Mitchell blasted a fastball into the abandoned, rain-soaked seats in right field to give the Indians their first runs and a 2–1 lead. Dale Mitchell, who five months earlier had flopped onto a dugout bench in Philadelphia and boldly informed a reporter that the Indians were going to win the pennant, gave his team a lead it would not relinquish. Mirroring Wally Westlake's heroics six days before, the homer was Mitchell's first and only of the season. And as it happened, it would prove to be the last of his career.

On Gromek's next pitch, Jim Hegan tomahawked a blast into left field. The baseball carried through the falling raindrops and landed in the empty seats just inside the foul pole. Though no one knew it at the time, Hegan had delivered the pennant.

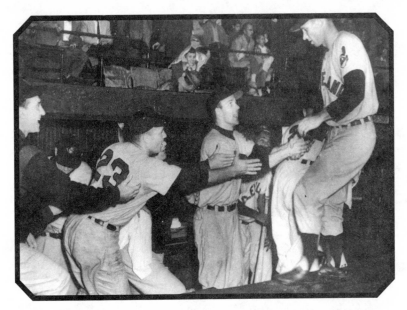

On a rainy Saturday afternoon in Detroit,
beloved Indians catcher Jim Hegan (right) hit the
home run that clinched the American League pennant.

After the Tigers scratched out a run in the bottom of the frame, rain delayed the game for forty-five minutes. The teams played the final inning veiled in darkness in an almost empty ballpark. Ray Narleski relieved Early Wynn and with two out in the ninth, he got Fred Hatfield to skid a weak grounder toward shortstop. The ball chopped through the saturated grass and puddled mud into the glove of Sam Dente, who dropped to one knee to corral it on its awkward path. He rose up and flipped the ball to Bobby Avila floating toward second. Avila snagged it and stepped on the bag, forcing out Harvey Kuenn. In the same fluid motion, Avila stepped toward Dente and they embraced. Players and coaches, who'd watched the final inning from the top step of the dugout waving towels and shouting like kids on the last day of school, spilled onto the field and embraced one another. "Ladies and gentlemen," the Briggs Stadium public-address announcer casually stated, "the Cleveland Indians have just won the pennant."

They left the mud and muck behind them as they marched down the dim tunnel and entered into the bright, warm clubhouse as American League champions. The subsequent celebration was energetic yet subdued, in part because much of the jubilation had been spent the previous Sunday but mostly because there was still work to do. This victory, their ninth straight, was number 107. Four more triumphs remained to secure their place in history.

The lasting image of the pennant-clinching celebration was provided by Vic Wertz. With a black crayon, someone had scribbled "We're In" across the top of Wertz's bald head. To the delight of teammates and reporters, Wertz bowed to deliver the message, which reflected his deep appreciation for the achievement. And after years of resisting the urge to try a different position, a healthy dose of serendipity had delivered Vic Wertz into this champagne-soaked locker room. "I had just about decided I'd have to spend the rest of my life second-guessing myself for the mistake when this chance came along," he said. "If I'm not the luckiest guy in the world, I'll do until somebody with a better claim to the title shows up . . . I'm the first baseman of a pennant-winner. Three months ago I wouldn't have believed it. Sometimes even now it seems like a dream." More than a half-century later, it still would.

As the celebration revved to full steam in the clubhouse, Al Lopez slipped away to his locker in the corner of the room and began undressing. He had been sprayed with champagne and congratulated by his players, but now he wanted the players to be the centerpiece of the celebration. Yet as he began to step into his trousers, he glanced around the corner of his locker and saw Larry Doby standing nonchalantly nearby with a steel bucket filled with ice cold water between his feet. Lopez, who'd seen *Press* reporter Frank Gibbons doused with water from the same bucket earlier, knew that he was Doby's next target.

Lopez spotted another writer stepping toward him with his notepad ready to ask some questions. The manager grabbed his shoes, balled up his pants and shoved them under his arm. Then he grabbed his jacket and thrust it at the reporter. "Here," he said quickly. "They won't suspect you. Make a bee line for the door and I'll follow." The reporter did as he was told, and the quiet, conservative Al Lopez, in the moment of the greatest triumph of his career, stepped into public wearing nothing but his underwear. Luckily, there was no one outside the clubhouse, and Lopez finished dressing before making his escape.

That evening, as the players celebrated with a team party at the Sheraton Cadillac Hotel, two telegrams arrived from Philadelphia. One was addressed to Al Lopez:

"Congratulations on your great management and leading of your players' determined drive for the 1954 American League pennant against such splendid New York Yankee opposition. Success to you, your coaches, and the Cleveland ballplayers in your bid for the world championship."

It had been sent by Casey Stengel. Lopez carefully held the telegram, as if it were made of spun gold, and re-read it, allowing a small smile to curl across his face. The student had finally beaten the Old Perfessor.

The other telegram was sent to the players as a group by their vanquished rivals:

"Congratulations to the Cleveland ballplayers on winning the 1954 American League pennant. We admired the clean method and hard fighting in which you gained your great triumph. We send a sincere desire for your success in the World Series.

"Sincerely, the New York Yankee ballplayers."

The party was upbeat but decidedly restrained. Many of the players' wives had joined the team in Detroit, and they danced with their triumphant husbands. A conga line was formed, and champagne flowed. Larry Doby sprayed Hank Greenberg with a shaken-up bottle. Greenberg, grinning through the foam, didn't mind a bit. All the criticisms of the past four years had evaporated. He was no longer the guy who screwed up the Indians but rather the shrewd architect of a champion. "I hope you win the World Series in four games," he told the players, "even though the ballclub makes no money on a four-game series." Good-natured laughs spiraled through the room. "Win it in four, if you can," he finished with a smile.

Doby, showing uncharacteristic levity, then joined Jim Hegan in singing along with a three-piece band playing at the party. "You know something?" he'd asked Gordon Cobbledick in the locker room. "I feel like I'm just winding up my rookie year. I've wasted a lot of time, but now it seems as if I'm a beginner. I'm just starting my baseball career. Whatever I make of myself, it starts from this point."

Such serious talk seemed out of context in the levity of the dingy clubhouse. "Hey," a teammate needled, "we just won a pennant, buddy. Aren't you gonna live it up a little? Aren't you even going to laugh?"

Doby grinned. "I'm laughing inside," he said. "I've had a lot of fun this year," he added, turning back to Cobbledick. "I never knew baseball could be so much fun. And I've learned a whole lot. I just wished I hadn't taken six years to learn it. I wish there'd been somebody to tell me all the things I've learned the hard way."

Cobbledick's eyebrows narrowed. "A good many people tried to tell you," he said. "But you had a wall around you. They couldn't get close enough so you could hear 'em." Doby's smile faded a bit as he contemplated the remark, looking around the room. "The wall's down," he said finally. "There ain't any wall now." He broke into a jitterbug, and his good spirits carried over to the party at the hotel that evening.

Al Lopez, who had been forced by his players to drink a few gulps of bubbly in spite of his tender stomach, smiled as he watched Doby's playfulness at the party. "There's the guy who makes the difference," he told the group gathered around him. "Without him . . ." Rather than finish the thought with words, he simply held out his right thumb and pointed it downward.

Nearby, in another small gathering of smiling friends, one of Doby's teammates brought back the ghost that had haunted the quiet athlete for his entire career. "It's taken seven long years for Larry to join the team," he said, motioning to Doby. Then he shook his head thoughtfully. "What a doggone shame." Cobbledick was more optimistic. He wrote that with his lesson learned, Doby had the opportunity to salvage what "still could be a distinguished career."

Back in Cleveland, the celebration also was muted. It was a rainy Saturday night and the downtown streets were nearly deserted. The only indication that anything extraordinary had happened that day scrolled across the electric news board on the Schofield Building overlooking East Ninth Street and Euclid: "Congratulations to the Cleveland Indians for winning the AL pennant." Unlike the explosion of joy after the dramatic finish to the 1948 pennant race, the '54 celebration was more of a gracious acknowledgement from a city that knew this was coming and felt it was well deserved. During the next few days, however, Cleveland's pride blossomed. All the major department stores took out ads in the newspapers congratulating the team. During station identification, one TV station began referring to its home city simply as the home of the American League champions. *Time* magazine noted that Republican George Bender had a slight edge over Democrat Tom Burke in their race for an Ohio Senate seat, but Bender was running a distant second to the Indians in public interest across the state. And plans were under way for a massive parade honoring the accomplishments of Cleveland's diamond heroes.

The Indians completed the sweep of the Tigers with their tenth straight win, then boarded a New York Central Mercury back to Cleveland. When it pulled into Union Terminal just before ten p.m., more than 2,500 fans gathered to greet their beloved team, jamming barriers and stairways leading to the lower levels of the station. Police officers cleared a canyon for the players to de-board, yet they were still mobbed. A young girl maneuvered through the throng as Al Rosen pushed his way through and planted a kiss on his cheek. Rosen, still hurting more than anyone in the terminal knew, couldn't help but smile.

The *Plain Dealer* stated the scene "climaxed as fantastic a season as ever a team has played in all the long history of baseball," a comment that echoed one made by Al Lopez in the jubilant locker room the previous evening. "It's been a great season," he said quietly. "This is a great team." Then, he added another thought that would prove to be eerily accurate. "It's a greater team than anybody knows."

31-ONE HUNDRED ELEVEN

Sam Sheppard wasn't getting away this time.

His prolonged bail hearing had stretched over the previous week, with William Corrigan jousting with his opponents, calling witnesses and attempting to turn back the wave of public opinion. He'd hired a private detective to continue the case the police had abandoned. His talk of "other suspects" was dismissed by county prosecutor Frank Cullitan as "red herrings" and "baseless suggestions." While deriding the Cleveland police and the court system, Corrigan turned his attention to the press, as he laid the groundwork for a motion to have the forthcoming trial moved out of Cuyahoga County.

"Under the guise of news," Corrigan explained in a statement, "the Cleveland newspapers and the newspapers generally throughout the United States have reported and editorialized on the case of Samuel Sheppard so that he was convicted in the minds of the public before he was arrested and charged. Every item that could be gathered that would make him appear unfavorably to the public was repeated over and over again."

During an interview in early September, Corrigan spelled it out in no uncertain terms: "You newspapers have convinced everyone that Sam did it." Corrigan even told his associates as they prepared for trial that their opponent wasn't the prosecutors or the police department, but the press. "They're just pawns on the chessboard," he said in one strategy meeting. "The newspapers are our opponents, and it's the newspapers we've got to fight."

Naturally, prosecutor John Mahon disagreed. He saw no media bias and wanted the trial to take place in Cuyahoga County. "Dr. Sheppard is no different than anyone else," he explained. "He can receive a fair trial here." As if on cue, coverage of the Sheppard case dwindled to nothing. Since late August, the story had moved from the front pages to deep within the papers. Thus, the details that followed in the next few weeks went largely unnoticed.

Two months into the investigation, the Cleveland police finally settled on a potential murder weapon: an orthopedic wrench found in the trunk of Sam's car. There had been no blood on the instrument or any other evidence to suggest that it was indeed what had been used to kill Marilyn Sheppard, but it would do.

With its work now complete, the Cleveland Police Department quietly passed along its bill to Bay Village like a waiter at a fancy restaurant. The cost for requesting help was almost $20,000, roughly two dollars per resident. It was so much for the modest city budget to bear that the expense would be folded into a two-mil operating levy up for voter approval in November.

In the meantime, Sam would sit in his cell and wait for October 18, the day the trial was scheduled to begin. The days stretched like saltwater taffy from Euclid Beach. One method of passing the time was taken away when jail officials no longer allowed him to examine x-rays brought by his father or brothers. A week before the World Series, in the rotunda of the courts building, with photographers nearby snapping photos of the process, county officials selected seventy-five names of citizens for the prospective jury pool for the trial. All seventy-five names were printed in the Cleveland papers.

Around him, life went on. Sam slipped a jail guard ten dollars to allow him to call his son once a week. That month, Chip began second grade at Rocky River Elementary School. One morning on his way to class, Chip dropped a textbook, and the cover flopped open on the floor. A girl reached down to pick it up and noticed Chip's name written in block letters on the first page. Her face immediately lit up with recognition. "Oh," she began innocently, "isn't that the name of the man who killed his wife?"

But these tidbits drew little attention. Clevelanders were eagerly looking forward to October—just a turn of the calendar away, when the eyes of the nation would settle upon its fair city for the World Series and then again for the Sheppard trial.

Keeping with the mood of their city, the Indians extended their winning streak to eleven games with a victory over the visiting Chicago White Sox on Monday night, giving Bob Feller his thirteenth and final victory of the season. Appropriately, it was also "We're Witcha' Hank" night at the ballpark. Anyone wearing one of the buttons supporting the embattled general manager distributed by a local laundry earlier in the year was given two free tickets to witness the 109th victory of the season.

These final few weeks of September were a glorious victory lap for Greenberg. He was asked to author an article for *Life* magazine titled "How We Beat the Yankees," which was teased across the cover and read by millions. In the lengthy, self-congratulatory piece, Greenberg proudly (to some, perhaps arrogantly) outlined the fashion in which he had turned the Indians' farm system into an arsenal with enough firepower to out-gun New York. "What we have been aiming for seems now to be accomplished," Greenberg wrote. "The Yankees have been caught and stopped . . . . Maybe the next voice you hear will be saying, 'Break up those Indians!'" But for once, Greenberg's self-confidence was backed by indisputable results. Labeled both a failure and a flop going into the season, Greenberg now had all of Cleveland behind him—many wearing the buttons to prove it.

Greenberg's Indians were now just one win away from matching the 1927 Yankees and perhaps correcting the course of baseball history. "That old line 'It's great to be a Yankee may suddenly become a hollow mockery," Chicago GM Frank Lane commented. "Maybe it's as great to be an Indian now." Indeed, like Lane, many baseball men were grateful to the Indians for shattering the Yankee monopoly. Baseball needed a fresh face, and both Cleveland and the Indians provided it.

On Tuesday afternoon, with a cool wind swirling an autumn flavor though the city, Cleveland hosted a grand parade for its team. The route covered eighteen miles going west on Euclid Avenue, starting at Ivanhoe Road on the east side and ending ninety minutes later at Rocky River Drive. The parade consisted of three marching bands placed on flatbed trucks and twenty-three cars, including sixteen brand-new convertibles cruising at a modest ten miles per hour to ensure the well-wishers got a good look at their heroes. In addition to each of the current players, arranged two by two in each convertible, five members of the 1920 world championship team would travel through the streets. Escorted by police motorcycles, the parade would be led by Mayor Celebrezze and Ohio Governor Frank Lausche—six weeks away from a decisive reelection victory over

James Rhodes at the polls. Schools let students out early to attend the parade, and business came to a standstill. Shops and restaurants along the route also got into the spirit. One luncheonette gave out free ice cream cones to kids.

Louis Seltzer had personally encouraged his citizens to attend, to commemorate this historic achievement. "Let's turn out by the thousands—by the tens of thousands—to give these 1954 Cleveland Indian pennant winners a real, rousing welcome," he wrote in the *Press*. "Let's cheer them on for the World Series. Let's give them such an ovation that they'll go into the Series and do to the Giants what they did to the Yankees."

As usual, what Louis Seltzer wanted, he got. More than a quarter-million people lined the streets to catch a glimpse of their champions. Players past and present waved at the fans, and Vic Wertz even tilted his bald head down to show off the message rewritten for this special occasion: "We're In."

The parade rolled past Cleveland Arena, where the hockey Barons had once again been crowned champions five months before, and cruised into the downtown area. It crossed East Ninth Street, coming within a few hundred yards of where one day a new baseball palace would be erected to save a doomed Indians franchise. It passed in the shadow of the offices of the *Cleveland Press*, where Louis Seltzer looked out upon his triumphant city with both pride and satisfaction.

At twenty till four, it wound through Public Square in the heart of a downtown that in two decades' time would be deemed lifeless. The players were showered with constant cheers that echoed from the sidewalks to the towering spires of the skyscrapers in which the powerful economic pistons of the city churned day after day. Along the way, the crowd could be heard in the Cuyahoga County jail less than a half-mile away from the route, where Sam Sheppard lay in his tiny cage, waiting for justice. Nearby in the criminal courts building, amidst the revelry of a city in love with its baseball team, prosecutors feverishly pieced together the case that would condemn the accused doctor to life imprisonment.

The parade crossed the Detroit Superior Bridge, passing over a river that would catch fire fifteen summers later. The celebratory march ended on Rocky River Drive, just a few miles away from where Marilyn Sheppard had been murdered seventy-nine days before. From there, the players traveled by chartered bus back to Municipal Stadium, where they prepared for that night's game. Perhaps still dizzy from the revelry of an afternoon of worship, they committed five errors that night and lost for the first time in two weeks.

They rebounded the next night to capture win number 110, then on Saturday afternoon on the lakefront, Early Wynn took a no-hitter into the ninth inning before the Tigers squeaked out a pair of safeties to produce a meaningless run in an 11–1 Cleveland triumph, their 111th. After weeks of conjecture and predictions, it finally put them above the 1927 Yankees as the greatest team in the history of the league. The debates began.

Mike Garcia sat beside Gordon Cobbledick in the clubhouse one day that week and asked the question on everyone's lips.

"You think this is a great ballclub?"

Cobbledick offered a wry smile. "Who, the Tigers?"

Garcia snorted. "You know who I mean," he said. "You think we're a great ballclub?"

More than a quarter-million people lined the streets
of Cleveland for an eighteen-mile parade paying
tribute to their pennant-winning Indians.

This time the *Plain Dealer*'s sports editor considered the question more carefully. He'd covered the Indians for the past thirty years and had seen some of the greatest teams ever.

"Let's put it this way," he said. "Twenty-five years from now, people are going to look in the book and see that the 1954 Cleveland Indians won more games than any ballclub before them ever won and they're going to say, 'That must have been a great ball club.'"

Garcia eyed Cobbledick, letting the comment hang in the air for a moment. It wasn't the answer he was looking for.

"You're ducking," the Bear responded. "This is a great ballclub."

And on Monday night, September 27, the greatest team in American League history once again returned to Union Station and boarded a train to New York, this time to face the National League champion Giants in the World Series, which would begin at the Polo Grounds on Wednesday afternoon. The collection of fans that had gathered to send the team off was puny compared to the massive gatherings that had welcomed them here a week before and at Hopkins Airport on Labor Day night, not to mention the historic parade six days earlier. It was just the Indians making another road trip to face an inferior team. When they returned to Cleveland on Friday to wrap up this magnificent season over the weekend, then there would be another reason for thousands to come together and celebrate. The few fans who waved good-bye to the Indians that night assumed they would only have to wait a couple of extra days before participating in another massive civic celebration. They had no way of knowing that a half-century later, they would still be waiting.

The players boarded the train and shortly after, with a blast of steam and a shriek of a whistle, it began rolling forward toward New York. On track thirteen.

The train burst through its own plumes of smoke and steam and vanished into the autumn night.

The summer was over.

W · I · N · T · E · R
Final Interlude

CHRISTMAS HAD SLOWLY WORKED ITS WAY into
Cleveland, and now, four days before the day itself, the city
was vibrant with the approaching holiday.

A sleek layer of snow, thickened each day by fresh flurries,
blanketed Cleveland and reflected in crystalline sparkles the colorful
displays on the houses and buildings. Public Square beamed with
holiday energy through the gunmetal afternoons and the dark
December evenings. Pine and spruce trees, ranging in price from $1.50
to $2.50, were being purchased across town and transported to homes
where families waited eagerly to decorate them. The warm glimmer of
store windows invited passersby to stop and gaze. Bundled in topcoats
and fedoras, shoppers waddled through slushy intersections in tune
with the red-and-green rotations of the traffic lights, and everywhere
Christmas carols echoed from static-clogged radios and the frozen lips
of carolers as if sung by distant choirs of angels.

But deep beneath the sweet symphony of Christmas, a buzz
swarmed to the surface like a giant circling wasp. It echoed through
the avenues and alleys of downtown Cleveland and slowly brought the
entire city to attention. It was the sound Cleveland—and the rest of the
nation, for that matter—had been anticipating for the last five days.
And, to a greater extent, for the last nine weeks.

The Sheppard jury gathers outside the
courthouse on a snowy December evening.

When the news of the
sounding buzzer reached the
squat, square building on East
Twenty-First Street that housed
the Cuyahoga County jail, chief
jailer Mike Ucello started the
wheels in motion. "Call the fourth
floor," he said, unable to keep the
excitement out of his voice, "and
tell Sheppard to get ready."

At the courthouse, the
sound of the buzzer began a
flurry of chaos. Reporters and
photographers who had sprawled
across the second floor of the
building for nearly a week,
treating it as if it were a summer
cabin in the mountains, sprang
to action and prepared for the
climax to what they believed was
the biggest news story Cleveland
had ever experienced. The floors
and tables of the corridors were
littered with paper cups, tattered
newspapers, crumpled cigarette
butts, and stacks of playing cards,

which had been used for poker and pinochle games. Reporters and bystanders had stretched out and fallen asleep on benches in abandoned courtrooms. But now, as the four o'clock hour drew near on this Tuesday afternoon, very possibly the day Sam Sheppard's second son would have been born, nobody slept.

They had a verdict.

The exhausted members of the jury—whom the reporters and followers of the case now knew on a first-name basis—had finally come to a decision and pressed the button in their deliberation room that lit the buzzer that served as their only means of communication with the outside world. They'd been dismissed at the conclusion of the trial on Friday morning, and one way or the other, were expected to come back swiftly with a verdict. Instead, after a half-day of deliberation on Friday, Saturday slipped away, and then Sunday, with no word. When the jurors were escorted to dinner during a one-hour break

between their afternoon and evening sessions, reporters and curious citizens approached and asked questions. Adhering to the instructions of Judge Edward Blythin, the jurors refused to talk about the case. They didn't even make eye contact with Sam Sheppard each evening when the cast of characters assembled back in the courtroom to report the jury had not yet reached a verdict and was to be sent back to its hotel for the night. When they reported without a decision Saturday night, Sam shook his head and muttered to bailiff Simon Streenstra, whom he'd gotten to know well over the previous two months, "Too long, Si, too long."

Yet it had been a long trial, longer than any other in the history of Cuyahoga County. Nine weeks. Two hundred and fourteen exhibits. Eighty-seven witnesses. Better than 10,000 pages and two million words of testimony. All followed by four days of silence as the jury deliberated for thirty-nine hours and twenty-seven minutes.

"My client is not in suspense," William Corrigan told reporters during the tense weekend. "He is ready to meet any fate. He is the calmest man in this building. That arises from his complete confidence in his innocence. He knows truth will prevail."

For Clevelanders, the trial was an anticlimax to the events of the summer—little more than a long-winded summary of all the evidence, theories, and counter-theories that had swept across the city in the time between Marilyn Sheppard's murder and her husband's arrest. The selection of the jury alone took nearly three weeks. All but one juror admitted during voir dire to reading about the case in the Cleveland papers. Prospective jurors later reported they'd received phone calls and threats at their homes after their names and addresses had appeared in the newspapers.

Not surprisingly, Louis Seltzer and the *Press* got in on the action. As the jury was being seated, the paper published one last inflammatory editorial, this one titled "But Who Will Speak for Marilyn?"

The first part correctly painted the picture of the upcoming trial as a dramatic presentation rather than an exhibition of justice. "Why, if you didn't know these were people and this was a real setting," the piece stated, "you would think you were watching a drama on television or a mystery play at a theater." The case was loaded with intriguing characters, not the least of which was the accused, his brothers, and his courtly, patriarchal father. "Then it hits you again," the editorial continued. "No, there's something—and someone—missing." The editorial then veered into a hypothetical conversation—though likely based on an actual interview—with one of the heroes of the story, James McArthur.

"'Sure,' says the detective chief. 'There always is. I'll tell you. It's the other side, the representatives of what in this case will be officially known as the corpus delicti, in other words, the body of the crime—in still other words: Marilyn Reese Sheppard.

"'There is no grieving mother—she died when Marilyn was very young.

"'There's no revenge-seeking brother nor sorrowing sister. Marilyn was an only child.'"

But rest assured, the hypothetical McArthur explains in the piece, that this side will be accounted for through the statements of testimony that will be given by the state's witnesses. "'Here is the complete story of Marilyn Reese Sheppard,'" McArthur says in the abstract editorial. "'How she lived, how, we think, she died. Her story will come into this courtroom through our witnesses.'"

The editorial ended on a thoughtful note. "Justice to Sam Sheppard," it wished. "And to Marilyn Sheppard." Implying, of course, that the two were mutually exclusive.

Once the jury was finally seated and the trial was set to begin, proceedings were halted for Election Day. Judge Edward Blythin, a former mayor of Cleveland, was re-elected as common pleas court judge by a dramatic five-to-one margin, and county prosecutor John Mahon, leading the prosecution in the case, won a bid for a separate common pleas judge seat.

The next day, with an early snow swirling through Bay Village, the jurors were bused to the Sheppard house. When they arrived, reporters and photographers were waiting for them. Overhead, a helicopter, something many below had never seen before, circled the scene and a photographer on board snapped pictures. He and the helicopter had been hired by the *Press*.

The day after, the parade of state witnesses, by now as well known as beloved characters from a favorite novel, began

Attorney William Corrigan (right) became
the face and voice of Sam Sheppard's defense.

to march into the courtroom: Lester Hoversten, Spencer Houk, Susan Hayes, Robert Schottke. And of course, Samuel Gerber. Just before Thanksgiving, the prosecution called a "bombshell" witness—a cousin of Marilyn's who told a story of Chip acting out and hitting his father, then Sam repeatedly striking him in fury. The *Press* dutifully offered a succinct translation in bold headline type: "Sam Called a Jekyll-Hyde."

All eyes eventually settled on Sam Sheppard as the trial unfolded. When photographs of Marilyn's beaten body were shown to the jury, Sam closed his eyes and stepped away from the table so he wouldn't have to look. His every action and expression was examined and discussed. "He had the air of a college boy coming home for the holidays," the *Press* intoned, "not a man on trial for his life." When Sam took the stand on December 9, he testified for three days. Over the course of his testimony, he answered "I don't know" or "I don't recall" more than 150 times. What new details or slightly altered variations of accounts that came out became the focus of much speculation.

In his own celebrated testimony, Samuel Gerber explained how he could make out the shape of a surgical instrument pressed into the spattering of blood on Marilyn's pillow. William Corrigan, perhaps in utter disbelief, did not aggressively cross-examine Gerber on this theory. Neighbor Don Ahern, who along with his wife, Nancy, had been the last person other than the murderer to see Marilyn Sheppard alive, testified that Sam had fallen asleep on the night of the murder with his jacket on, not that he'd taken it off before falling asleep as Ahern had told police just after the murder. Esther Houk stated that Sam's shoulders were dry when she saw him the next morning, yet she wasn't asked to either repeat or rebuke her original statements made to police that his hair, shoes, and pants had been wet.

The closing arguments cut through the noise to what both felt was the heart of the case. Assistant prosecutor Thomas Parrino encouraged the jury to struggle with the logic of the killer if it wasn't Sam. "If the burglar was in that room and took the time and trouble to strike all those vicious blows against Marilyn," he said, "I ask you why the assailant did not use that same instrument, not to hit Sam thirty-five times, but to strike one single blow against him. A burglar does not want to leave a living witness at the scene of a crime." Sam's "injuries," belittled along the way, were explained by the prosecution as the result of a desperate, failed suicide attempt in which he'd thrown himself off the cliff between the house and the beach. The newly elected John Mahon took the argument to another level. "Why, this house was full of phantoms that night," he said with a sneer. "The phantom burglar, the phantom killer, and then they charge the defendant with the murder." Then, with a wry smile, he added, "The phantoms did all that, ladies and gentlemen."

Corrigan countered with his own questions for the jurors to ponder, namely, how the prosecution could rail away for nine weeks without explaining how, with what, or why Marilyn Sheppard was killed. Corrigan also ended with a flourish. "We are approaching the Christmas season," he said, "when God came down to Earth to set man free and establish on Earth the principle of freedom. Unless we American lawyers and we American jurors do our part in maintaining that freedom in this case, we have failed in our duties."

Finally, at 4:12 p.m. on the Tuesday before Christmas, after five long days of arguments and agreements, of public scrutiny and celebrity treatment,

the jury foreman, James Bird, looked around the smoke-filled deliberation room at the weary faces of his eleven compatriots. "Is everyone satisfied?" he asked. Slowly, all eleven nodded. Bird, a night cashier at Union Terminal, then pressed the button that signaled the buzzer and sent Cleveland into motion.

Humanity swelled into Judge Blythin's wood-paneled courtroom, with the selected reporters returning to their appropriate places in the four rows of tables near the bench. Sam Sheppard, two days away from his thirty-first birthday, was led into the courtroom wearing a crisp blue suit. The muffled conversation died as the solemn-faced jurors entered the room and filed into their box. William Corrigan studied them and, with his decades of experience, made a spot assessment. He leaned over to Sam. "Steady yourself," he whispered. "I don't think the verdict's good. They're going to convict you." Sam's face tensed into a paper-thin frown and he bit his lips. His heart fluttered. Bailiff Eddie Francis stepped to the front of the courtroom and announced, "Everybody please rise." The crowd stood as Blythin mounted the bench, his carefully combed white hair seeming to glow in contrast to his black robe. It was 4:30 p.m.

The spectators slid back into their seats and Blythin turned to the jury. "Ladies and gentlemen," he said in the Welch accent that had added another layer of flavor to the proceedings, "have you arrived at a verdict?"

James Bird rose, holding an envelope. "We have," he said, and held it out. Francis stepped over to the box and took the envelope, then slowly moved back toward the judge, his hands trembling. The courtroom sat in perfect silence as Blythin's eyes scanned the decision. Sam, sitting at the defendant table, closed his eyes. In his hand he clenched a small silver crucifix so tightly it left indentations on his palms.

Blythin read the verdict aloud. "We the jury," he began slowly, "being duly impaneled and sworn, do find the defendant, Samuel H. Sheppard . . ."

Though the pause between clauses was just a fraction of a second, inside the courtroom, it seemed as though the world had stopped.

". . . not guilty of murder in the first degree."

Sam's eyes shot open. An audible gasp rippled through the courtroom. For that one powerful moment, Sam Sheppard was an innocent man. His thin lips began to relax and even curl into a smile of relief.

Then Blythin, knowing what was going through the minds of Sam and every other person in the room, spoke again.

"But," he began again, this time quicker and more forcefully, "guilty of murder in the second degree."

Sam's jaw, which had just unclenched slightly from its vice-like state, dropped open, and the gasp of air he drew into it echoed through the room. The doctor slumped. William Corrigan, who had fought for Sam every day for the past five months, automatically dropped his hand on his client's shoulder. It was difficult to tell whether this gesture was to support Sam or himself.

Sam's two brothers nearby felt their faces flush with fury. The room buzzed with whispers that quickly escalated in volume. Reporters in their private box in the front of the room leaped out of their seats and raced for the doors to get to the nearest telephone. But the bailiffs barred the doors, preventing anyone from leaving until the proceedings were complete. The only people who knew the truth were trapped in this courtroom. The world would have to wait for the news.

Order was restored and Blythin looked at the jury. "Is this your verdict, ladies and gentlemen?" he asked. Twelve heads nodded grimly. Corrigan

Reporters and editors in the *Cleveland Press* newsroom await the verdict in the Sam Sheppard murder trial.

stood and requested that the jury be polled. One by one, the bailiff called out the names of the jurors, and while the tone and cadence varied from firm and decisive to somber whispers, each answer was the same: "Yes."

In that minute of confirmation, Sam shook his head slowly as if disagreeing with each individual juror. He continually licked his lips. Then, for the first time, the judge looked directly at the defendant—now a convicted murderer.

"Dr. Sam Sheppard," he called, "you will come up here, please."

Sam rose on wobbly legs and was escorted by the bailiff to stand before the judge. His face still carrying the weight and shock of the morning of July 4, he slowly stepped forward and stopped at the base of the bench. Now, for the first time in the entire trial, he was closer to the judge than the reporters.

"This jury has found you guilty of murder in the second degree," Blythin said sternly and succinctly. "Do you have anything to say?"

As if a grammar school boy about to make a presentation before his class, Sam's feet shifted nervously and he half-turned to face the jury.

"I would like to say, sir," he said in a clear, firm voice, "that I am not guilty." The furious scratching of pencils on the notepads of the reporters was almost as loud as Sam's words. "I feel there have been facts," he continued, "presented to this court that definitely prove that I could not have performed this crime."

He turned back to face Blythin, who replied simply, "This jury has found otherwise."

In the time it took Blythin to take a new breath, he shifted the proceedings in an unexpected direction. "It is now the judgment of this court . . ."

Corrigan quickly understood what was happening. As Blythin's words echoed through the chamber, Corrigan rose and interrupted. "Why sentence him now," he shouted to Blythin, "before I file a motion for a new trial?"

Blythin glared at him and offered perhaps the most preposterous statement of the entire trial. "This case will be handled the same way as any other," he said. A few feet to his left, the eighty reporters scribbled in their notepads as if volunteer stenographers.

Corrigan turned away from the judge with a dismissive wave of his hand. "Oh, go ahead," he sighed. "It's just indicative of the way this whole thing has been conducted."

"The judgment of this court," Blythin began again, "is that you be confined in the Ohio State Penitentiary, there to remain for the rest of your natural life."

Corrigan moved to the jury box and began to speak to the jurors.

"Mr. Corrigan," Blythin's voice boomed, "I wish that you would have no communication with any of the jurors while this court is in session. Please desist."

Corrigan's head snapped back to the bench. "The case is finished," he shouted. "They can talk. I have a right to talk to the jurors. I want the record to show my exception."

Blythin sighed. "Let the record show," he said, "that Mr. Corrigan tried to speak to one or more of the jurors while court was in session."

Corrigan closed his eyes and steadied himself, allowing rationality to return. "All right," he said softly, "I apologize." He returned to the table.

"Your apology is accepted," Blythin replied. "We have known each other too many years for our friendship to be broken by this."

As the judge spoke, his bailiff approached Sam and reattached the handcuffs to his wrists. Sam turned to look back at his brothers and their weeping wives. He offered a nod that carried all of the emotion they shared.

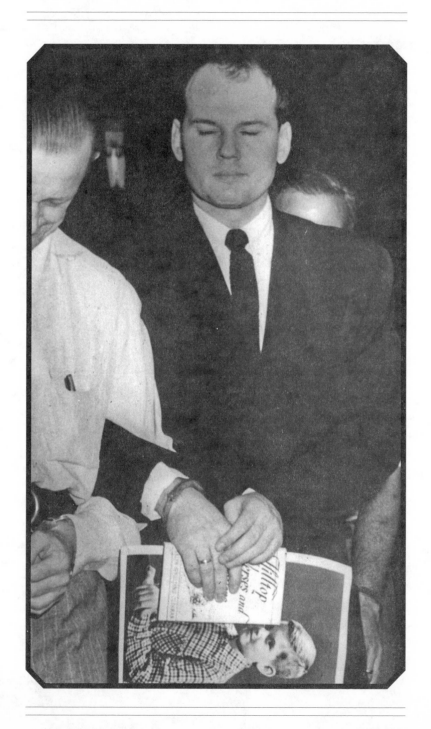

Blythin thanked the members of the jury for their patience and service, noting that they were "a credit to the community and to the jury system of our country." As he instructed them that they were not obligated to be interviewed by reporters, Sam was escorted out of the courtroom, turning to look again at the jury. The *Plain Dealer* described it as "a last, terrible look back at the jury that had branded him a brutal murderer. His eyes burned in an angry scowl." Then he was gone, marched through the corridors of the building back to the cold, metallic county jail.

Blythin then nodded to the jury. "Thank you very much," he said, and motioned to his bailiff. "You are now dismissed." It was 4:48 p.m., and the trial of Sam Sheppard was over.

The chamber doors opened, and now reporters raced through them, shouting the news and desperately seeking pay telephones. Finally, the rest of the world could learn the news. All three of Cleveland's television stations and most radio stations interrupted their programming as the news crackled across the airwaves. The switchboards of the *Press* and *Plain Dealer*, which had been choked for days with phone calls, both local and long-distance, about the status of the case, now lit up like the Christmas trees on Playhouse Square. Longtime employees said only the Lindbergh landing and the later kidnapping trial matched the interest of the Sheppard verdict. The previous day, United Press International had released its list of the top ten stories of 1954, as voted by its wire editors across the country. Alongside the U.S. testing of a hydrogen bomb, the Brown vs. Board of Education decision, and the Army-McCarthy

Sam Sheppard is led away from the courtroom after being sentenced to life in prison. He holds a photograph of his son, Chip.

hearings was the trial of Sam Sheppard.

For the first time, Cleveland's newspapers assessed how its various media outlets covered the case. From this swarm of self-congratulatory prose, many took notice of the insightful commentary offered about the case on radio station WGAR by an up-and-coming hometown reporter. His name was Jack Perkins, and in the decades to come he would achieve national prominence as a reporter for NBC and later as the host of the popular Biography program on the cable network A&E.

Yet the timing of the dramatic climax proved to be the worst-case scenario for Louis Seltzer. With that day's Press already printed and on its way to its readers, Seltzer and Co. had to wait an extra twenty-four hours to deliver the news. Thus, for all of the Press's involvement in and impact on the case, it was the Plain Dealer that broke the story in print to Cleveland.

Naturally, when Wednesday's Press hit the stands, readers paging through found a short epilogue commentary on the editorial page. Under the headline "A Tragic Episode Ends," the Press informed Cleveland that it could be proud of the work of the Sheppard jury and the decision it had reached. "Again that great rock of American liberty, the jury system, stood strong and upright," it read. "In the midst of emotion and prejudice, it stayed firm and fair." Then, as a final, surreal mark of punctuation, the Cleveland Press closed its own book on the Sam Sheppard case. "Somehow, in some dark way, this case became too much a part of all our lives. Too interesting. Too important. Let the tragic episode end now. For always."

And though the timing of the final act was damaging by any editor's standard, Louis Seltzer could sit back in the Press newsroom, put his feet up on a desk, and leaf through Wednesday's edition of the paper with pride. Even a day late, he sold 30,000 extra copies that afternoon.

It carried the hearty comments of agreement from all the key players. Mayor Anthony Celebrezze pronounced his belief that the defendant had received a fair trial and that the verdict was justified by the evidence presented. "I especially would like to commend the Cleveland Police Department for its fine work in investigating the murder and in preparing the case for trial," the mayor added. In the same spirit, victorious James McArthur declared that "justice prevailed." Samuel Gerber commented that "The verdict fits my estimation of the case." Even Marilyn's family members felt it was a just verdict. A cousin added a comment that would echo through the years: "We knew Sam and liked him, but he acted like a guilty man."

Stephen Sheppard expressed his utter frustration in six sharp words: "You can't beat a stacked deck." Les Hoversten, the houseguest who'd suddenly left the afternoon of the murder, was sorry to hear the news. "I have no basis to think Sam is guilty," he said. "I am still at a total loss to understand how he could possibly do it, what could have motivated it." Within a matter of weeks, Hoversten left the country for Europe. Spencer Houk carefully danced around the question, saying simply that he respected the verdict. Susan Hayes, about to fade back into obscurity as quickly as she'd tumbled into fame, had no comment.

Yet while the Cleveland papers were glowing in their praise of the jury and its decision, out-of-town reporters were less impressed. "No two people who sat through the trial saw it in quite the same light," wrote the *New York Herald Tribune*. The associate editor of the *Toledo Blade* was even more harsh: "Almost from the moment Marilyn Sheppard's body was found, the *Press* took over the roles of detective, sheriff, prosecutor, judge, and jury." Celebrezze reflected the feeling of many trial observers in voicing a distaste for these interlopers from other cities, saying they were giving the city a "black name." Yet Dorothy Kilgallen, a well-known New York gossip columnist sent to cover the trial, noted in a syndicated piece that ran across the nation that the prosecution hadn't proven Sam Sheppard was guilty "any more than they proved there are pin-headed men on Mars." The Cleveland papers chose not to run her column.

More disturbing was an account Kilgallen would later tell of when she was called into Blythin's chambers prior to the trial. The judge, eager to meet her, was curious why she was covering the case. Kilgallen was surprised by the question and replied that it had all the ingredients of a good story, primarily centering on the mystery surrounding the murder. "Mystery?" Blythin supposedly replied. "It's an open-and-shut case. He's guilty as hell. There's no question about it." Blythin was dead when Kilgallen revealed this

story ten years after the verdict, but his family disputed the tale.

Their work completed, the jurors were escorted out by police officers into blinding flashes of cameras and questions from reporters. The questions went unanswered, as the jurors had agreed beforehand not to make any comments. Stephen and Betty Sheppard, alongside Richard Jr. and Dorothy Sheppard, pushed their way through the crowd that clogged the corridor to the courtroom. They had to return home to tell their parents, both of whom had just returned home from the hospital—Richard Sr. for a bout of pleurisy and Ethel after a cerebral stroke—and to tell young Chip, who would spend the first of many Christmases without his mother or father.

As people swarmed out of the courts building, Sam reached the fourth floor of the jail, where dozens of eager faces hung before him, awaiting the news. "They found me guilty of second-degree murder," Sam called out as casually as if reporting the score of a ballgame. The faces of guards and prisoners alike wilted in silence. There seemed to be no appropriate reply.

As dusk fell over the holiday landscape on this, the shortest day of the year, Sam stepped into his cell and the door slid shut behind him. Sleep did not come easily that night as the doctor envisioned a lifetime of imprisonment not as a possibility, but as a stark reality. A long winter, which would officially begin for the rest of Cleveland at 4:25 the following morning, had started early for Sam Sheppard. Outside, in the darkness, a new flurry of snow showers as dry as sand swirled across downtown, adding another layer of holiday cheer to this city in the midst of celebration.

The thin, membranous snowflakes of that December night were quite different from the ones that fell in Columbus, Ohio, on a gray April morning sixteen years later. These were wet and fluffy, unrealistically large, which fit the surreal atmosphere of snow showers this late in the year. They caked on the well-kept yard of a small, squat house nestled in a quiet neighborhood on the east side of the city, which on this morning had drawn police and emergency medical personnel. Yet their fervor was dramatically less than on the morning in Bay Village when Marilyn Sheppard was found dead. The death of Sam Sheppard was an altogether different brand of tragedy.

Once a young doctor on the brink of a long and fulfilling career, Sam Sheppard, in the spring of 1970, was practicing medicine in a friend's dining room. He'd closed his small office on the main thoroughfare of the Columbus suburb of Gahanna the previous fall and moved it to the residence he shared with his friend and trainer George Strickland (no relation to the Indians' 1954 shortstop), a friend from his college days who encouraged Sam to enter the world of professional wrestling. After his first match in a high school gymnasium in Waverly in August of 1969, Sam married Strickland's twenty-year-old daughter Colleen—his second marriage in three years—and the new couple moved into the Stricklands' house.

Sam had been sick over the weekend with what appeared to be the flu. His temperature spiked at 104 degrees on Sunday, and he could barely walk. Like on the night of Marilyn's death, Sam was asleep on a couch in the living room, this time on a foldout bed. Colleen and her mother, Betty, heard Sam stumble out of bed three times during the night before finally, at three a.m., they hurried to his side. They helped him to the kitchen, where he asked to be let go so he could stand alone. For a moment, he did. Then he lost his balance and crashed to the floor between the kitchen and dining room, cracking his head against the wall on the way down. As his wife and mother-in-law bent down to help him up, he called them off. With Strickland out of town, Sam knew he was too heavy for them to carry back to the sofa bed. He wanted to be left on the floor. Colleen and her mother scurried through the house collecting pillows and blankets to create a makeshift bed on the floor of the dining room, where he often saw patients with Betty's assistance. Now he demanded she give him a shot of Librium, a tranquilizer, to help him sleep. She did so, and they left him on the floor to spend the remainder of the night.

Two hours later, as dawn began to break, Betty checked on Sam and found him flailing his arms and hands around, crying deliriously, "Do you know what's happening?" She comforted him, and he went back to sleep.

When she checked on him two hours after that, Sam lay motionless on the dining room floor where they'd left him. He wasn't breathing and had no pulse. Betty attempted to give him mouth-to-mouth resuscitation. As she did, she smelled a coppery aroma coming from within Sam, which she interpreted as internal bleeding. It was no use. Sam Sheppard was dead.

Wearing only a pair of sweatpants and socks, his body lay twisted on the floor of the dining room—fittingly, the last place he practiced medicine. He was forty-six years old. When he was buried, the Stricklands picked out a nice blue suit for him, much like the suit he'd worn the day he'd been convicted, and placed his white surgery coat and several medical instruments in his coffin. But something still didn't seem right. Finally they decided that Sam needed one more item to look truly natural. A pair of dark sunglasses was gently placed over his eyes.

Prior to the weekend illness, Sam had been going through life as he'd done for the past year. He was scheduled to compete in a wrestling match in two weeks and had kept in touch with his remaining family members. Yet for as sudden as it was, his death was not at all a surprise. The Franklin County coroner revealed that Sam had not only been prescribing drugs for himself, but had been drinking heavily for years—as much as two fifths of vodka a day—and the likely cause of death was the mixture of alcohol with such a heavy tranquilizer.

Neither his brother Stephen nor his son, Chip, both in Europe at the time of his death, would attend the funeral. The Stricklands were also informed that there was no more room in the Sheppard family plot in Cleveland. Thus, Sam would be buried in Columbus in a disjointed ceremony attended primarily by reporters and photographers. "In many ways Sam Sheppard's life was an open book," the Reverend Alan Davis of Bay Village said during the eulogy. "But much remains a mystery, as it should be, known only to God."

On the day after Sam Sheppard's death, a modest crowd at frosty Municipal Stadium watched the Cleveland Indians open the 1970 season with a lethargic 8–2 loss to Baltimore. Eighty-five more losses would follow that summer, with Alvin Dark, the 1954 New York Giants captain, serving as manager, and it would prove to be the second in a string of seven consecutive losing campaigns. The franchise had entered the worst decade in its history.

The rhapsody of 1954 faded quicker for the Indians than anyone could have imagined. The much-anticipated 1955 season turned out to be little more than a repeat of the three frustrating campaigns that preceded '54. Almost lost amidst the fervor of the Sheppard trial in November, the Indians appeared to shore up their already solid lineup by trading for six-time All-Star outfielder Ralph Kiner, who'd hit 200 home runs in a five-year stretch with Pittsburgh. When Vic Wertz heard of the trade, he thought it was a joke. It took him several minutes to believe that he wasn't being fooled. "Next year we'll not only win the pennant," Wertz declared, "we'll also win the World Series." Between the addition of Kiner's big bat and the inevitable promotion of the already legendary Herb Score from Indianapolis, plus the return of the remaining cast of characters from the '54 onslaught, a dynasty appeared possible. Score was as good as advertised, winning sixteen games and American League Rookie of the Year honors, but Kiner and the rest of the gang fell short of expectations. Early Wynn and Bob Lemon combined to win thirty-five games, but Mike Garcia struggled to an 11–13 mark with a 4.02 ERA. Ray Narleski and Don Mossi continued their roles in putting out late-inning fires, joined by part-time starters Art Houtteman and Bob Feller. Only Hal Newhouser failed to assume his key role from 1954, appearing in just two games before being released in mid-May and calling it a career.

While the pitching was still strong, the offense seemed to remain in its World Series funk. Kiner hit just .243 with a modest eighteen home runs. Bobby Avila's batting average dipped seventy points. Al Rosen became a shadow of his 1953 form, hitting .244 with twenty-one homers and only eighty-one RBI. Larry Doby's average actually jumped almost twenty points, but he knocked in fifty less runs. Vic Wertz continued his steady contributions but was shelved for the season in July when he was afflicted not with injury, but with polio—three months after Jonas Salk announced the creation of his vaccine but two years before it became widely available.

As they did the year before, the Indians started slowly before finding their rhythm. But that rhythm wasn't as rhythmic as 1954, and the Yankees were just as good. Yogi Berra explained that the Yankees had to win the pennant in '55 because they couldn't stand to watch another World Series like the one of 1954. Speaking to a Rotary Club in Stamford, Connecticut, two months after the Series, Yankees pitcher Eddie Lopat explained the October sweep in more trite terms: "That's what happens when you put amateurs in the Series."

Naturally, the Yankees' sour grapes stirred up the embers of Cleveland's fury. "Of all the people least entitled to make cracks about the Indians, the Yankees should head the list," Ed McAuley wrote in the *Cleveland News*. "If they were so superbly talented, why didn't they finish ahead of our Tribesmen?"

In early July, the Indians were eight games back but rallied to catch New York by the end of the month, then surged to a two-game lead with nine games to play. Fifty-two weeks after the now-mythical Yankee Doubleheader in Cleveland, Herb Score pitched six strong innings to propel Cleveland to a 3–2 win in the second game of a twin-bill before 65,000 at Yankee Stadium that seemed to indicate the Tribe was in the driver's seat, defeating the Yankees for the thirteenth time in twenty-two games—an even better clip than they'd managed in 1954.

Cleveland ended an otherwise successful road trip by blowing a one-run lead in the late innings to lose in Washington then came home for a weekend series with the fifth-place Detroit Tigers. Just as it had the September before, Cleveland was already preparing for the World Series, with hotels once again flooded with requests. Coinciding perfectly with the pre-emptive celebration, however, the Indians staged a revival of the horrors of the fall of '54.

On Friday night, with the Municipal Stadium box office selling World Series tickets outside, former Indian Steve Gromek held Cleveland to three hits in six innings of relief as

Detroit won, 3–0, while the Yankees rallied for two runs in the bottom of the ninth to topple the Red Sox and pull back into a tie for first. On Saturday afternoon, the Indians went 0-for-11 with runners in scoring position as the Tigers won again, permitting the Yankees to take over sole possession of first. The wheels then officially came off the wagon on Sunday as Mike Garcia was battered in a six-run sixth inning and the Tigers cruised to a 10–3 triumph. The Indians scored only four runs in the three-game sweep, leaving thirty-one runners on base while hitting an abysmal 1-for-25 with runners in scoring position. In less than forty-eight hours, a one-game lead had mutated into a two-game deficit with only five to play. Naturally, it proved too much as the Yankees clinched the pennant three days later.

With Lemon, Wynn, and Score all winning twenty games— marking the third time in six years a trio of Cleveland pitchers had reached the twenty-win plateau in the same season—they finished second again in 1956, but this time a distant nine games back. The magic of 1954 was long gone, and by the end of the '57 season, so were the majority of the men who had been the idols of the city three years before.

Two weeks after the Indians completed their sixth-place 1957 season, the team's board of directors voted to dismiss Hank Greenberg as general manager, even though he had a year remaining on his contract. Team president Mike Wilson justified the decision in two words: "Fan reaction." He added, "The fans insisted on it." Greenberg remained on the team's board of directors but maintained a silent animosity toward the city and the fans who had forced him out. He proclaimed, "Baseball is dead in Cleveland" and fought to move the team to Minneapolis. His fellow board members, primarily native Clevelanders, refused to go along and bought Greenberg out in 1958.

He moved on to Chicago, becoming the vice president of the White Sox, and stewed silently as Frank Lane, formerly Chicago's GM, took over for Greenberg in Cleveland and gutted his carefully constructed farm system, trading away potential superstars for marginal returns. Thirty years would pass before the Indians would invest in their farm system like they had under Greenberg. A quarter-century after leaving, Greenberg's bitterness still festered. "The closest I ever want to get to Cleveland is 30,000 feet away," he said, "while I'm in an airplane flying over the city on my way to New York."

Al Rosen, who'd never returned to full health after his rocky 1954 season, had taken pay cuts after the '54 and '55 campaigns and then decided he'd had enough when Hank Greenberg gave him an obvious lowball offer going into 1957. Rosen walked away from the game at the age of thirty-three, opening up a place in the lineup for a rookie outfielder from Fargo, North Dakota, named Roger Maris. Yet he, too, would soon be gone, one of a long line of mindless trades that pillaged the Cleveland organization.

Bobby Avila's meteoric rise to batting champion was matched by a stunning plunge. His average went from .341 in 1954 to .272 in 1955 to .224 in 1956. After two more mediocre seasons, Avila was traded away. His career batting average was .281, sixty points below his high-water mark of 1954.

Much less patience was shown with Larry Doby when his production fell off. Following what was perceived as a sub-par campaign for Doby in 1955, Hank Greenberg wanted Chicago's All-Star shortstop Chico Carrasquel to ignite Cleveland's sluggish offense and was thrilled when the White Sox asked for Doby in return. When Al Lopez was told of the trade on a Tampa golf course, he said he was so happy he shot his best score of the year.

Greenberg glowed with pride at what he thought was another shrewd trade, even after he received a phone call from an irate black woman who denounced him, saying that many blacks felt the Indians had treated Doby unfairly. Greenberg thought little of it at the time, but history would prove the caller correct.

Not surprisingly, Doby, whose loneliness defined him in Cleveland, wasn't missed, and it would be years before Cleveland truly appreciated his talent. "Larry Doby, whose opportunities for immortality in baseball ended where his complexes began—at the neckline—was in a new green pasture today," Franklin Lewis wrote coldly in the Press the day he was traded. "Highly gifted, he was frequently morose, sullen, and upon occasion, downright surly to his teammates and his public." Ironically, after two solid years in Chicago, Doby was traded back to the Indians in 1958 and saw limited action off the bench. He wrapped up his career with the White Sox a year later, having amassed 1,500 hits, 250 home runs, and nearly a thousand RBI. In 1998, he was enshrined in baseball's Hall of Fame.

He joined Al Lopez in Cooperstown, inducted as a manager twenty years earlier after winning more than 2,400 major league games. After five second-place finishes in six years in Cleveland, Lopez stepped aside before public opinion turned against him after the 1956 season, taking over the reins of the White Sox. This time, Greenberg didn't try to talk him out of leaving. Still, he was surprised at Lopez's decision and even approached Gordon Cobbledick to inquire why Lopez had left. "On account of you," Cobbledick replied, further fueling Greenberg's grudge against the city and its media.

Lopez's .617 winning percentage still tops the list of all managers in Cleveland history. The majority of his career triumphs, however, came in Chicago, where he guided the White Sox for eleven years after leaving Cleveland. Interestingly, Lopez's most memorable season with the Sox brought together several other strands of the '54 Indians. In addition to having Larry Doby on the bench and Hank Greenberg in the front office, the 1959 White Sox lineup included Al Smith and their top pitcher was Early Wynn, who were traded away together in 1957. Wynn won twenty-two games for Lopez in 1959, earning the Cy Young Award and propelling Chicago to the pennant in a heated race with the Indians. Clinging to a one-game lead in late August, Lopez and the White Sox rolled into Municipal Stadium and delivered a devastating four-game sweep that crippled the Tribe's shot at the pennant. Yet the '59 Indians were just a shadow of the team that had won 111 games five years before. Only two players from the 1954 team—George Strickland and Mike Garcia—remained on the 1959 squad, which would prove to be Cleveland's last pennant contender for thirty-five years.

Garcia, who'd injured his back pitching on a wet mound in spring training the year before, was used primarily as a reliever that season, his final one in a Cleveland uniform. His fortunes dropped dramatically after 1954, losing more games than he won in '55 and '56. Similarly, Bob Lemon ran out of magic after his final twenty-win season in 1956, dropping to 6–11 the next year before being released midway through 1958. Bob Feller ended his career after the 1956 season. Art Houtteman was able to avoid the bad luck that had plagued his early career for one more season before his ERA swelled to 6.56 in 1956 and he was sold to Baltimore in '57.

Even the two young colts in the Indians' first true bullpen failed to leave a truly lasting impression. Ray Narleski was a workhorse in 1955, appearing in sixty games and saving a league-high nineteen. When he was shifted into the starting rotation over the following two years, he lost much of what had made him valuable as a reliever. He won twenty-four games over the next two years, but also surrendered more runs than ever before. Likewise, Don Mossi's fortunes sunk when he became a regular starter in 1957. Appropriately, Narleski and Mossi were traded away together in a package deal with Detroit in 1958 that shipped longtime Indians nemesis Billy Martin to Cleveland.

As the remnants of the Big Three faded, Herb Score's star rose, and he was on the brink of becoming one of the greatest pitchers in baseball history. As expected, he made the Indians' roster in spring training in 1955, and in his major-league debut in Detroit, he struck out nine in a complete-game victory. Score would post an ERA of 2.85 while leading all of baseball in strikeouts and was the overwhelming choice for American League Rookie of the Year. He was even better the following season, going 20–9 with a 2.53 ERA while collecting 263 strikeouts—seventy-one more than his closest competition. After striking out Yogi Berra looking at a wicked slider in 1956, Score chuckled when he came to bat later and Berra spoke to him. "Aw, Herbie," Yogi sighed, "you don't need that pitch. It ain't fair."

Going into his third year in 1957, Score was not only the Indians' ace but widely considered the best pitcher in baseball. Just before the season began, the Boston Red Sox offered the Indians a million dollars for Score—a colossal amount for the time. The Indians turned them down. "Herb is to pitching what Mantle is to hitting," Hank Greenberg said that spring. "Mantle is the only hitter around with the potential to break Babe Ruth's home run record. Herb is the only pitcher who can become another Bob Feller or a second Lefty Grove."

It all changed on a cool May evening on the lakefront. Making his fifth start of the season, Score was struck in the face by a line drive hit by Yankee second baseman Gil McDougald, shattering his eye socket. With blood gushing from his ears, nose, and mouth, Score was carried from the field and taken to a hospital, where doctors feverishly worked to prevent him from losing his eye. Score kept his eye but sat out the remainder of the season as the Indians slipped into sixth place, posting their first losing record in eleven years.

He returned in 1958, and after pitching a complete-game three-hit shutout against Chicago in his third start, it appeared he would pick up right where he left off. Yet that spring he suffered a shoulder injury that decimated his comeback campaign, limiting him to just two more starts. While the eye injury is often pointed to as the turning point of Score's doomed career, it was actually the shoulder injury of '58 that proved insurmountable. He went 9–11 with a 4.50 ERA in 1959 then was traded away to, fittingly, Chicago, where he attempted another fruitless comeback with

Al Lopez in 1960. After winning thirty-six games in his first two seasons, Herb Score would win just nineteen more over his last six, going down in history as one of the most tragic stories the game had ever seen. "I would not do anything to denigrate the great career of Sandy Koufax," Al Rosen would say years later. "But I've got to tell you: I can't believe that Sandy Koufax was any better than Herb Score could have been."

Yet Score, as humble and kind as he was talented, never saw his life as anything but blessed. When his playing career ended, he entered the expanding world of broadcasting, and for thirty years he was the radio voice of the Indians. For most of that time, Score delivered descriptions of miserable teams sloshing away in meaningless seasons. It only seemed fair that Score's hard-luck life in baseball should end on the game's grandest stage. After announcing that 1997 would be his last season behind the microphone, the Indians made

an improbable postseason run, and Herb Score's final broadcast turned out to be Game Seven of the World Series. Appropriately, the Indians blew a ninth-inning lead and lost, denying Cleveland its first baseball title in five decades.

The duration of Score's star-crossed career almost perfectly paralleled Sam Sheppard's life in prison. As Score soared through his first major-league season, Sam was transferred to the Ohio Penitentiary to begin his life sentence. In six months, his medical career had ended, his son was being raised by his brothers, and he'd endured the sudden deaths of his wife, his unborn son, his mother, and his father.

Eighteen days after her son was found guilty of murder, with her husband Richard in grave condition in the hospital with a hemorrhaging gastric ulcer, Ethel Sheppard committed suicide in her home, shooting herself in the head. The note she left for Stephen mirrored the despondency of the entire family: "Dear Steve, I just can't manage without Dad. Thanks for everything – Mother." What Sam never knew until later was that his mother had also tried to kill herself during the trial. Eleven days after her suicide, Sam's father also perished from his stomach condition, which had worsened dramatically over the previous six months.

The final member of Sam Sheppard's household also came to an undignified end. Kokie the dog, perhaps the only living being besides Sam to know what happened that night, was given away.

As Sam spent his first month in prison, his family was finally permitted access to the house on Lake Road. They brought in forensic scientist Dr. Paul Leland Kirk to give many pieces of evidence their first true inspection. By examining fibers found under Marilyn's fingernails and the splatters of blood in the house, Kirk suggested that a third person may have been in the house that night. He estimated the murder weapon was probably a flashlight. Not only did this suggestion make more sense than Sam using his own surgical tools—and then imprinting them in the blood on the pillow—but it may have explained the mysterious paint chip found on the bed that could never be identified. It may have been a paint chip from the shaft of a flashlight. Adding weight to the theory, a flashlight was found on the beach by a neighbor of the Sheppards a year after the murder.

Kirk compiled his findings in a lengthy report, which William Corrigan built into a motion for a new trial. It was denied. Corrigan died in 1961, and in the months that followed, a young attorney from Boston named F. Lee Bailey replaced him as Sam Sheppard's lead counsel. Several other appeals were filed over the next few years but each stalled. Then in the summer of 1964, just over a year after Marilyn Sheppard's father killed himself with a shotgun, a writ of habeas corpus filed in federal district court was ruled upon, setting the wheels in motion for an historic Supreme Court decision.

Judge Carl Weinman agreed that Sam's rights had been denied during the trial. "If there ever was a trial by newspaper," he stated, "this is a perfect example." He labeled the entire episode a "mockery of justice." The decision mirrored the warnings William Corrigan had shouted upon deaf ears in 1954. "When newspapers can do what they have done to Dr. Sheppard," he said in a written statement that summer, "it is time for newspapers to begin to examine their conscience and consider the conditions that they are creating. Perhaps wise newspaper publishers might begin to have a slight twinge of fear in the methods resorted to in the reporting of the Sheppard case and the stirring of the public to a condition that verged on mob reaction.

"If they listen closely, they may hear the creaking of the ropes backstage, which can indicate that the curtain may be beginning to fall on the constitutional guarantees of the individual and the press."

On July 16, 1964, two weeks shy of the ten-year anniversary of his original arrest, Sam Sheppard was released from prison as Weinman's decision slowly ground its way through the upper echelon of the legal machinery. Two years later, the case Sheppard vs. Maxwell reached the United States Supreme Court, which ruled eight to one that Sam Sheppard had not received a fair trial and outlined parameters for how the media could cover a case, ensuring that the defendant received just proceedings. The Court ruled that back in the hectic days of 1954, the Sheppard case had been infected by "massive, pervasive, and prejudicial publicity," that "bedlam had reigned at the courthouse," which had taken on a "carnival atmosphere." Essentially

every quality of the trial was judged
a mistake. The charges were either
to be dropped or Sam Sheppard
was to be put on trial again.
Naturally, it couldn't end like that.
Cuyahoga County decided to retry
Sam Sheppard.

The retrial began in October
of 1966 and, by design, received
only a fraction of the attention of
the original proceedings twelve
years before. No cameras were
permitted in the courtroom; no
press table was installed. The
jurors were sequestered for the
duration. With energetic and
flamboyant F. Lee Bailey leading
Sam's defense, the prosecution
could never ride the wave of
momentum it found in '54. The
most dramatic moment of the
trial was during Bailey's cross-
examination of Samuel Gerber,
when he took the coroner to task
in a fashion William Corrigan
never could have achieved.

"Now Dr. Gerber," Bailey
inquired at one point, "as a basic
principle of crime investigation,
it was of course important

to preserve the scene in its
original condition until it could
be completely examined and
investigated, true?"

"Yes, sir," Gerber replied.

"Did you permit at 11:30
on the morning of July 4 certain
newsmen to go through the house
and take pictures?"

"Two people from the
Cleveland Press," Gerber said.

Bailey's eyebrows raised in
melodramatic lawyer fashion.

"From the *Cleveland Press*?"
he asked in disbelief.

Gerber justified the decision
by saying he accompanied them.

"You were with both of them
at all times?" Bailey asked.

"Yes, sir," Gerber replied.

"And the one from the *Plain
Dealer*?"

"They came at the same
time."

"But they were in the house
with your permission?"

"That was my permission,"
Gerber said, "with the chief of
police's permission, yes, they
were there, and they had the same

courtesy as the members of the *Cleveland Press* had."

Bailey then turned to Gerber's proclamation about the murder weapon being a surgical instrument, which Gerber said had left a bloody imprint on Marilyn's pillow.

"And you never produced one, did you?" Bailey queried.

"No, sir," Gerber answered.

"Now, produce one if you can."

"I can't," Gerber said.

"Doctor," Bailey continued, "could you tell us where we could find one of the instruments compatible with what you may see there [in the outline on the pillow], where one of those would be located?"

"Any surgical store. But I hunted all over the United States, and I couldn't find one."

Bailey's tone slipped into astonishment.

"You never could find one in twelve years?"

Attorney F. Lee Bailey (left), Sam Sheppard (center), and his new wife, Ariane Tebbenjohanns (right), celebrate after Sheppard is freed from prison.

After being declared not guilty of Marilyn's murder, Sam Sheppard (top) rides away toward a new life with second wife, Ariane (center), and son, Chip (bottom).

"Well," Gerber said, "I didn't look that long."

"Well, you hunted all over the United States to find something to fit that?"

"Yes," Gerber replied. "I found plenty of things close to it, but . . ."

Any doubt of the outcome vanished as Gerber left the stand, clearly overmatched.

On November 16, 1966, Sam Sheppard was found not guilty of the murder of his wife.

In the eyes of the legal system, he was an innocent man and was free to restart his life. In reality, Sam Sheppard's life sentence continued.

His attempt to resurrect his medical career was derailed when he was fingered in two malpractice suits. Not only was he instantly recognized wherever he went, but a weekly reminder of his story was broadcast to the nation every week on ABC. *The Fugitive* premiered in September of 1963, weaving the story of Richard Kimble, a doctor who was convicted of murdering his wife in their home and sentenced to life in prison. But Kimble knew the real killer was a one-armed man, and after the train carrying him to the penitentiary crashed, enabling Kimble to escape, he spent the next four years trying to find his wife's murderer while he is pursued by a determined police detective. Roy Huggins, the creator of the show, denied that the premise of *The Fugitive* was based on Sam Sheppard, but

the similarities are too evident for there not to have been some influence—whether intentional or otherwise—or for the public appetite for such a series not to have been whet by the Sheppard case. Yet once Sam Sheppard was released from prison and his conviction overturned, the popularity of Dr. Richard Kimble's adventures dwindled. Less than a year after the conclusion of Sam Sheppard's second trial, *The Fugitive* ended its run, with Richard Kimble finally catching the one-armed man and proving his innocence.

For Sam Sheppard, this process—and that of simply re-entering the world—proved much more difficult. Whether deserved or not, the destruction of his 1954 life followed by ten years in prison had permanently damaged him, and his remaining six years could most graciously be described as bizarre.

Two days after he was released from prison in 1964, Sam Sheppard married Ariane

Tebbenjohanns, a German woman with whom he'd corresponded in prison. Their marriage lasted through the entire retrial process, but they eventually separated and divorced in 1969. Tebbenjohanns claimed Sam had been abusive, and she had feared for her life. After his death, she revealed that they had discussed the details of Marilyn's murder many times and that when she left Germany to marry him, she believed he was innocent. When asked if the real story was how Sam presented it in court, she answered cryptically, "In certain ways." When asked if she still believed he was innocent in 1970, she replied, "I don't wish to comment about that."

However cruel Sam may have been to his second wife, he was equally punishing to himself, drinking heavily and going through dramatic mood swings. The expenses associated with the retrial had cost Sam nearly $200,000, and still a generation away from being able to feed a celebrity culture that would have

lapped up any interview Sam would have granted or book or film he would have produced, he had little opportunity to get on his feet again.

After moving to Columbus to get away from the glare of publicity and attempt to salvage his medical practice, in 1969, Sam began his wrestling career at the behest of old friend George Strickland. He would participate in more than forty matches over the next seven months, adopting the less-than-subtle nickname "Killer." He married Strickland's daughter Colleen, who was twenty-five years younger than him.

The Sam Sheppard of 1969, leathery and graying, was a mere shadow of the boyish physician he'd been fifteen years earlier. In many ways, he personified the rapid decline of his hometown. The Cleveland of 1969 was a hollowed-out shell of the Best Location in the Nation Sam Sheppard knew in 1954.

The opening of the St. Lawrence Seaway did provide a

boost, but did not deliver the dramatic, defining changes hoped for at its creation. Cleveland's manufacturing base, once the rock of the city's economy, began to waver, with several companies either folding or moving elsewhere—a plague that spread across the Midwestern factory towns that had turned America into a world power. Similarly, suburban shopping destinations such as the Meadowbrook Merchandise Mart and the Southgate shopping center, which opened across Northfield Road a year later, began drawing customers into the outskirts of Cuyahoga County and away from the downtown department stores. There became fewer reasons to go downtown at all.

Downtown Cleveland, like many other metropolitan areas in America in the 1960s and 1970s, quickly crumbled. Well-known reporter Philip W. Porter wrote a column in the Plain Dealer in the spring of 1954 forecasting a bleak future if the proper action wasn't taken in the then-foreign realm of "urban redevelopment."

"Something needs to be done to downtown Cleveland, that's for sure," Porter wrote. "No new office buildings in a quarter century, no new big hotels in longer than that. Several tall buildings torn down in the last half-dozen years to make room for smaller ones. Auto traffic getting thicker, fewer people using public transportation to come downtown, more shopping centers being built in suburbs.

"A real opportunity awaits a political and civic leader big enough to pick up this ball and run with it. Today there seems no one in sight with enough money, stature, or time to do it."

As that ball remained untouched, Cleveland's population dipped. From the seventh-largest city in 1950, it dropped to number eight in the 1960 census, then tenth in 1970. By 2000, Cleveland's population was just over half of what it was in 1950. Porter would later refer to this golden era of the 1950s as Cleveland's "era of coasting."

And toiling in the background like a macabre soundtrack were the Indians, falling from one of the most respected franchises in sports in the 1940s and 1950s to the most disgraced. Forty-one years would pass between Cleveland's 1954 pennant and its next one, and with the installation of divisional play in 1969, the Indians went twenty-five years without placing higher than fourth. Over that same period, they managed a winning record only four times—the same total of 100-loss campaigns they suffered through. Municipal Stadium, once celebrated for its mammoth size and splendor, became the spurge of baseball, mirroring the aging city it called home.

The Indians and their hometown experienced a long-overdue renaissance in the mid-1990s. The opening of Jacobs Field—and the Indians' metamorphosis into one of baseball's elite franchises served as the centerpiece of a downtown revitalization that pointed Cleveland in the right direction and redefined it as a city willing to stand up and fight back.

The music genre that Alan Freed helped launch in Cleveland in the 1950s was honored by the construction of the Rock and Roll Hall of Fame along the Lake Erie shore. A new arena was built, bringing high-profile concerts and Cleveland's NBA team from the meadows of Summit County back downtown where they belonged. Cleveland Browns Stadium replaced Municipal Stadium and served as the home of the reborn Browns—making Cleveland the first and only city to see a pro sports franchise move away but still keep every morsel of its heritage.

Though the grimy era of the 1960s and 1970s was gradually rinsed away, along with the "Mistake by the Lake" moniker, Cleveland's hard-luck reputation—in sports and beyond—persists.

Accordingly, the 1954 team still hangs over the city like an archangel. Suffering fans still look back to the picture of the '54 team, the greatest in American League history, and smile sadly. That team not only represented a brighter time and a bolder Cleveland but also the moment everything changed. The team still looms like a specter over the game, representing all that can go right and wrong in a single season. The 1954 Indians became baseball's *Titanic*—so spectacular and glorious that the only fitting fate would be disaster.

Twice the team's 111-victory plateau was exceeded. In 1998, the New York Yankees won 114 games and much was made of their breaking the record. Yet the '98 Yankees played eight more games than the '54 Indians, as Major League Baseball shifted from a 154-game schedule to 162 in 1961. Naturally, few fans took notice that the Yankees of 1998 held a winning percentage of just .704—seventeen points

lower than the .721 posted by the 1954 Indians. Three years later, the Seattle Mariners topped that, winning a remarkable 116 for a percentage of .716. One more victory and the 2001 Mariners would have reached .722 and secured their spot as the greatest team in American League history. Not only did they fall one game shy of history they were promptly eliminated in the playoffs by the Yankees, who'd won twenty-one fewer games during the regular season.

The Mariners' fall completed a remarkable hat trick: it ensured that the three most successful teams in the modern history of Major League Baseball all failed to win a World Series. The 2001 Mariners and 1954 Indians stand alongside the statistical Goliath of all time, the 1906 Chicago Cubs, who posted an incredible record of 116–36 for a .763 winning percentage, then lost the World Series in six games to the cross-town White Sox, whose record was twenty-three games worse. The

'98 Yankees, the 1909 Pittsburgh Pirates (110–42, .724), and of course, the heralded 1927 Yankees stand as the only teams of the six modern ones ever to record a winning percentage better than .700 and then go on to win the World Series.

Then and now, the argument has been made that the 1954 Indians only were successful because of the weakness of that year's American League. To be sure, this was a team that mopped up on inferior competition, posting a record of 75–13 against the four teams that made up the league's second division— compared to 36–30 against the clubs that finished second, third, and fourth. Thus the 1954 Yankees became just the fourth team in baseball history to win 100 games and not reach the postseason. It's only happened four times since, most recently by the 1993 San Francisco Giants. In the current, six-division "wild card" format of baseball, it is virtually impossible for this to occur again.

Ironically, the 103 victories proved to be the finest showing of Casey Stengel's storied career. Though he'd win seven world titles and ten pennants, Stengel never won more games than he did in 1954. But it wasn't enough. "Señor beat me," Stengel would say simply years later, "and you could look it up."

The AL's weakness in 1954 was cited as an explanation for the Indians' World Series collapse. The Giants, pundits argued, had an inferior record because they played in a tougher league and were therefore better prepared for the Fall Classic. Yet this belief hadn't been expressed the previous five seasons when the Yankees won their pennants then clobbered their National League opposition in the World Series. The American League was certainly no worse in 1954 than it was in 1953 or 1955, when the Yankees took the pennant without winning 100 games. Likewise, the American League standings of 1954 very closely resemble those of 1927, when the Yankees won 110 and earned the title of the greatest team of all time. "If a New York team had won 111 games as we did that season," Hank Greenberg once said, "we'd never hear the end of it."

Baseball is the one team sport in which strength of schedule has never been a viable argument. So many games are played, and even in an era of interleague play and unbalanced schedules, every team will play every other team in its league every year. No baseball team coasts to 100 victories through a "cupcake" schedule. The game is not designed this way, eschewing style points and rewarding consistency over everything else. Since the advent of the 162-game season, a proverb has emerged to account for the differences between a first- and last-place club: Every team will win fifty-four games, every team will lose fifty-four, and what it does with the other fifty-four determines the success of the season. Though the

math would be slightly different, the 1954 Indians not only won all of the fifty-four games in question, they grabbed another handful from the loss column and turned them into victories. Nitpicking at a Major League Baseball team winning 72 percent of its games over the course of a full season is like criticizing a pitcher for hurling a perfect game against a last-place team.

It's also important to keep in mind that Babe Ruth, Lou Gehrig and Co. swatted their way to the title without having to face a single black pitcher. Nor did Waite Hoyt or Herb Pennock have to worry about any Latino hitters. True, in 1954 the game was not as racially diverse as it would become, but it was integrated with some of the greatest hitters and pitchers of all time. And as Willie Mays proved with his improbable catch in the Polo Grounds, just one player—of any skin color—can dramatically alter a postseason series.

The '54 Indians' lineup,

highlighted by a Jewish third baseman, a black center fielder, and a Mexican second baseman, all led by a Latino manager, could be considered baseball's first truly modern team, mixing not just one minority but several, basing overall personnel judgment on talent rather than skin color or ethnicity. Yet the true hallmark of this team, what it will forever be known for, is the finest pitching staff in baseball history.

Four Hall of Famers. More than 1,400 total career victories. The game's first left-hand/right-hand duo in the bullpen. The 1954 Indians' team ERA was 2.78, the lowest since the end of the dead-ball era, and would only be topped in the pitcher-friendly era of the 1960s, when the league's cumulative batting average fell below .240. In 1954, the cumulative batting average for Major League Baseball was .261. Fifty years later, it was a comparable .263. However, the top team ERAs were almost a full run higher in 2004 than that of the '54 Indians.

Yet for their dominance and significance, when discussions arise concerning the greatest baseball teams of all time, the 1954 Indians are often left out. The culture of American sport is to honor those teams and players who won on the grandest stage, regardless of how they got there. In the five decades since the Indians were swept by the Giants, teams that won roughly as many games as they lost over the course of the long season have been crowned world champions and have earned a revered spot in the annals of the sport.

Now that their 111 victories no longer stand as a record, their first-glance place in history has been taken away. And almost in the same motion, Cleveland was equally affected.

It only seemed fitting that a summer defined by the *Cleveland Press* would close with Louis Seltzer providing the last word. An editorial the Monday after the conclusion of the 1954 World Series assured its readers that

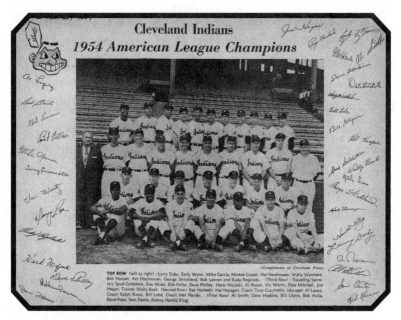

TOP ROW (left to right): Larry Doby, Early Wynn, Mike Garcia, Mickey Grasso, Hal Newhouser, Wally Westlake, Bob Hooper, Art Houtteman, George Strickland, Bob Lemon and Rudy Regalado. (Third Row): Traveling Secretary Spud Goldstein, Don Mossi, Bob Feller, Dave Philley, Hank Majeski, Al Rosen, Vic Wertz, Dale Mitchell, Jim Hegan, Trainer Wally Bock. (Second Row) Ray Narleski, Hal Naragon, Coach Tony Cuccinello, Manager Al Lopez, Coach Ralph Kress, Bill Lobe, Coach Mel Harder. (First Row) Al Smith, Dave Hoskins, Bill Glynn, Bob Avila, Dave Pope, Sam Dente, Batboy Harold Klug.

The 1954 Cleveland Indians—the greatest team
in American League history.

Cleveland would continue its reign as the Best Location in the Nation:

"Our coveted reputation as 'The City of Champions' has, by a cruel turn of events, been somewhat shaken for the moment, but let no one—in New York or anywhere else—gain the false notion that Cleveland has permanently relinquished its claim to the title."

The 1954 Browns wound up rallying from their sluggish start and defeating the Detroit Lions for the NFL Championship, avenging three straight title-game losses. The Browns would win it all again in 1955 with its original core group, led by coach Paul Brown and Hall of Fame quarterback Otto Graham, then capture one more surprising championship in 1964. They haven't won one since.

The Cleveland Barons would win two more Calder Cups, then as the National Hockey League grew in popularity in the United States, the Barons

sunk to the middle of the pack
in the American Hockey League,
which by the 1960s was viewed
as clearly inferior to the NHL.
With attendance at now-rickety
Cleveland Arena dwindling,
the Barons, like many other
downtown businesses, fled for
greener pastures, moving to
Jacksonville in 1973. A ramshackle
second version of the team
emerged when the California
Golden Seals of the NHL moved to
Cleveland in 1976 and adopted the
Barons nickname. But after two
unremarkable seasons, Cleveland
lost the Barons once again, this
time watching the team merge
with the Minnesota North Stars.

"The Indians, specially, gave
Cleveland a great thrill this summer,"
the *Press* editorial affirmed on
October 4, 1954. *"They won more
games in their league than any team
ever won before. It may be that they
tired themselves out in doing that.
Whatver the reason for their faltering
play in the World Series, they did bring
the pennant—which was something
we shouldn't forget."*

The Indians would not bring
another pennant until 1995, their
second season playing in Jacobs
Field. After the original Browns
franchise moved to Baltimore
the following year, Cleveland
Municipal Stadium was destroyed
and its remnants pushed into Lake
Erie to form a man-made reef.

*"The teams with which the
championships were brought to
Cleveland need to be reorganized,
strengthened, infused with new and
younger blood and talent. That
applies to the diamond, the gridiron,
the rink, and wherever sports are
played. That's really what caught up
with us—and what catches up with
any sports, any business, any human
endeavor, and the moral of all this is
quite plain for all to see."*

Cleveland, like many
rust-belt cities, endured never-
before-seen challenges in the
last quarter of the twentieth
century. The construction of
easy-access freeways fueled the
dispatch of thousands from
Greater Cleveland into the
suburbs, leaving many old city

neighborhoods to deteriorate into slums "as vast and as wretched as are to be found anywhere in the country," the *Plain Dealer* would describe. Underlying racial tension exploded in the black neighborhood of Hough in the summer of 1966 during a four-day riot that killed four people and resulted in millions of dollars of property damage. Two years later, Cleveland police and black militants engaged in a shootout in Glenville that left ten dead and dozens wounded.

The Cleveland Public School system decayed into one of the worst in the nation. Department stores and theaters closed. Crime worsened. Empty factories littered the horizon. By the 1970s, downtown Cleveland looked like a bombed-out European city in the months following World War II.

"All of this is interesting in a city that has been accustomed to championships all along the way."

Cleveland's last world-championship year was also the last year Sam Sheppard spent in prison. In the half-century prior, Cleveland celebrated six world championships. In the half-century since, none.

Even after his acquittal, Sam Sheppard could never quite earn the triumph of justice he sought. In his years in prison, a viable suspect emerged in Richard Eberling, who in 1954 was a window washer who had the Sheppards as a client. It was learned he'd washed their windows on the Friday before the murder. In 1959, a ring that belonged to Marilyn Sheppard was found among Eberling's possessions. He admitted stealing it, but from Richard Sheppard's house long after Marilyn's death. He became the perfect alternative—an ideal "one-armed man"—for the Sheppards in the years to come, particularly when he was convicted of the murder of a wealthy widow in 1989. All future blood tests seeking to identify a third sample centered on Eberling, who, bizarrely, admitted he'd cut his hand during a job at the Sheppards and likely dripped blood throughout the house. No test was able to conclusively prove that Eberling was in the house that night, nor did any jailhouse confessions stick. Fellow inmates claimed Eberling confessed to killing Marilyn Sheppard, but others said Eberling told them he'd discovered that Sam Sheppard and Spencer Houk were gay lovers having an affair and that they conspired to kill Marilyn. This version was closer to F. Lee Bailey's hypothesis: that Esther Houk caught Spencer with Marilyn that night and beat her to death in a rage, then forced her husband to help her cover it up.

Eberling died in 1998, but he still served as the key alternative to the final legal procedure pertaining to the death of Marilyn Sheppard. In 1995, Sam Jr., long having grown out of the "Chip" nickname, sued the state of Ohio on the grounds that his father had been wrongfully accused of his mother's murder. The state won the case in 2000,

proving that Sam Sheppard could not be effectively considered "innocent" of the crime.

In the process of this final case, Sam Sheppard's body was exhumed in Columbus in 1997 to attain DNA samples for blood testing. It was later cremated, and after forty-three years apart, Sam was rejoined with Marilyn. His remains were placed beside hers and those of their unborn child—either as two lovers reunited or a killer and his victim trapped together in a nightmarish purgatory. Either way, they rest together in a labyrinth of a crypt lined with red carpet and marbled walls, with the eternal lilt of fresh flowers hanging in the chilled, still air.

"But a 'City of Champions' behaves like a champion. It wins and loses with a smile. It looks for another day—works, trains, and builds to recapture the championships that have been momentarily lost."

Beginning in 1954, Cleveland's teams developed a tendency not just to lose championships but to lose them in colossally heartbreaking fashion.

In an eight-year period, the Browns would see three seasons of destiny derailed by apparent acts of God—a poorly thrown pass at the precise wrong moment, an impossible last-minute score, and a heart-wrenching fumble.

The Cavaliers, Cleveland's National Basketball Association entry founded in 1970, were denied a world championship in their magical sixth year because their leading scorer broke his foot in the last practice session before the conference finals.

In Herb Score's final game as a broadcaster, the Indians were two outs away from their first world championship in forty-nine years, but squandered the lead and lost Game Seven of the World Series in extra innings. A decade later, another Indians team stood one victory away from another pennant, this time with a probable World Series victory just over the horizon, only to implode in three straight lopsided defeats to the Boston Red Sox.

"That title of 'City of Champions' belongs to Cleveland. We will bring it back. Losing the World Series and getting set back on the pro gridiron may turn out after all to be good for us—if, in the best tradition of Cleveland, we dig in harder, plan better, and give it everything we've got."

From the mid-1950s on, poor planning became as regular an occurrence in Cleveland as winter snowstorms. Overseeing the twilight of the Best Location in the Nation was Anthony Celebrezze, who coasted along with the city to become its first and only five-term mayor. By the time Sam Sheppard's conviction was pitched to the curb by the U.S. Supreme Court in 1966, Celebrezze was serving as Secretary of Health, Education, and Welfare for President Lyndon Johnson. After that, perhaps ironically, given the miscarriage of justice he oversaw in the summer of 1954, Celebrezze finished his career as a federal judge for the Sixth District Court of Appeals.

The historic rejection of his work in the Sheppard case also glazed over Dr. Samuel Gerber. He would remain Cuyahoga County's coroner for another thirty-two years before retiring in 1986 due to poor health with two years remaining in his final term. He died five months later at the age of eighty-eight.

Louis Seltzer also continued to thrive through the following decades. The year Sam Sheppard was released from prison, *Time* magazine named the *Cleveland Press* as one of the ten best newspapers in the country. Seltzer resigned as editor of the *Press* the year of the retrial, later serving on the advisory board for the Pulitzer Prize. He died in 1980, and symbolically, two years later, the *Press* folded, following the same course as many afternoon papers across the nation. Despite the result of the second trial and the rebuke of his actions as journalism evolved, Seltzer always insisted he did the right thing by persecuting Sam Sheppard

that summer. "We believed," Seltzer said in one of many public speeches he gave that fall of 1954, "that the *Press*'s larger obligation in this case was to the whole community."

"What happened was yesterday. Today is another day. Tomorrow is another opportunity. That's the way of a 'City of Champions'—looking ahead, planning ahead, thinking ahead. Champions are made that way. Cleveland was made that way."

Nine years after the Cuyahoga River caught fire in 1969, Cleveland became the first major American city since the Great Depression to declare bankruptcy when it couldn't pay back fourteen million dollars in loans to six local banks. Thirty years later, despite admirable efforts that improved the city and provided hope for the future, *Forbes* magazine listed Cleveland as one of the nation's ten fastest-dying cities. An even more infamous title was awarded by *Forbes* in 2010 when Cleveland was named the most miserable city in America.

"And that's why the title of 'City of Champions' belongs to Cleveland.

"And always will!"

The shadows cast from that summer of 1954 still cloud the city in darkness.

The ugliness of the Sam Sheppard case—whether the original result was correct or not—is held up in journalism and law classes as the embodiment of everything that can go wrong with the American justice system. "The clouds still hang over Cleveland," author Jack Harrison Pollack would write in 1972. Similarly, memories of the shining Cleveland of the mid-1950s often provide as much pain as nostalgic satisfaction. Those who'd experienced the Best Location in the Nation knew that it could no longer live up to the name.

Alas, the city endures. It suffers silently, absorbing the bad jokes and fighting to shed the shoddy reputation with which it has been saddled. To those on the outside, it seems as though whenever the days are warm and enchanting in northeast Ohio, winter is always looming just over the horizon. To them, it is a city haunted by itself, attempting in vain to return to a bygone era ripped away.

Yet, as always, Cleveland perseveres, its citizens cherishing their city no matter what its perception and appreciating the golden days when they come. In the meantime, they're left with memories of what once was, and the hope that even in the depths of the darkest winter, someday summer will come again.

END NOTES

PRELUDE

The description of the Cuyahoga River fire and the snapshot of the city in 1969 comes from the *Plain Dealer* and the *Cleveland Press* as well as *The Encyclopedia of Cleveland History* (Edited by David D. Van Tassel and John J. Grabowski, Indiana University Press, 1987) and *Time* magazine ("Environment: The Cities: The Price of Optimism," Aug. 1, 1969). The account of Sam Sheppard's wrestling debut and his status in 1969 was drawn from the *Waverly News*, *Columbus Dispatch*, and *Chillicothe Gazette*. In this section and many that followed, details of game descriptions were gleaned from www.baseball-reference. com. Quotes and descriptions of Sam Sheppard's death come from the *Plain Dealer*, the *Press*, the *Columbus Citizen-Journal*, and the *Columbus Dispatch*.

AUTUMN: THE FIRST INTERLUDE

Descriptions of Game One of the 1954 World Series and the days leading up to the World Series come from *The Sporting News*, the *Plain Dealer*, the *Press*, the *New York Times*, and *Sports Illustrated* ("1..2..3..4..& BINGO," Roger Kahn, Oct. 11, 1954), *The 1954 World Series Film* (Major League Baseball Productions, 1991), the Mutual Broadcasting System radio broadcast of the game, and www.baseball-reference.com. I also drew from several books: *Cleveland Sports Legends: The 20 Most Glorious and Gut-Wrenching Moments of All Time* (Bob Dyer, Gray & Co., 2003);

Endless Summers: The Fall and Rise of the Cleveland Indians (Jack Torry, Diamond Communications, Inc., 1995); and *The Cleveland Indians Encyclopedia 3rd Edition* (Russell Schneider, Sports Publishing LLC, 2004).

CHAPTER 1: NOW OR NEVER

Accounts of the 1954 Indians' spring training and preseason activities come from the *Plain Dealer*, the *Press*, and *The Sporting News*, and the Society for American Baseball Research's Baseball Biography Project (www.bioproj.sabr.org). Descriptions of Hank Greenberg and his background come from the *Plain Dealer*, the *Press*, www.bioproj. sabr.org, *Hank Greenberg: The Story of My Life* (Hank Greenberg with Ira Berkow, Triumph Books, 2001), *Endless Summers: The Fall and Rise of the Cleveland Indians* (Jack Torry, Diamond Communications, Inc., 1995); *Look* magazine ("Will the Indians Fold Again?, Tim Cohane, Aug. 10, 1954); *Life* magazine ("How We Got Into the Series," Hank Greenberg, Sept. 27, 1954). In this chapter and others to follow, details of games, pennant races, and trades come from www.baseball-reference.com. Details of Sam and Marilyn Sheppard's California vacation come from the *Plain Dealer*, the *Press*, and *The Wrong Man* (James Neff, Random House, 2001).

CHAPTER 2: EMPIRE OF FREEDOM

The origin of the "Best Location in the Nation" phrase as well as Cleveland's 20th century history and details of current events in United States and Cleveland in 1954 comes from the *Plain Dealer*, the *Press*, the *Toledo Blade*, *The Encyclopedia of Cleveland History* (Edited by David D. Van Tassel and John J. Grabowski, Indiana University Press, 1987); *Cleveland: The Best-Kept Secret* (George E. Condon, Doubleday &

Co. Inc., 1967); and *The Summer of 54* (Thomas Kelly, Vista Books, 1994). Louis Seltzer's background was gathered from the *Press*; *The Summer of 54* (Thomas Kelly, Vista Books, 1994); *Mockery of Justice* (Cynthia L. Cooper and Sam Reese Sheppard, Northeastern University Press, 1995); *Dr. Sam: An American Tragedy* (Jack Harrison Pollack, Henry Regnery Company, 1972); *My Brother's Keeper* (Dr. Stephen Sheppard with Paul Holmes; David McKay Company, Inc., 1964); *Cleveland: The Best-Kept Secret* (George E. Condon, Doubleday & Co. Inc., 1967; and *The Years Were Good* (Louis B. Seltzer, The World Publishing Company, 1956).

CHAPTER 3: A SATURDAY NIGHT TOWN

In this chapter and ones that follow, descriptions of the Indians' season on and off the field, events around the league and the state of Major League Baseball in 1954 come from *The Sporting News*, the *Plain Dealer* and the *Press*. See above for accounts of Cleveland current events. My portraits of Bob Lemon, Early Wynn, and Mike Garcia were drawn from *The Sporting News*, the *Plain Dealer*, and the *Press*, as well as *The Cleveland Indians Encyclopedia 3rd Edition* (Russell Schneider, Sports Publishing LLC, 2004); *Endless Summers: The Fall and Rise of the Cleveland Indians* (Jack Torry, Diamond Communications, Inc., 1995); www.bioproj.sabr.org; and www.baseball-reference.com.

CHAPTER 4: STORM CLOUDS

See above for accounts of Indians action on and off the field and Cleveland current events. In illustrating Sam and Marilyn Sheppard's background, I drew upon the *Plain Dealer*, the *Press*, and several books: *Mockery of Justice* (Cynthia L. Cooper and Sam Reese Sheppard, Northeastern University Press, 1995); *Dr. Sam: An American Tragedy* (Jack Harrison Pollack, Henry Regnery Company, 1972); *My Brother's*

Keeper (Dr. Stephen Sheppard with Paul Holmes; David McKay Company, Inc., 1964); *The Sheppard Murder Case* (Paul Holmes, David McKay Company Inc., 1961); *Endure and Conquer* (Dr. Sam Sheppard; The World Publishing Company; 1966); *The Wrong Man* (James Neff, Random House, 2001); *Dr. Sam Sheppard on Trial: The Prosecutors and the Marilyn Sheppard Murder* (Jack P. DeSario and William D. Mason, Kent State University Press, 2003); and *When the Husband is the Suspect* (F. Lee Bailey with Jean Rabe, Tom Doherty Associates, 2008). Details of the Cleveland Barons history and their 1954 title came from the *Plain Dealer*, the *Press*, *Forgotten Glory: The Story of Cleveland Barons Hockey* (Gene Kiczek, Blue Line Publications, 1994), and the official website of the American Hockey League, www.theahl.com. My portrait of Al Rosen is drawn from *The Sporting News*, the *Plain Dealer*, the *Press*, Collier's magazine ("How Rosen Rocks Em," Hal Lebovitz, May 28, 1954); *Time* magazine (Sport: Top of the League, July 5, 1954); *The Summer of 54* (Thomas Kelly, Vista Books, 1994); *Endless Summers: The Fall and Rise of the Cleveland Indians* (Jack Torry, Diamond Communications, Inc., 1995); *The Cleveland Indians Encyclopedia 3rd Edition* (Russell Schneider, Sports Publishing LLC, 2004); www.bioproj.sabr.org; and www.baseball-reference.com.

CHAPTER 5: THE CHASM OF RIDICULOUSNESS

See above for accounts of Indians action on and off the field and Cleveland current events. Descriptions of Frederic Wertham's crusade against comic books and the state of the industry in the 1950s come from the *Plain Dealer*, the *Press*, *Superman: From the Thirties to the Seventies* (Introduction by E. Nelson Bridwell, Bonanza Books, 1971); *Superman vs. Hollywood* (Jake Rossen, Chicago Review Press, 2008); and *Men of Tomorrow* (Gerard Jones, Basic Books, 2004). My portrait of Larry Doby is drawn from *The Sporting News*, the *Plain Dealer*, the *Press*; *Pride Against Prejudice* (Joseph Thomas Moore, Greenwood Press, 1988); *The Summer of 54* (Thomas Kelly, Vista Books, 1994); *Endless Summers: The Fall and Rise of the Cleveland Indians* (Jack Torry, Diamond Communications, Inc., 1995); *The Cleveland Indians Encyclopedia 3rd Edition* (Russell Schneider, Sports Publishing LLC, 2004); *Cleveland Sports Legends: The 20 Most Glorious and Gut-Wrenching Moments of All Time* (Bob Dyer, Gray & Co., 2003); www.bioproj.sabr.org; and www.baseball-reference.com.

CHAPTER 6: A TRIPLE INTO THE GRAVESTONES

See above for accounts of Indians action on and off the field and Cleveland current events. My portrait of Alan Freed is drawn from the *Plain Dealer*, the *Press*, and *Big Beat Heat* (Alan Freed and the Early Years of Rock & Roll (John A. Jackson, Schirmer Books, 1991).

CHAPTER 7: HARD LUCK

See above for accounts of Indians action on and off the field and Cleveland current events. My portrait of Art Houtteman is drawn from *The Sporting News*, the *Plain Dealer*, the *Press*; *The Summer of 54* (Thomas Kelly, Vista Books, 1994); *The Cleveland Indians Encyclopedia 3rd Edition* (Russell Schneider, Sports Publishing LLC, 2004); www.bioproj.sabr. org; and www.baseball-reference.com.

AUTUMN: THE SECOND INTERLUDE

Descriptions of Game Two of the 1954 World Series come from *The Sporting News*, the *Plain Dealer*, the *Press*, the *New York Times*, and *Sports Illustrated* ("1..2..3..4..& BINGO," Roger Kahn, Oct. 11, 1954), *The 1954 World Series Film* (Major League Baseball Productions, 1991), the Mutual Broadcasting System radio broadcast of the game, and www.

baseball-reference.com. I also drew from several books: *Cleveland Sports Legends: The 20 Most Glorious and Gut-Wrenching Moments of All Time* (Bob Dyer, Gray & Co., 2003); *Endless Summers: The Fall and Rise of the Cleveland Indians* (Jack Torry, Diamond Communications, Inc., 1995); and *The Cleveland Indians Encyclopedia 3rd Edition* (Russell Schneider, Sports Publishing LLC, 2004).

CHAPTER 8: BLEED AND BELIEVE

See above for accounts of Indians action on and off the field and Cleveland current events. My portrait of Vic Wertz and the trade for him is drawn from *The Sporting News, the Plain Dealer*, the *Press, The Summer of 54* (Thomas Kelly, Vista Books, 1994); *The Cleveland Indians Encyclopedia 3rd Edition* (Russell Schneider, Sports Publishing LLC, 2004); and www.baseball-reference.com. My portrait of Bobby Avila is drawn from *The Sporting News*, the *Plain Dealer*, the *Press, The Cleveland Indians Encyclopedia 3rd Edition* (Russell Schneider, Sports Publishing LLC, 2004); and www.baseball-reference.com. The description of the Painesville woman's possible encounter with Marilyn Sheppard comes from the *Plain Dealer*, the *Press*, and *The Wrong Man* (James Neff, Random House, 2001).

CHAPTER 9: TWO AGING ACES

See above for accounts of Indians action on and off the field and Cleveland current events. My portrait of Bob Feller is drawn from *The Sporting News*, the *Plain Dealer*, the *Press, The Summer of 54* (Thomas Kelly, Vista Books, 1994); *The Cleveland Indians Encyclopedia 3rd Edition* (Russell Schneider, Sports Publishing LLC, 2004); *Bob Feller: Ace of the Greatest Generation* (John Sickels, Brassey's Inc., 2004); *Now Pitching: Bob Feller* (Bob Feller with Bill Gilbert, Carol Publishing Group, 1990; and www.baseball-reference.com. My portrait of Hal Newhouser is drawn from *The Sporting News*, the *Plain Dealer*, the *Press*, *The Summer of 54* (Thomas Kelly, Vista Books, 1994); *The Cleveland Indians Encyclopedia 3ʳᵈ Edition* (Russell Schneider, Sports Publishing LLC, 2004); and www. baseball-reference.com. My portrait of Wally Westlake is drawn from *The Sporting News*, the *Plain Dealer*, the *Press*, *The Summer of 54* (Thomas Kelly, Vista Books, 1994; www.bioproj.sabr.org, and www.baseball-reference.com.

CHAPTER 10: SEVEN MINUTES OF SILENCE

See above for accounts of Indians action on and off the field and Cleveland current events. My portrait of Al Lopez is drawn from *The Sporting News*, the *Plain Dealer*, the *Press*, *The Summer of 54* (Thomas Kelly, Vista Books, 1994); *Endless Summers: The Fall and Rise of the Cleveland Indians* (Jack Torry, Diamond Communications, Inc., 1995); *The Cleveland Indians Encyclopedia 3ʳᵈ Edition* (Russell Schneider, Sports Publishing LLC, 2004); *Al Lopez: The Life of Baseball's El Senor* (Wes Singletary, McFarland & Co., 1999); and www.baseball-reference.com. The account of the June boat accident outside the Sheppard house comes from *Mockery of Justice* (Cynthia L. Cooper and Sam Reese Sheppard, Northeastern University Press, 1995).

CHAPTER 11: THE SPHINX AND THE HOWITZER

See above for accounts of Indians action on and off the field and Cleveland current events. My portrait of Arnold Palmer comes from the *Plain Dealer*, the *Press*, *A Golfer's Life* (Arnold Palmer w/James Dodson, Ballantine Books, 1999); and *Arnold Palmer: Memories, Stories, and Memorabilia from a Life On and Off the Course* (Arnold Palmer, Stewart, Tabari & Chang, 2004). My portrait of Don Mossi and Ray Narleski comes from *The Sporting News*, the *Plain Dealer*, the *Press*, *The Summer of 54* (Thomas Kelly, Vista Books, 1994); *The Cleveland Indians Encyclopedia 3rd Edition* (Russell Schneider, Sports Publishing LLC, 2004); and www. baseball-reference.com. My portrait of Herb Score is drawn from *The Sporting News*, the *Plain Dealer*, the *Press*, *Endless Summers: The Fall and Rise of the Cleveland Indians* (Jack Torry, Diamond Communications, Inc., 1995); and the *Saturday Evening Post* ("Cleveland's Left-Handed Lightning, Hal Lebovitz, May 11, 1957).

CHAPTER 12: THE NIGHT BEFORE

See above for accounts of Indians action on and off the field and Cleveland current events. My account of the events in Cleveland on July 3 come from *Plain Dealer*, the *Press*, *Ohio UFOs (and many others)* (I. Scott, Greyden Press, 1997); and www.ufodna.com. My portrait of the Sheppards' activities on July 3 are drawn from *Plain Dealer*, the *Press*, and several books: *Mockery of Justice* (Cynthia L. Cooper and Sam Reese Sheppard, Northeastern University Press, 1995); *Dr. Sam: An American Tragedy* (Jack Harrison Pollack, Henry Regnery Company, 1972); *My Brother's Keeper* (Dr. Stephen Sheppard with Paul Holmes, David McKay Company, Inc., 1964); *The Sheppard Murder Case* (Paul Holmes, David McKay Company Inc., 1961); *Endure and Conquer* (Dr. Sam Sheppard, The World Publishing Company, 1966); *The Wrong Man* (James Neff, Random House, 2001); *Dr. Sam Sheppard on Trial: The Prosecutors and the Marilyn Sheppard Murder* (Jack P. DeSario and William D. Mason, Kent State University Press, 2003); *When the Husband is the Suspect* (F. Lee Bailey with Jean Rabe, Tom Doherty Associates, 2008); *They Died Crawling* (John Stark Bellamy II, Gray & Co., 1995); and *The Maniac in the Bushes* (John Stark Bellamy II, Gray & Co., 1997).

AUTUMN: THE THIRD INTERLUDE

Descriptions of Game Three of the 1954 World Series come from *The Sporting News*, the *Plain Dealer*, the *Press*, the *New York Times*, and *Sports Illustrated* ("1..2..3..4..& BINGO," Roger Kahn, Oct. 11, 1954), *The 1954 World Series Film* (Major League Baseball Productions, 1991), the Mutual Broadcasting System radio broadcast of the game, and www.baseball-reference.com. I also drew from several books: *Cleveland Sports Legends: The 20 Most Glorious and Gut-Wrenching Moments of All Time* (Bob Dyer, Gray & Co., 2003); *Endless Summers: The Fall and Rise of the Cleveland Indians* (Jack Torry, Diamond Communications, Inc., 1995); and *The Cleveland Indians Encyclopedia 3ʳᵈ Edition* (Russell Schneider, Sports Publishing LLC, 2004).

CHAPTER 13: THEY'VE KILLED MARILYN

My account of Marilyn Sheppard's murder and the morning after come from the *Plain Dealer* and the *Press*, as well as several books: *Mockery of Justice* (Cynthia L. Cooper and Sam Reese Sheppard, Northeastern University Press, 1995); *Dr. Sam: An American Tragedy* (Jack Harrison Pollack, Henry Regnery Company, 1972); *My Brother's Keeper* (Dr. Stephen Sheppard with Paul Holmes, David McKay Company, Inc., 1964); *The Sheppard Murder Case* (Paul Holmes, David McKay Company Inc., 1961); *Endure and Conquer* (Dr. Sam Sheppard, The World Publishing Company, 1966); *The Wrong Man* (James Neff, Random House, 2001); *Dr. Sam Sheppard on Trial: The Prosecutors and the Marilyn Sheppard Murder* (Jack P. DeSario and William D. Mason, Kent State University Press, 2003); *When the Husband is the Suspect* (F. Lee Bailey with Jean Rabe, Tom Doherty Associates, 2008); *They Died Crawling* (John Stark Bellamy II, Gray & Co., 1995); and *The Maniac in the Bushes* (John Stark Bellamy II, Gray & Co., 1997). My portrait of Samuel Gerber is drawn from the above sources as well as *In the Wake of the Butcher* (James Jessen Badal, Ken State University Press, 2001); *Torso: The Story of Eliot Ness and the Search for a Psychopathic Killer* (Steven Nickel, John F. Blair, Publisher, 1989); and *The Encyclopedia of Cleveland History* (Edited by David D. Van Tassel and John J. Grabowski, Indiana University Press, 1987). Dialogue between Sam Sheppard and detectives was drawn from *Endure and Conquer* (Dr. Sam Sheppard, The World Publishing Company, 1966) and *Dr. Sam: An American Tragedy* (Jack Harrison Pollack, Henry Regnery Company, 1972).

CHAPTER 14: THE LOST WEEKEND

See above for accounts of Indians action on and off the field and Cleveland current events.

CHAPTER 15: THE STRONG ARM OF THE LAW

In this chapter and others, my account of the Marilyn Sheppard murder investigation is drawn from the *Plain Dealer* and the *Press*, as well as several books: *Mockery of Justice* (Cynthia L. Cooper and Sam Reese Sheppard, Northeastern University Press, 1995); *Dr. Sam: An American Tragedy* (Jack Harrison Pollack, Henry Regnery Company, 1972); *My Brother's Keeper* (Dr. Stephen Sheppard with Paul Holmes, David McKay Company, Inc., 1964); *The Sheppard Murder Case* (Paul Holmes, David McKay Company Inc., 1961); *Endure and Conquer* (Dr. Sam Sheppard, The World Publishing Company, 1966); *The Wrong Man* (James Neff, Random House, 2001); *Dr. Sam Sheppard on Trial: The Prosecutors and the Marilyn Sheppard Murder* (Jack P. DeSario and William D. Mason, Kent State University Press, 2003); *When the Husband is the Suspect* (F. Lee Bailey with Jean Rabe, Tom Doherty Associates, 2008); *They Died Crawling* (John Stark Bellamy II, Gray & Co., 1995);

and *The Maniac in the Bushes* (John Stark Bellamy II, Gray & Co., 1997). The dialogue between Sam Sheppard and detectives during the murder reenactment comes from the *Press*.

CHAPTER 16: THE CLEVELAND SPECTACLE

My account of the All-Star Game is drawn from *The Sporting News*, the *Plain Dealer*, the *Press*, *The Summer of 54* (Thomas Kelly, Vista Books, 1994); and *Cleveland Sports Legends: The 20 Most Glorious and Gut-Wrenching Moments of All Time* (Bob Dyer, Gray & Co., 2003).

CHAPTER 17: MR. CLEVELAND TO THE RESCUE

See above for accounts of Indians action on and off the field, Cleveland current events, and the Marilyn Sheppard murder investigation, in addition to *The Years Were Good* (Louis B. Seltzer, The World Publishing Company, 1956).

CHAPTER 18: STEAMED UP

See above for accounts of Indians action on and off the field, Cleveland current events, and the Marilyn Sheppard murder investigation, in addition to *Look* magazine ("Will the Indians Fold Again?", Tim Cohane, Aug. 10, 1954).

CHAPTER 19: GET THAT KILLER

See above for accounts of Indians action on and off the field, Cleveland current events, and the Marilyn Sheppard murder investigation. My account of the Marilyn Sheppard murder inquest is drawn from *Plain Dealer* and the *Press*, as well as several books: *Mockery of Justice* (Cynthia L. Cooper and Sam Reese Sheppard, Northeastern University Press, 1995); *Dr. Sam: An American Tragedy* (Jack Harrison

Pollack, Henry Regnery Company, 1972); *My Brother's Keeper* (Dr. Stephen Sheppard with Paul Holmes, David McKay Company, Inc., 1964); *The Sheppard Murder Case* (Paul Holmes, David McKay Company Inc., 1961); *Endure and Conquer* (Dr. Sam Sheppard, The World Publishing Company, 1966); *The Wrong Man* (James Neff, Random House, 2001); *Dr. Sam Sheppard on Trial: The Prosecutors and the Marilyn Sheppard Murder* (Jack P. DeSario and William D. Mason, Kent State University Press, 2003); *When the Husband is the Suspect* (F. Lee Bailey with Jean Rabe, Tom Doherty Associates, 2008); *They Died Crawling* (John Stark Bellamy II, Gray & Co., 1995); and *The Maniac in the Bushes* (John Stark Bellamy II, Gray & Co., 1997).

CHAPTER 20: LIKE A HOLLYWOOD MOVIE

See above for accounts of Indians action on and off the field, Cleveland current events, and the Marilyn Sheppard murder investigation.

CHAPTER 21: BRING HIM IN

See above for accounts of Indians action on and off the field, Cleveland current events, and the Marilyn Sheppard murder investigation. Dialogue from Sam Sheppard's arrest and arraignment comes from the *Plain Dealer* and the *Press*. Descriptions of Sam's thoughts during this episode come from *Endure and Conquer* (Dr. Sam Sheppard, The World Publishing Company, 1966). Additional material used for my account of Larry Doby's catch came from *The Baseball Research Journal* ("Larry Doby's 'The Catch,'" Ken Saulter, Summer 2010), and *Municipal Stadium: Memories on the Lakefront Volume 1, 4th edition* (Edited by George E. Cormack, Instant Concepts Inc., 2005).

CHAPTER 22: THE GUNS OF AUGUST

See above for accounts of Indians action on and off the field, Cleveland current events, and the Marilyn Sheppard murder investigation. My account of the Homer Wentworth incident comes from the *Plain Dealer*.

CHAPTER 23: A GHOUL'S PARADISE

See above for accounts of Indians action on and off the field, Cleveland current events, and the Marilyn Sheppard murder investigation. My account of Alfred Kreke's sermon comes from the *Plain Dealer*. The dialogue between detectives and Sam during questioning is drawn from *Dr. Sam: An American Tragedy* (Jack Harrison Pollack, Henry Regnery Company, 1972). The account of and dialogue from the confrontation between Stephen Sheppard and Spencer Houk comes from the *Plain Dealer* and the *Press*.

CHAPTER 24: DESTINY

See above for accounts of Indians action on and off the field and Cleveland current events. The description of the birth of Sports Illustrated comes from the *Press*, *Time* magazine ("The Press: *Sports Illustrated*, Vol. 1, No. 1," Aug. 16, 1954), and *Sports Illustrated* (Aug. 16, 1954).

CHAPTER 25: WHAT EVIDENCE IS THERE?

See above for accounts of the Marilyn Sheppard murder investigation. The dialogue between Stephen Sheppard and David Kerr comes from *Endure and Conquer* (Dr. Sam Sheppard, The World Publishing Company, 1966). The account of and dialogue from Sam Sheppard's second arrest is drawn from the *Plain Dealer* and the *Press*.

CHAPTER 26: NOT THE FOLDING-UP TYPE

See above for accounts of Indians action on and off the field, Cleveland current events, and the Marilyn Sheppard murder investigation. The account of Johnny Carson's national television debut comes from the *Plain Dealer* and *Time* magazine ("Radio: The Week in Review," July 30, 1954).

AUTUMN: THE FOURTH INTERLUDE

Descriptions of Game Four of the 1954 World Series come from *The Sporting News*, the *Plain Dealer*, the *Press*, the *New York Times*, and *Sports Illustrated* ("1..2..3..4..& BINGO," Roger Kahn, Oct. 11, 1954), *The 1954 World Series Film* (Major League Baseball Productions, 1991), the Mutual Broadcasting System radio broadcast of the game, and www.baseball-reference.com. I also drew from several books: *Cleveland Sports Legends: The 20 Most Glorious and Gut-Wrenching Moments of All Time* (Bob Dyer, Gray & Co., 2003); *Endless Summers: The Fall and Rise of the Cleveland Indians* (Jack Torry, Diamond Communications, Inc., 1995); and *The Cleveland Indians Encyclopedia 3rd Edition* (Russell Schneider, Sports Publishing LLC, 2004).

CHAPTER 27: WHAMMY BE DAMNED

See above for accounts of Indians action on and off the field, Cleveland current events, and the Marilyn Sheppard murder investigation. The account of the Indians' airport pep rally comes from the *Plain Dealer* and the *Press*.

CHAPTER 28: THE YANKEE DOUBLEHEADER, ACT ONE

My portrait of the Yankee Doubleheader is drawn from *The Sporting News*, the *Plain Dealer*, the *Press*, *Sports Illustrated* ("The

Twilight of the Gods," Roger Kahn, Sept. 20, 1954), and *The Cleveland Indians Encyclopedia 3rd* Edition (Russell Schneider, Sports Publishing LLC, 2004.

CHAPTER 29: THE YANKEE DOUBLEHEADER, ACT TWO

See above for the account of the Yankee Doubleheader. The account of the premiere of *Satins & Spurs* and *Lassie* comes from the *Plain Dealer*, the *Press*, and *Filmed TV Drama 1952-1958* (William Hawes, McFarland & Co., 2002).

CHAPTER 30: WE'RE IN

See above for accounts of Indians action on and off the field and Cleveland current events.

CHAPTER 31: ONE HUNDRED ELEVEN

See above for accounts of Indians action on and off the field, Cleveland current events, and the Marilyn Sheppard murder investigation, in addition to *Life* magazine ("How We Got Into the Series," Hank Greenberg, Sept. 27, 1954). My portrait of the Indians' victory parade is drawn from the *Plain Dealer* and the *Press*.

THE FINAL INTERLUDE: WINTER

My accounts of the Sam Sheppard murder trial and its aftermath are drawn from come from the *Plain Dealer* and the *Press*, as well as several books: *Mockery of Justice* (Cynthia L. Cooper and Sam Reese Sheppard, Northeastern University Press, 1995); *Dr. Sam: An American Tragedy* (Jack Harrison Pollack, Henry Regnery Company, 1972); *My Brother's Keeper* (Dr. Stephen Sheppard with Paul Holmes, David McKay Company, Inc., 1964); *The Sheppard Murder Case* (Paul Holmes, David McKay Company

Inc., 1961); *Endure and Conquer* (Dr. Sam Sheppard, The World Publishing Company, 1966); *The Wrong Man* (James Neff, Random House, 2001); *Dr. Sam Sheppard on Trial: The Prosecutors and the Marilyn Sheppard Murder* (Jack P. DeSario and William D. Mason, Kent State University Press, 2003); *When the Husband is the Suspect* (F. Lee Bailey with Jean Rabe, Tom Doherty Associates, 2008); *They Died Crawling* (John Stark Bellamy II, Gray & Co., 1995); *The Maniac in the Bushes* (John Stark Bellamy II, Gray & Co., 1997); and *The Years Were Good* (Louis B. Seltzer, The World Publishing Company, 1956). The description of Sam Sheppard's death comes from the *Plain Dealer*, the *Press*, the *Columbus Dispatch*, and the *Columbus Citizen-Journal*. My descriptions of the Indians after 1954 is drawn from *The Sporting News*, the *Plain Dealer*, the *Press*, *Endless Summers: The Fall and Rise of the Cleveland Indians* (Jack Torry, Diamond Communications, Inc., 1995); *Hank Greenberg: The Story of My Life* (Hank Greenberg with Ira Berkow, Triumph Books, 2001), *The Cleveland Indians Encyclopedia 3rd Edition* (Russell Schneider, Sports Publishing LLC, 2004); *Pride Against Prejudice* (Joseph Thomas Moore, Greenwood Press, 1988); the *Saturday Evening Post* ("Cleveland's Left-Handed Lightning, Hal Lebovitz, May 11, 1957); *Al Lopez: The Life of Baseball's El Senor* (Wes Singletary, McFarland & Co., 1999), and www. baseball-reference.com.

ABOUT THE AUTHOR

J onathan Knight is the author of six books on Cleveland sports history. A member of the Society for American Baseball Research and a columnist for the popular website theclevelandfan .com, he is a graduate of Ohio University's nationally renowned E.W. Scripps School of Journalism and has twice been named Sportswriter of the Year by the Ohio Prep Sportswriters Association. He lives in Columbus, Ohio.